D1096667

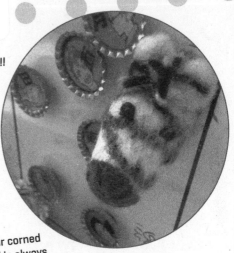

Thank you for picking up *Haikyu!!* volume 33! When I create each chapter, I start by writing out a detailed outline. But whenever I try to type the word *shiteshimau* (to wind up) in Japanese, the autocorrect always tries to change it to *shimauma* (zebra). And it always tries to change *conbi* (combo) to *conbiifu* (corned beef).

"Here the Karasuno first year corned beef zebra taking the block" is always how it ends up.

HARUICHI FURUDATE began his manga career when he was 25 years old with the one-shot *Ousama Kid* (King Kid), which won an honorable mention for the 14th Jump Treasure Newcomer Manga Prize. His first series, *Kiben Gakuha, Yotsuya Sensei no Kaidan* (Philosophy School, Yotsuya Sensei's Ghost Stories), was serialized in *Weekly Shonen Jump* in 2010. In 2012, he began serializing *Haikyu!!* in *Weekly Shonen Jump*, where it became his most popular work to date.

HAIKYU!!

VOLUME 33
SHONEN JUMP Manga Edition

Story and Art by
HARUICHI FURUDATE

Translation **1 ADRIENNE BECK**
Touch-Up Art & Lettering **2 ERIKA TERRIQUEZ**
Design **3 JULIAN [JR] ROBINSON**
Editor **4 MARLENE FIRST**

HAIKYU!! © 2012 by Haruichi Furudate
All rights reserved.
First published in Japan in 2012 by SHUEISHA Inc., Tokyo.
English translation rights arranged by SHUEISHA Inc.

The stories, characters and incidents mentioned
in this publication are entirely fictional.

No portion of this book may be reproduced or transmitted
in any form or by any means without written permission
from the copyright holders.

Printed in the U.S.A.

Published by VIZ Media, LLC
P.O. Box 77010
San Francisco, CA 94107

10 9 8 7 6 5 4 3 2 1
First printing, July 2019

VIZ MEDIA
viz.com

PARENTAL ADVISORY
HAIKYU!! is rated T for Teen and
is recommended for ages 13
and up for mild language.

SHONEN JUMP
shonenjump.com

HAIKYU!!

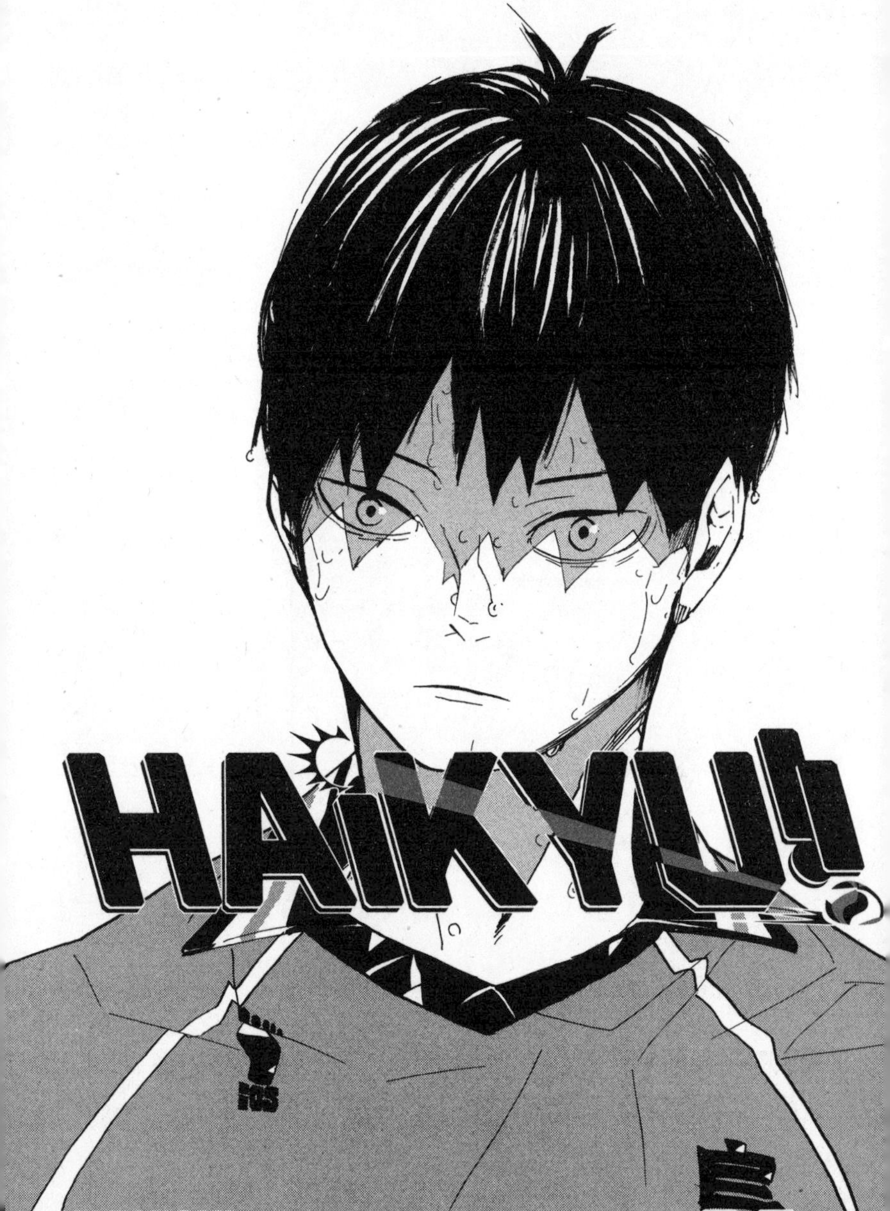

HARUICHI FURUDATE

MONSTERS' BALL

33

Karasuno High School Volleyball Club

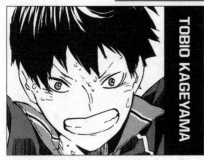

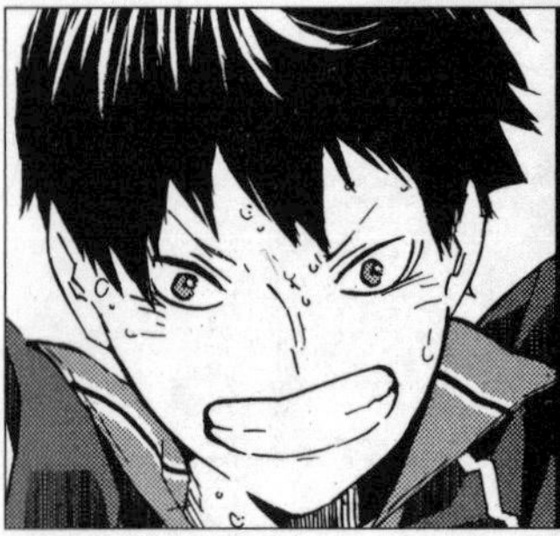
TOBIO KAGEYAMA

1ST YEAR / SETTER
His instincts and athletic talent are so good that he's like a "king" who rules the court. Demanding and egocentric.

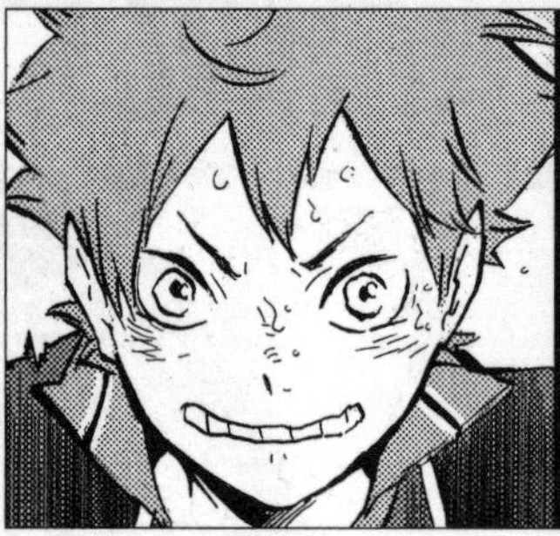
SHOYO HINATA

1ST YEAR / MIDDLE BLOCKER
Even though he doesn't have the best body type for volleyball, he is super athletic. Gets nervous easily.

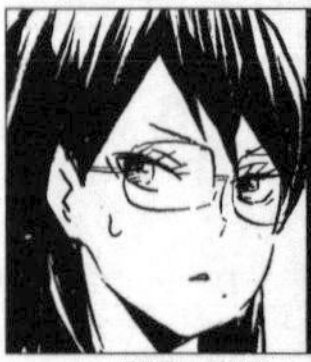
KIYOKO SHIMIZU

3RD YEAR
MANAGER

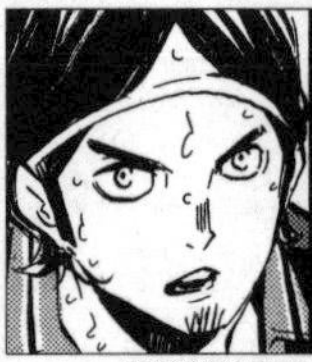
ASAHI AZUMANE

3RD YEAR
WING SPIKER

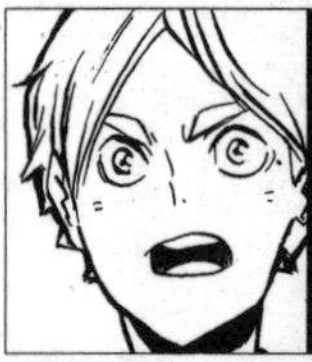
KOUSHI SUGAWARA

3RD YEAR (VICE CAPTAIN)
SETTER

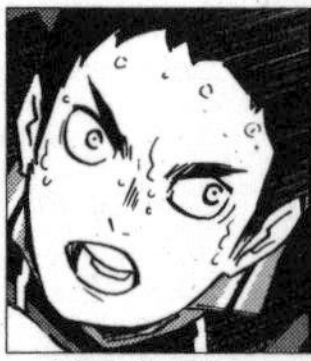
DAICHI SAWAMURA

3RD YEAR (CAPTAIN)
WING SPIKER

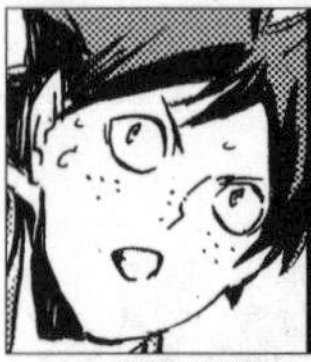
TADASHI YAMAGUCHI

1ST YEAR
MIDDLE BLOCKER

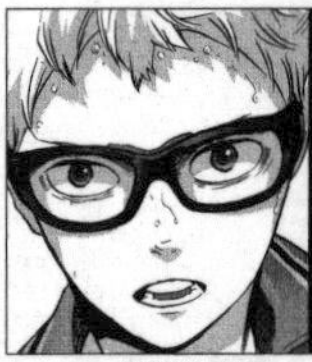
KEI TSUKISHIMA

1ST YEAR
MIDDLE BLOCKER

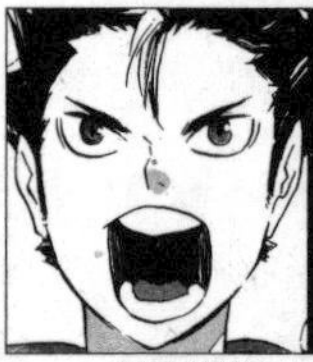
YU NISHINOYA

2ND YEAR
LIBERO

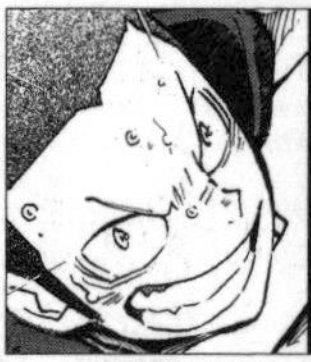
RYUNOSUKE TANAKA

2ND YEAR
WING SPIKER

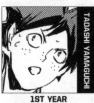

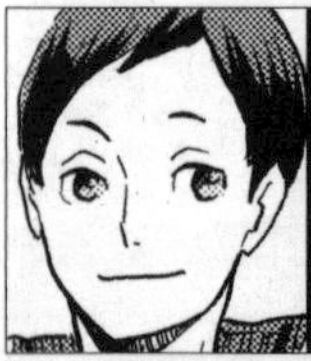
CHIKARA ENNOSHITA

2ND YEAR
WING SPIKER

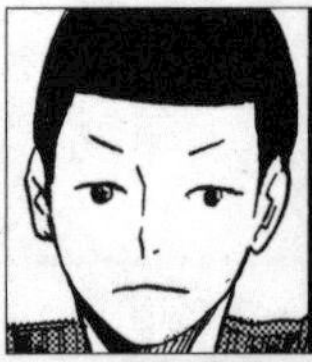
KAZUHITO NARITA

2ND YEAR
MIDDLE BLOCKER

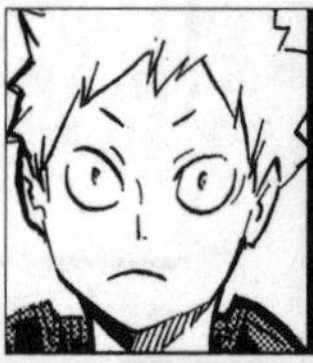
HISASHI KINOSHITA

2ND YEAR
WING SPIKER

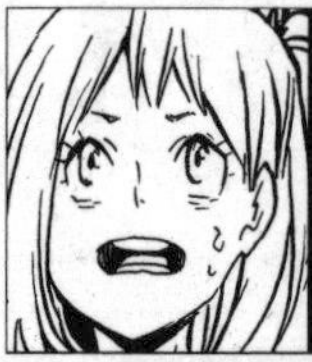
HITOKA YACHI

1ST YEAR
MANAGER

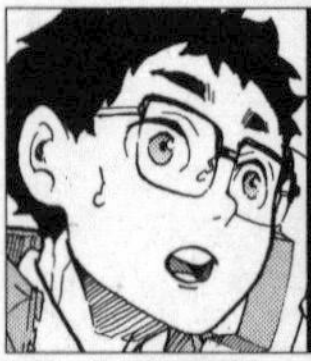
ITTETSU TAKEDA

ADVISER

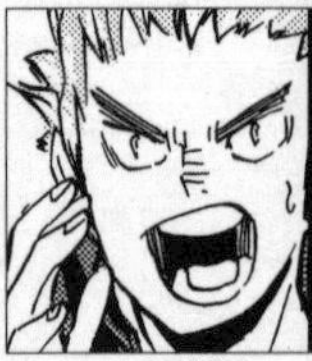
KEISHIN UKAI

COACH

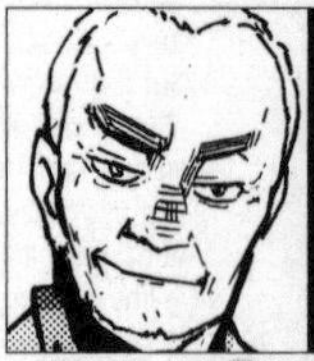
IKKEI UKAI

FORMER HEAD COACH

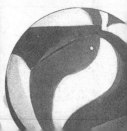

CHARACTERS

NATIONAL SPRING TOURNAMENT ARC

Inarizaki Volleyball Club

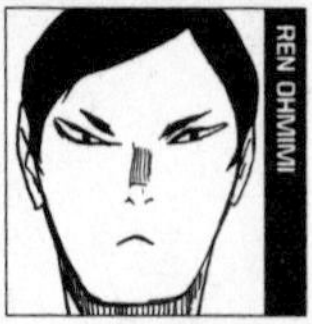
REN OHMIMI
3RD YEAR
MIDDLE BLOCKER

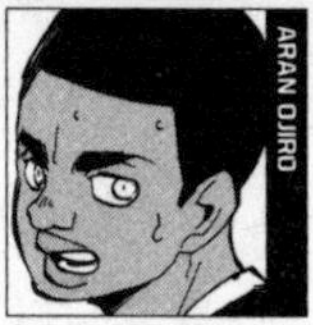
ARAN OJIRO
3RD YEAR
WING SPIKER

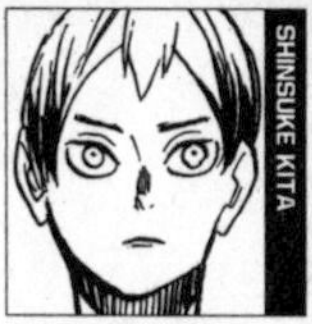
SHINSUKE KITA
3RD YEAR (VICE CAPTAIN)
WING SPIKER

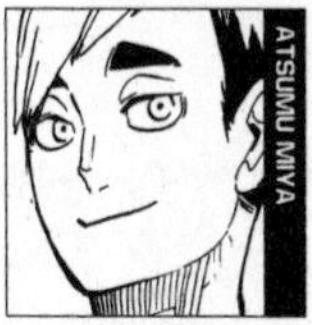
ATSUMU MIYA
2ND YEAR
SETTER

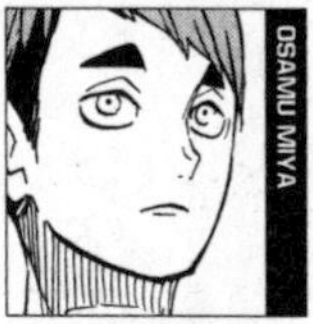
OSAMU MIYA
2ND YEAR
WING SPIKER

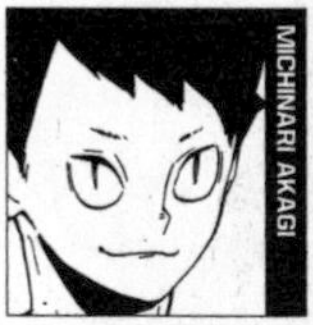
MICHINARI AKAGI
3RD YEAR
LIBERO

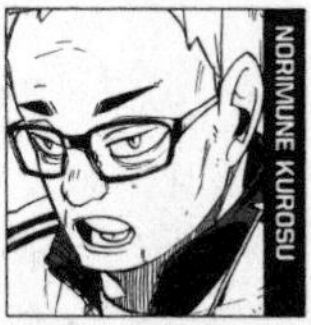
NORIMUNE KUROSU
HEAD COACH

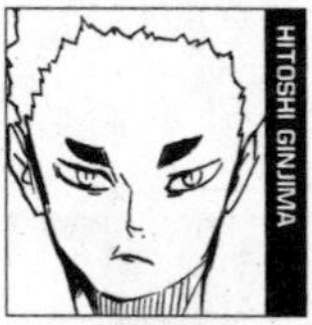
HITOSHI GINJIMA
2ND YEAR
WING SPIKER

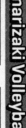

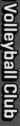

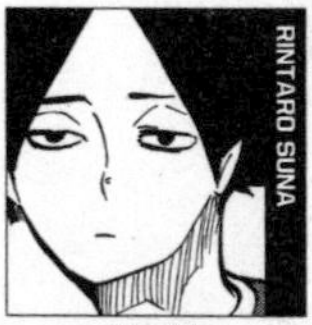
RINTARO SUNA
2ND YEAR
MIDDLE BLOCKER

Nekoma Volleyball Club

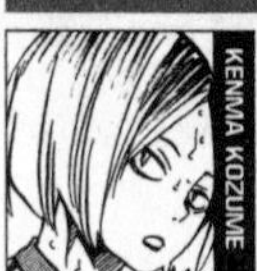
KENMA KOZUME
2ND YEAR
SETTER

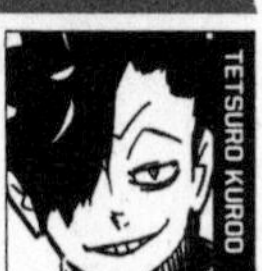
TETSURO KUROO
3RD YEAR
MIDDLE BLOCKER

Karasuno Cheer Squad

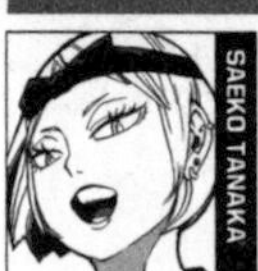
SAEKO TANAKA

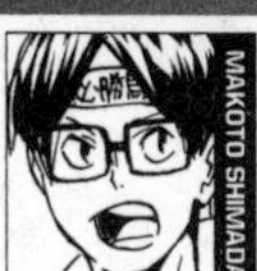
MAKOTO SHIMADA

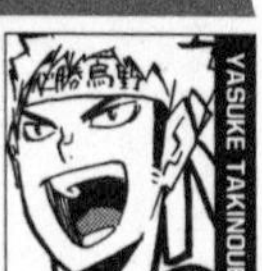
YASUKE TAKINOUE

Ever since he saw the legendary player known as "the Little Giant" compete at the national volleyball finals, Shoyo Hinata has been aiming to be the best volleyball player ever! He decides to join the volleyball club at his middle school and gets to play in an official tournament during his third year. His team is crushed by a team led by volleyball prodigy Tobio Kageyama, also known as "the King of the Court." Swearing revenge on Kageyama, Hinata graduates middle school and enters Karasuno High School, the school where the Little Giant played. However, upon joining the club, he finds out that Kageyama is there too! The two of them bicker constantly, but they bring out the best in each other's talents and become a powerful combo. The Spring Tournament begins! On day 2, Inarizaki and Karasuno are duking it out in the third set when Atsumu Miya's superb setting gives Inarizaki the lead! Things look bleak for Karasuno, but a perfect save by Hinata of all people lifts the team's spirits. Azumane and Sawamura score another point to tie things up, but Inarizaki gets to match point first. Kageyama leads Tanaka into an amazing line shot to keep Karasuno out of immediate danger, but the fierce back-and-forth continues. Then, on one critical play, Tsukishima makes the decision to forgo a desperate block and instead trust Hinata to make the dig!

HAIKYU!!

33 MONSTERS' BALL

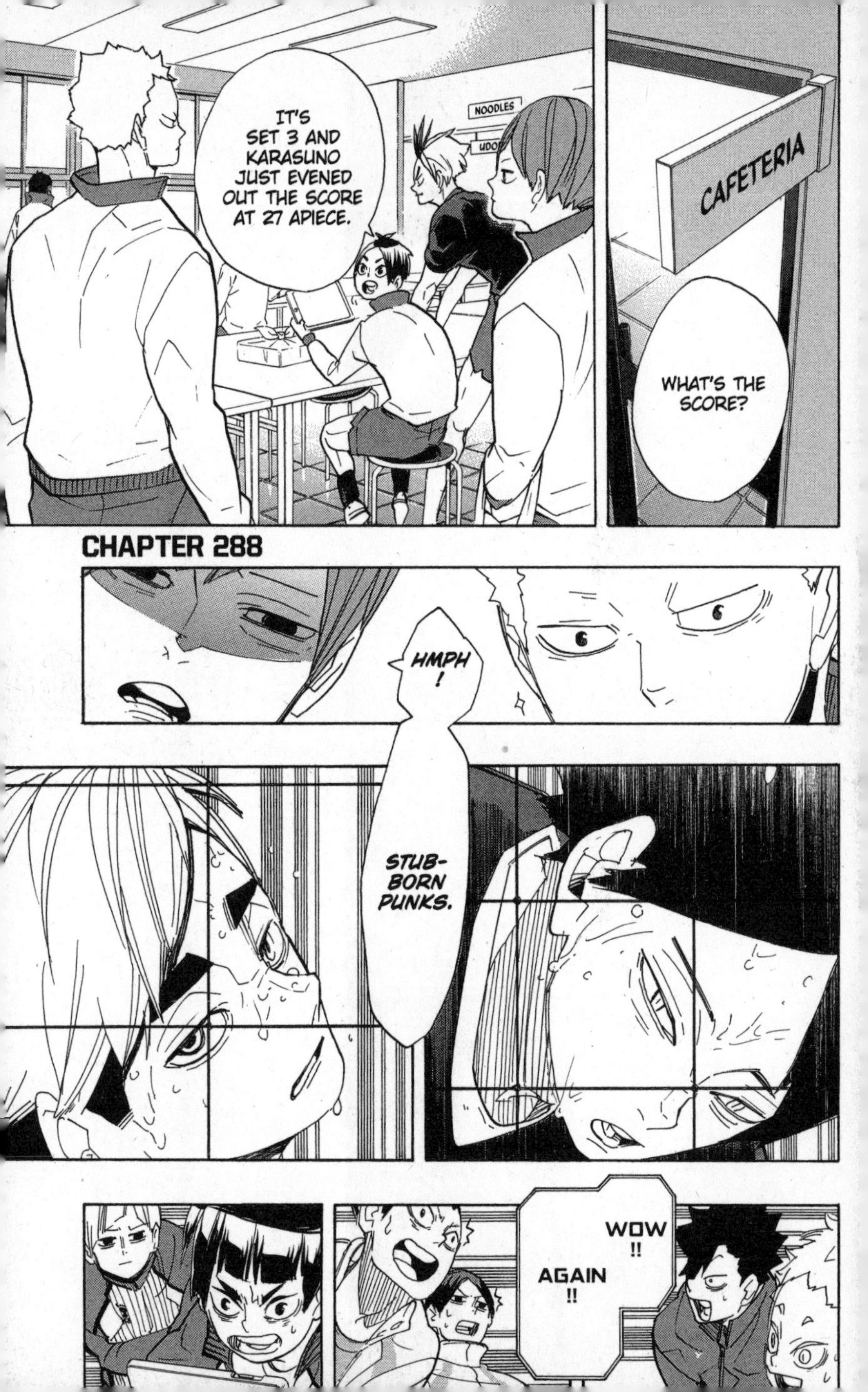
CAFETERIA
WHAT'S THE SCORE?
NOODLES
UDO
IT'S SET 3 AND KARASUNO JUST EVENED OUT THE SCORE AT 27 APIECE.
CHAPTER 288
HMPH!
STUBBORN PUNKS.
WOW!!
AGAIN!!

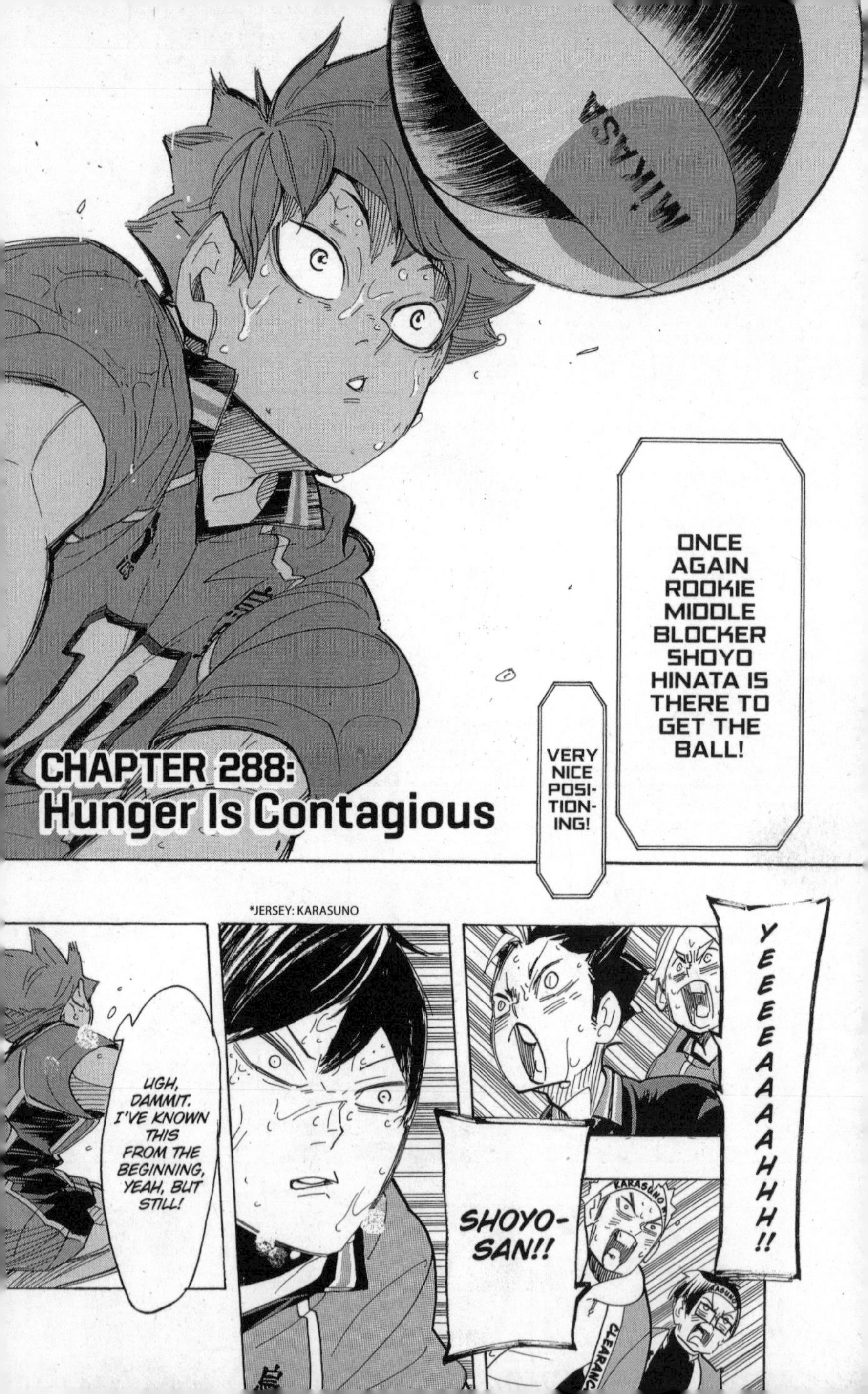
MIKASA
ONCE AGAIN ROOKIE MIDDLE BLOCKER SHOYO HINATA IS THERE TO GET THE BALL!
VERY NICE POSI-TION-ING!
CHAPTER 288:
Hunger Is Contagious
*JERSEY: KARASUNO
YEEEEAAAAAHHHH!!
SHOYO-SAN!!
UGH, DAMMIT. I'VE KNOWN THIS FROM THE BEGINNING, YEAH, BUT STILL!

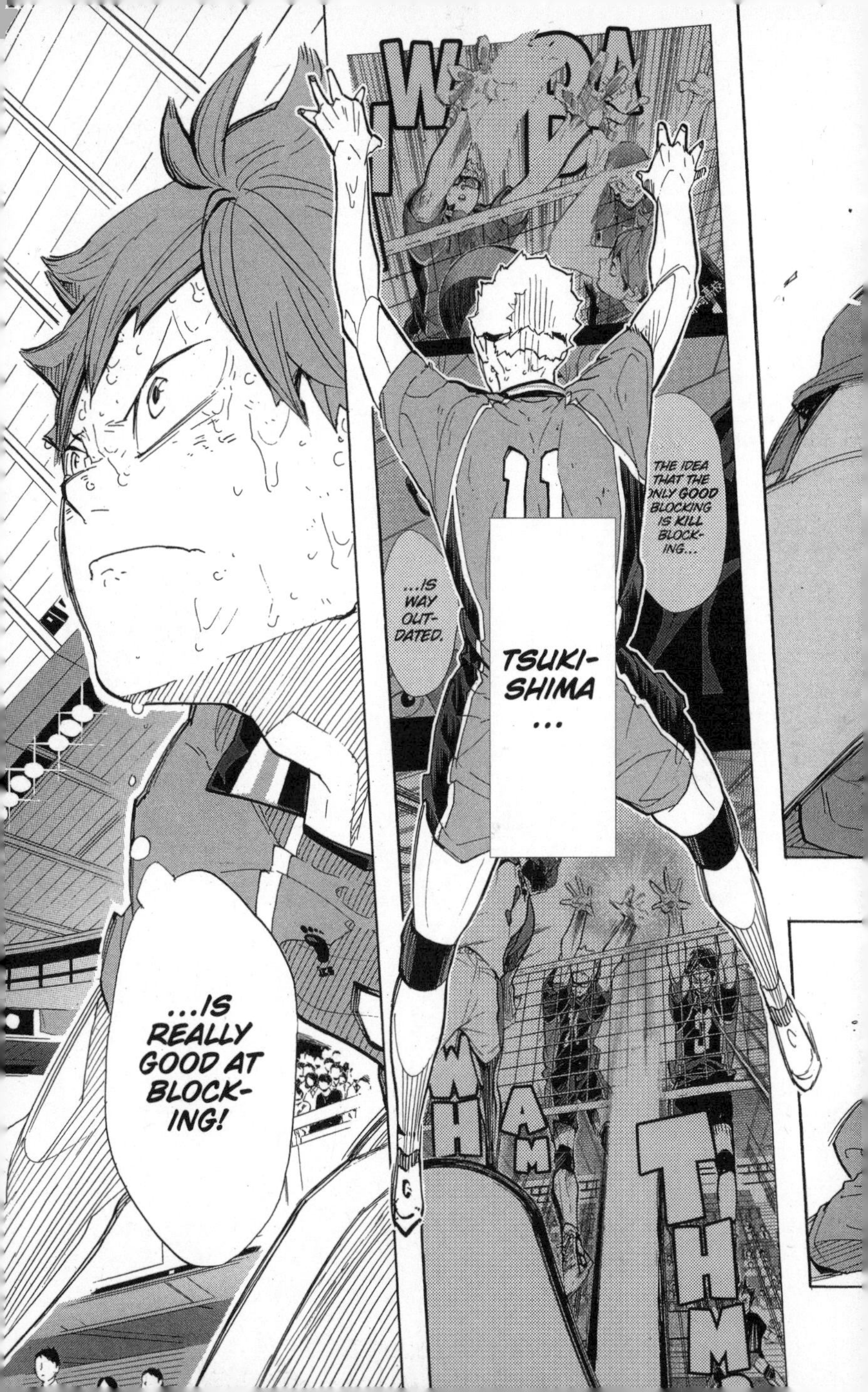
THE IDEA THAT THE ONLY GOOD BLOCKING IS KILL BLOCKING...
...IS WAY OUTDATED.
TSUKISHIMA...
WHAM
...IS REALLY GOOD AT BLOCKING!

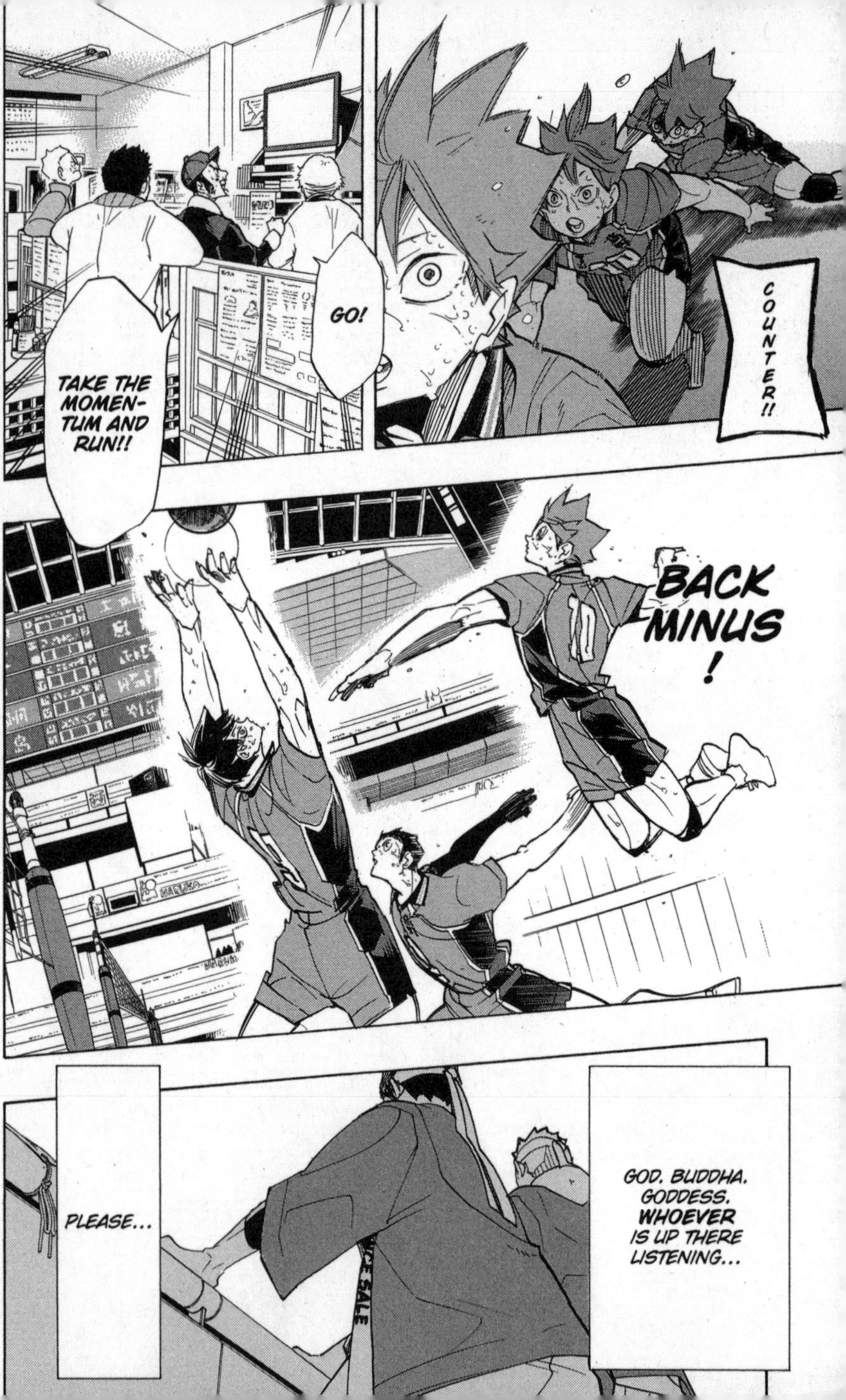
COUNTER!!
GO!
TAKE THE MOMENTUM AND RUN!!
BACK MINUS!
GOD. BUDDHA. GODDESS. WHOEVER IS UP THERE LISTENING...
PLEASE...

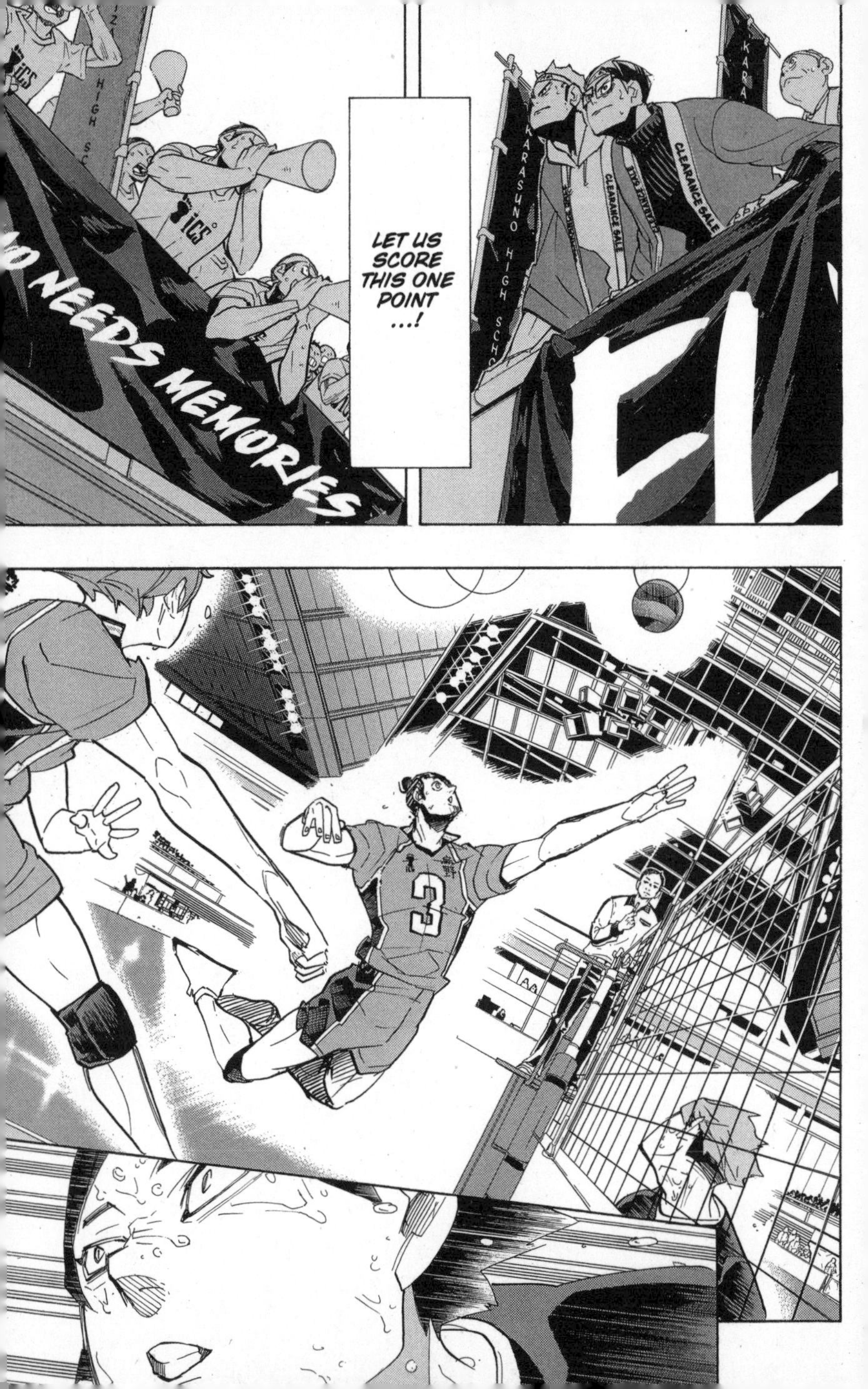
KARASUNO HIGH SCHO
CLEARANCE SALE
CLEARANCE SALE
LET US SCORE THIS ONE POINT ...!
HIGH SC
O NEEDS MEMORIES

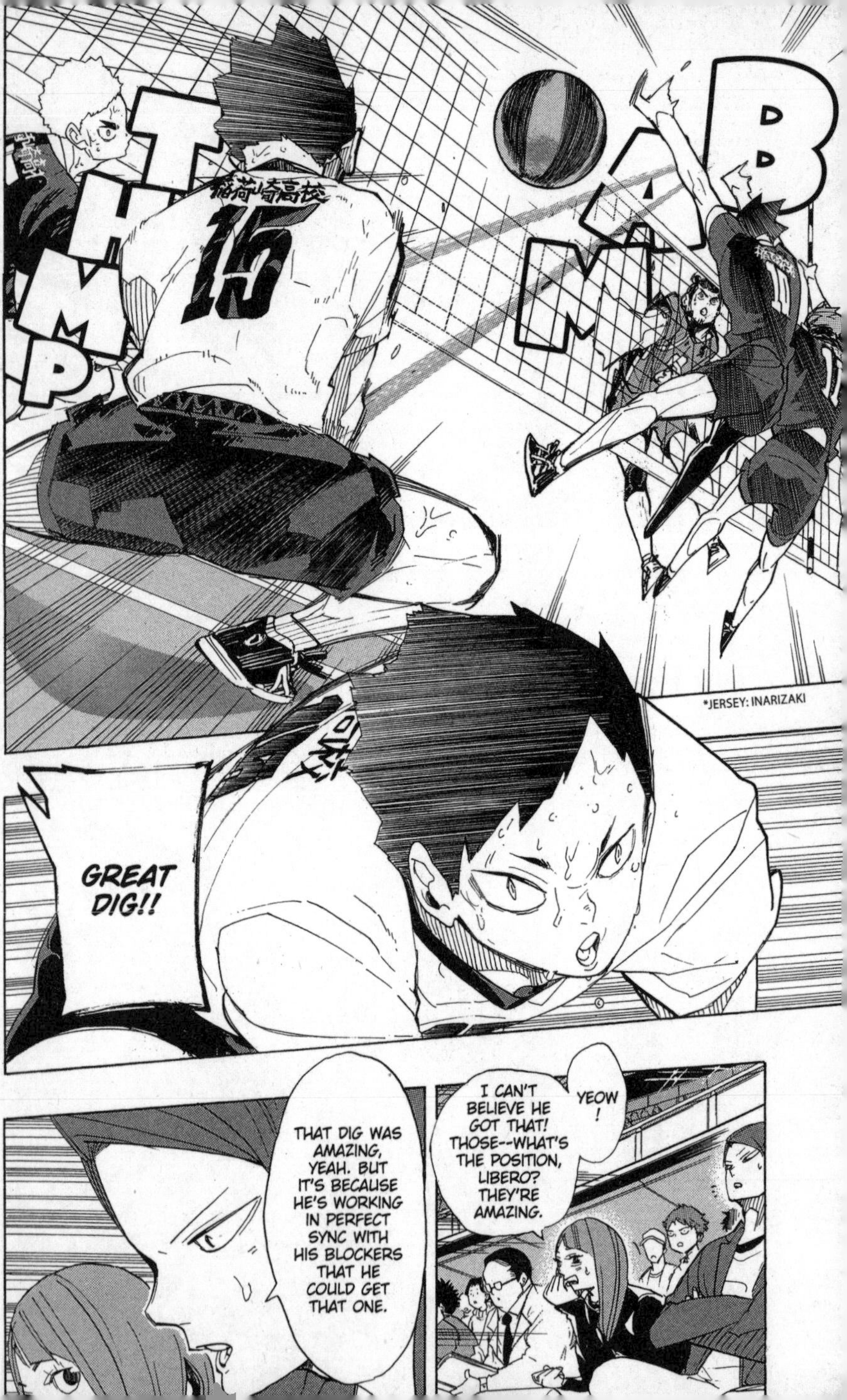
BAM
THUMP
*JERSEY: INARIZAKI
GREAT DIG!!
YEOW!
I CAN'T BELIEVE HE GOT THAT! THOSE--WHAT'S THE POSITION, LIBERO? THEY'RE AMAZING.
THAT DIG WAS AMAZING, YEAH. BUT IT'S BECAUSE HE'S WORKING IN PERFECT SYNC WITH HIS BLOCKERS THAT HE COULD GET THAT ONE.

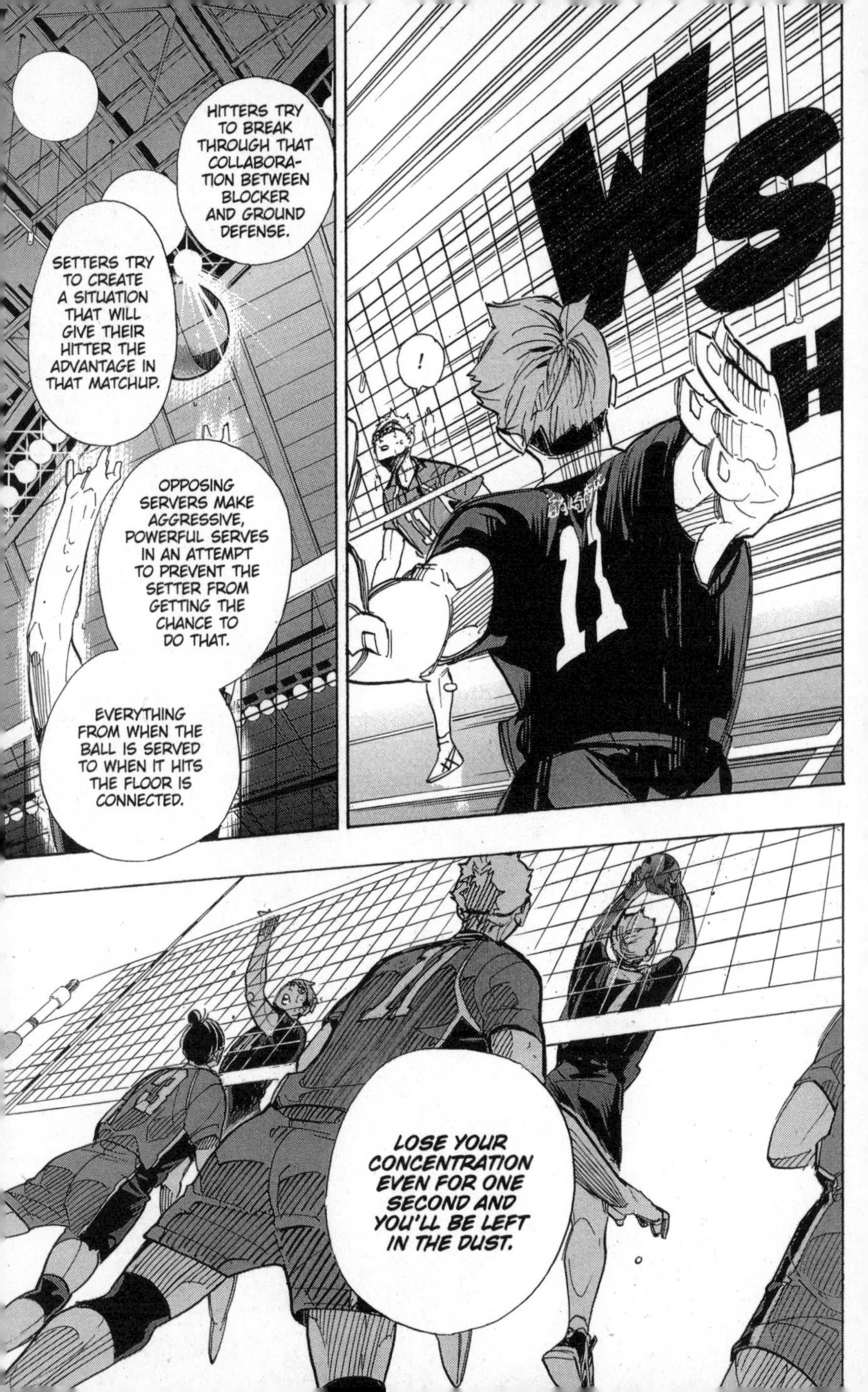
WSH
!
HITTERS TRY TO BREAK THROUGH THAT COLLABORATION BETWEEN BLOCKER AND GROUND DEFENSE.
SETTERS TRY TO CREATE A SITUATION THAT WILL GIVE THEIR HITTER THE ADVANTAGE IN THAT MATCHUP.
OPPOSING SERVERS MAKE AGGRESSIVE, POWERFUL SERVES IN AN ATTEMPT TO PREVENT THE SETTER FROM GETTING THE CHANCE TO DO THAT.
EVERYTHING FROM WHEN THE BALL IS SERVED TO WHEN IT HITS THE FLOOR IS CONNECTED.
LOSE YOUR CONCENTRATION EVEN FOR ONE SECOND AND YOU'LL BE LEFT IN THE DUST.

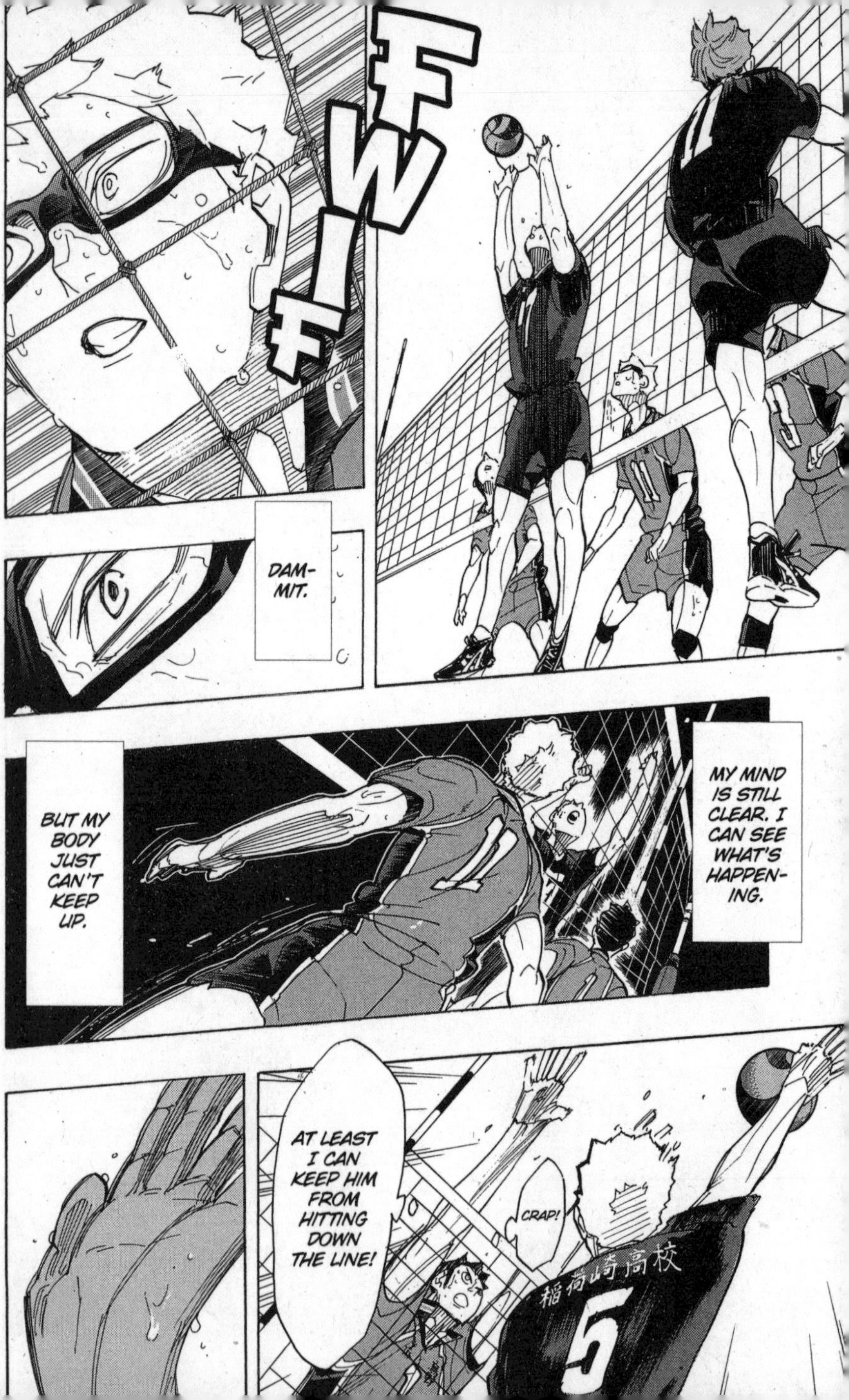
FWIF
DAM-MIT.
MY MIND IS STILL CLEAR. I CAN SEE WHAT'S HAPPENING.
BUT MY BODY JUST CAN'T KEEP UP.
AT LEAST I CAN KEEP HIM FROM HITTING DOWN THE LINE!
CRAP!
稲荷崎高校
5

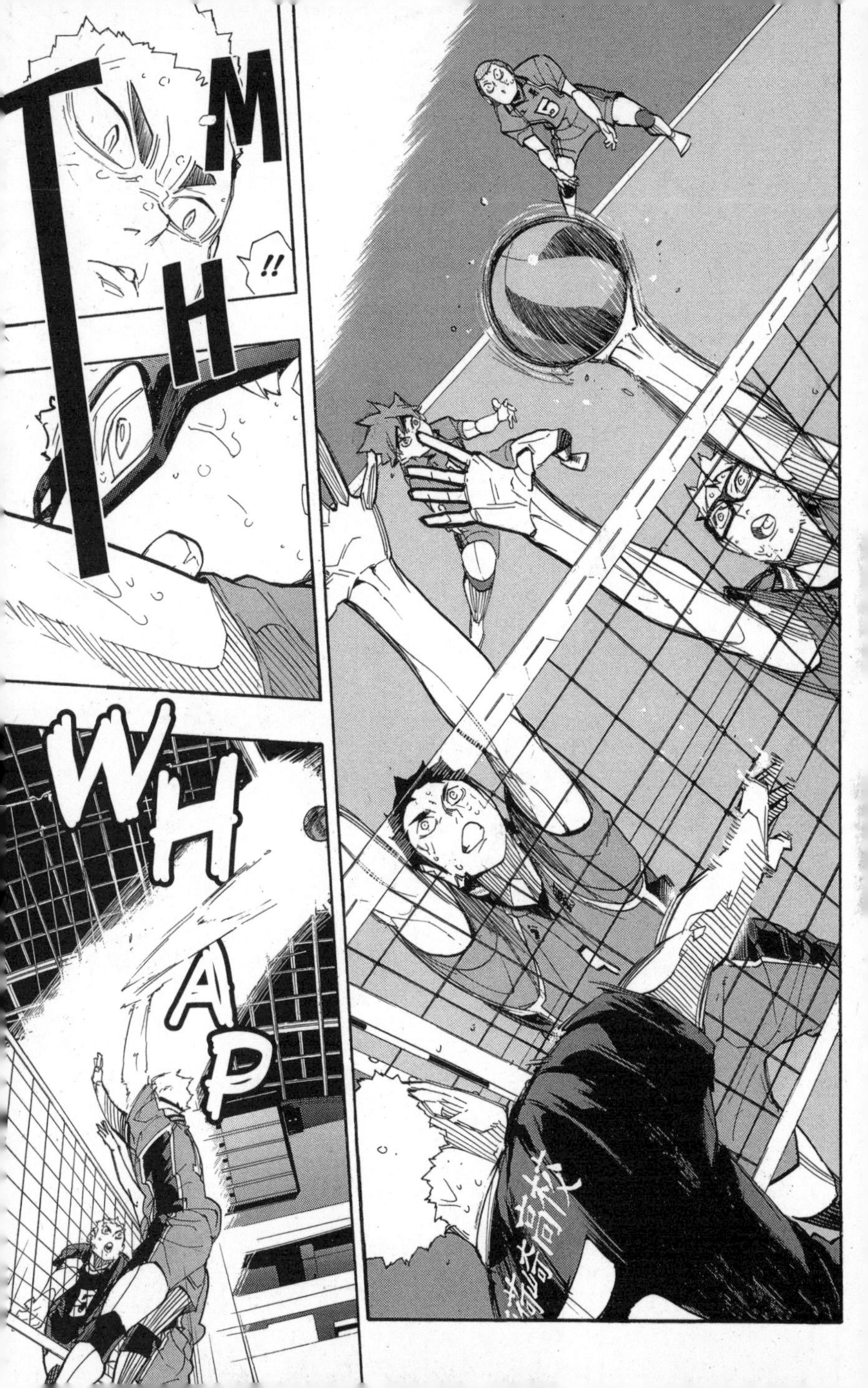
!!
WHAP

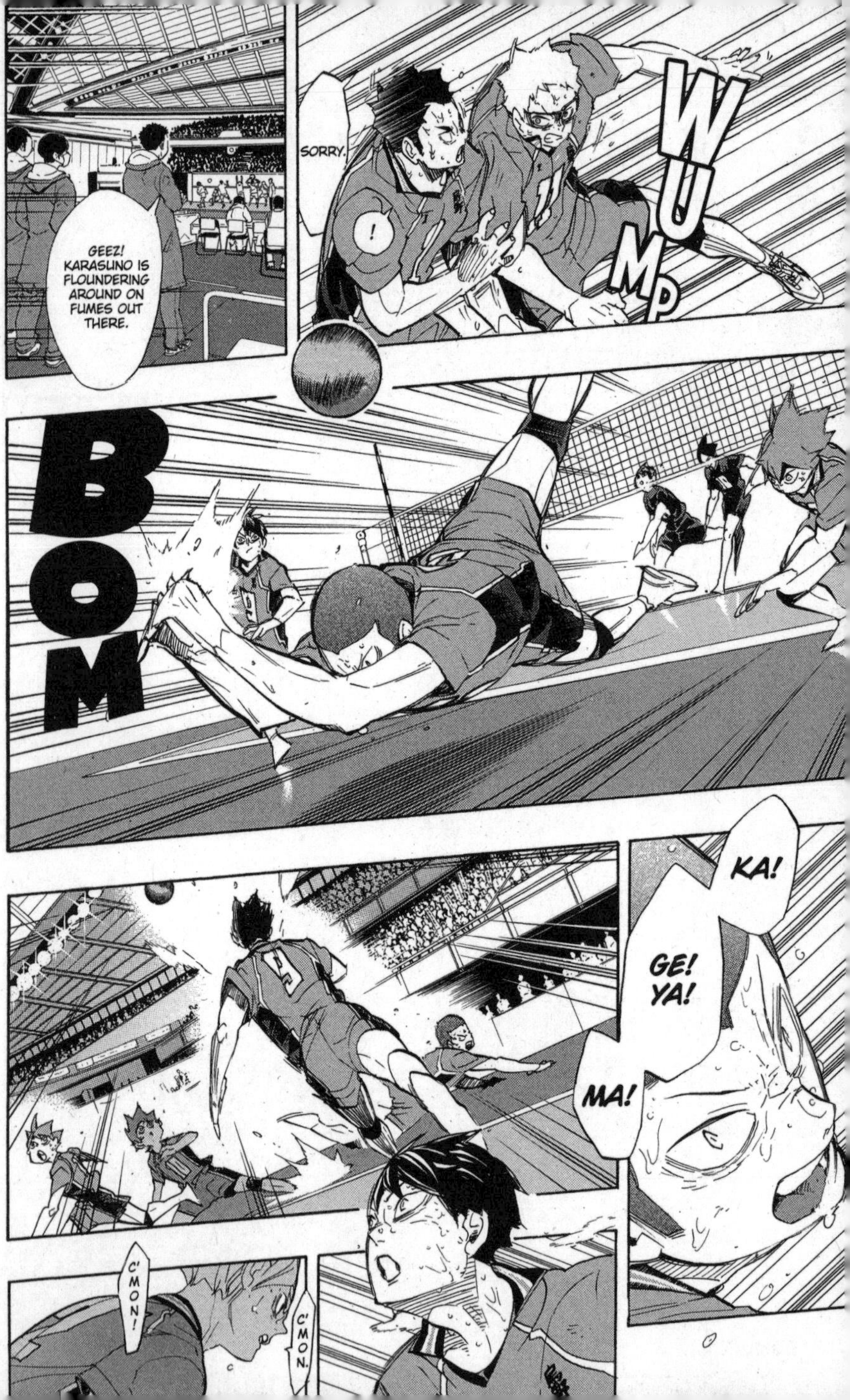
WUMP
SORRY.
!
GEEZ! KARASUNO IS FLOUNDERING AROUND ON FUMES OUT THERE.
BOM
KA!
GE! YA!
MA!
C'MON.
C'MON!

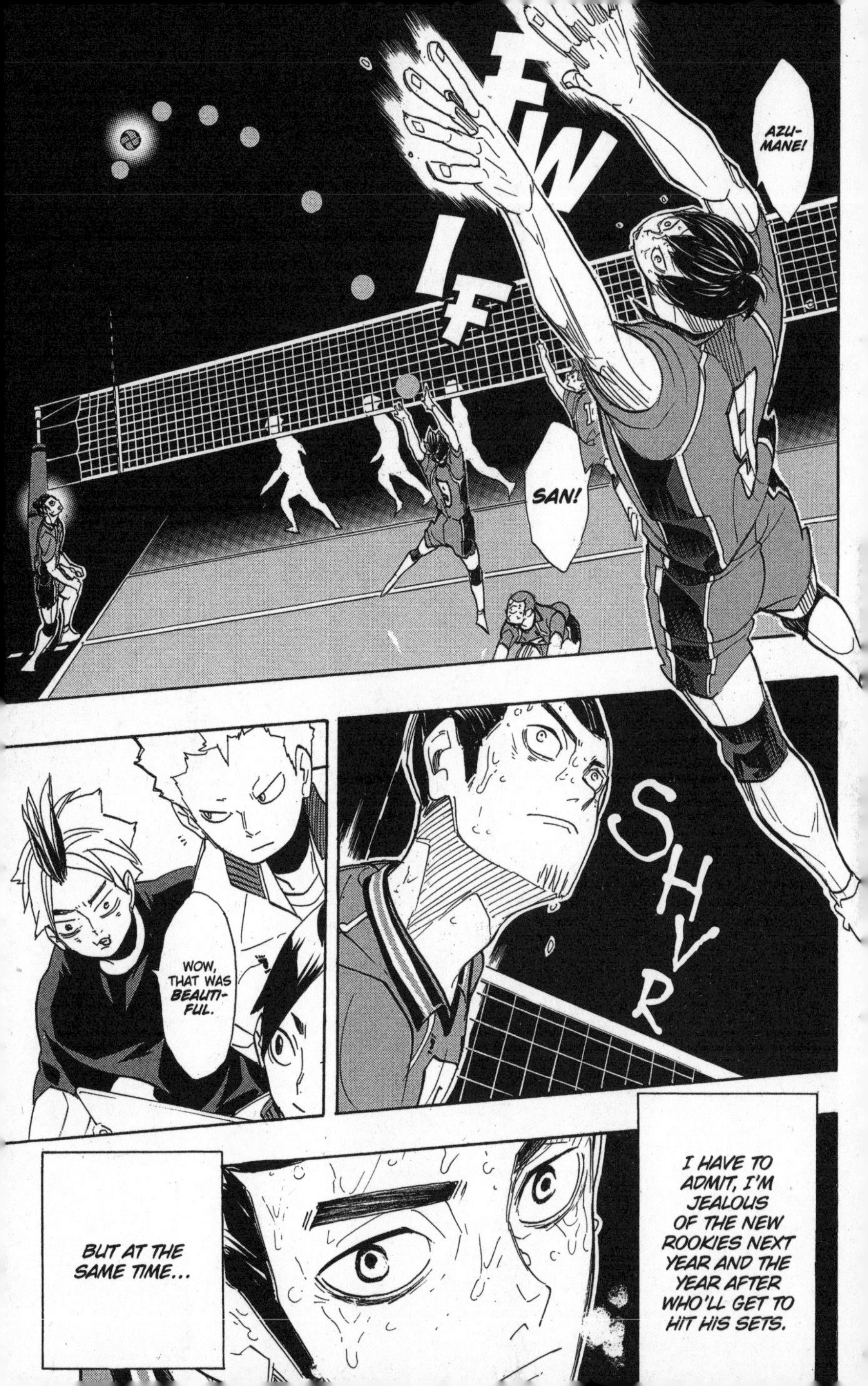
FWIF
AZU-MANE!
SAN!
SHVR
WOW, THAT WAS BEAUTI-FUL.
I HAVE TO ADMIT, I'M JEALOUS OF THE NEW ROOKIES NEXT YEAR AND THE YEAR AFTER WHO'LL GET TO HIT HIS SETS.
BUT AT THE SAME TIME...

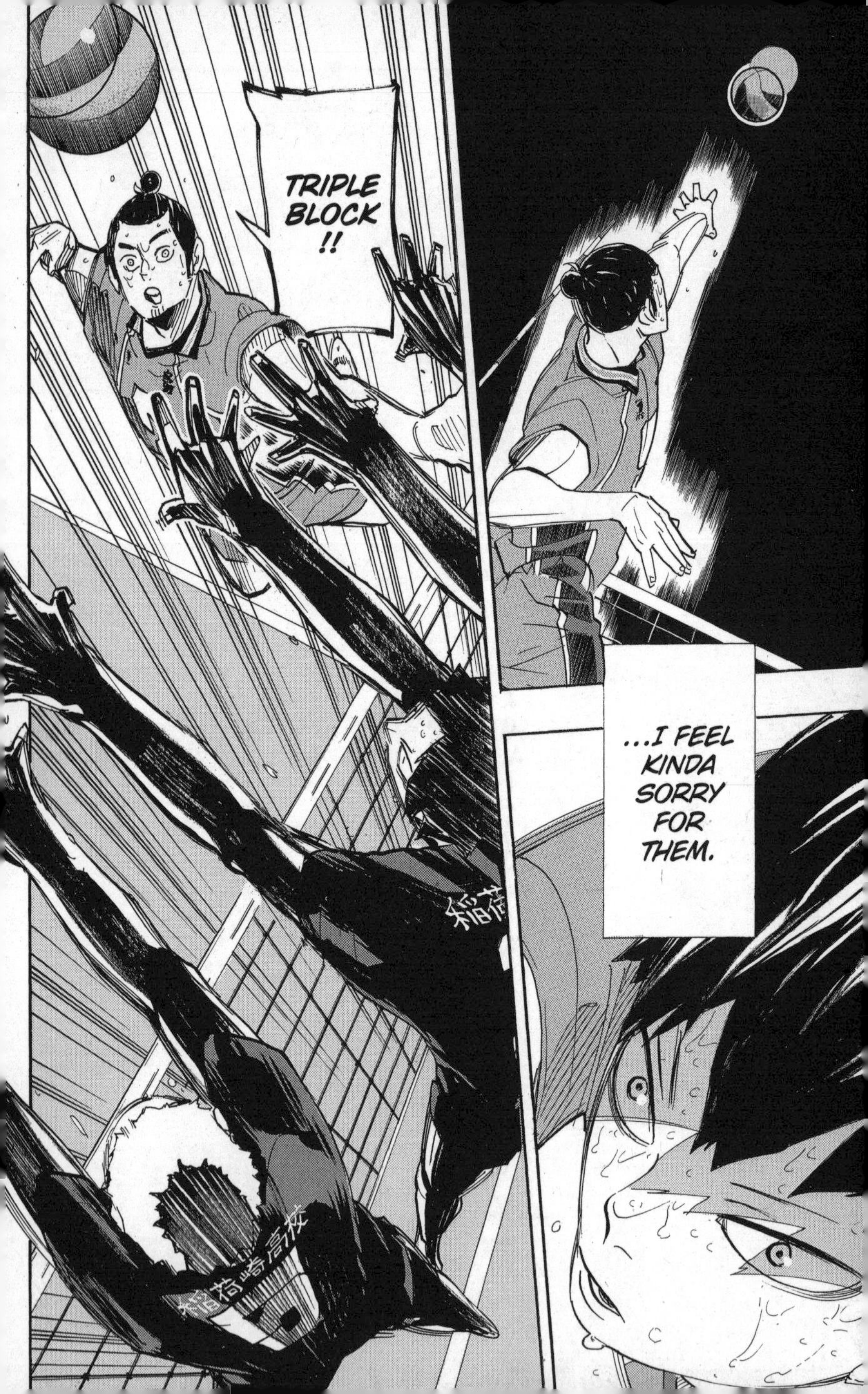
...I FEEL KINDA SORRY FOR THEM.
TRIPLE BLOCK !!
稲荷崎高校

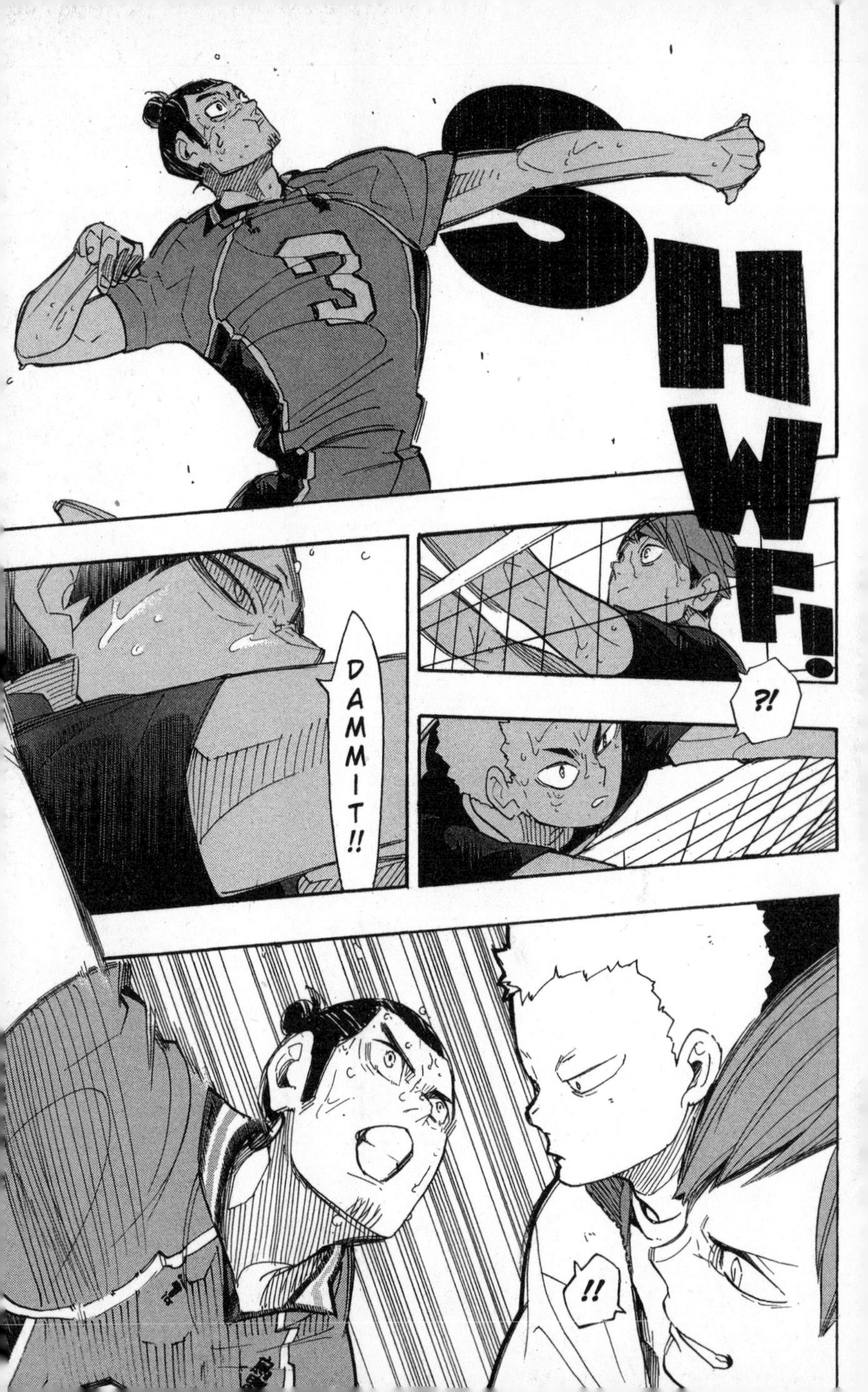
SHWFF!!
?!
DAMMIT!!
!!

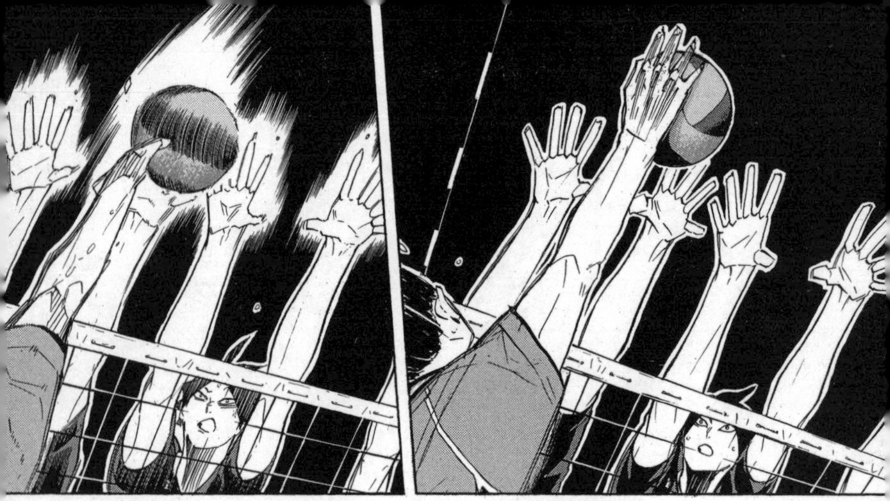

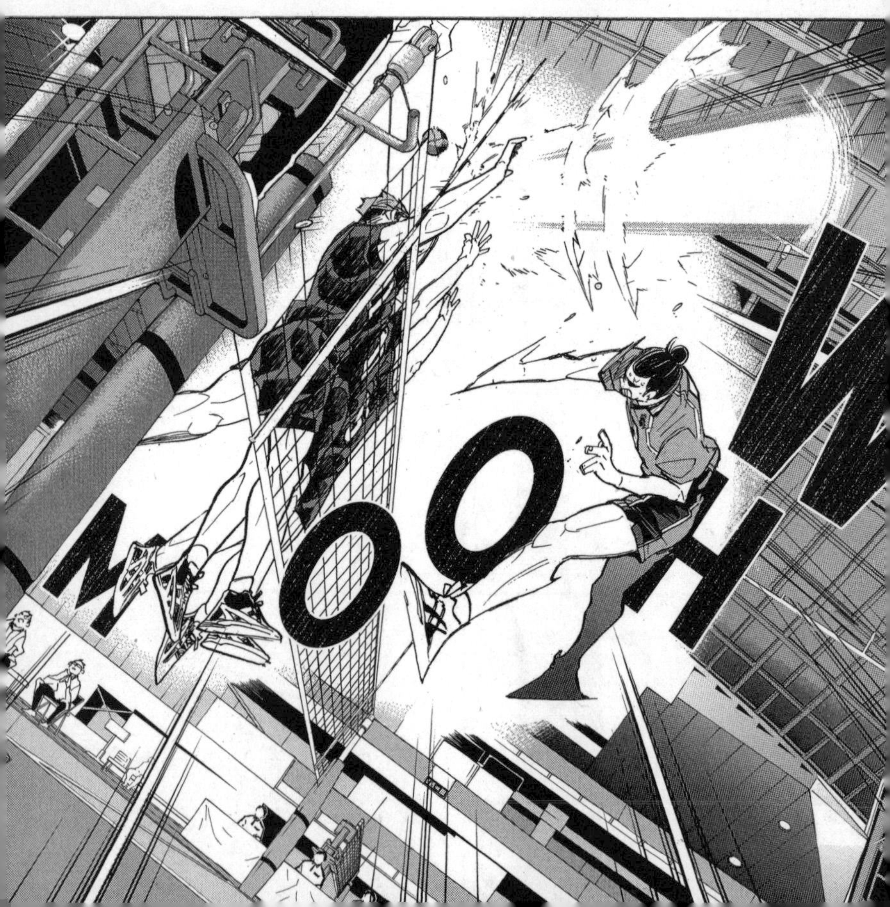
WHOOM

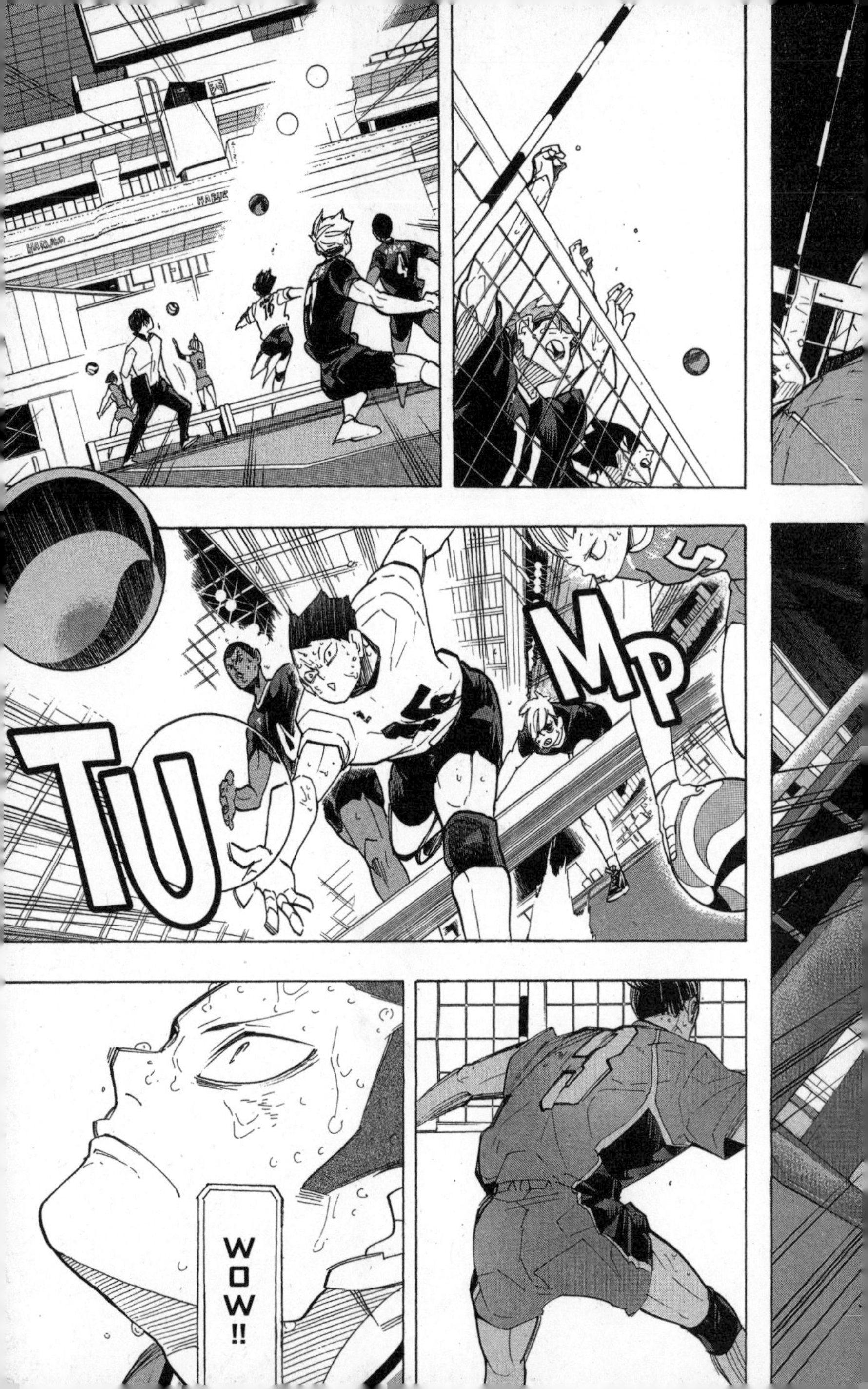
TMP
WOW!!

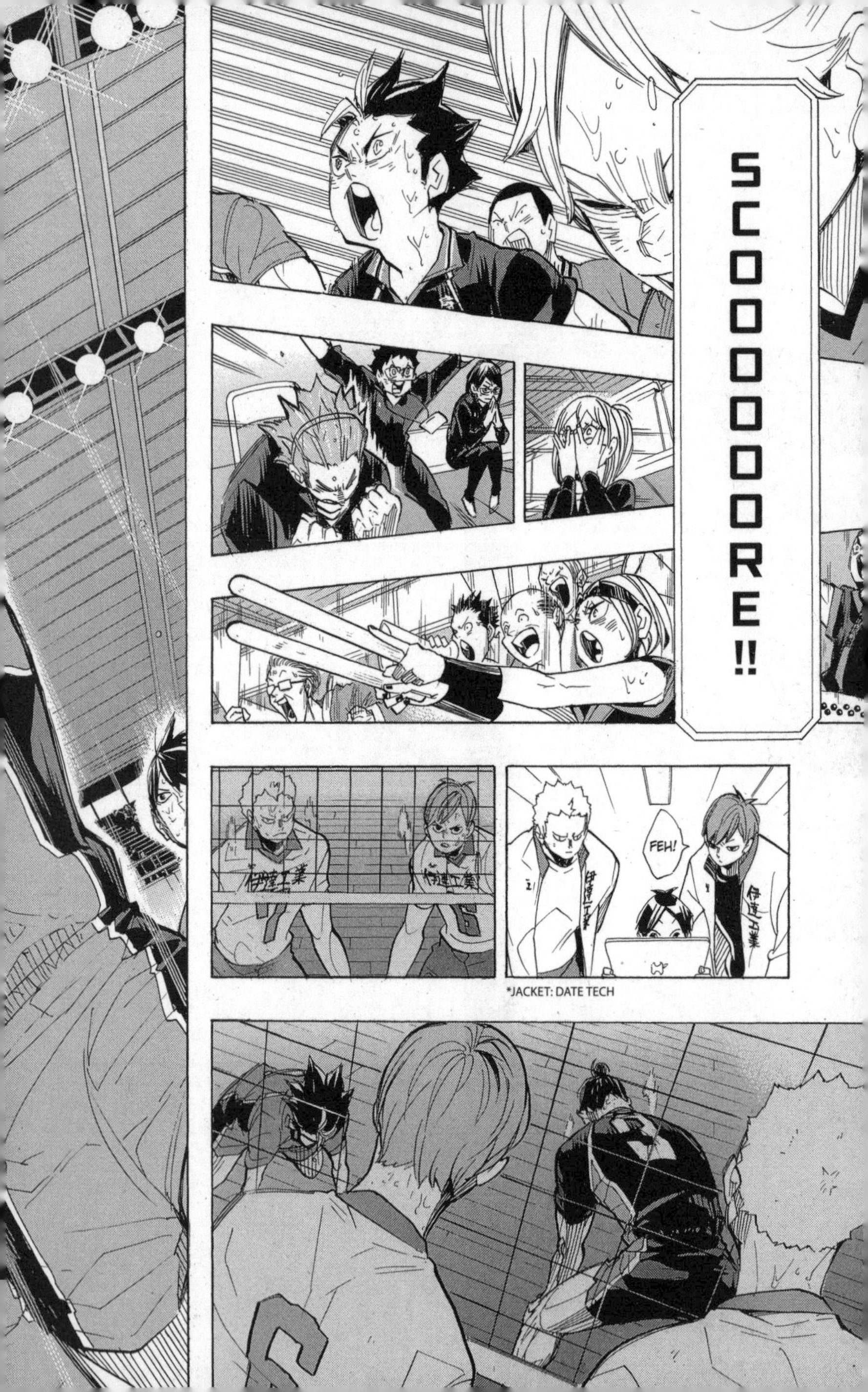
SCOOOOOOORE!!
FEH!
伊達工業
*JACKET: DATE TECH

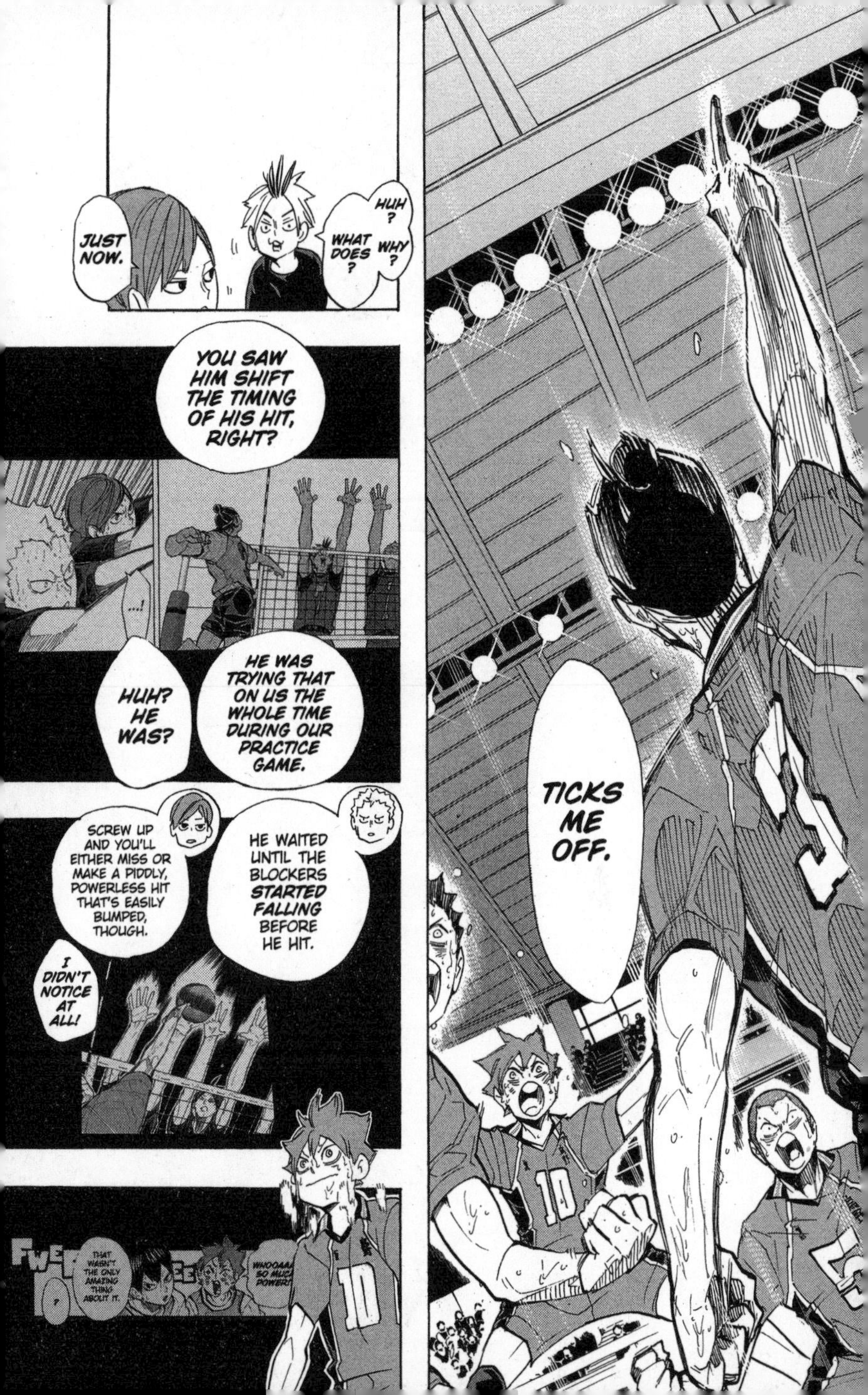
TICKS ME OFF.
HUH? WHY?
WHAT DOES?
JUST NOW.
YOU SAW HIM SHIFT THE TIMING OF HIS HIT, RIGHT?
...!
HE WAS TRYING THAT ON US THE WHOLE TIME DURING OUR PRACTICE GAME.
HUH? HE WAS?
HE WAITED UNTIL THE BLOCKERS STARTED FALLING BEFORE HE HIT.
SCREW UP AND YOU'LL EITHER MISS OR MAKE A PIDDLY, POWERLESS HIT THAT'S EASILY BUMPED, THOUGH.
I DIDN'T NOTICE AT ALL!
WHOOAA! SO MUCH POWER!
THAT WASN'T THE ONLY AMAZING THING ABOUT IT.

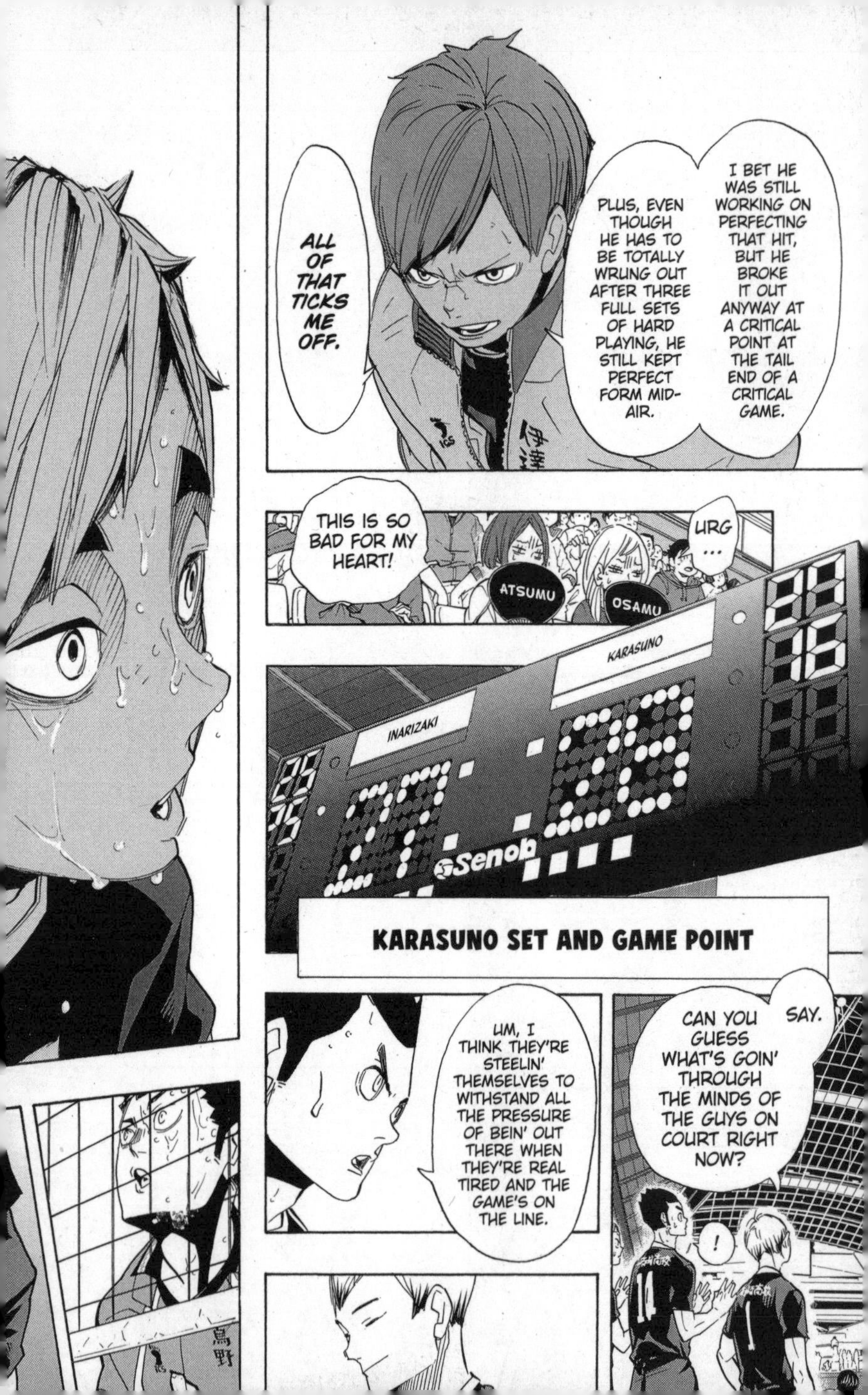
I BET HE WAS STILL WORKING ON PERFECTING THAT HIT, BUT HE BROKE IT OUT ANYWAY AT A CRITICAL POINT AT THE TAIL END OF A CRITICAL GAME.
PLUS, EVEN THOUGH HE HAS TO BE TOTALLY WRUNG OUT AFTER THREE FULL SETS OF HARD PLAYING, HE STILL KEPT PERFECT FORM MID-AIR.
ALL OF THAT TICKS ME OFF.
URG ...
THIS IS SO BAD FOR MY HEART!
ATSUMU
OSAMU
KARASUNO
INARIZAKI
Senob
KARASUNO SET AND GAME POINT
SAY.
CAN YOU GUESS WHAT'S GOIN' THROUGH THE MINDS OF THE GUYS ON COURT RIGHT NOW?
!
UM, I THINK THEY'RE STEELIN' THEMSELVES TO WITHSTAND ALL THE PRESSURE OF BEIN' OUT THERE WHEN THEY'RE REAL TIRED AND THE GAME'S ON THE LINE.

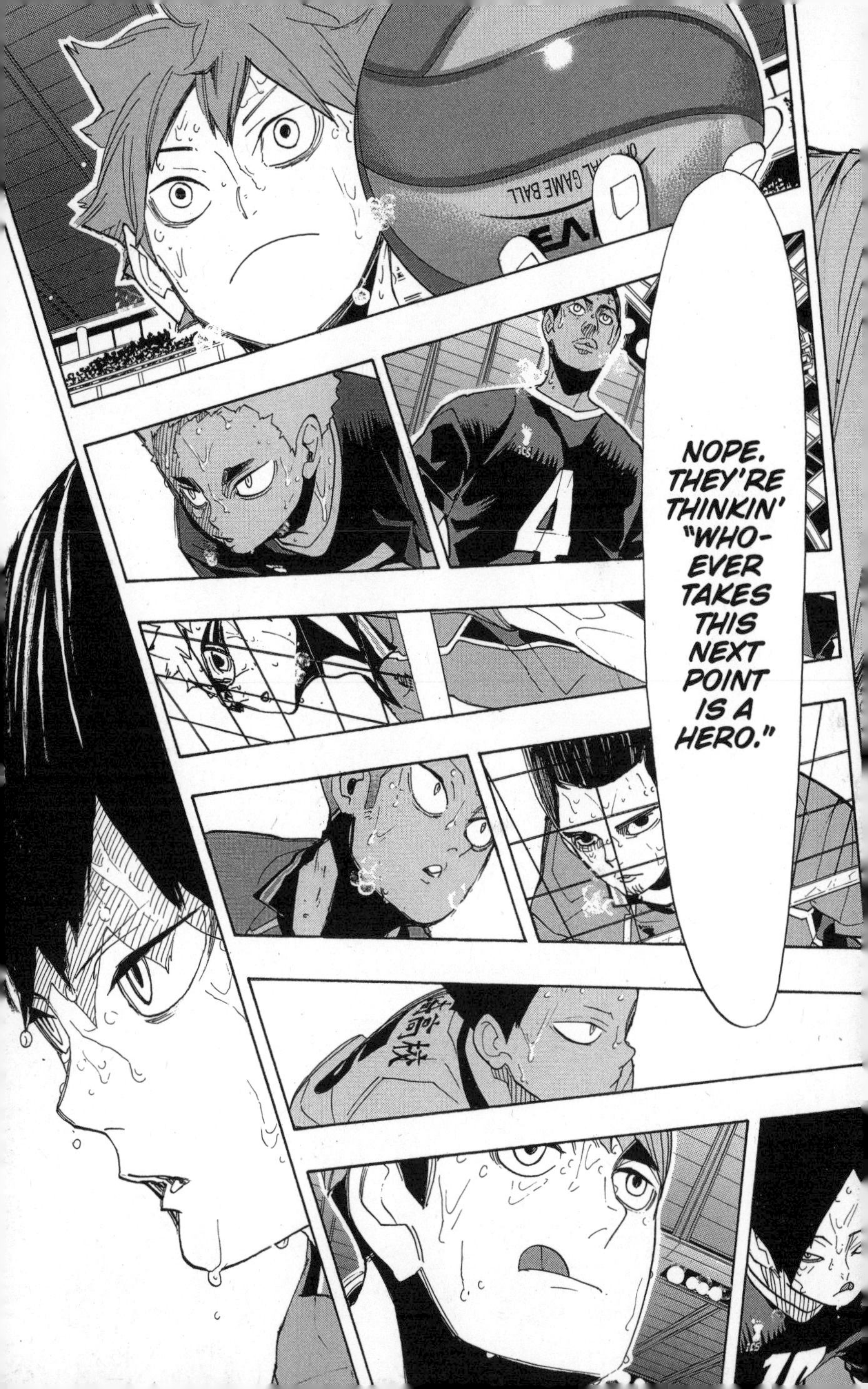
NOPE. THEY'RE THINKIN' "WHO-EVER TAKES THIS NEXT POINT IS A HERO."

HAIKYU!!

CHAPTER 289: Take It Easy: Part 2

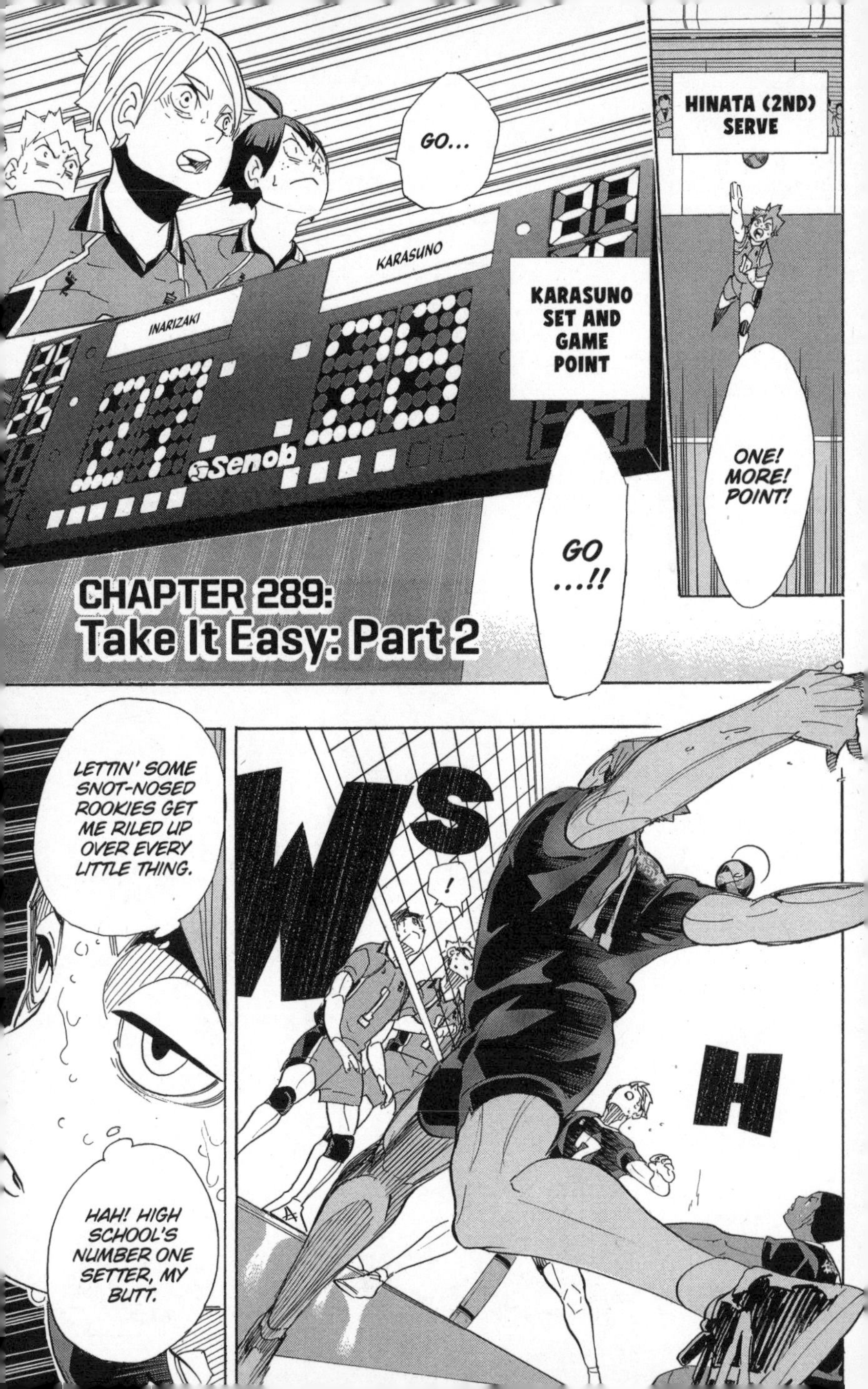
HINATA (2ND) SERVE
ONE! MORE! POINT!
GO...
KARASUNO
INARIZAKI
Senob
KARASUNO SET AND GAME POINT
GO ...!!
!
LETTIN' SOME SNOT-NOSED ROOKIES GET ME RILED UP OVER EVERY LITTLE THING.
HAH! HIGH SCHOOL'S NUMBER ONE SETTER, MY BUTT.

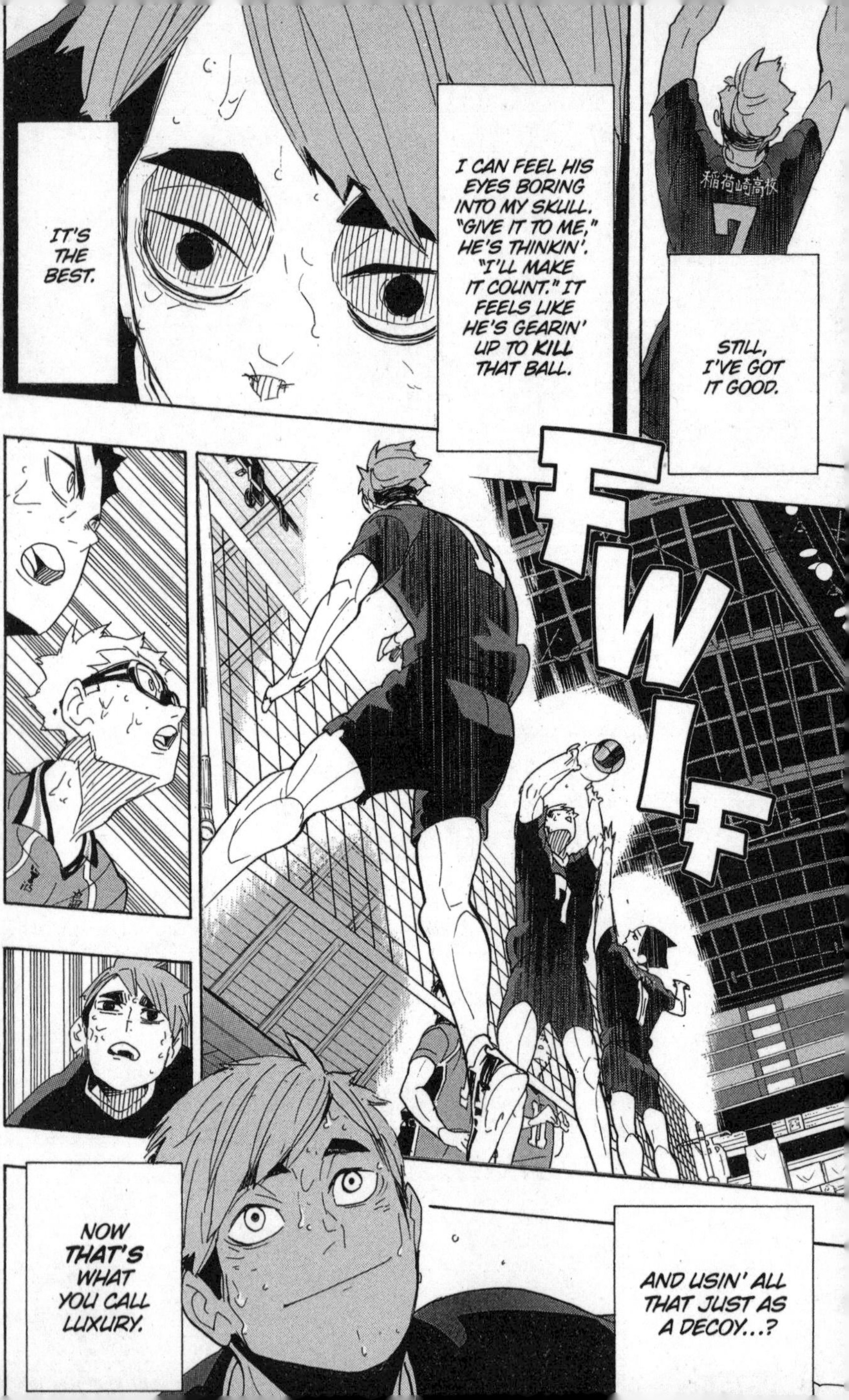
I CAN FEEL HIS EYES BORING INTO MY SKULL. "GIVE IT TO ME," HE'S THINKIN'. "I'LL MAKE IT COUNT." IT FEELS LIKE HE'S GEARIN' UP TO KILL THAT BALL.
STILL, I'VE GOT IT GOOD.
IT'S THE BEST.
FWIF
AND USIN' ALL THAT JUST AS A DECOY...?
NOW THAT'S WHAT YOU CALL LUXURY.

INARIZAKI	KARASUNO
28	28

UH, *I'M* THE ONE DOING THE ATTACKING, THANKS.

Heh.

NO WAY AM I LETTIN' MY ATTACKS GET BUMPED ALL DAY LONG.

YEAH.

...BUT SO FAR HE'S DOING A GOOD JOB OF KEEPING HIMSELF DISCI-PLINED.

THE TWINS' QUICK IS A NEW TOY I'M SURE ATSUMU IS JUST DYIN' TO PLAY WITH...

THE MIYA TWINS MAY NOT HAVE USED THEIR NEW SUPER-QUICK SET THAT MANY TIMES, BUT IT HAS LEFT A DEFINITE IMPRESSION ON KARASUNO. ATSUMU MIYA IS MAKING CLEVER USE OF EVEN THE SIMPLE THREAT OF THAT ATTACK NOW.

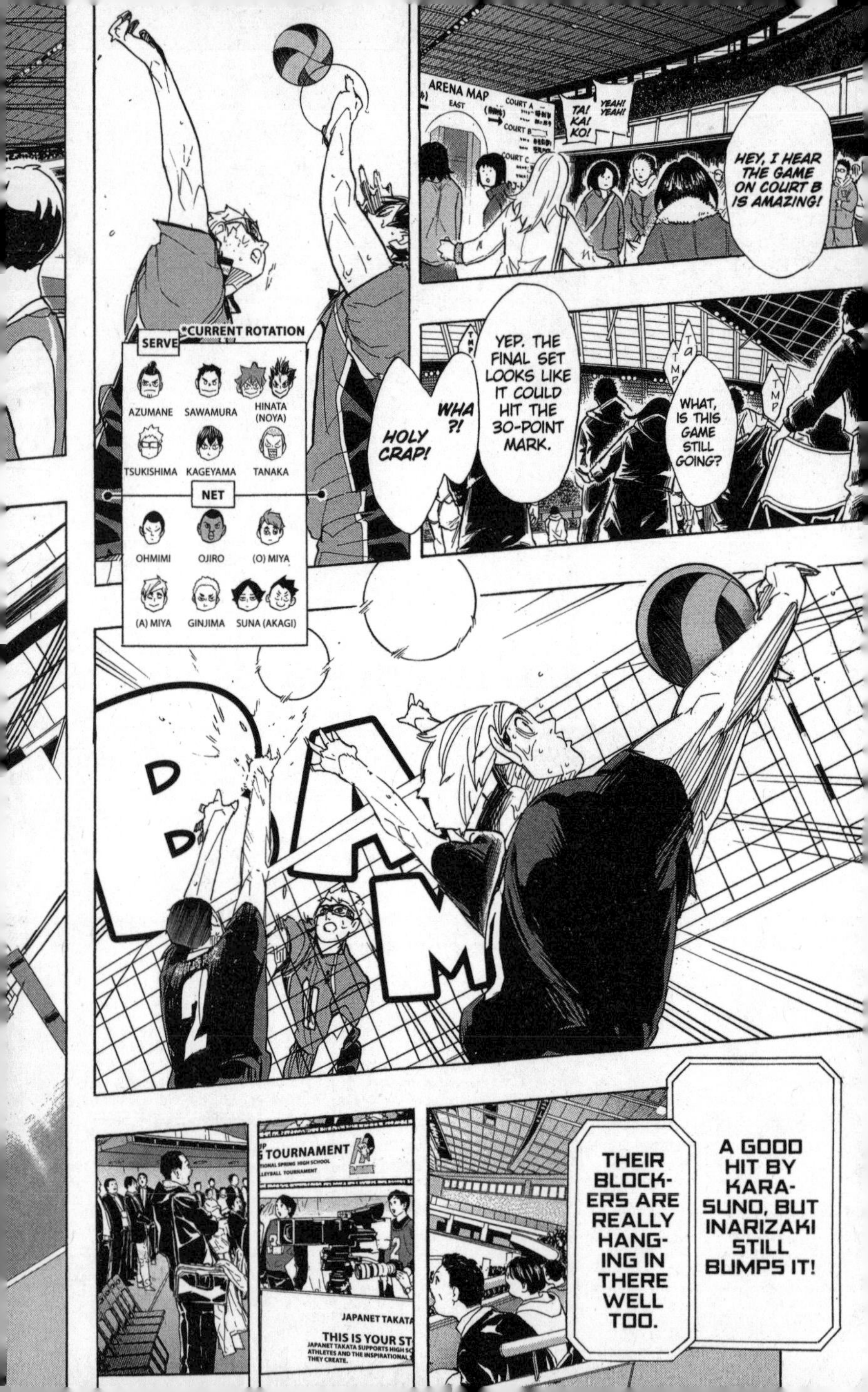

ARENA MAP
EAST
COURT A
COURT B
COURT C
TA! KA! KO!
YEAH! YEAH!
HEY, I HEAR THE GAME ON COURT B IS AMAZING!
TMP
TMP
TMP
TMP
WHAT, IS THIS GAME STILL GOING?
YEP. THE FINAL SET LOOKS LIKE IT COULD HIT THE 30-POINT MARK.
WHA?!
HOLY CRAP!
*CURRENT ROTATION
SERVE
AZUMANE
SAWAMURA
HINATA (NOYA)
TSUKISHIMA
KAGEYAMA
TANAKA
NET
OHMIMI
OJIRO
(O) MIYA
(A) MIYA
GINJIMA
SUNA (AKAGI)
DDAM
A GOOD HIT BY KARA-SUNO, BUT INARIZAKI STILL BUMPS IT!
THEIR BLOCK-ERS ARE REALLY HANG-ING IN THERE WELL TOO.
TOURNAMENT
JAPANET TAKATA
THIS IS YOUR ST

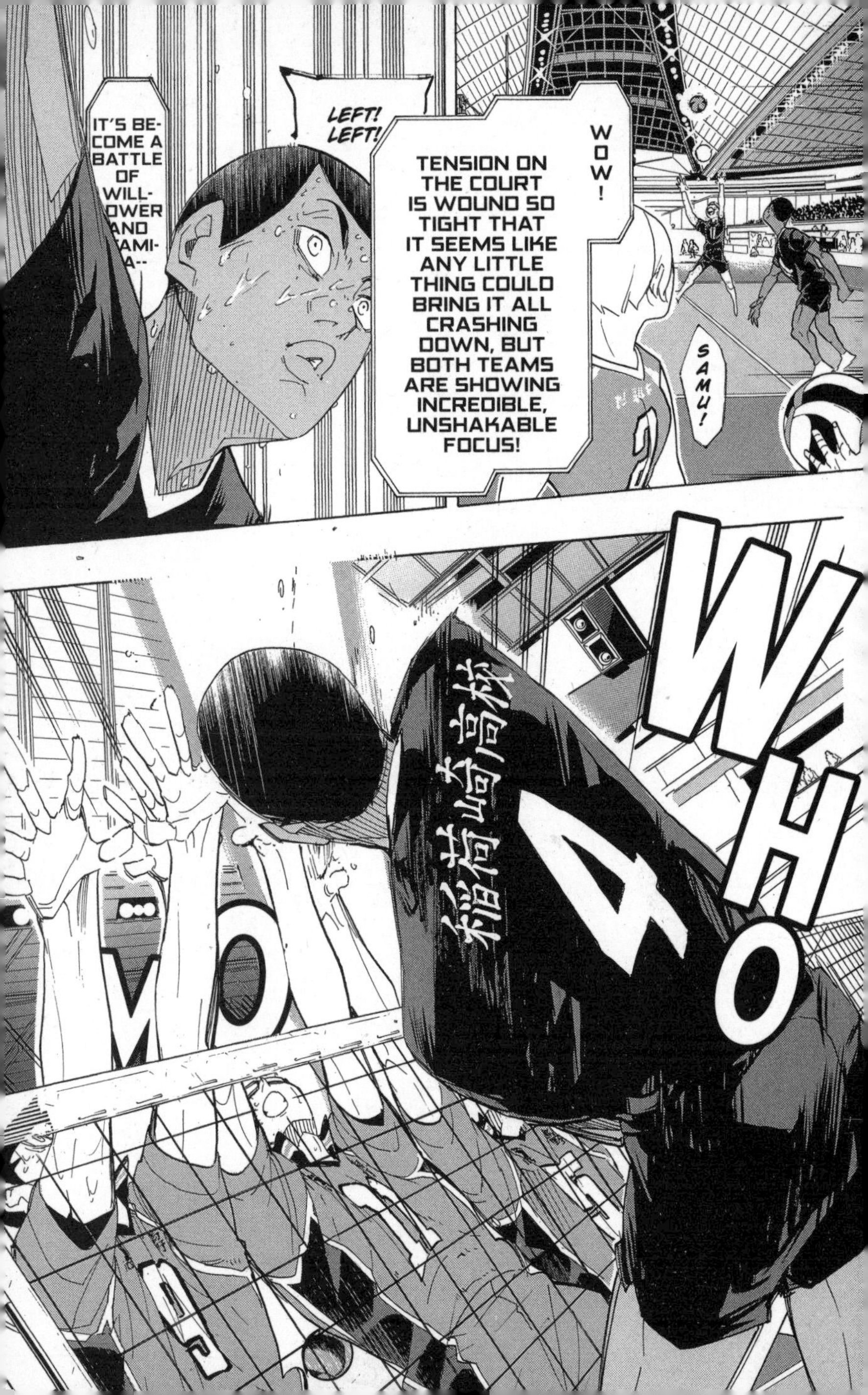
WOW!
TENSION ON THE COURT IS WOUND SO TIGHT THAT IT SEEMS LIKE ANY LITTLE THING COULD BRING IT ALL CRASHING DOWN, BUT BOTH TEAMS ARE SHOWING INCREDIBLE, UNSHAKABLE FOCUS!
SAMU!
LEFT! LEFT!
IT'S BE-COME A BATTLE OF WILL-
OWER
AND
AMI-
A--
稲荷崎高校
WHOO

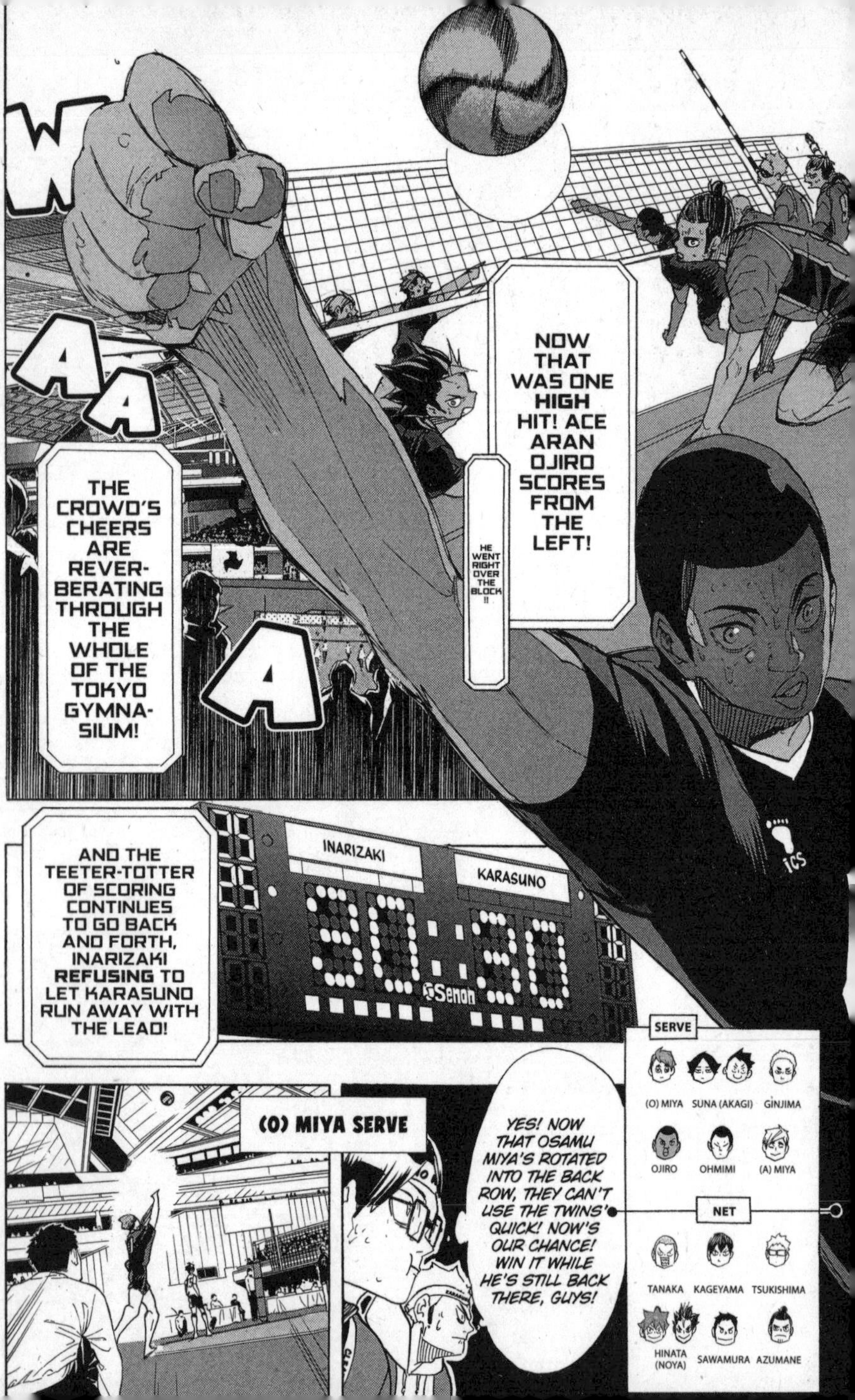
NOW THAT WAS ONE HIGH HIT! ACE ARAN OJIRO SCORES FROM THE LEFT!
HE WENT RIGHT OVER THE BLOCK!!
THE CROWD'S CHEERS ARE REVERBERATING THROUGH THE WHOLE OF THE TOKYO GYMNASIUM!
WAAAA
INARIZAKI
KARASUNO
30 : 30
AND THE TEETER-TOTTER OF SCORING CONTINUES TO GO BACK AND FORTH, INARIZAKI REFUSING TO LET KARASUNO RUN AWAY WITH THE LEAD!
SERVE
(O) MIYA
SUNA (AKAGI)
GINJIMA
OJIRO
OHMIMI
(A) MIYA
NET
TANAKA
KAGEYAMA
TSUKISHIMA
HINATA (NOYA)
SAWAMURA
AZUMANE
YES! NOW THAT OSAMU MIYA'S ROTATED INTO THE BACK ROW, THEY CAN'T USE THE TWINS' QUICK! NOW'S OUR CHANCE! WIN IT WHILE HE'S STILL BACK THERE, GUYS!
(O) MIYA SERVE

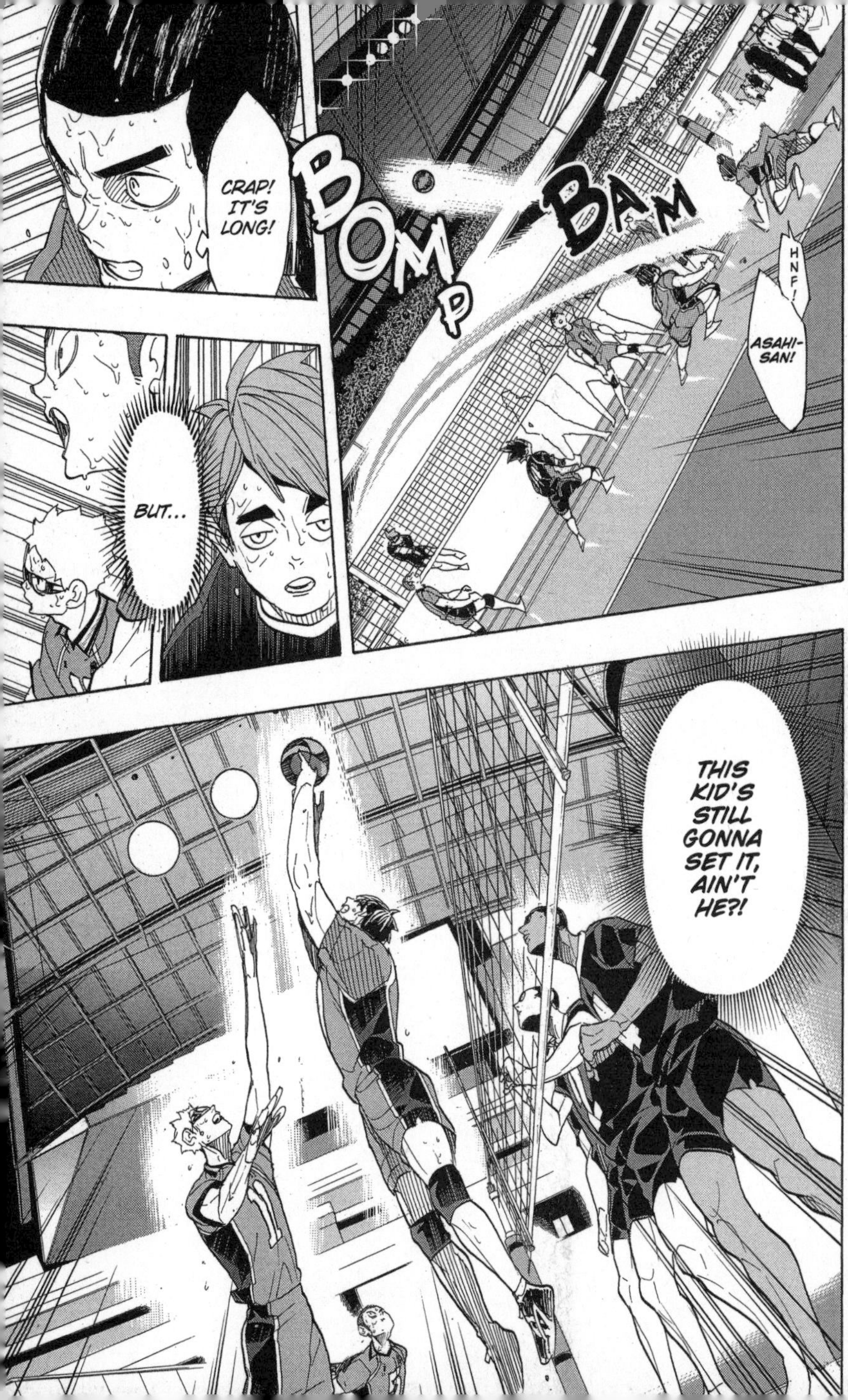
BOMP
BAM
HNF!
ASAHI-SAN!
CRAP! IT'S LONG!
BUT...
THIS KID'S STILL GONNA SET IT, AIN'T HE?!

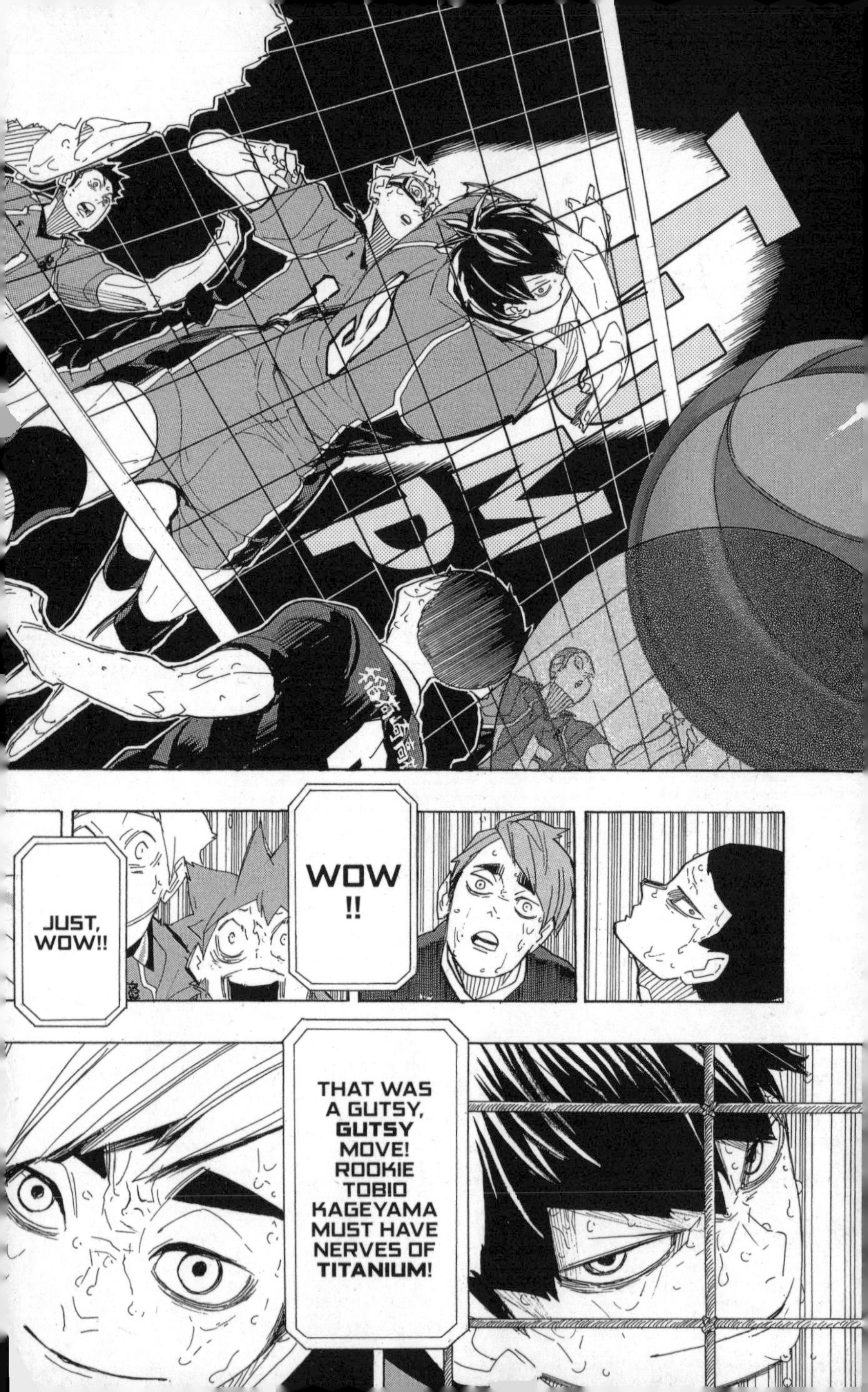
WOW !!
JUST, WOW!!
THAT WAS A GUTSY, GUTSY MOVE! ROOKIE TOBIO KAGEYAMA MUST HAVE NERVES OF TITANIUM!

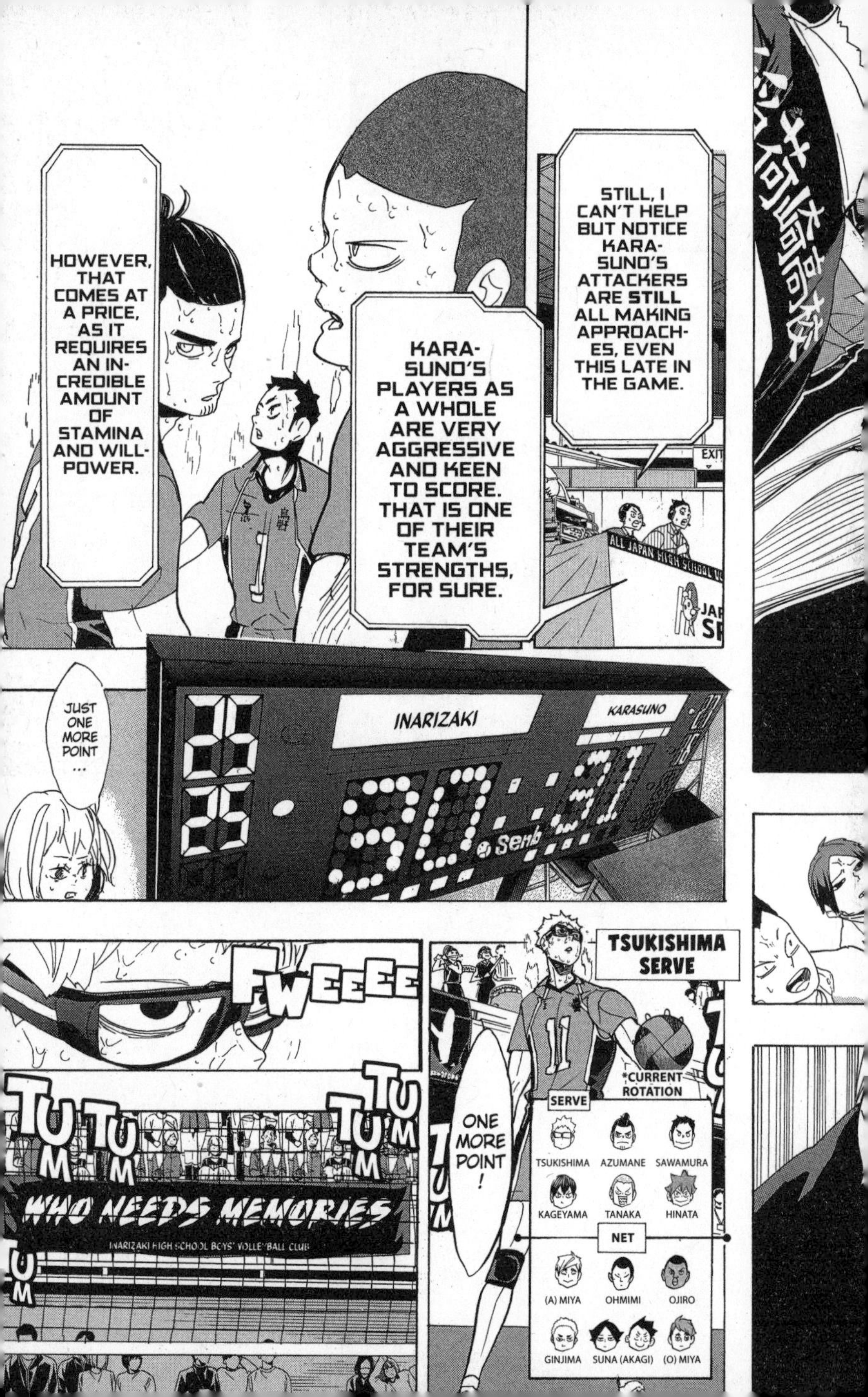
STILL, I CAN'T HELP BUT NOTICE KARA-SUNO'S ATTACKERS ARE STILL ALL MAKING APPROACH-ES, EVEN THIS LATE IN THE GAME.
EXIT
ALL JAPAN HIGH SCHOOL VO
KARA-SUNO'S PLAYERS AS A WHOLE ARE VERY AGGRESSIVE AND KEEN TO SCORE. THAT IS ONE OF THEIR TEAM'S STRENGTHS, FOR SURE.
HOWEVER, THAT COMES AT A PRICE, AS IT REQUIRES AN IN-CREDIBLE AMOUNT OF STAMINA AND WILL-POWER.
KARASUNO
INARIZAKI
JUST ONE MORE POINT ...
TSUKISHIMA SERVE
TUTUM
*CURRENT ROTATION
SERVE
TSUKISHIMA
AZUMANE
SAWAMURA
KAGEYAMA
TANAKA
HINATA
NET
(A) MIYA
OHMIMI
OJIRO
GINJIMA
SUNA (AKAGI)
(O) MIYA
ONE MORE POINT !
FWEEEE
TUTUM
TUTUM
WHO NEEDS MEMORIES
INARIZAKI HIGH SCHOOL BOYS' VOLLEYBALL CLUB

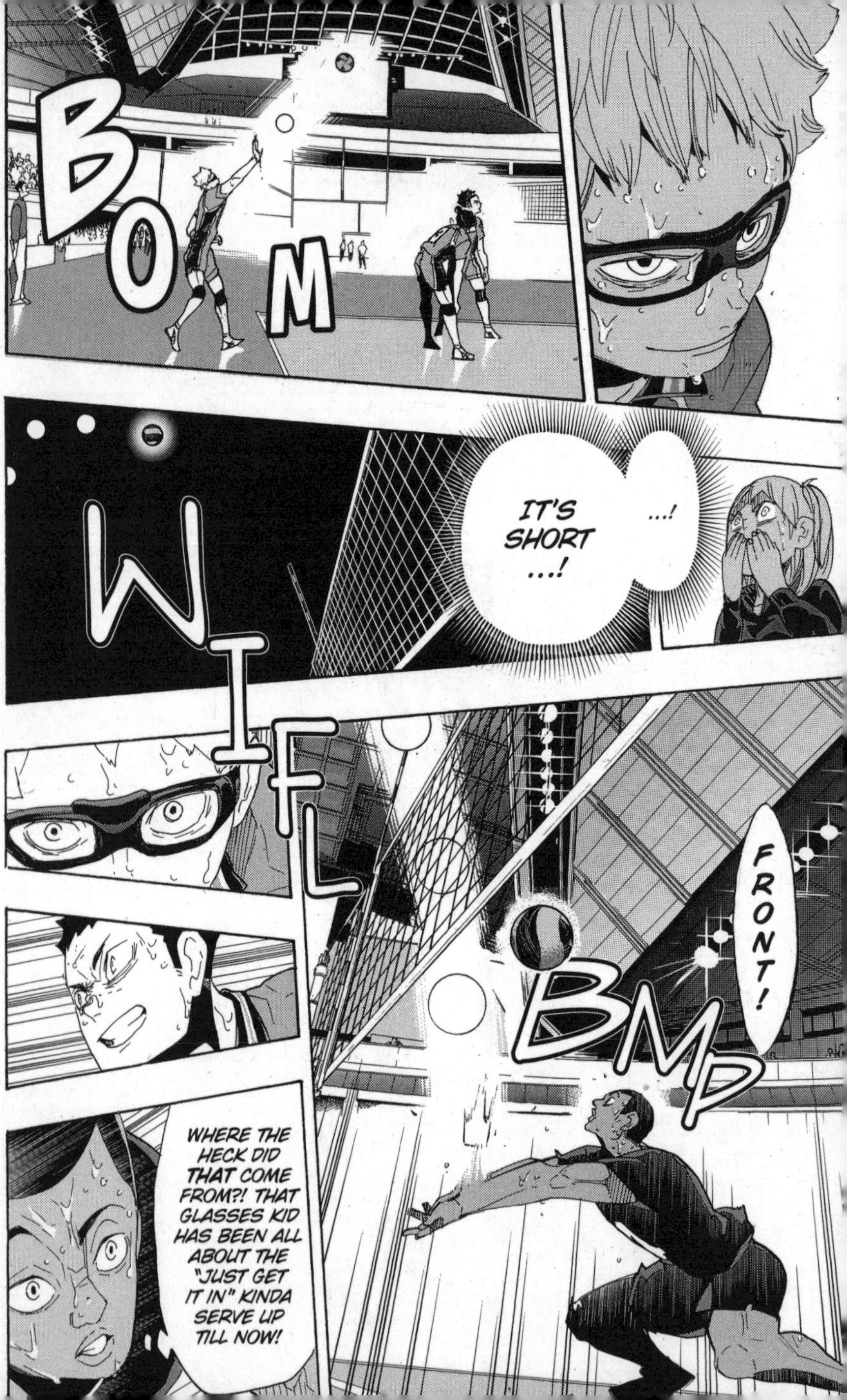
BOOM
...!
IT'S SHORT ...!
WIFFL
FRONT!
BMP
WHERE THE HECK DID THAT COME FROM?! THAT GLASSES KID HAS BEEN ALL ABOUT THE "JUST GET IT IN" KINDA SERVE UP TILL NOW!

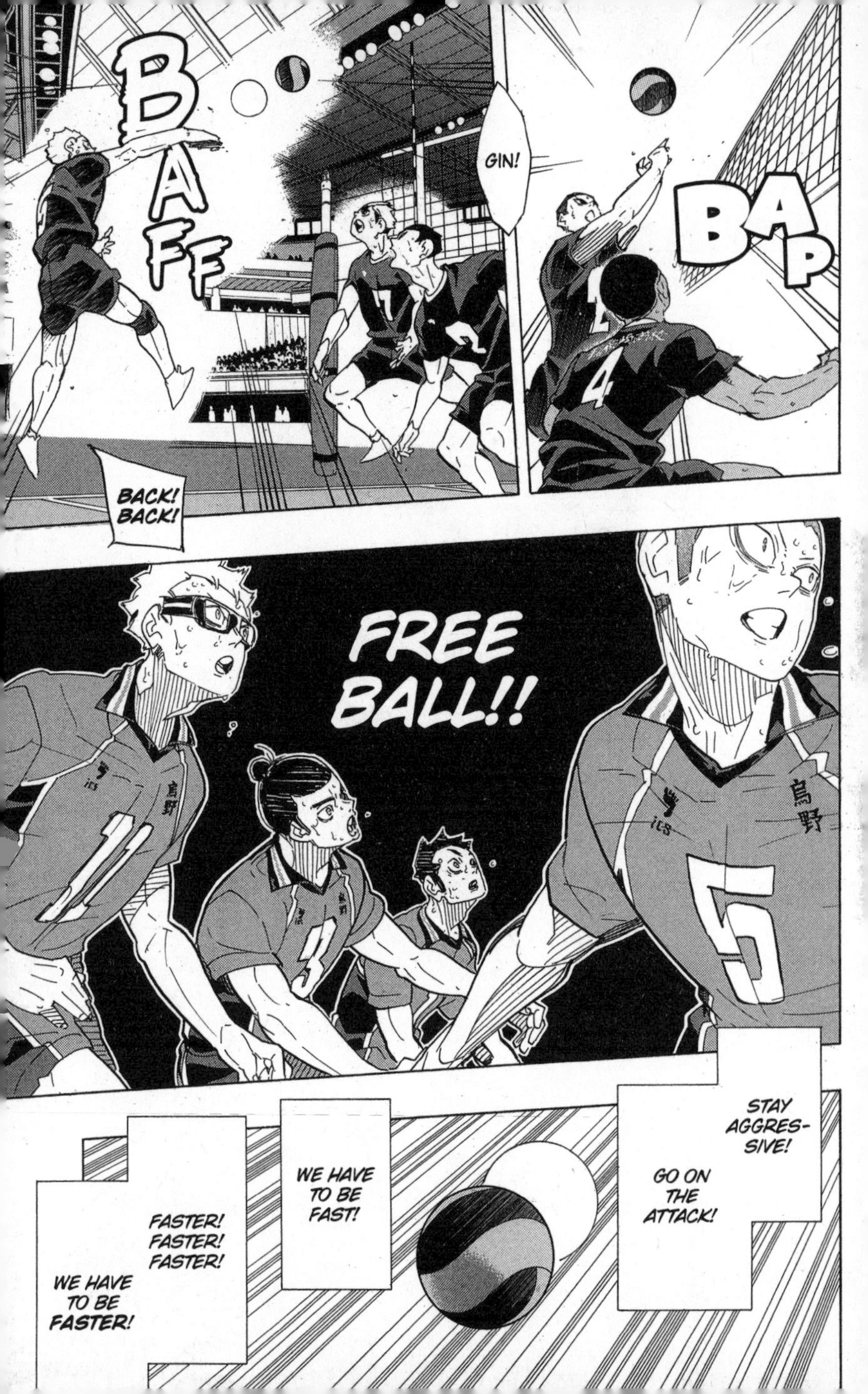
GIN!
BAP
BAFF
BACK! BACK!
FREE BALL!!
STAY AGGRES-SIVE!
GO ON THE ATTACK!
WE HAVE TO BE FAST!
FASTER! FASTER! FASTER!
WE HAVE TO BE FASTER!

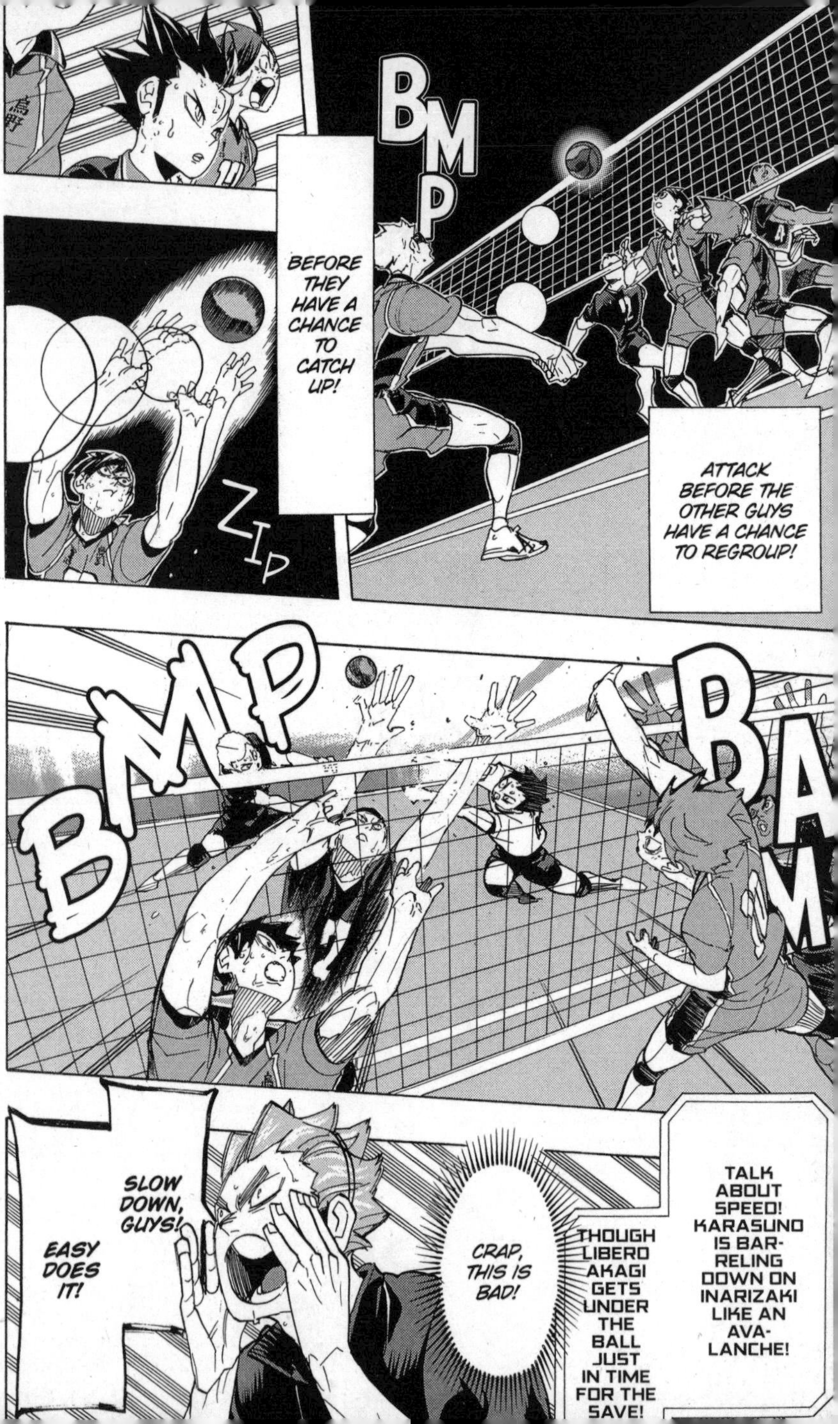
BMP
ATTACK BEFORE THE OTHER GUYS HAVE A CHANCE TO REGROUP!
BEFORE THEY HAVE A CHANCE TO CATCH UP!
ZIP
BAM
BMP
TALK ABOUT SPEED! KARASUNO IS BAR-RELING DOWN ON INARIZAKI LIKE AN AVA-LANCHE!
THOUGH LIBERO AKAGI GETS UNDER THE BALL JUST IN TIME FOR THE SAVE!
CRAP, THIS IS BAD!
SLOW DOWN, GUYS!
EASY DOES IT!

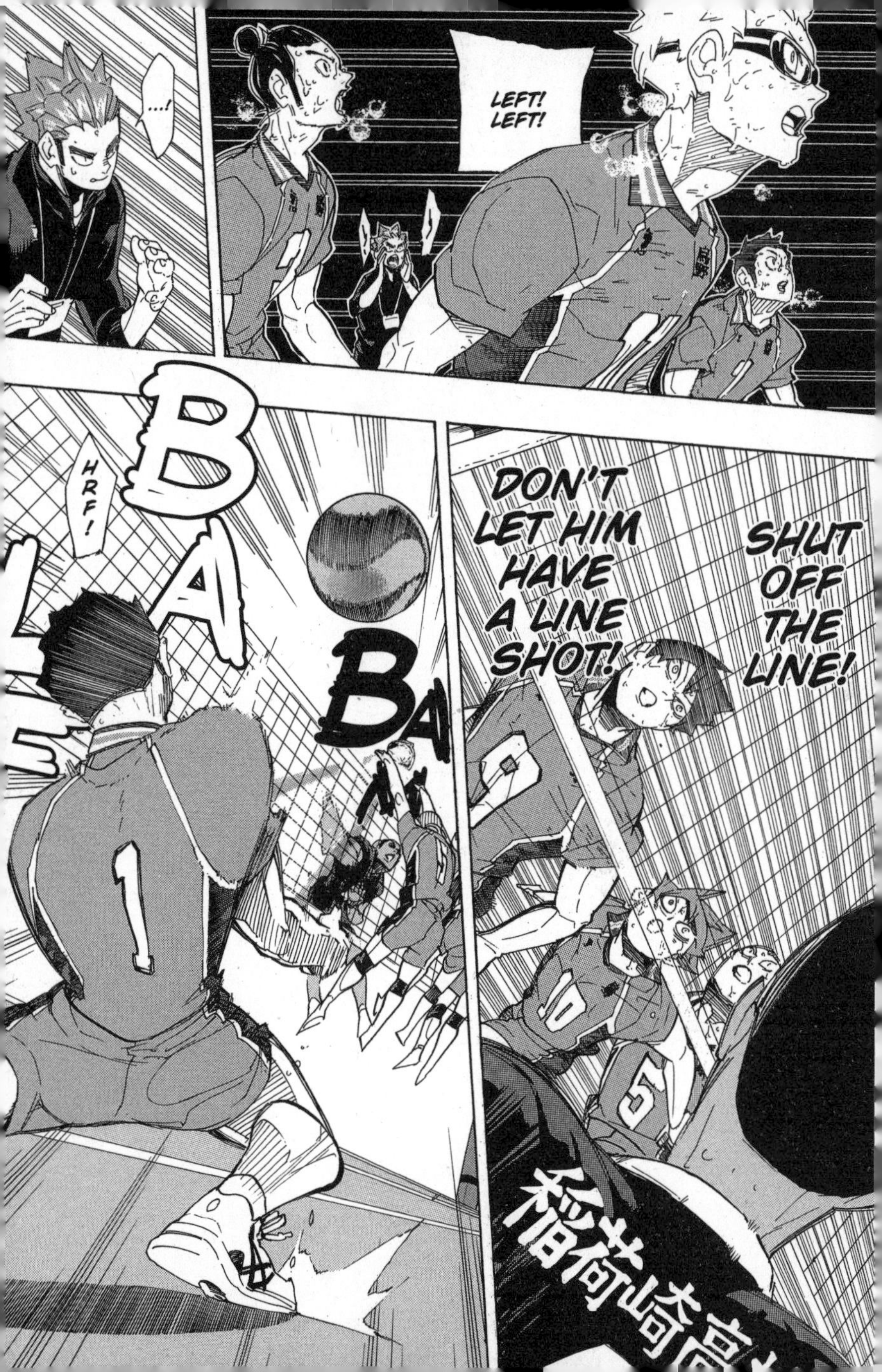
LEFT! LEFT!
...!
SHUT OFF THE LINE!
DON'T LET HIM HAVE A LINE SHOT!
HRF!
BA
BA

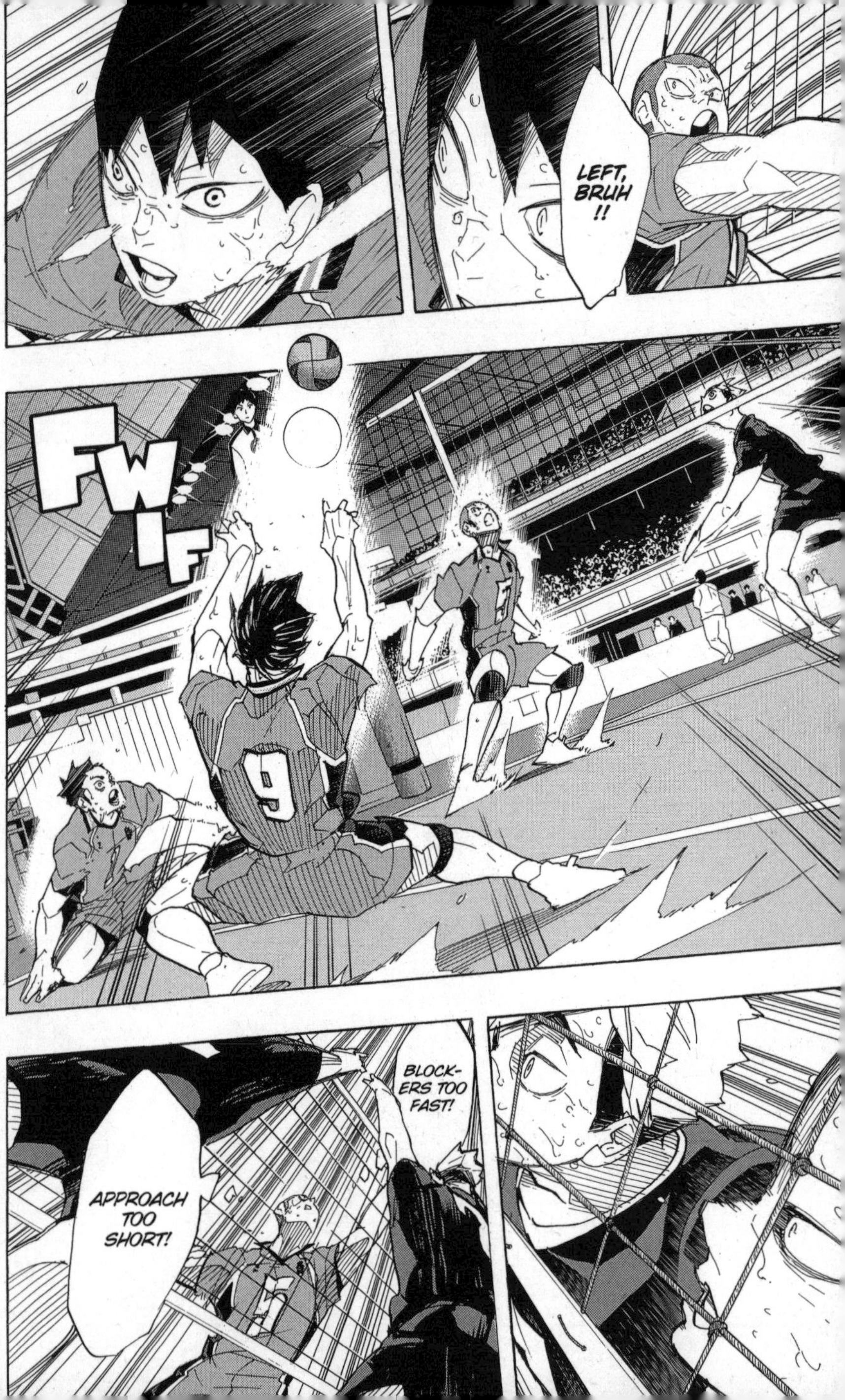
LEFT, BRUH !!
FWIF
BLOCKERS TOO FAST!
APPROACH TOO SHORT!

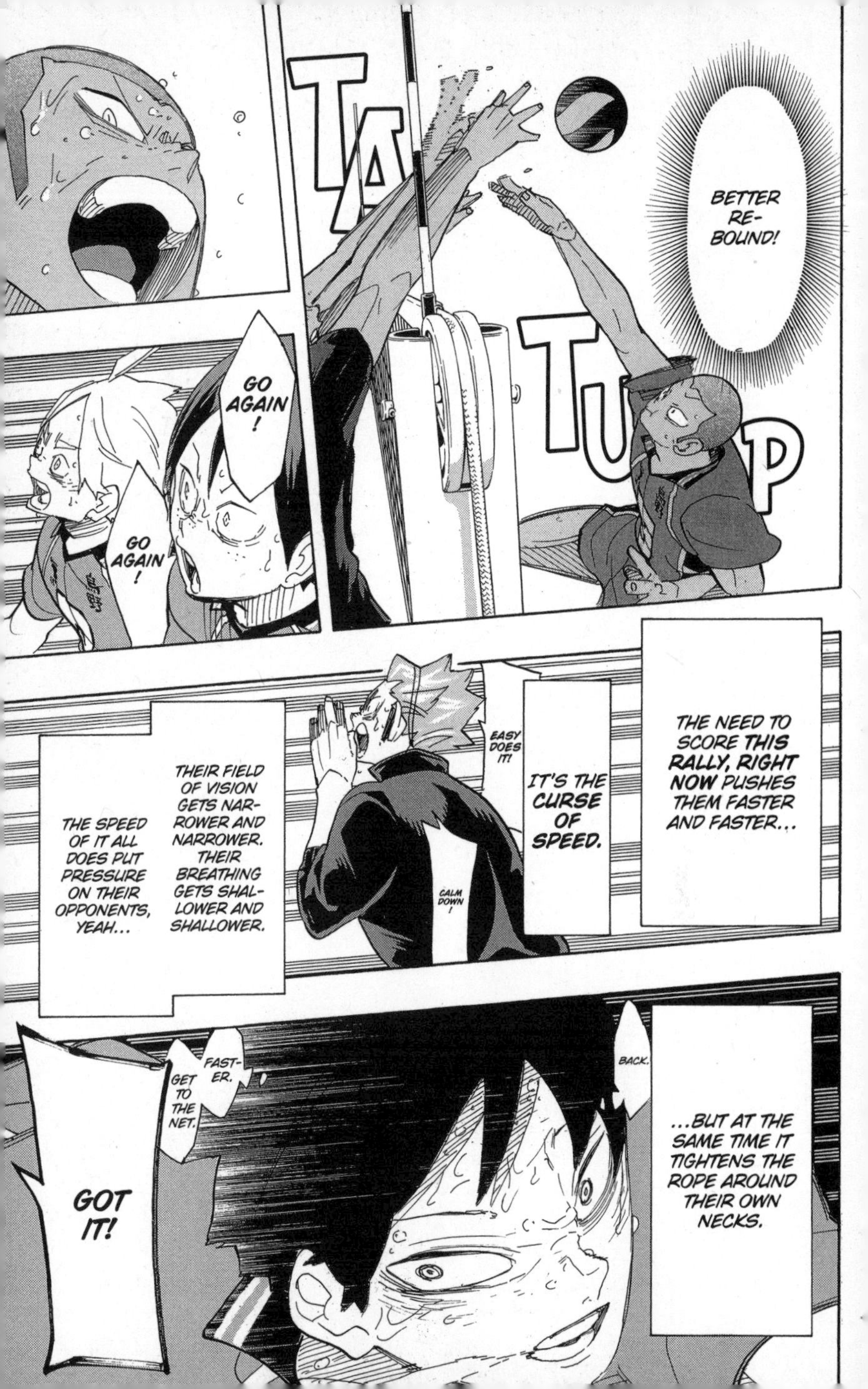
BETTER RE-BOUND!
GO AGAIN!
GO AGAIN!
THE NEED TO SCORE THIS RALLY, RIGHT NOW PUSHES THEM FASTER AND FASTER...
IT'S THE CURSE OF SPEED.
EASY DOES IT!
CALM DOWN!
THEIR FIELD OF VISION GETS NAR-ROWER AND NARROWER. THEIR BREATHING GETS SHAL-LOWER AND SHALLOWER.
THE SPEED OF IT ALL DOES PUT PRESSURE ON THEIR OPPONENTS, YEAH...
...BUT AT THE SAME TIME IT TIGHTENS THE ROPE AROUND THEIR OWN NECKS.
BACK.
FAST-ER.
GET TO THE NET.
GOT IT!

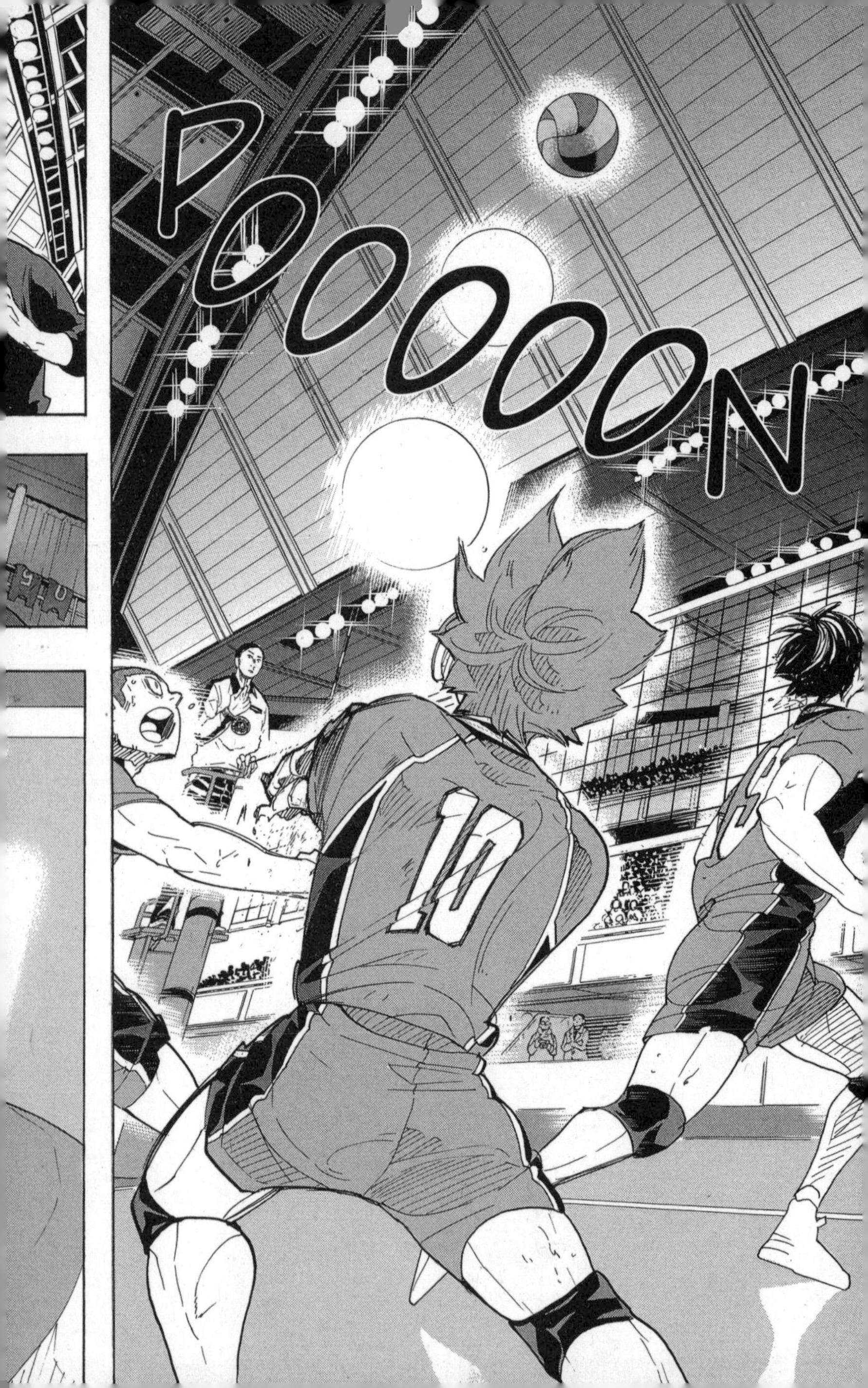
POOOOON

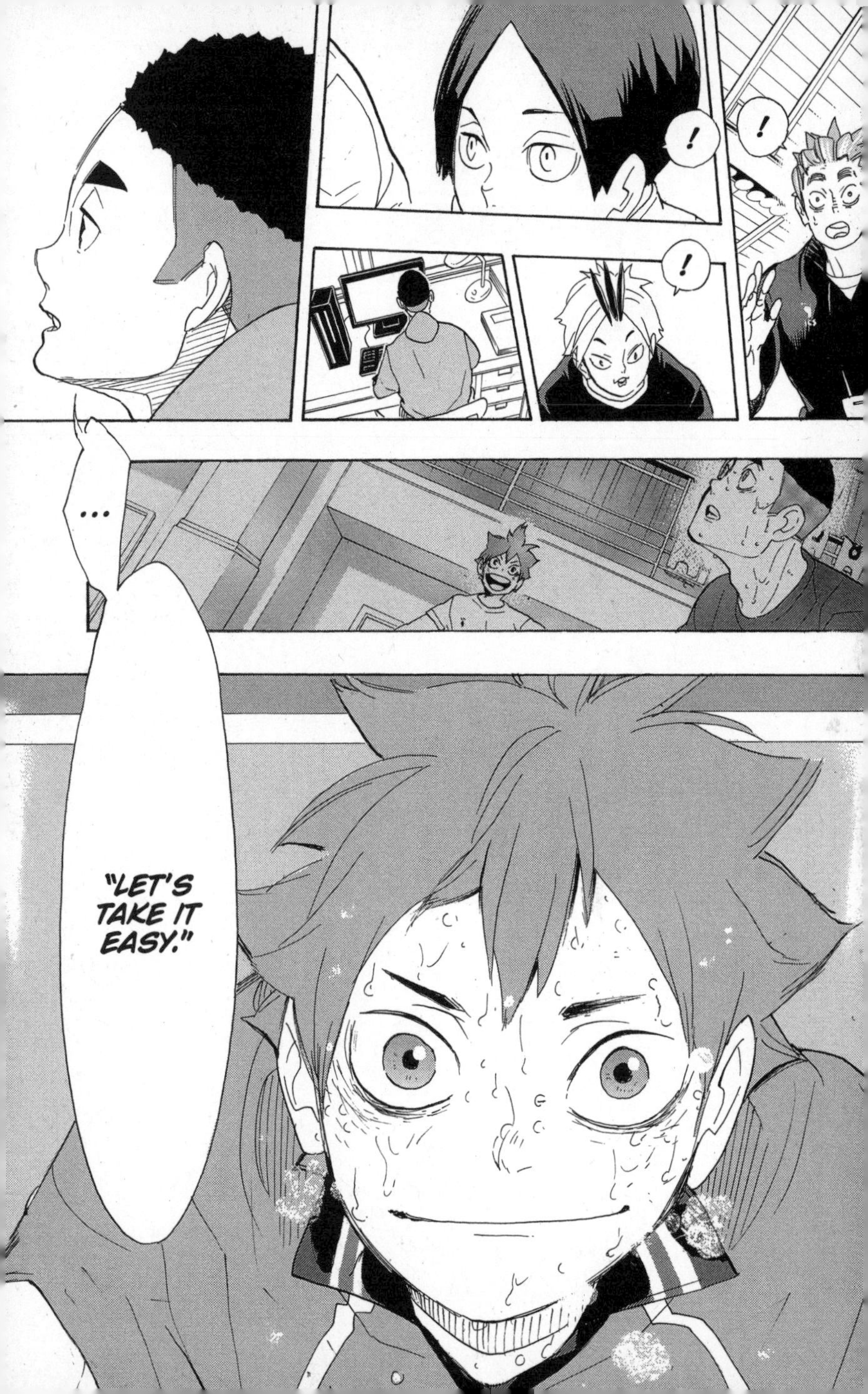
!
!
!
...
"LET'S TAKE IT EASY."

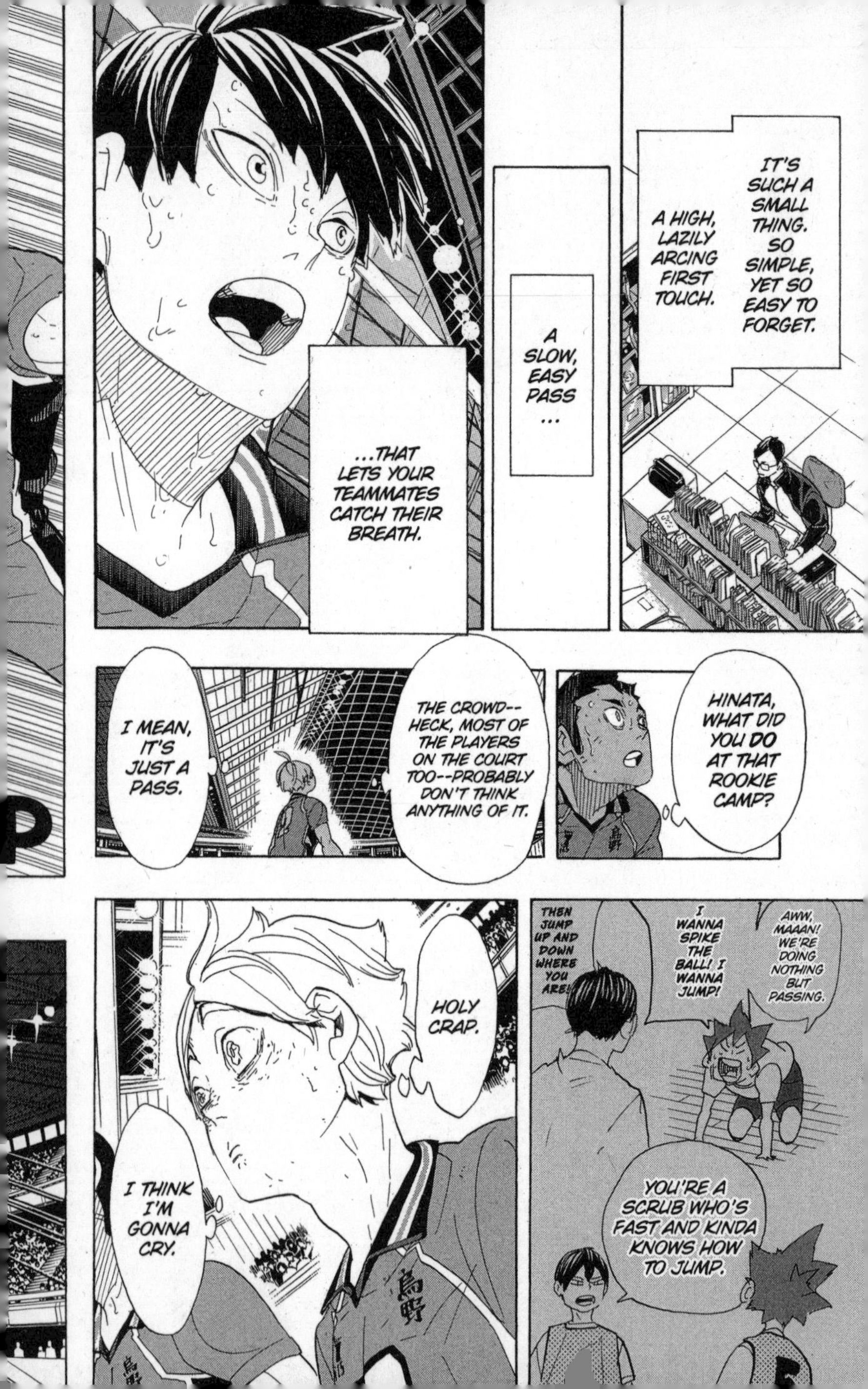
IT'S SUCH A SMALL THING. SO SIMPLE, YET SO EASY TO FORGET.
A HIGH, LAZILY ARCING FIRST TOUCH.
A SLOW, EASY PASS ...
...THAT LETS YOUR TEAMMATES CATCH THEIR BREATH.
HINATA, WHAT DID YOU DO AT THAT ROOKIE CAMP?
THE CROWD--HECK, MOST OF THE PLAYERS ON THE COURT TOO--PROBABLY DON'T THINK ANYTHING OF IT.
I MEAN, IT'S JUST A PASS.
AWW, MAAAN! WE'RE DOING NOTHING BUT PASSING.
I WANNA SPIKE THE BALL! I WANNA JUMP!
THEN JUMP UP AND DOWN WHERE YOU ARE!
YOU'RE A SCRUB WHO'S FAST AND KINDA KNOWS HOW TO JUMP.
HOLY CRAP.
I THINK I'M GONNA CRY.

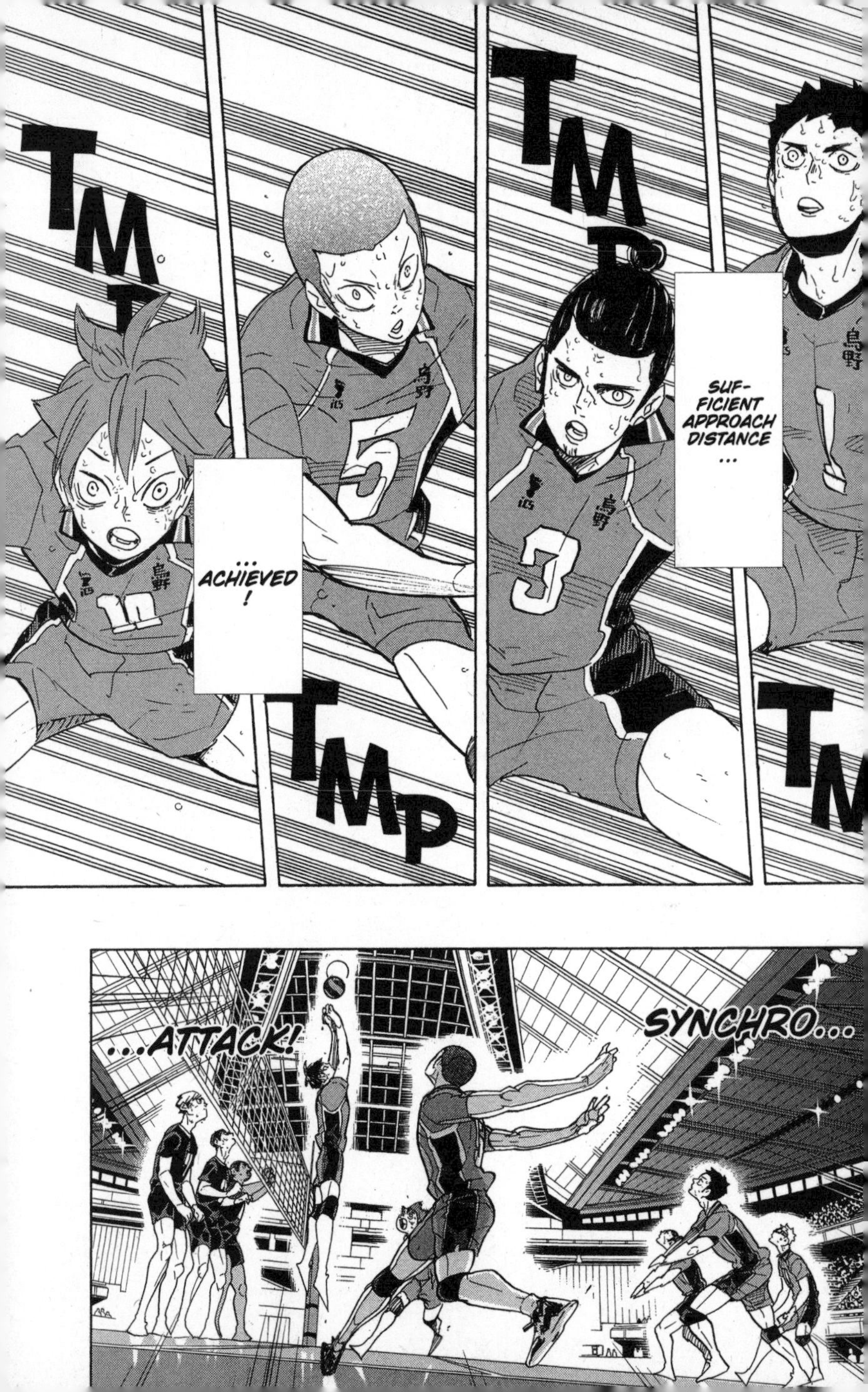

SUF-FICIENT APPROACH DISTANCE ...
TM
TMP
TMP
... ACHIEVED !
TM
SYNCHRO...
...ATTACK!

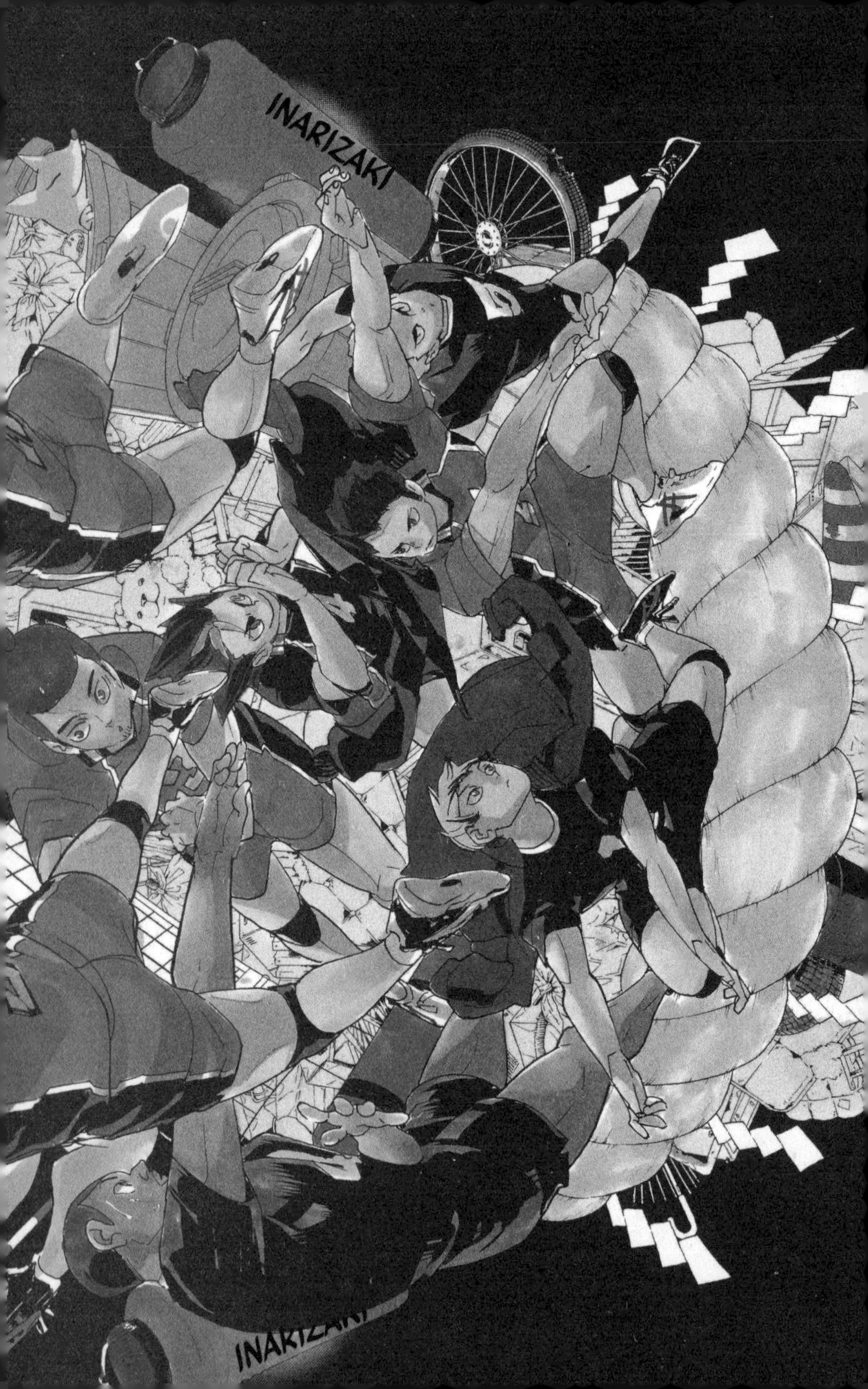
INARIZAKI
INARIZAKI

CHAPTER 290:
Monsters' Ball

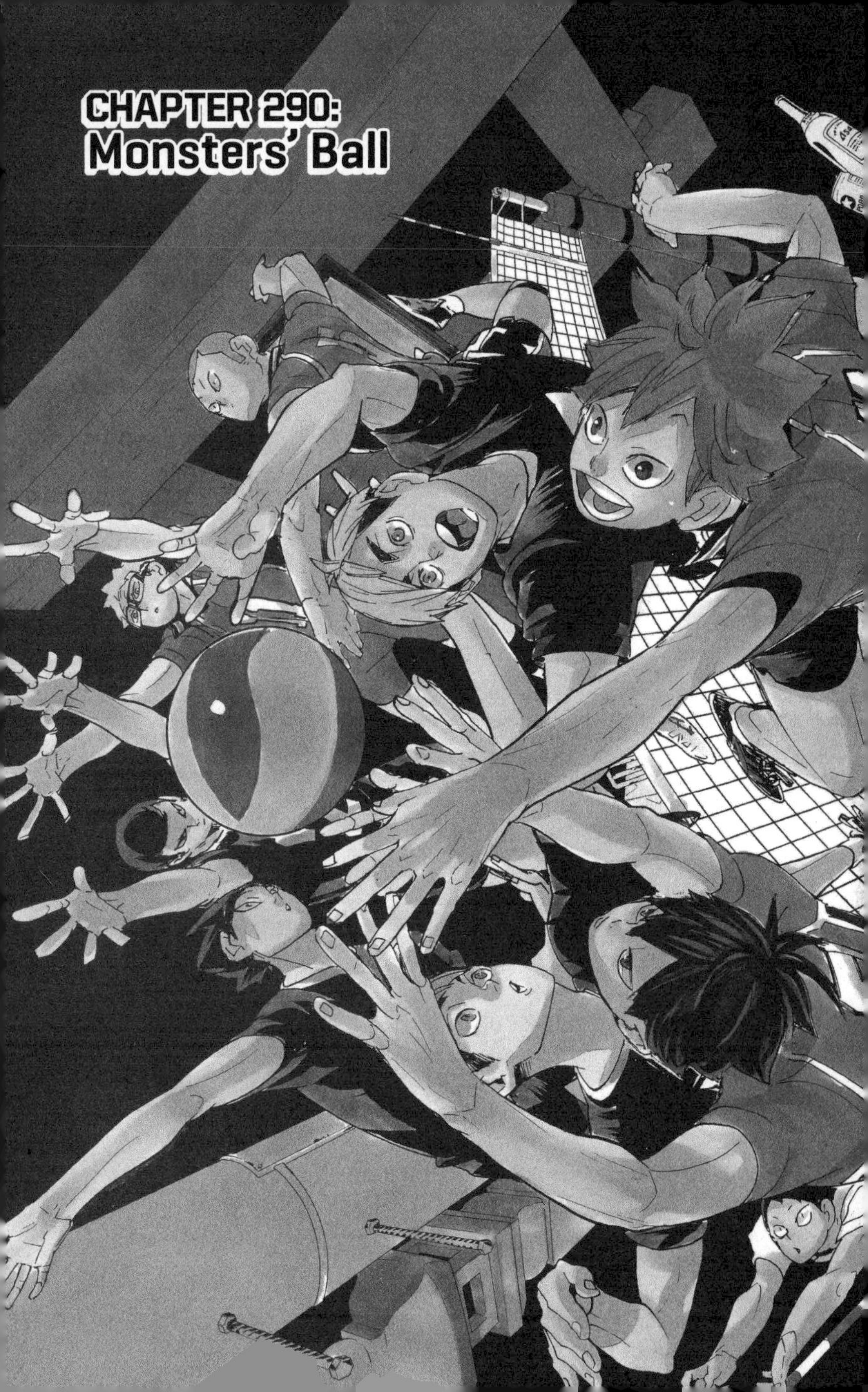

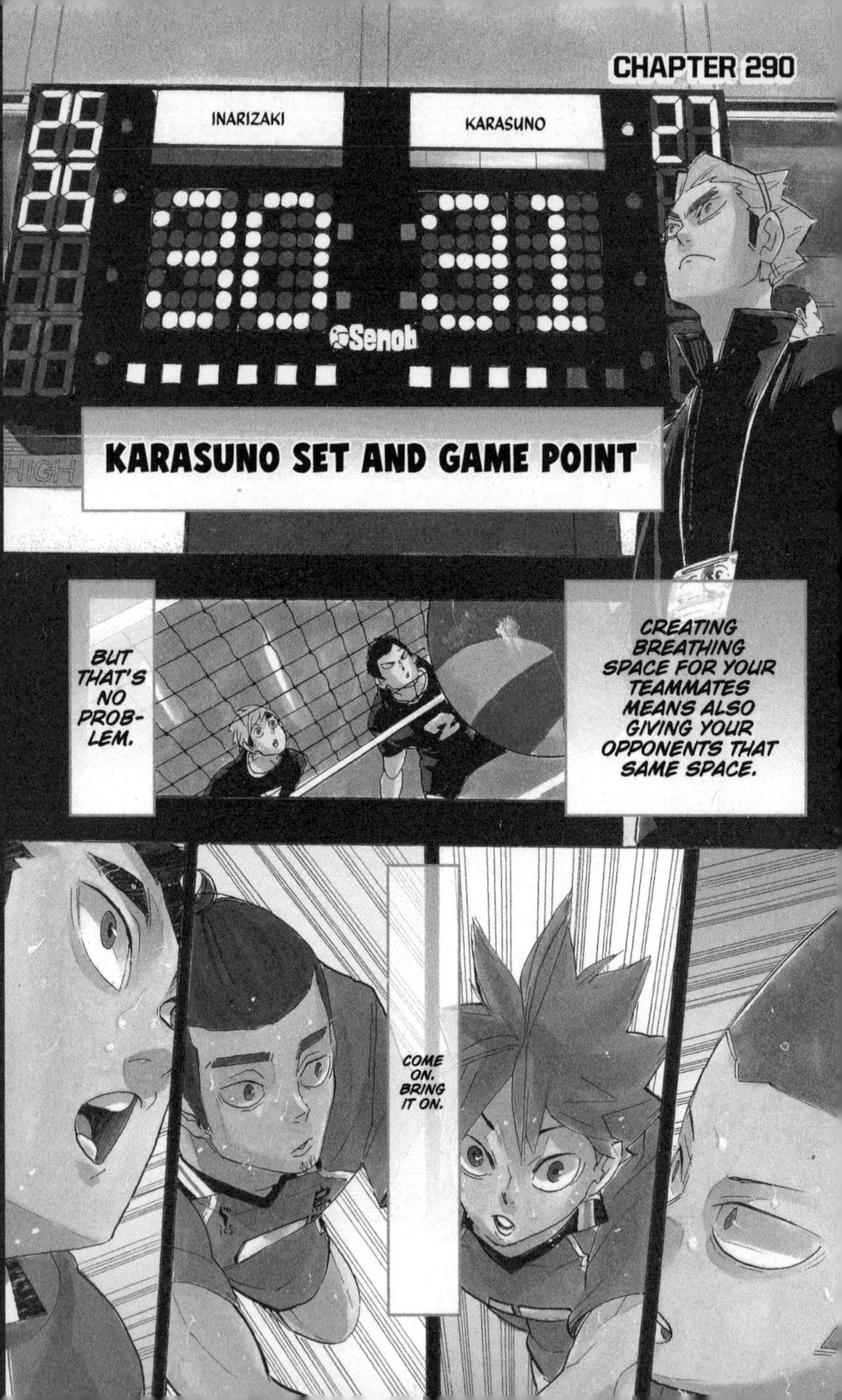
CHAPTER 290
INARIZAKI
KARASUNO
KARASUNO SET AND GAME POINT
CREATING BREATHING SPACE FOR YOUR TEAMMATES MEANS ALSO GIVING YOUR OPPONENTS THAT SAME SPACE.
BUT THAT'S NO PROB-LEM.
COME ON. BRING IT ON.

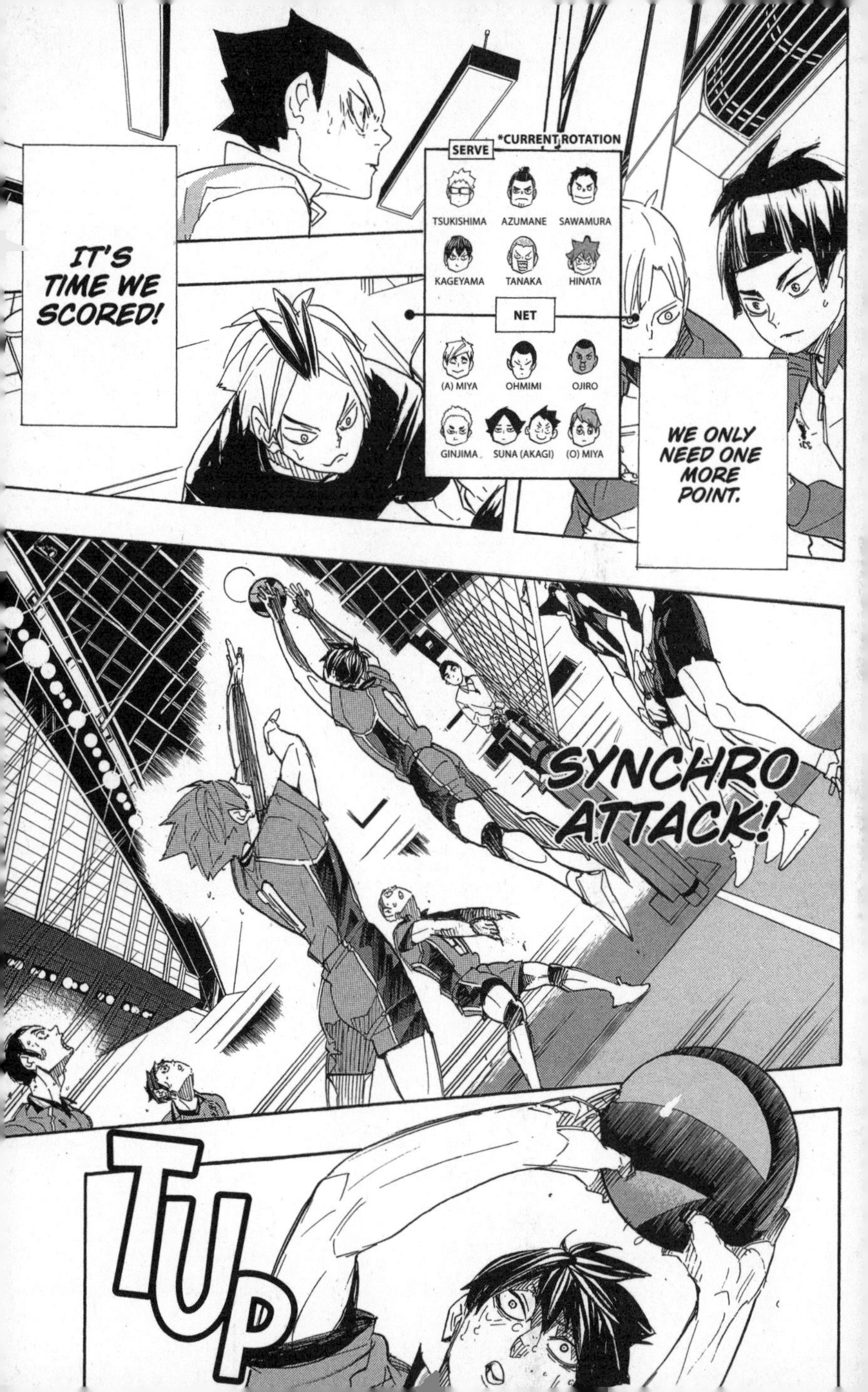

*CURRENT ROTATION
SERVE
TSUKISHIMA
AZUMANE
SAWAMURA
KAGEYAMA
TANAKA
HINATA
NET
(A) MIYA
OHMIMI
OJIRO
GINJIMA
SUNA (AKAGI)
(O) MIYA
WE ONLY NEED ONE MORE POINT.
IT'S TIME WE SCORED!
SYNCHRO ATTACK!
TUP

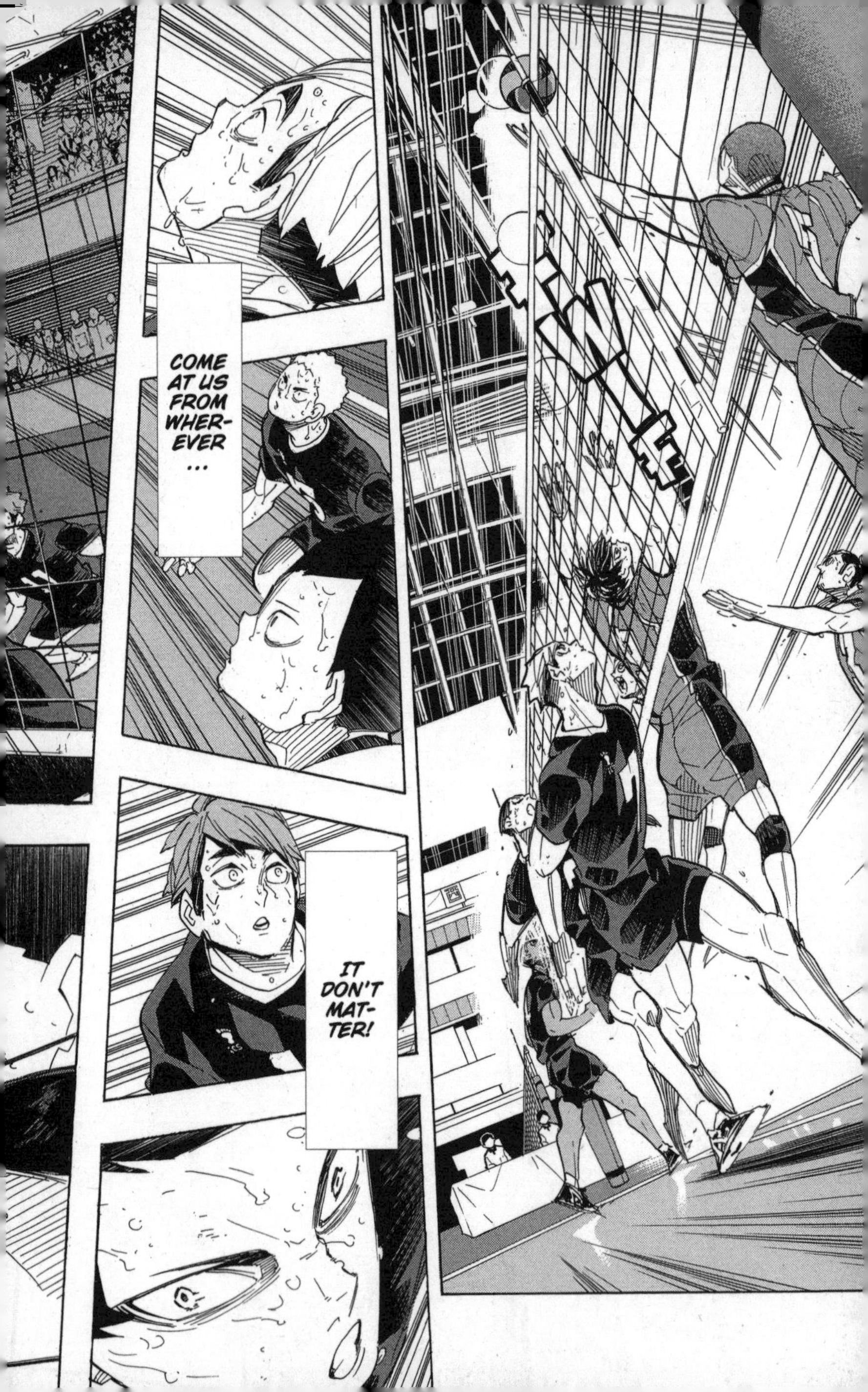
COME AT US FROM WHER-EVER ...
IT DON'T MAT-TER!

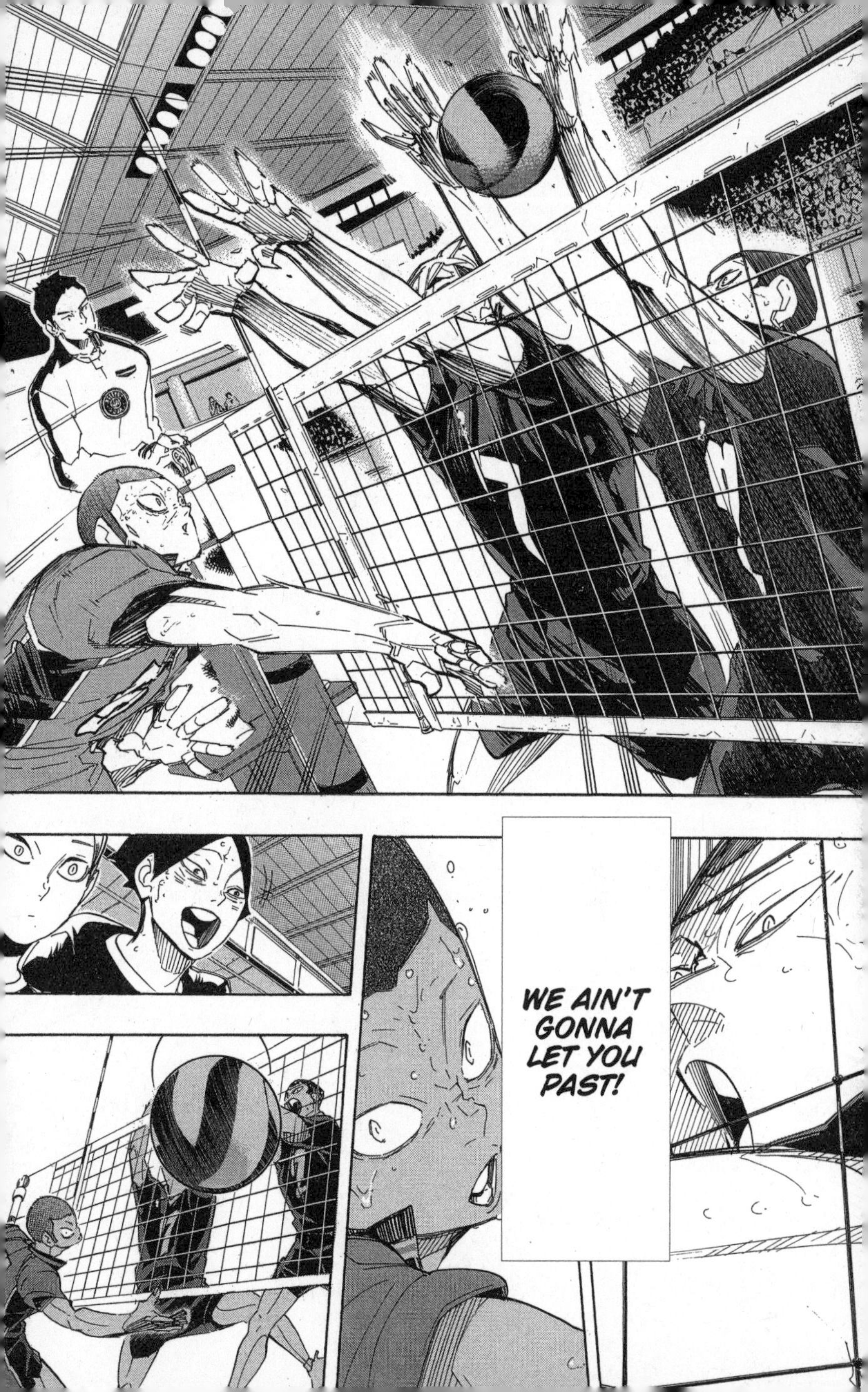
WE AIN'T GONNA LET YOU PAST!

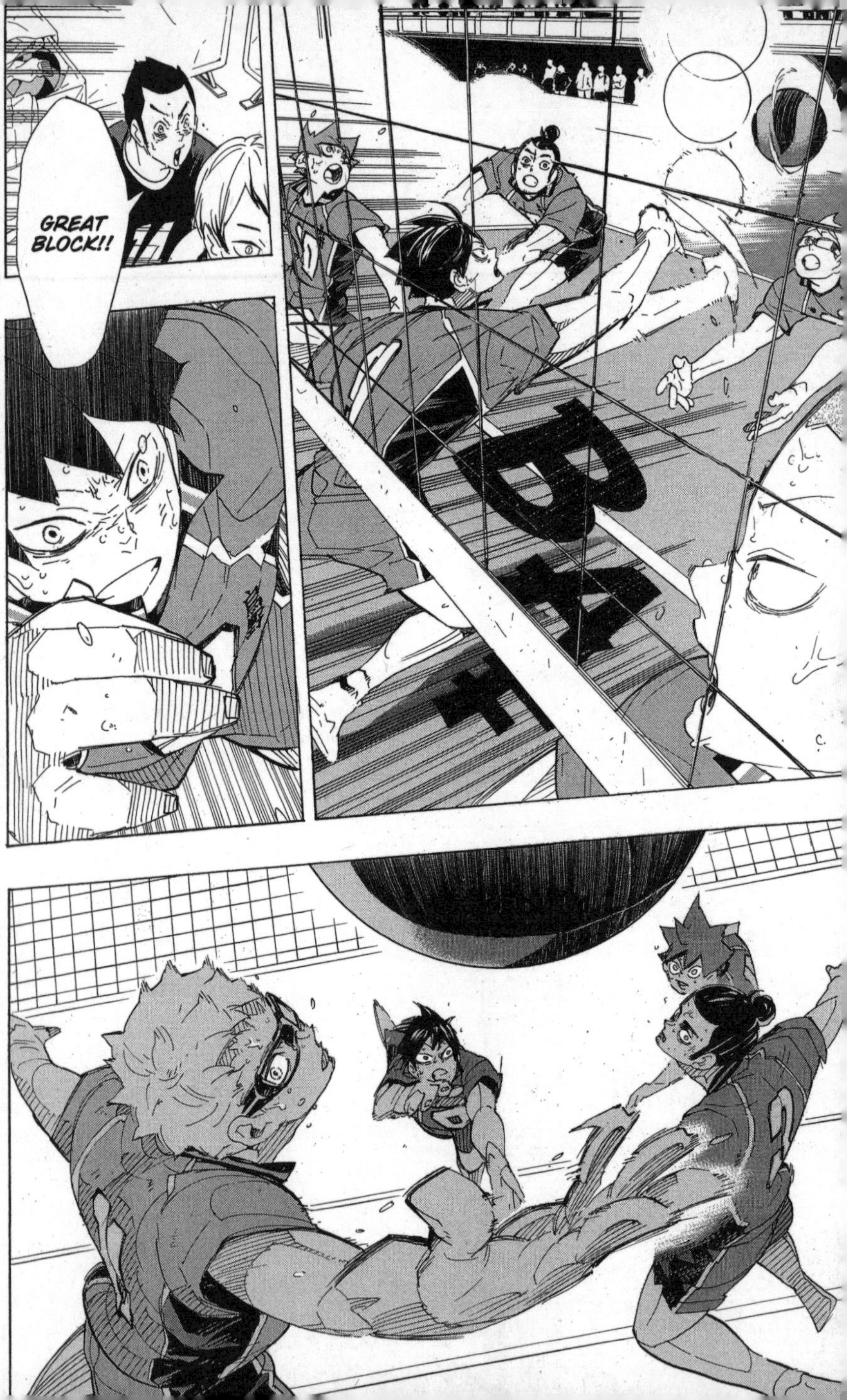
GREAT BLOCK!!

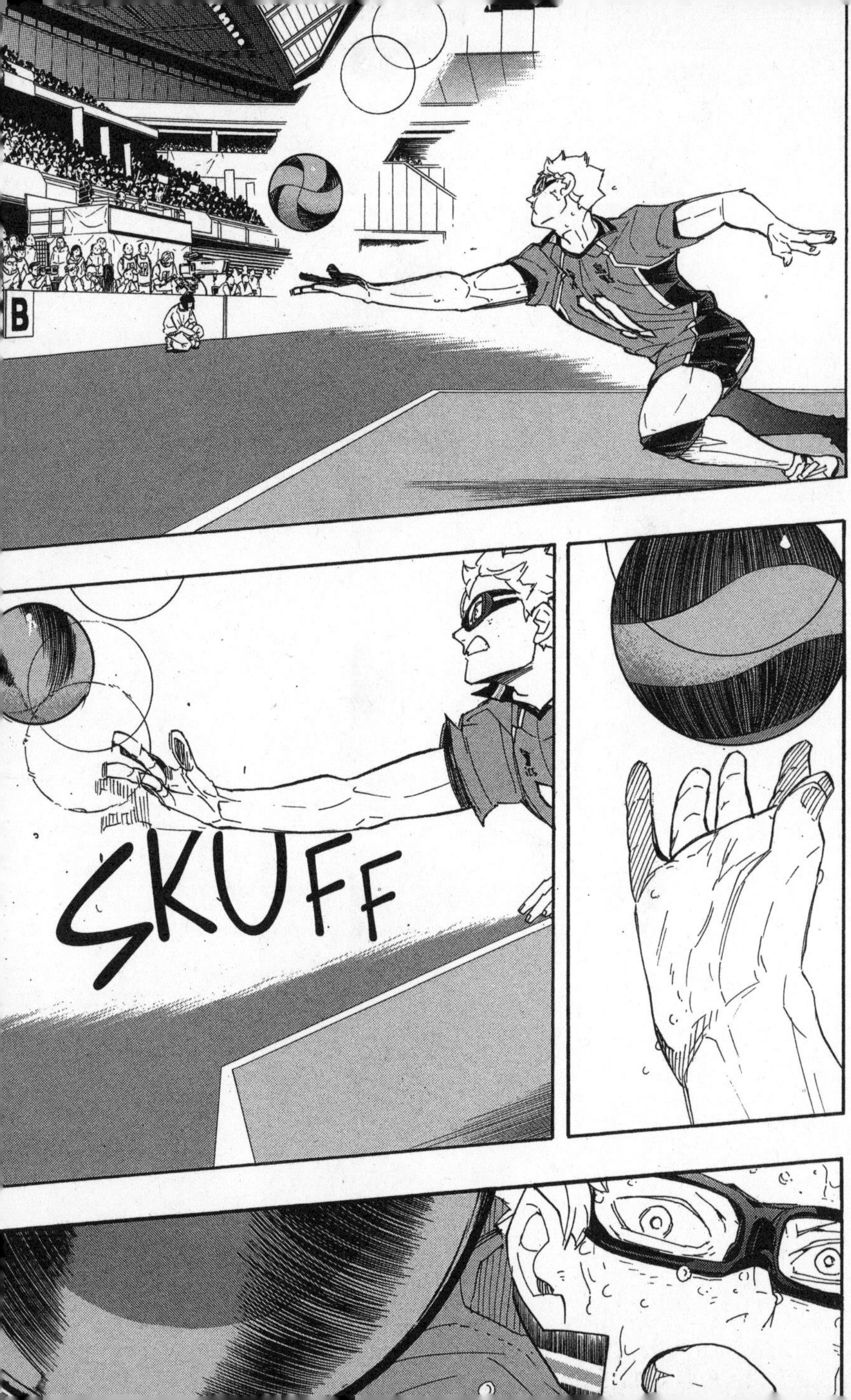
B
SKUFF

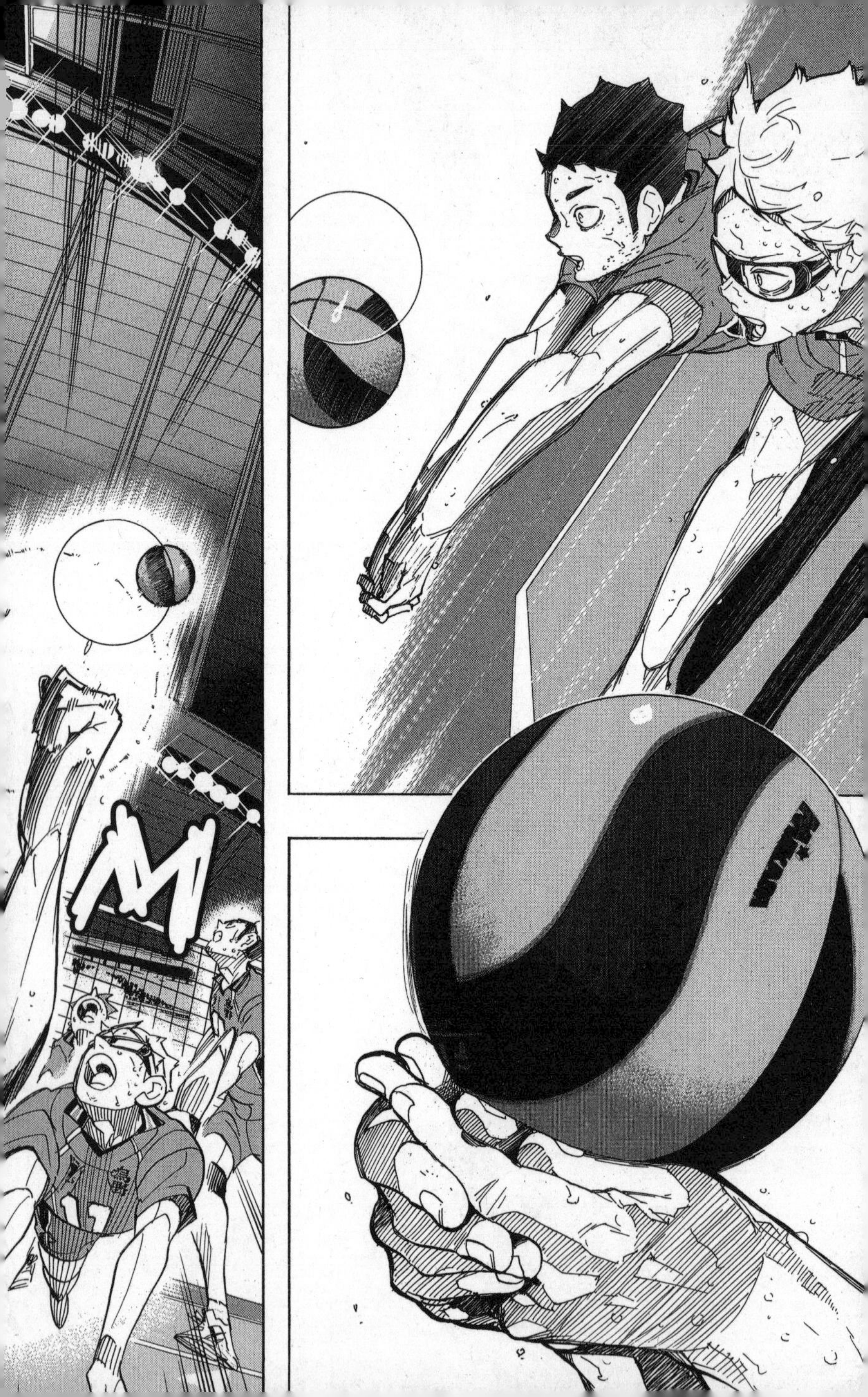

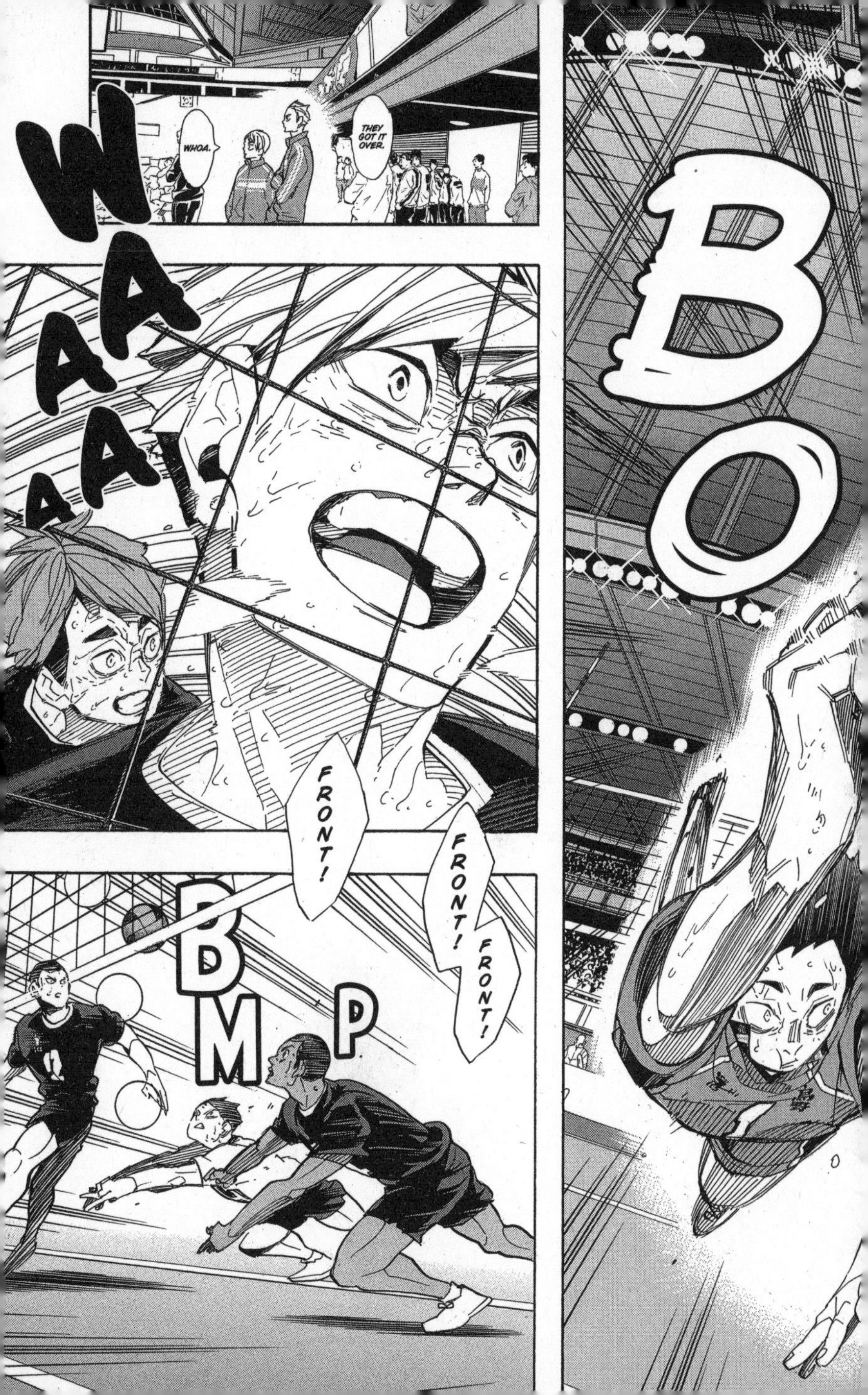
BO
WAAAA
THEY GOT IT OVER.
WHOA.
FRONT!
FRONT!
FRONT!
FRONT!
BMP

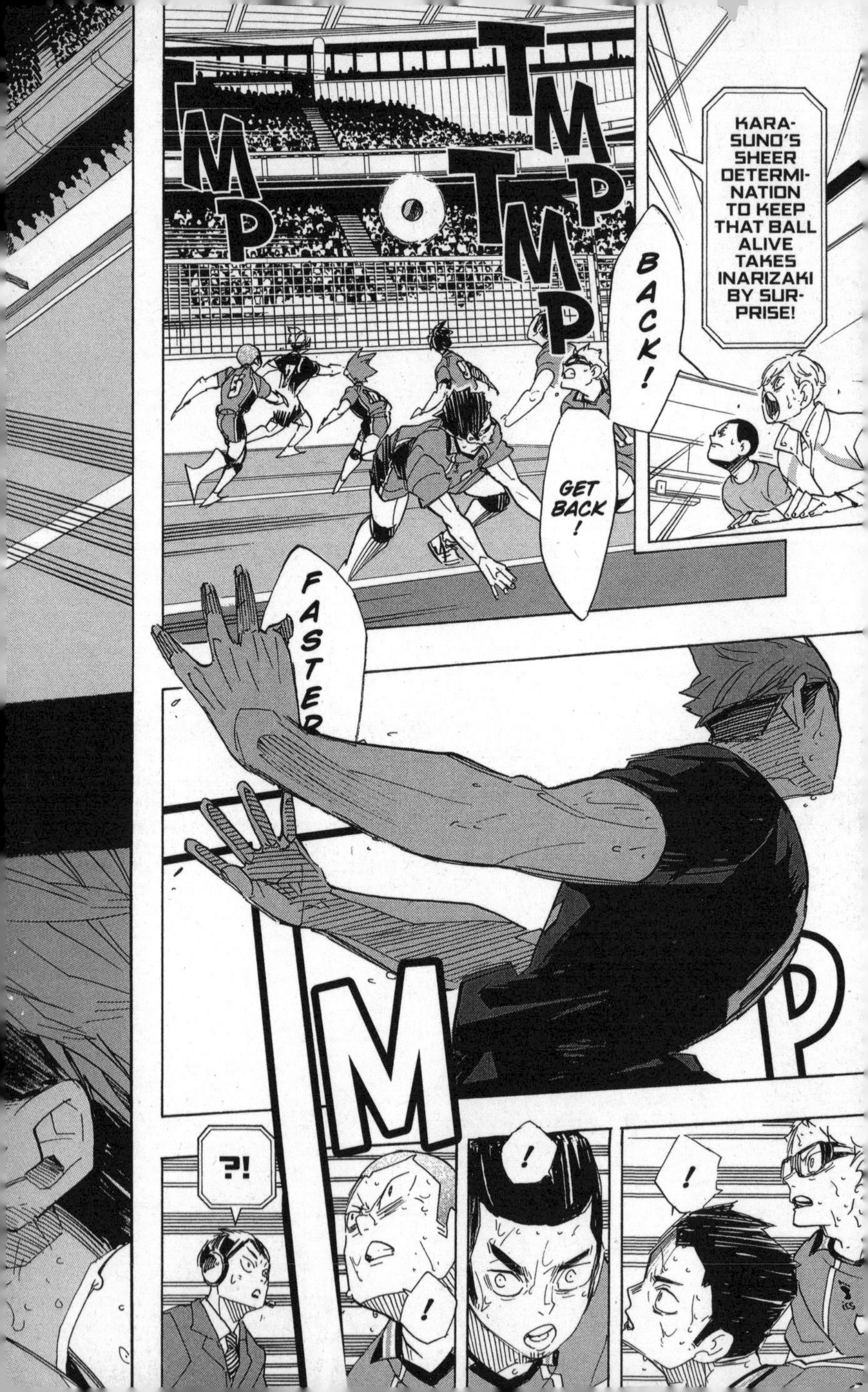
KARA-SUNO'S SHEER DETERMINATION TO KEEP THAT BALL ALIVE TAKES INARIZAKI BY SURPRISE!
BACK!
GET BACK!
FASTER
TMP TMP TMP TMP
MP
?!
!
!
!

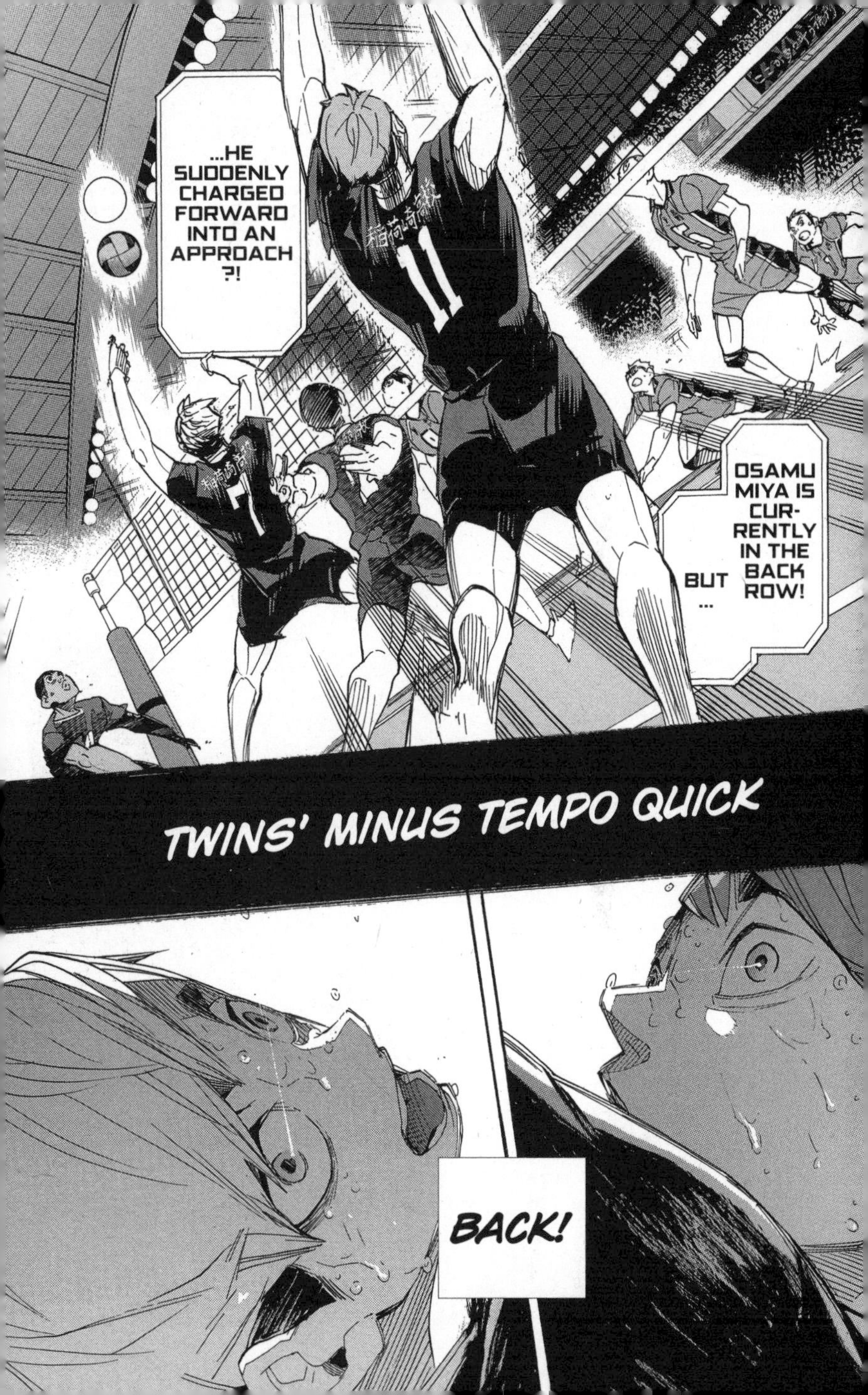
OSAMU MIYA IS CUR-RENTLY IN THE BACK ROW!
BUT...
...HE SUDDENLY CHARGED FORWARD INTO AN APPROACH?!
TWINS' MINUS TEMPO QUICK
BACK!

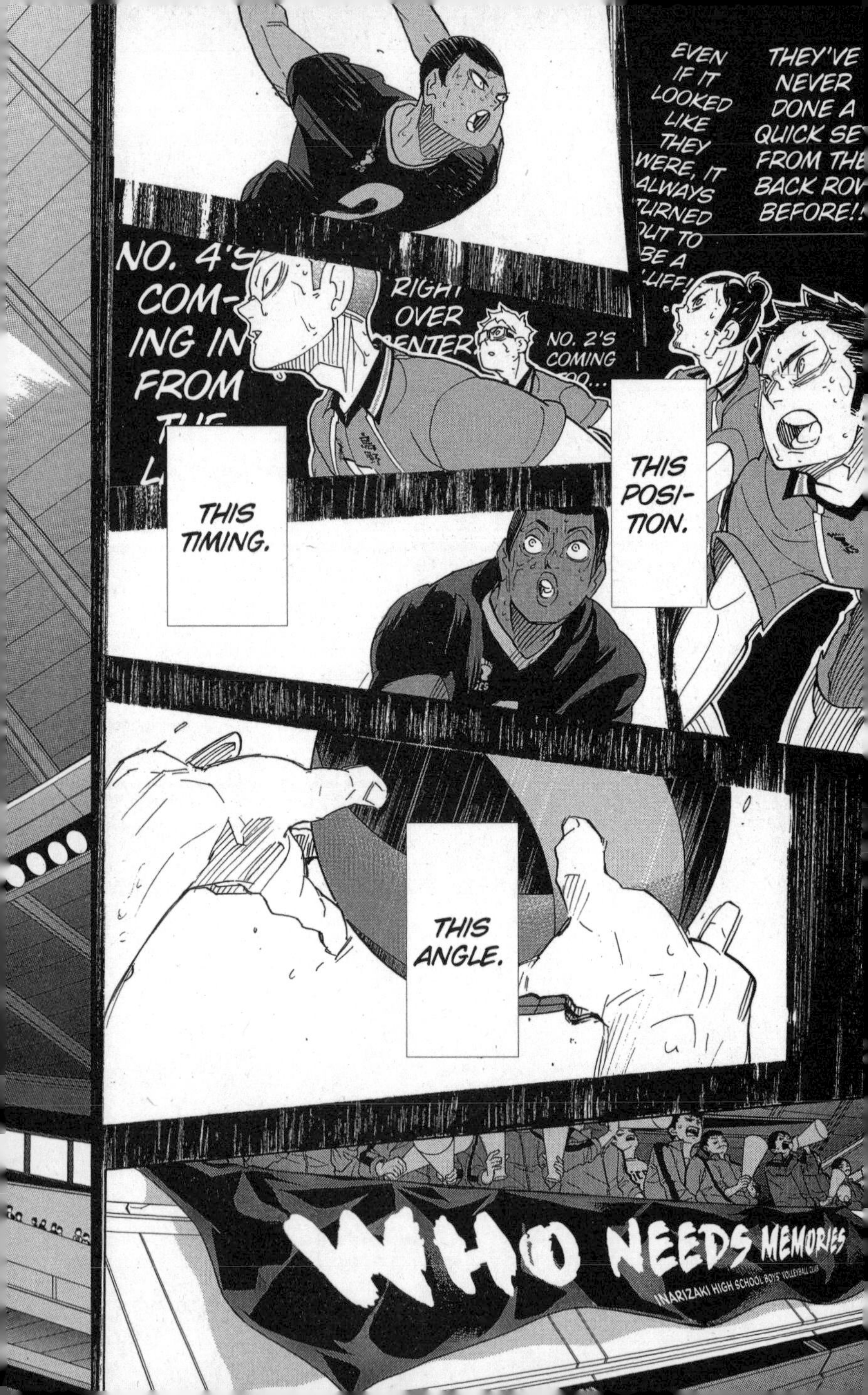

THEY'VE NEVER DONE A QUICK SET FROM THE BACK ROW BEFORE!!
EVEN IF IT LOOKED LIKE THEY WERE, IT ALWAYS TURNED OUT TO BE A BLUFF!
NO. 2'S COMING TOO...
RIGHT OVER CENTER.
NO. 4'S COMING IN FROM THE
THIS POSITION.
THIS TIMING.
THIS ANGLE.
WHO NEEDS MEMORIES
INARIZAKI HIGH SCHOOL BOYS' VOLLEYBALL CLUB

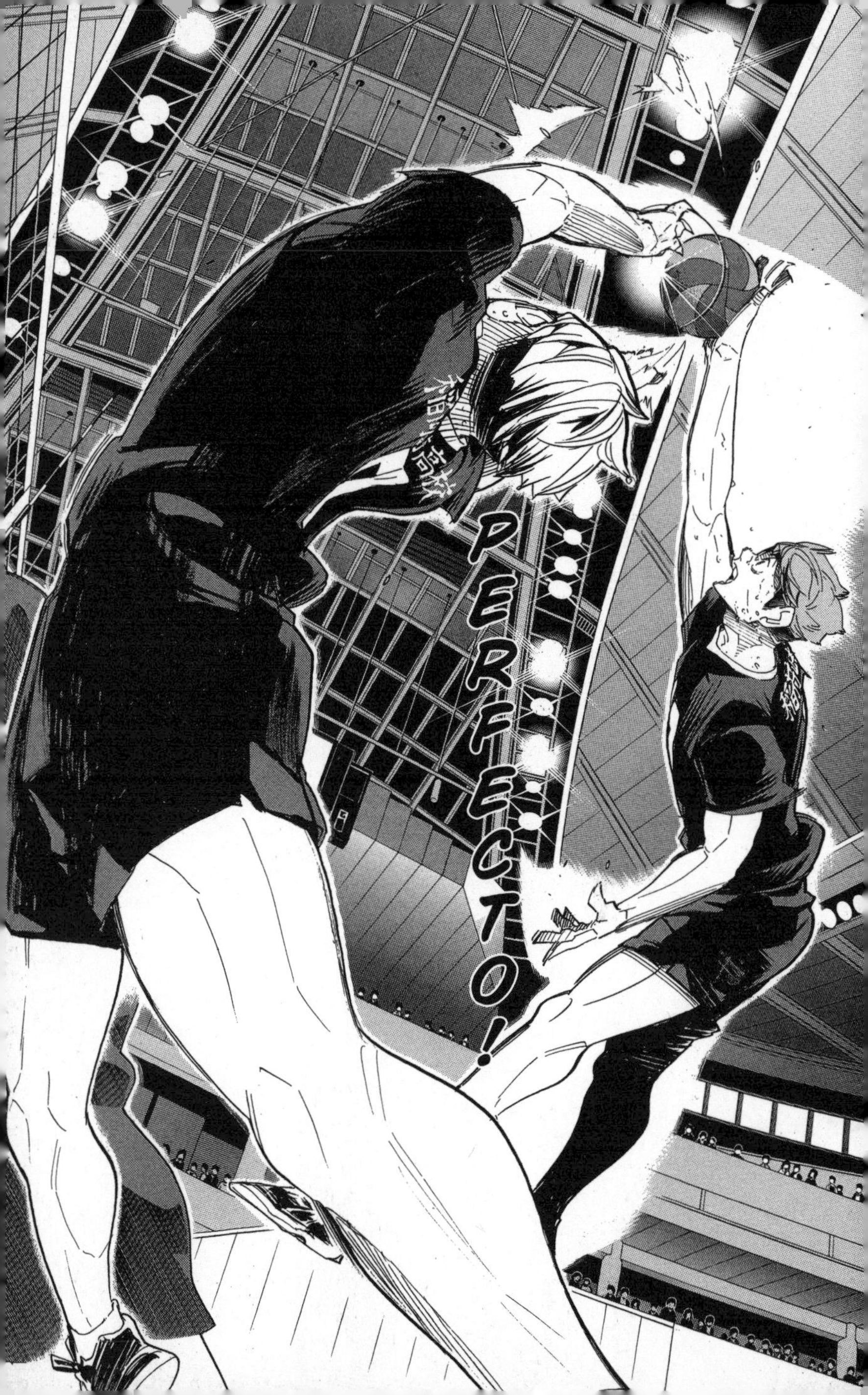
PERFECTO!

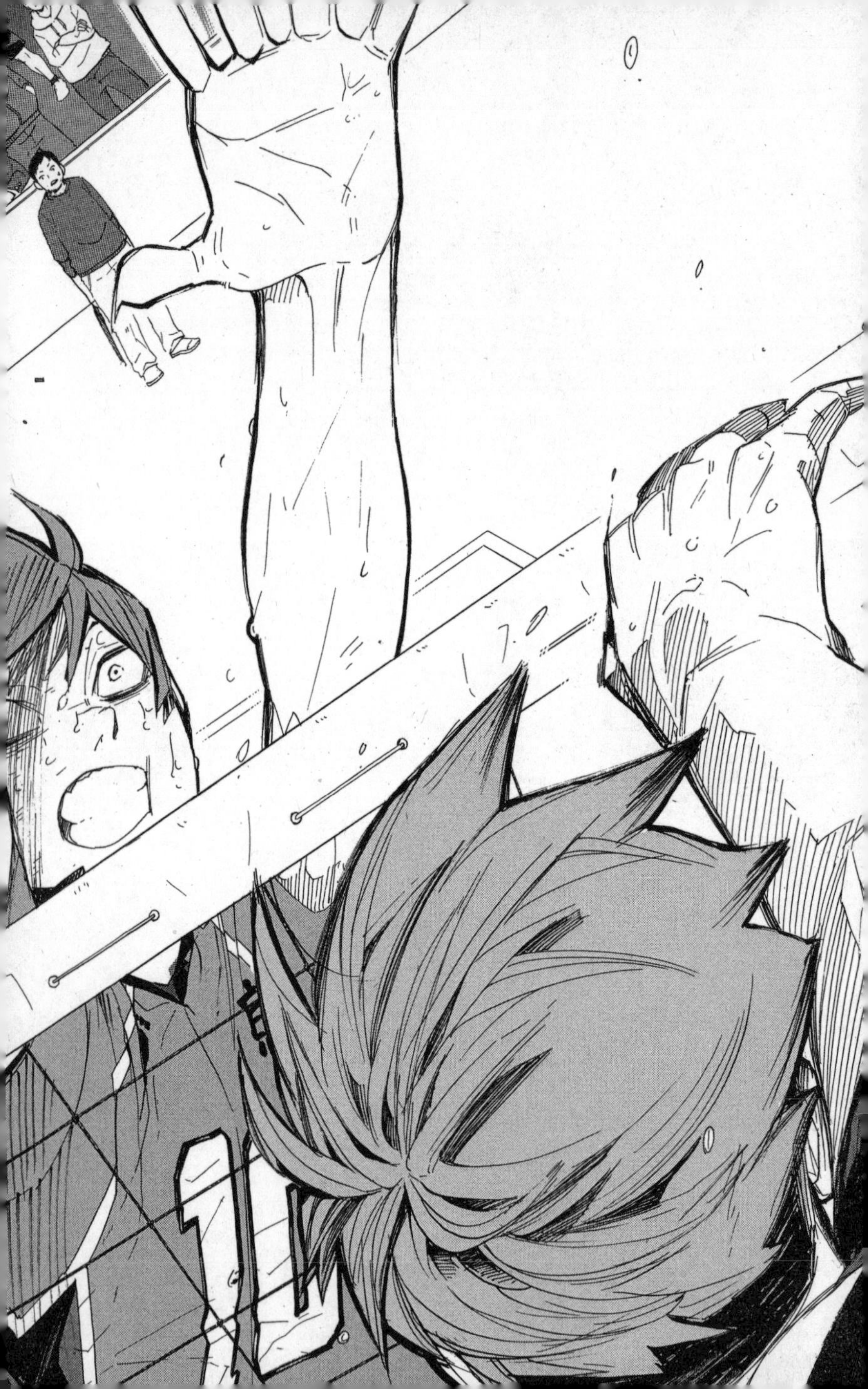

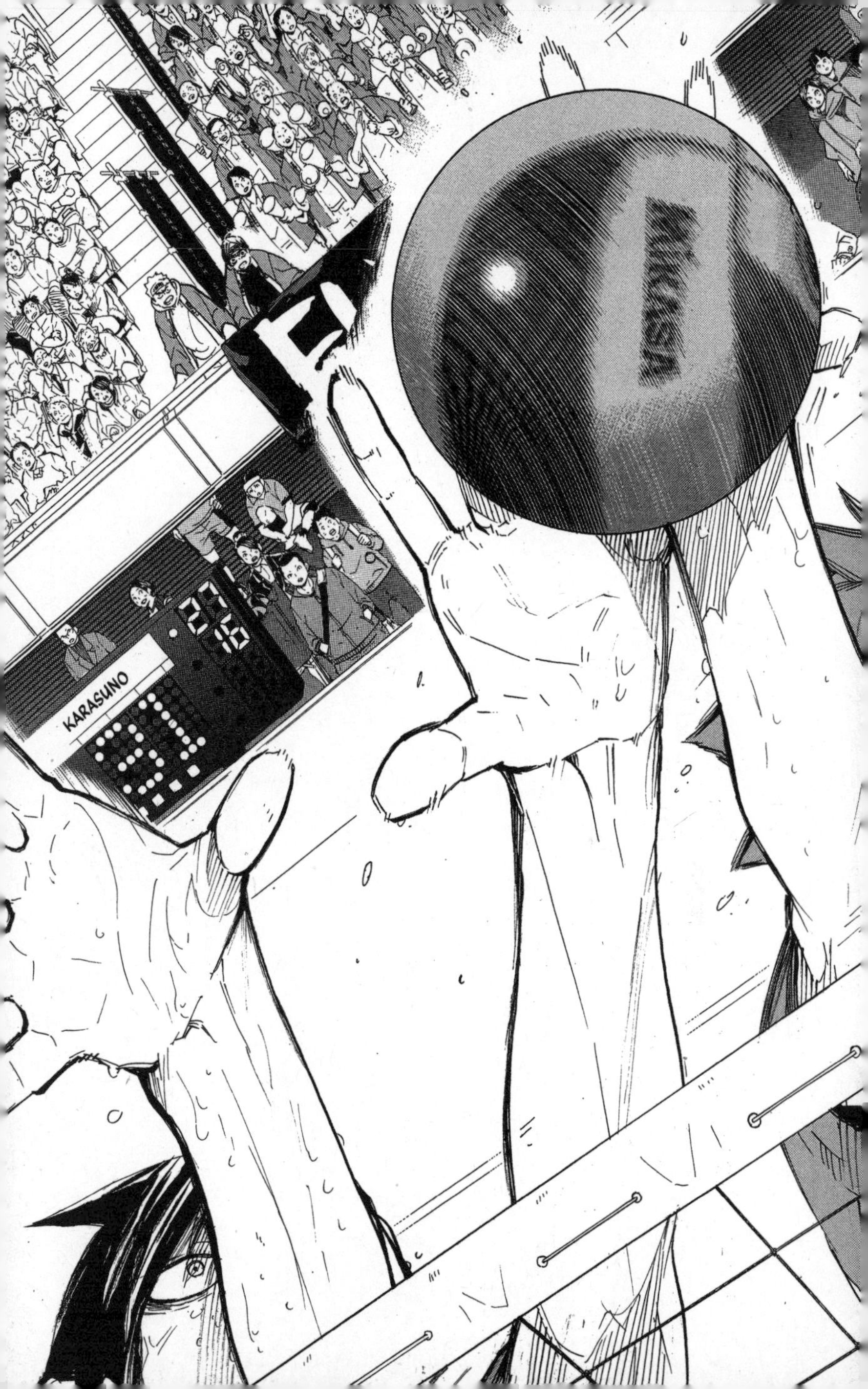
KARASUNO

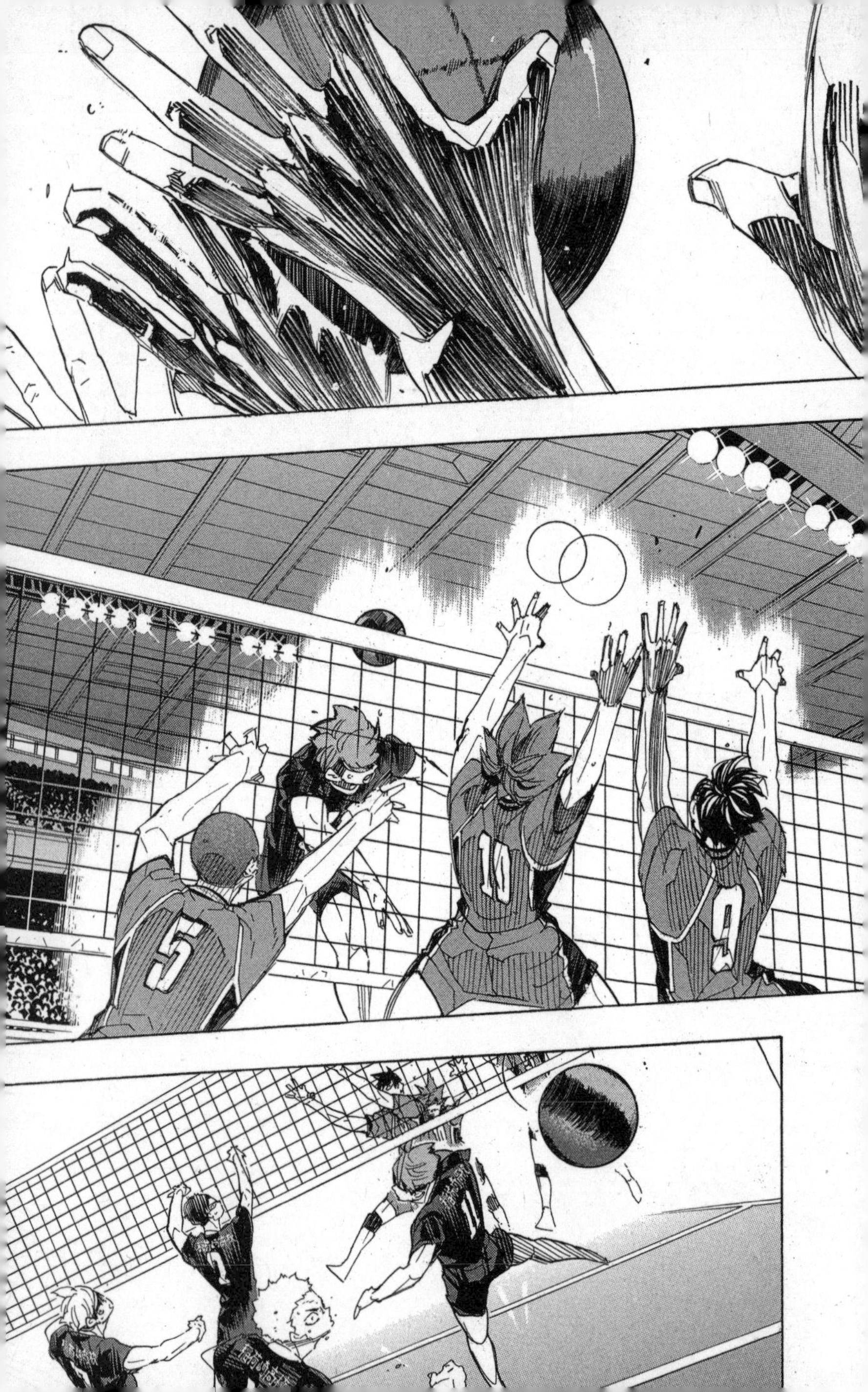

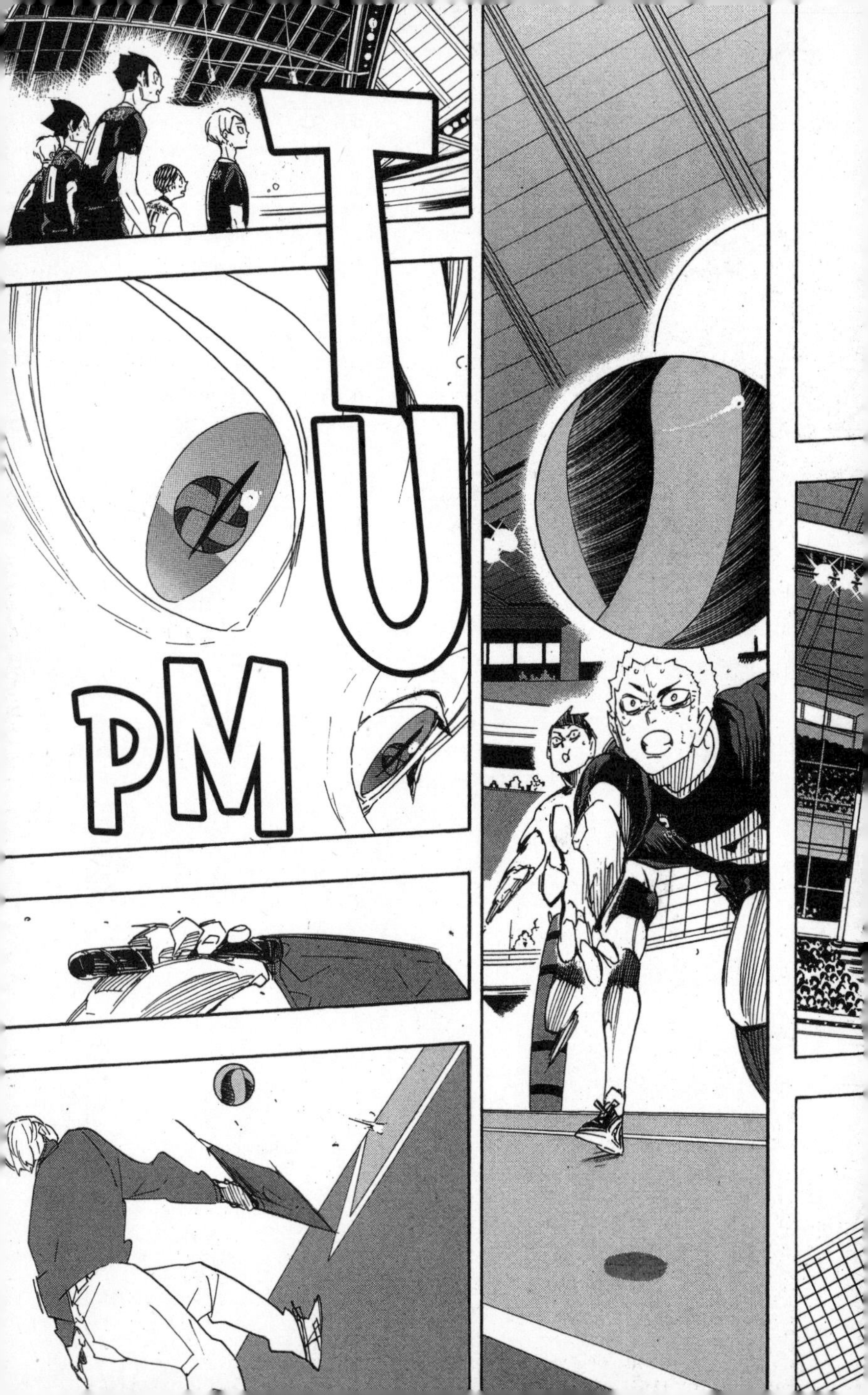
TU
PM

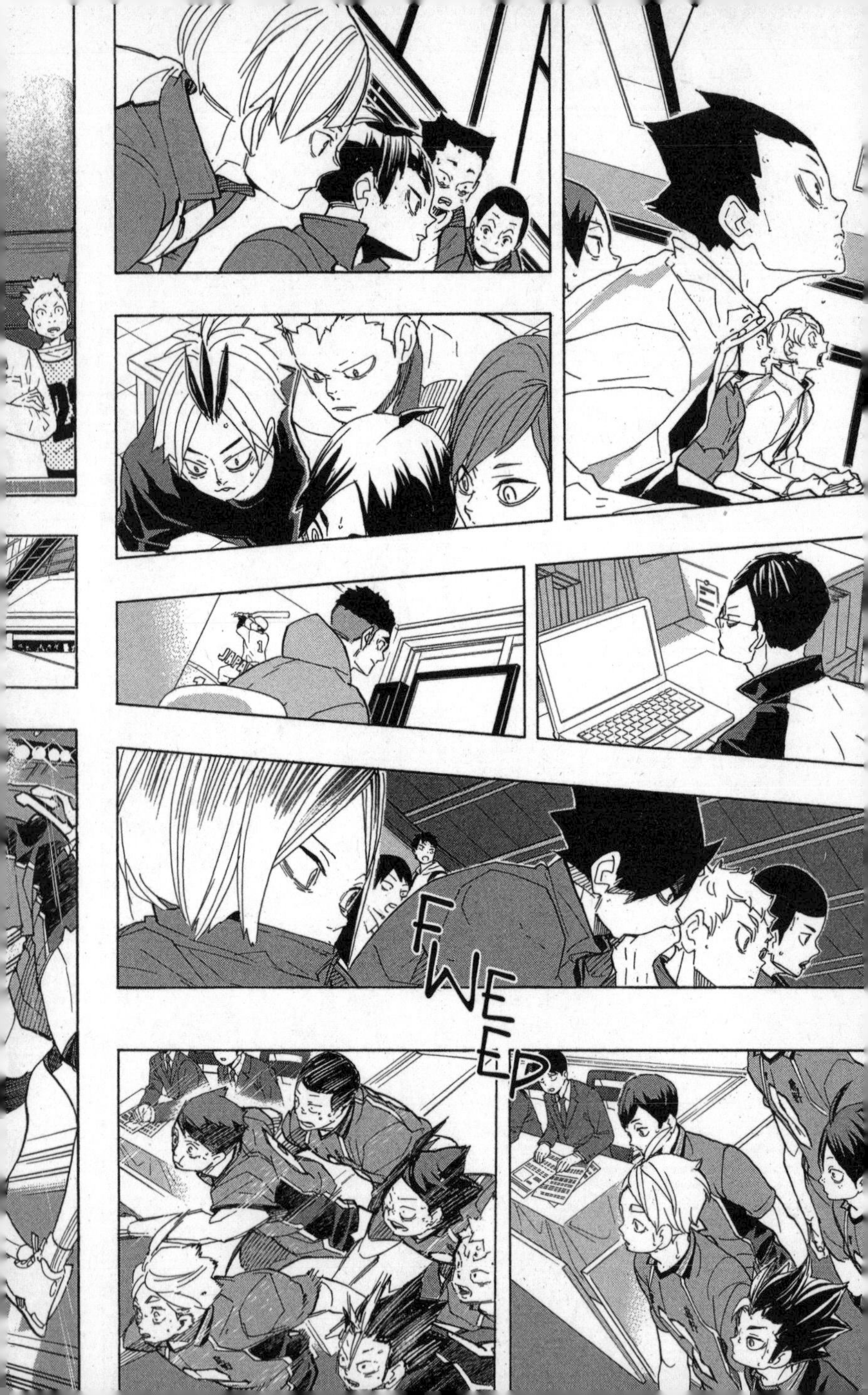
FWEEP

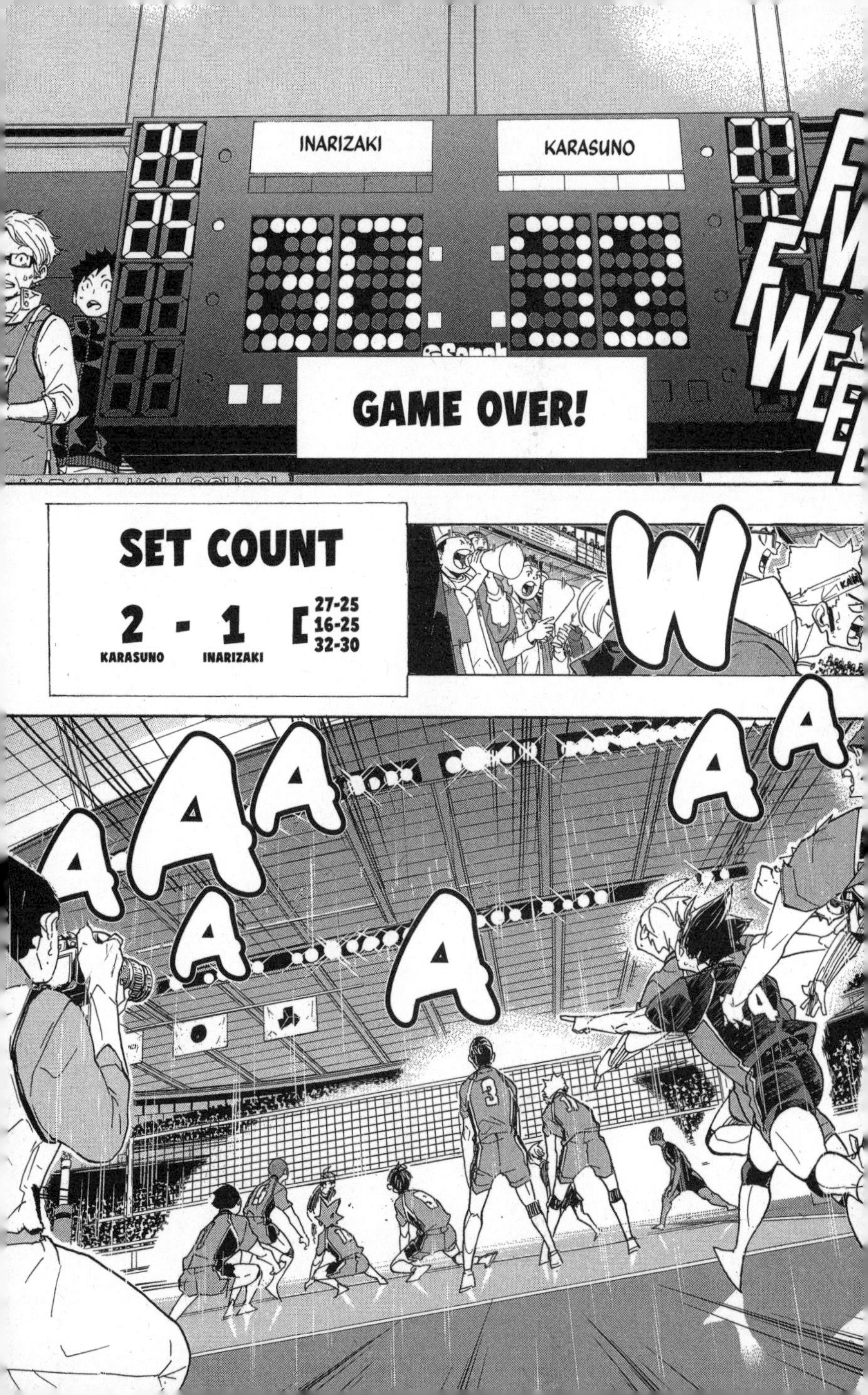
FWEEE
INARIZAKI
KARASUNO
GAME OVER!
W
SET COUNT
2 - 1
KARASUNO
INARIZAKI
27-25
16-25
32-30
AAAA
AAA

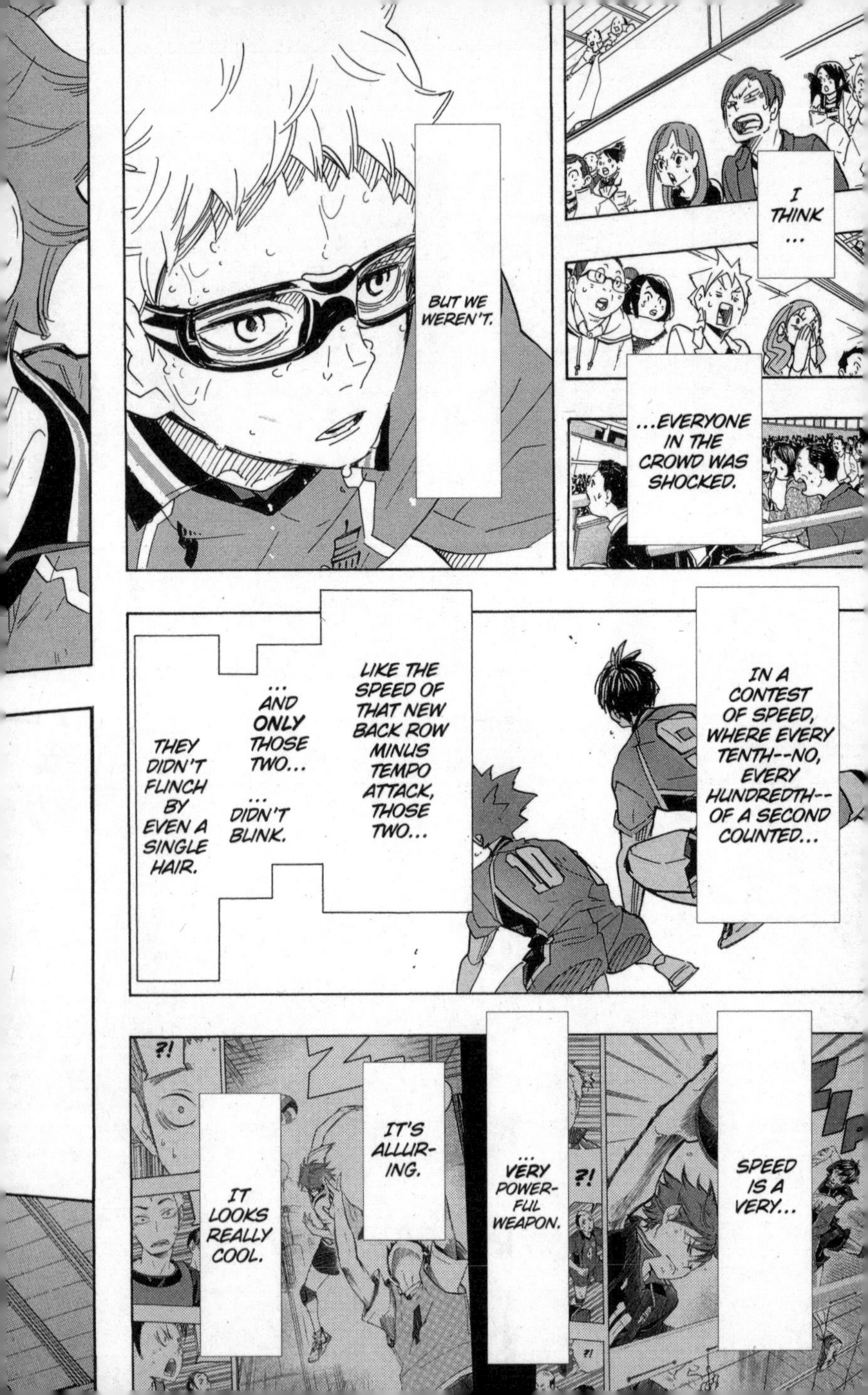
I THINK...
...EVERYONE IN THE CROWD WAS SHOCKED.
BUT WE WEREN'T.
IN A CONTEST OF SPEED, WHERE EVERY TENTH--NO, EVERY HUNDREDTH--OF A SECOND COUNTED...
LIKE THE SPEED OF THAT NEW BACK ROW MINUS TEMPO ATTACK, THOSE TWO...
...AND ONLY THOSE TWO...
...DIDN'T BLINK.
THEY DIDN'T FLINCH BY EVEN A SINGLE HAIR.
SPEED IS A VERY...
?!
...VERY POWERFUL WEAPON.
IT'S ALLURING.
IT LOOKS REALLY COOL.
?!

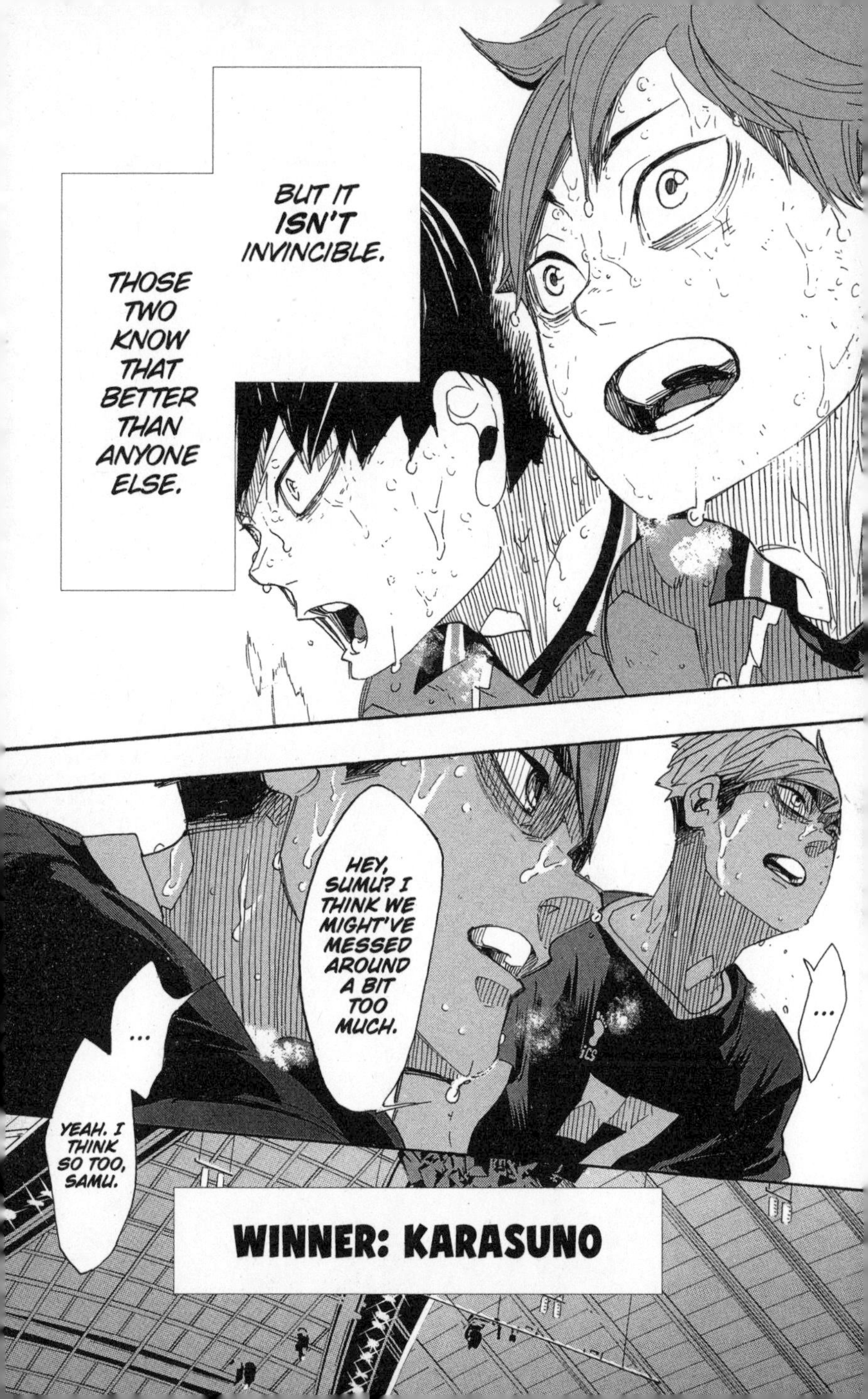
BUT IT ISN'T INVINCIBLE.
THOSE TWO KNOW THAT BETTER THAN ANYONE ELSE.
HEY, SUMU? I THINK WE MIGHT'VE MESSED AROUND A BIT TOO MUCH.
...
...
YEAH. I THINK SO TOO, SAMU.
WINNER: KARASUNO

HAIKYU!!

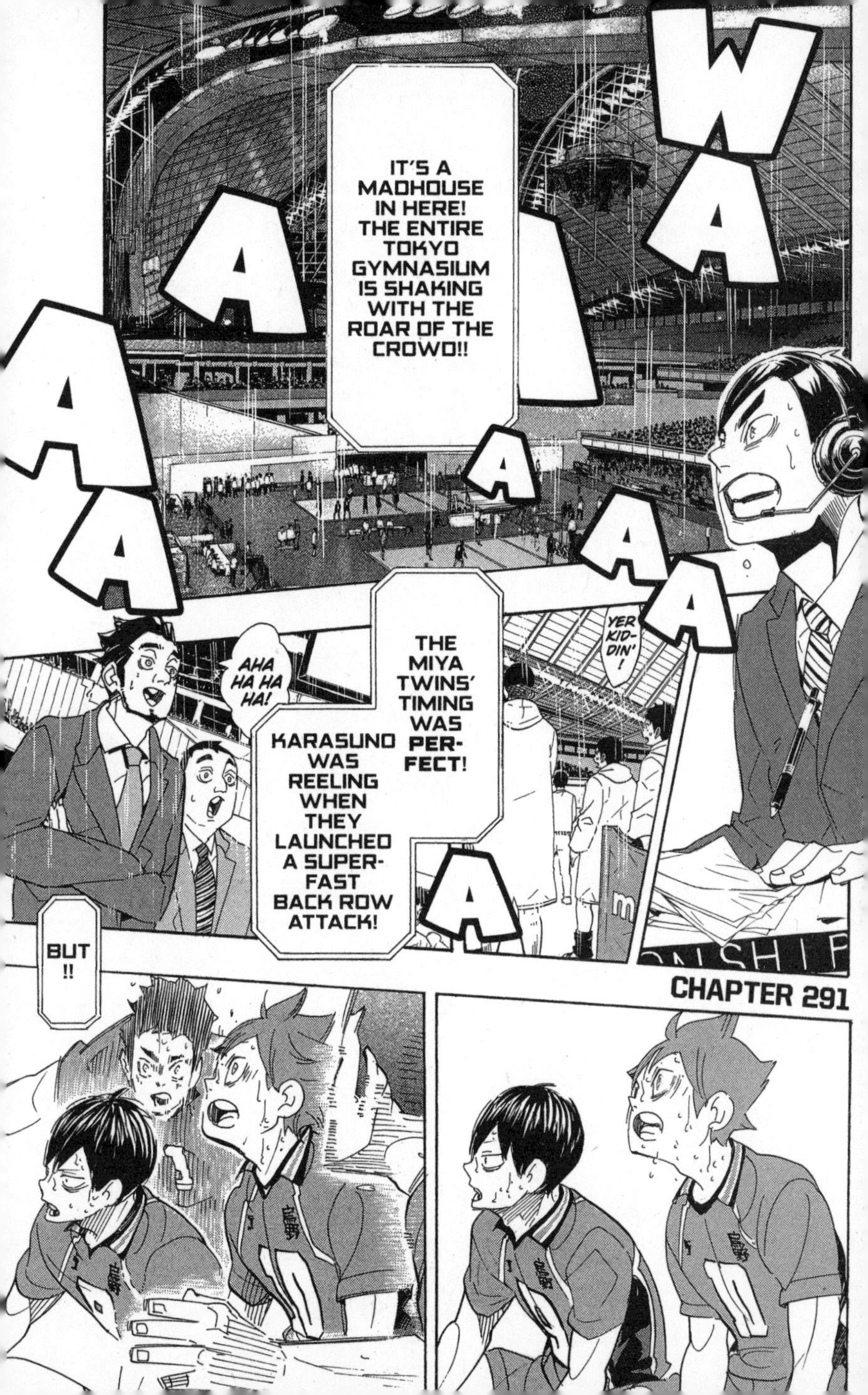
WAAAAAAAA
IT'S A MADHOUSE IN HERE! THE ENTIRE TOKYO GYMNASIUM IS SHAKING WITH THE ROAR OF THE CROWD!!
YER KID-DIN'!
THE MIYA TWINS' TIMING WAS PER-FECT!
KARASUNO WAS REELING WHEN THEY LAUNCHED A SUPER-FAST BACK ROW ATTACK!
AHA HA HA HA HA!
BUT !!
CHAPTER 291

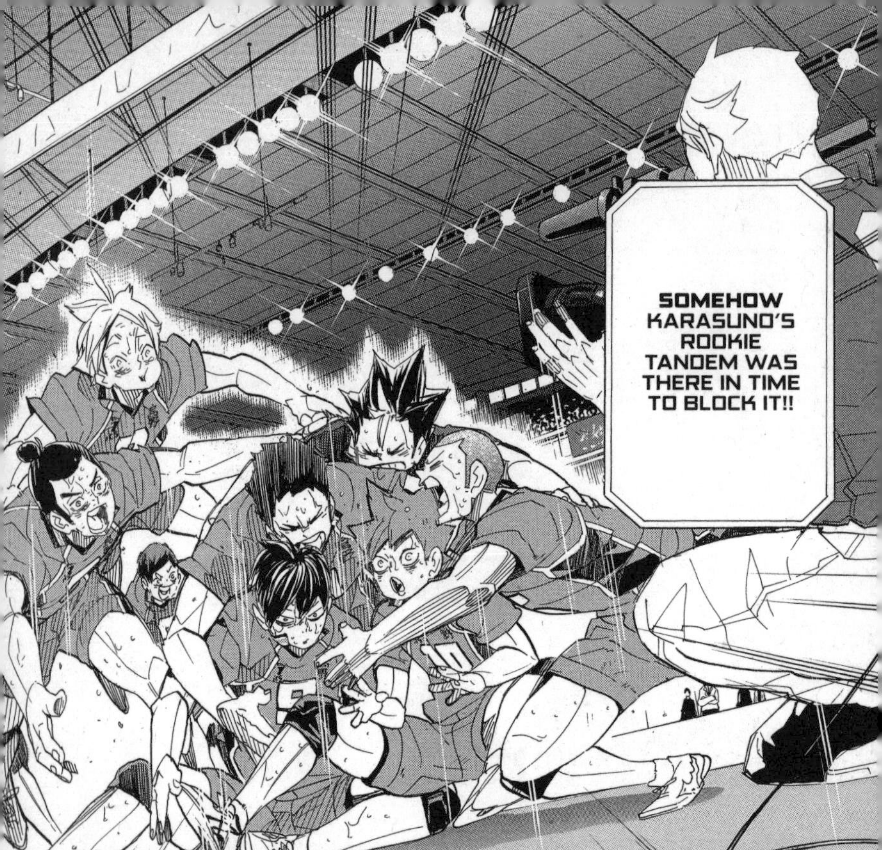
SOMEHOW KARASUNO'S ROOKIE TANDEM WAS THERE IN TIME TO BLOCK IT!!

CHAPTER 291: A Day of Change

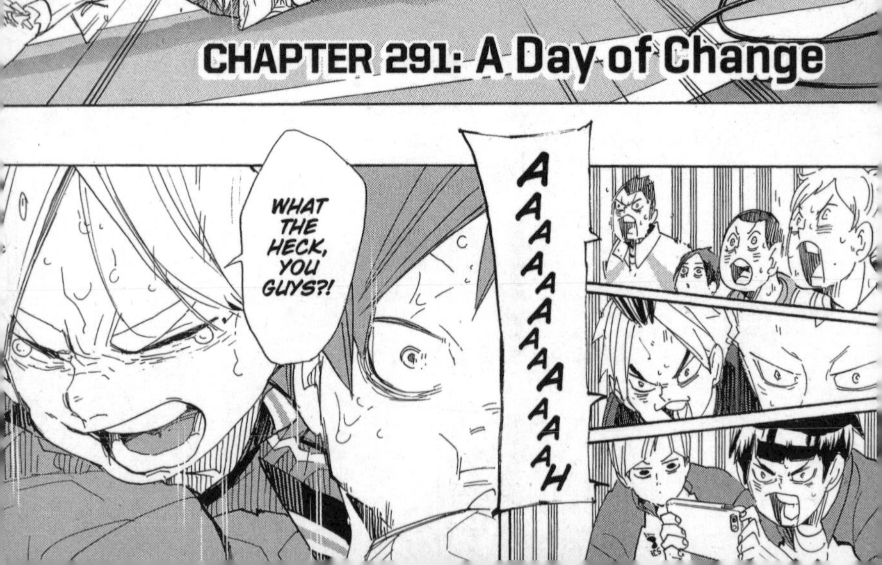
AAAAAAAAAAAAH
WHAT THE HECK, YOU GUYS?!

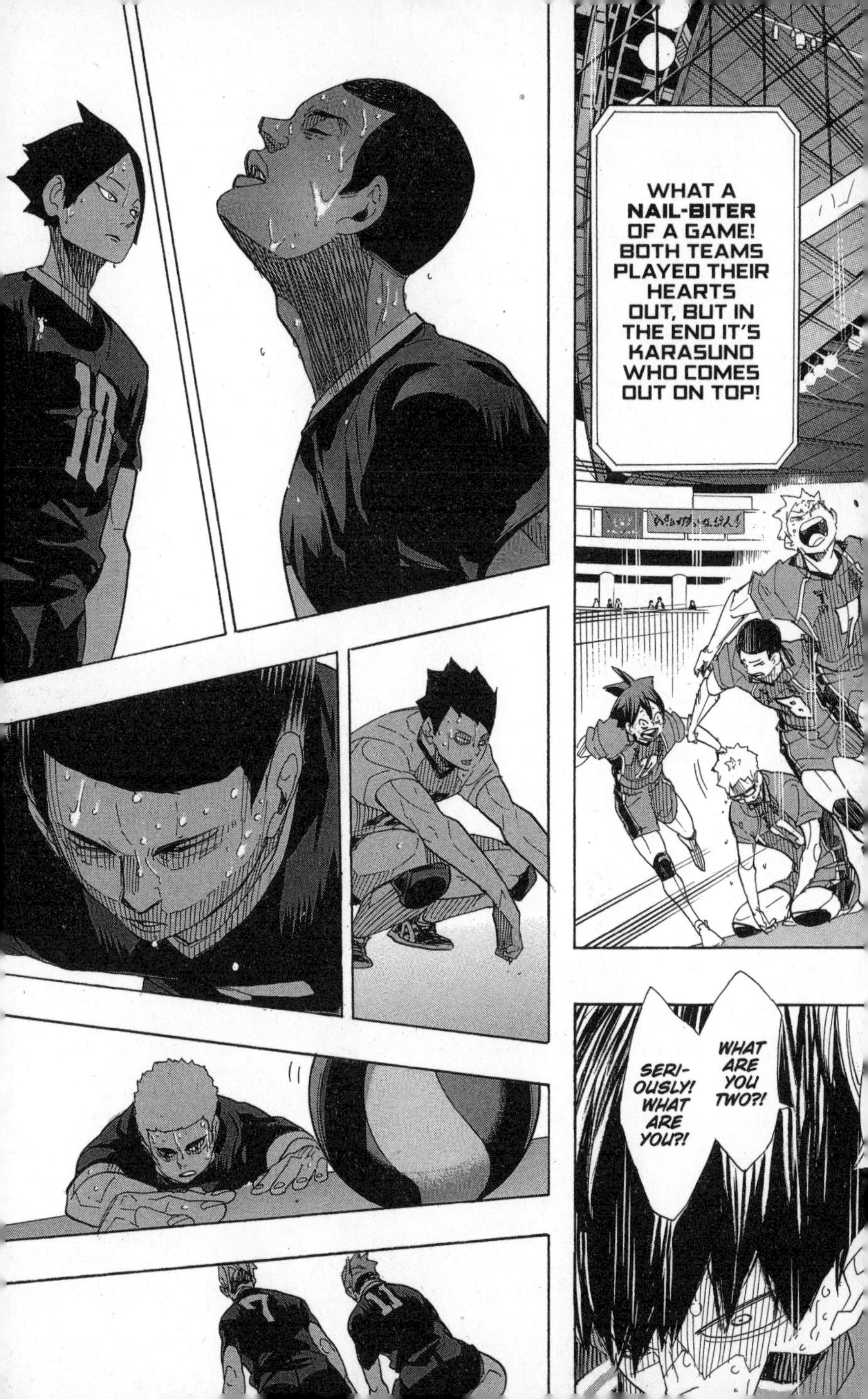
WHAT A NAIL-BITER OF A GAME! BOTH TEAMS PLAYED THEIR HEARTS OUT, BUT IN THE END IT'S KARASUNO WHO COMES OUT ON TOP!
WHAT ARE YOU TWO?!
SERI-OUSLY! WHAT ARE YOU?!

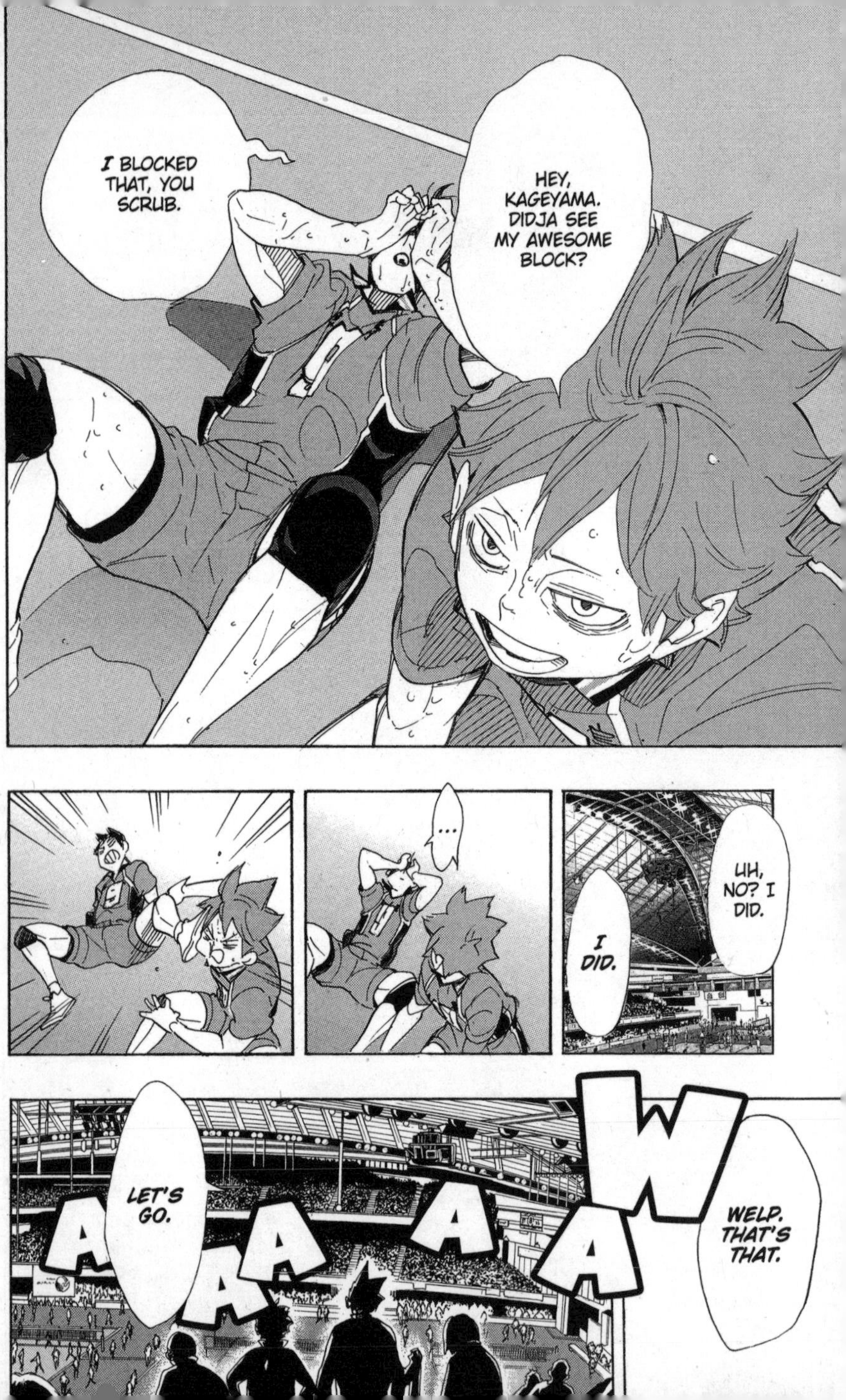
HEY, KAGEYAMA. DIDJA SEE MY AWESOME BLOCK?
I BLOCKED THAT, YOU SCRUB.
UH, NO? I DID.
I DID.
...
WELP. THAT'S THAT.
WAAAAAA
LET'S GO.

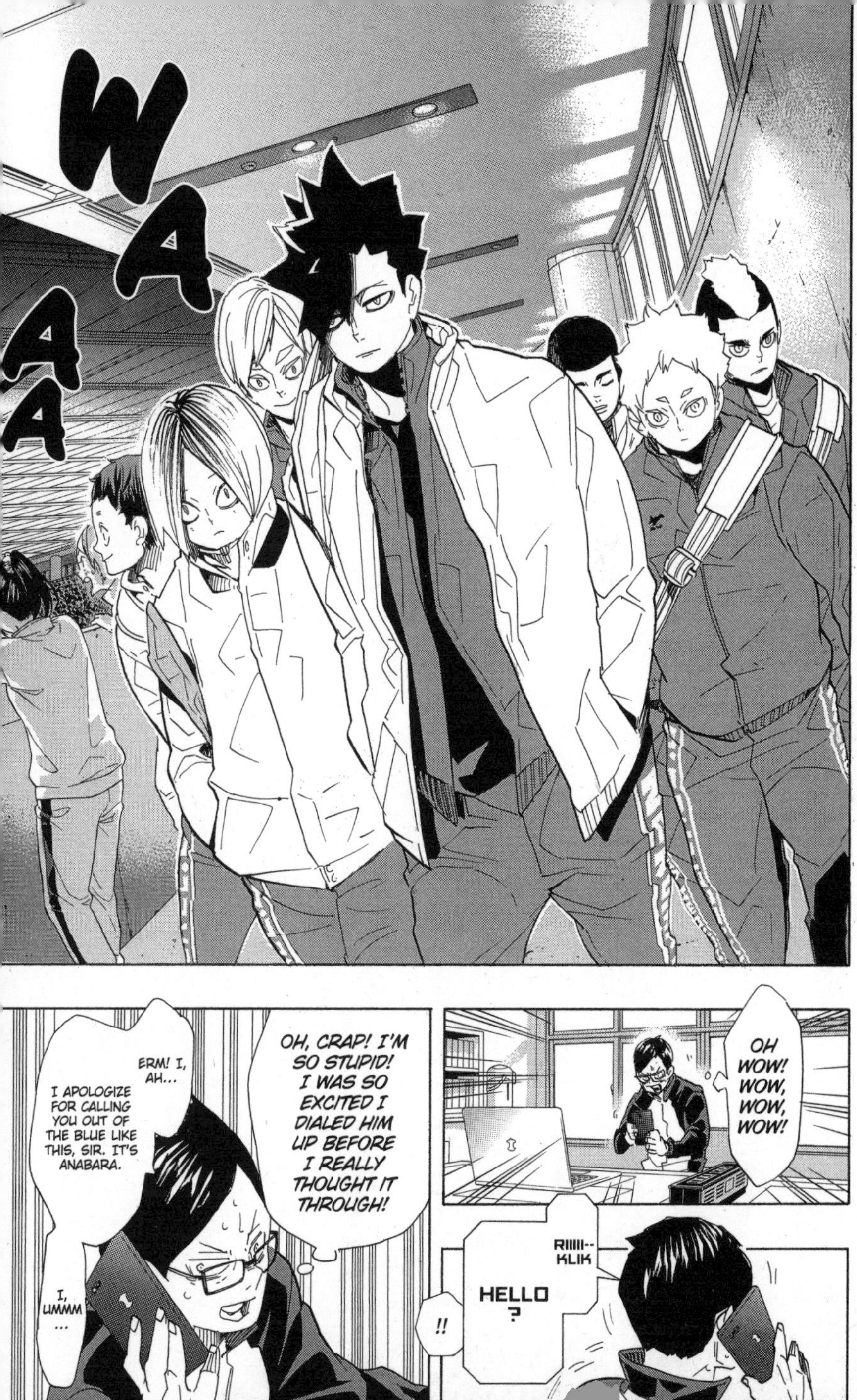
WAAAA
OH WOW! WOW, WOW, WOW!
RIIII--KLIK
HELLO?
!!
OH, CRAP! I'M SO STUPID! I WAS SO EXCITED I DIALED HIM UP BEFORE I REALLY THOUGHT IT THROUGH!
ERM! I, AH...
I APOLOGIZE FOR CALLING YOU OUT OF THE BLUE LIKE THIS, SIR. IT'S ANABARA.
I, UMMM ...

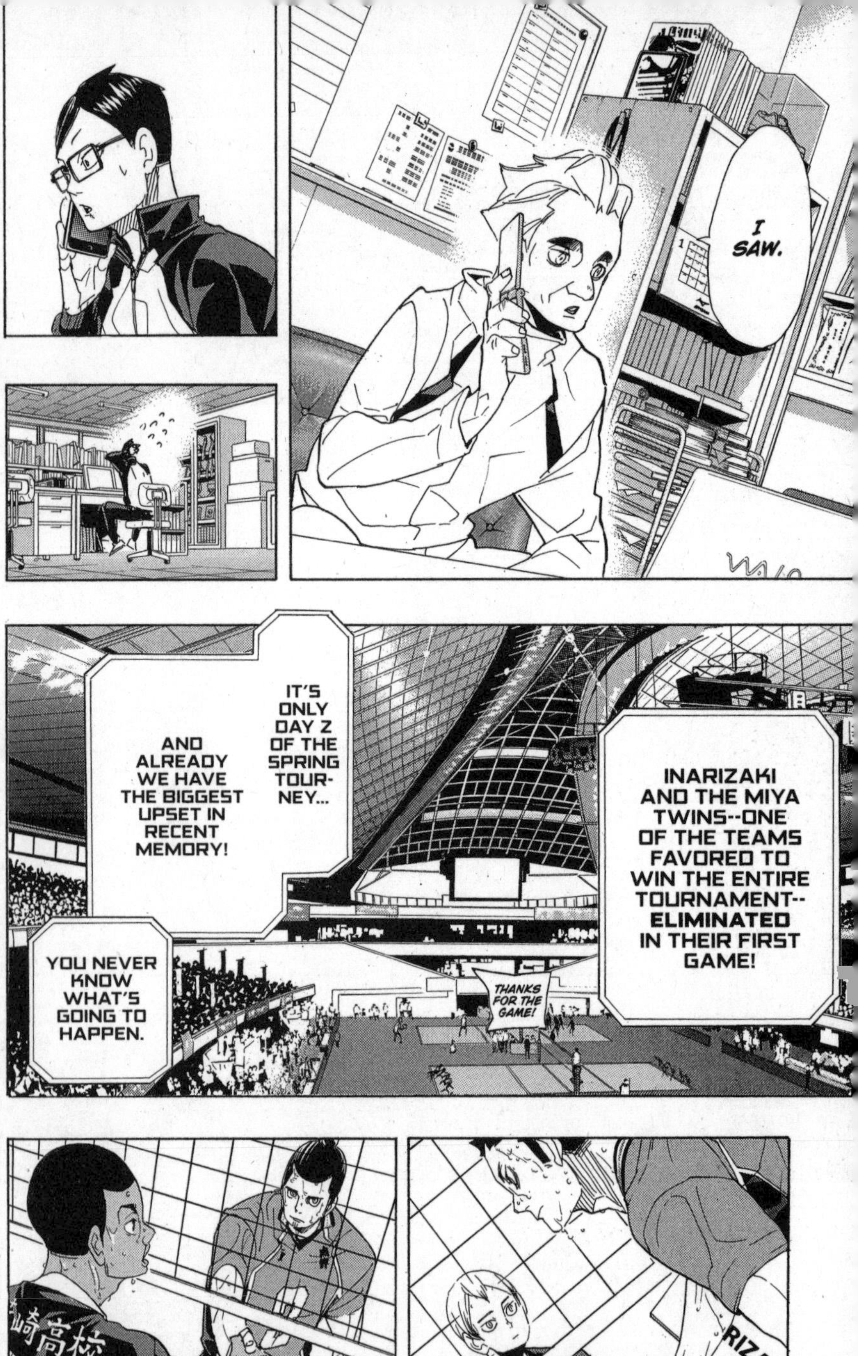
I SAW.
INARIZAKI AND THE MIYA TWINS--ONE OF THE TEAMS FAVORED TO WIN THE ENTIRE TOURNAMENT--ELIMINATED IN THEIR FIRST GAME!
THANKS FOR THE GAME!
IT'S ONLY DAY 2 OF THE SPRING TOUR-NEY...
AND ALREADY WE HAVE THE BIGGEST UPSET IN RECENT MEMORY!
YOU NEVER KNOW WHAT'S GOING TO HAPPEN.
RIZAKI
崎高校

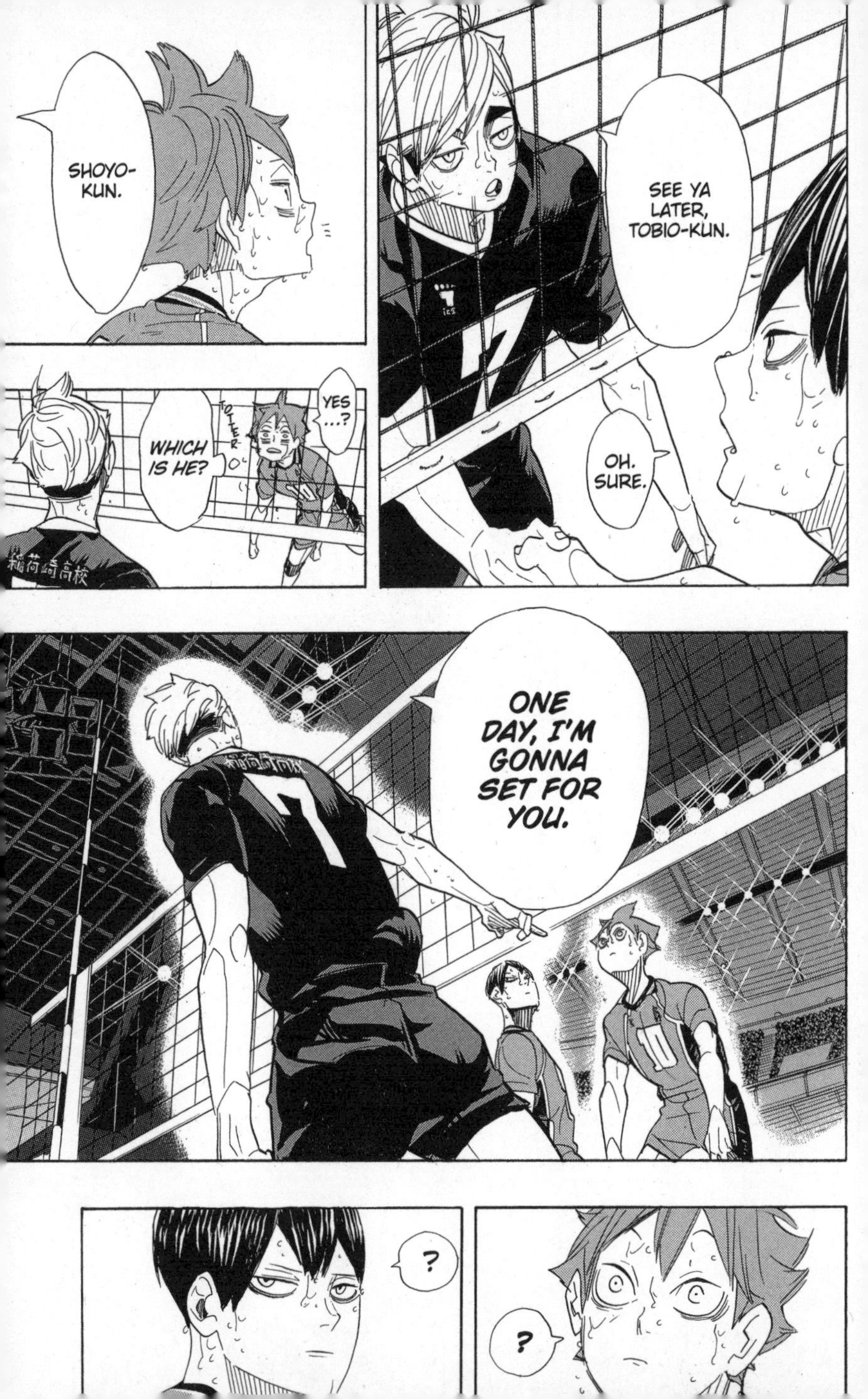
SEE YA LATER, TOBIO-KUN.
OH. SURE.
SHOYO-KUN.
YES ...?
TOTTER
WHICH IS HE?
ONE DAY, I'M GONNA SET FOR YOU.
?
?

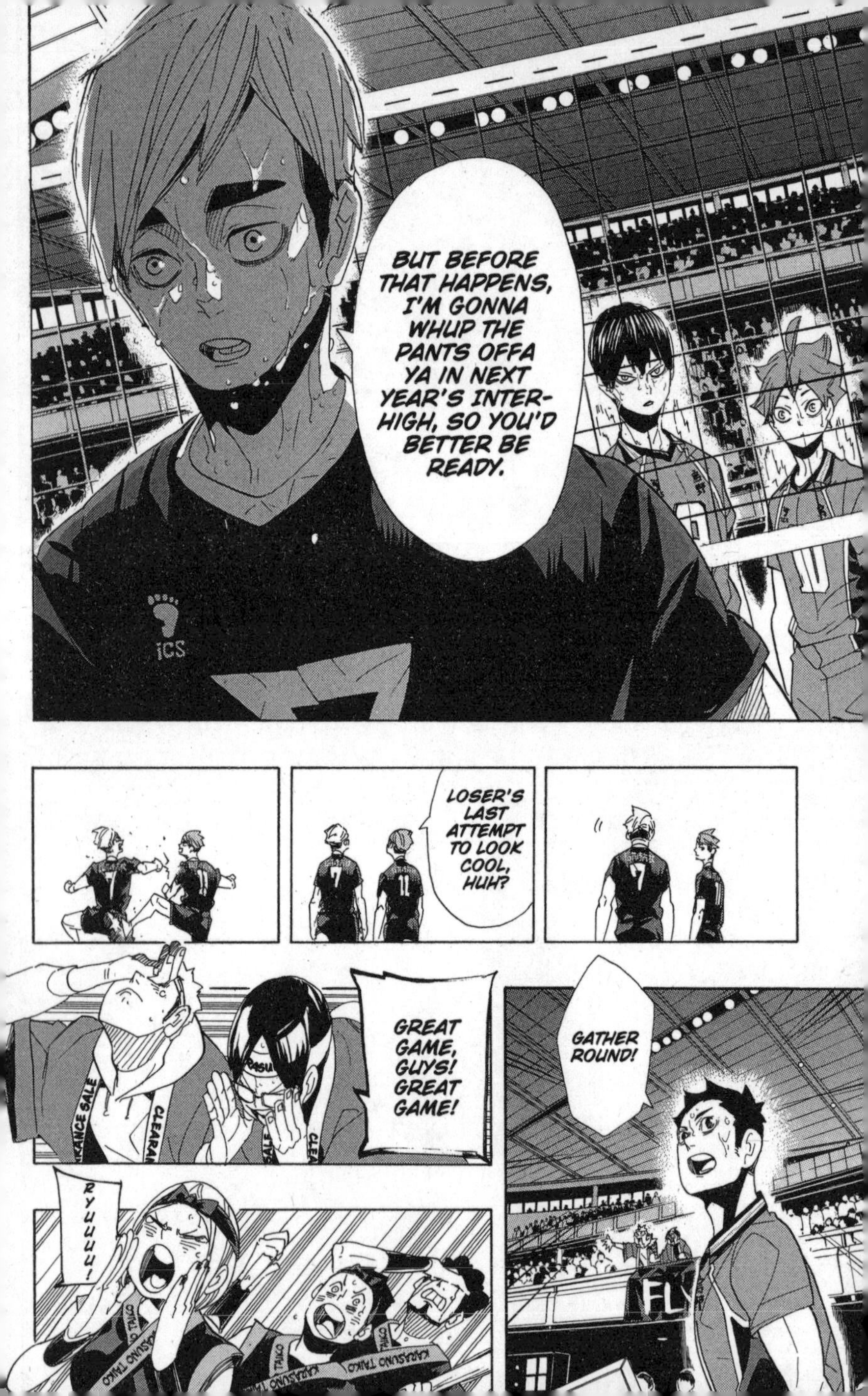
BUT BEFORE THAT HAPPENS, I'M GONNA WHUP THE PANTS OFFA YA IN NEXT YEAR'S INTER-HIGH, SO YOU'D BETTER BE READY.
LOSER'S LAST ATTEMPT TO LOOK COOL, HUH?
GATHER ROUND!
GREAT GAME, GUYS! GREAT GAME!
RYUUUU!

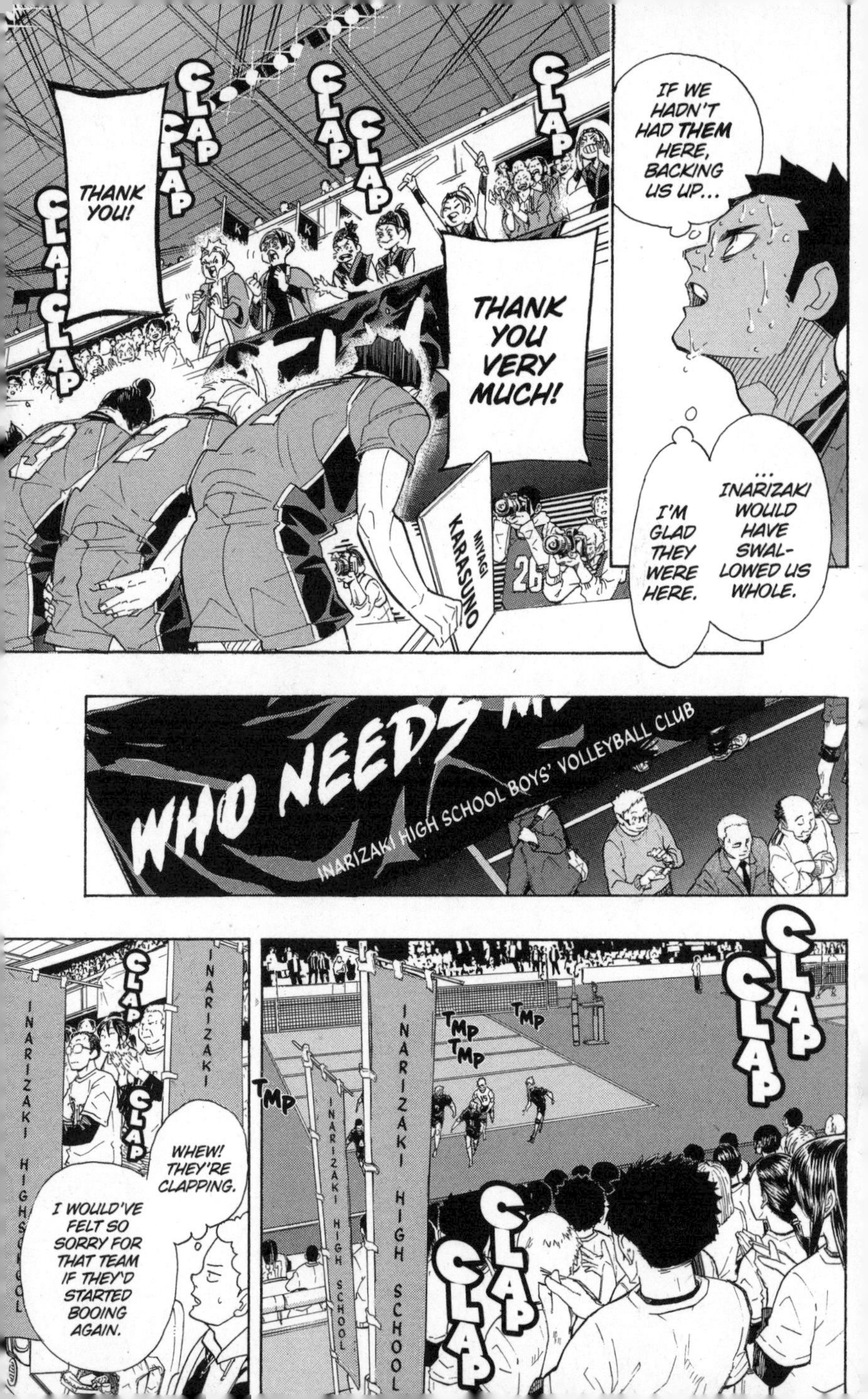
IF WE HADN'T HAD THEM HERE, BACKING US UP...
...INARIZAKI WOULD HAVE SWALLOWED US WHOLE.
I'M GLAD THEY WERE HERE.
CLAP
CLAP CLAP
CLAP CLAP
THANK YOU!
CLAP CLAP
THANK YOU VERY MUCH!
MIYAGI KARASUNO
WHO NEEDS
INARIZAKI HIGH SCHOOL BOYS' VOLLEYBALL CLUB
CLAP CLAP
TMP
TMP
TMP
TMP
INARIZAKI HIGH SCHOOL
INARIZAKI HIGH SCHOOL
CLAP CLAP
INARIZAKI
INARIZAKI HIGH SCHOOL
CLAP CLAP
WHEW! THEY'RE CLAPPING.
I WOULD'VE FELT SO SORRY FOR THAT TEAM IF THEY'D STARTED BOOING AGAIN.

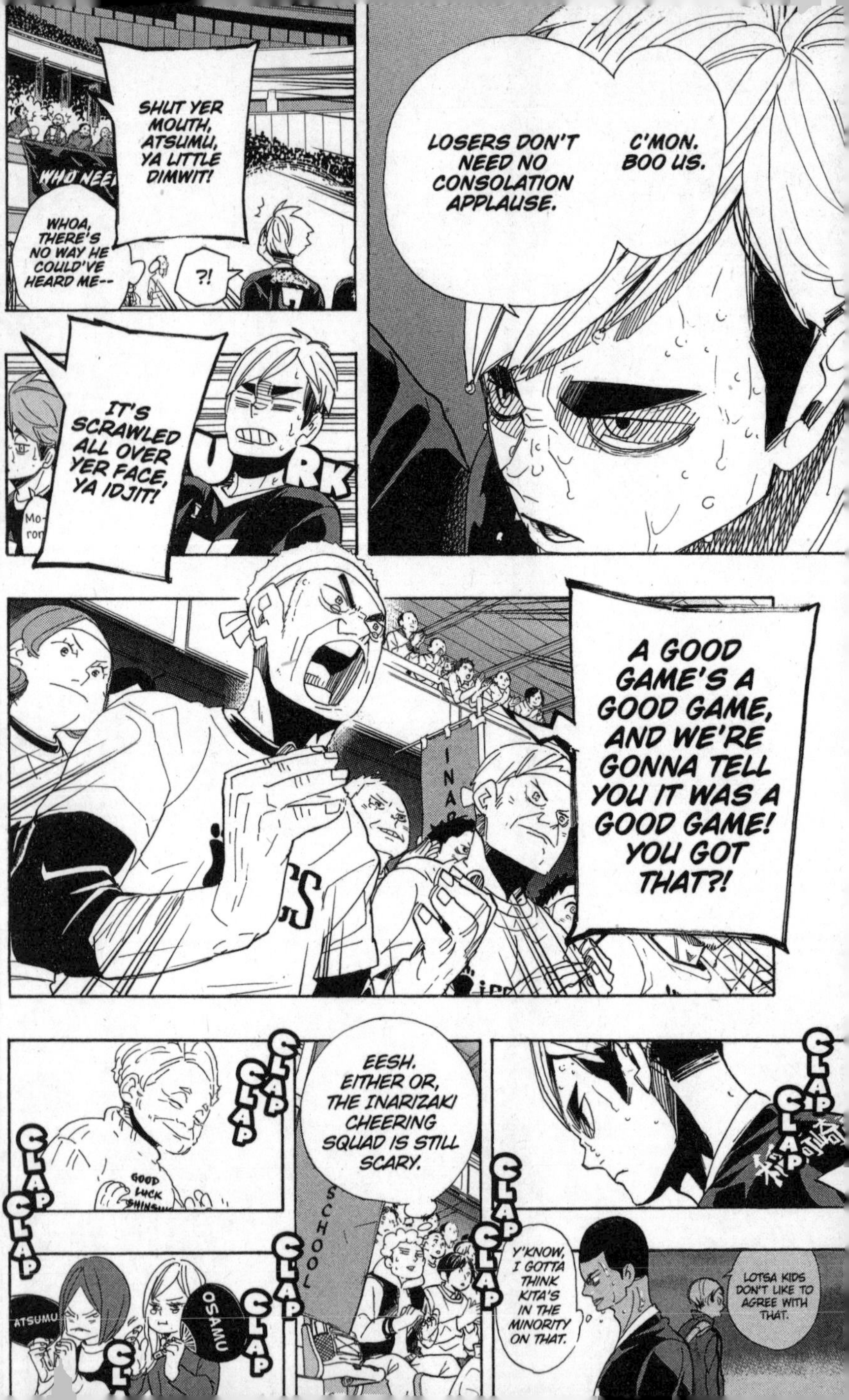
C'MON. BOO US.
LOSERS DON'T NEED NO CONSOLATION APPLAUSE.
SHUT YER MOUTH, ATSUMU, YA LITTLE DIMWIT!
?!
WHOA, THERE'S NO WAY HE COULD'VE HEARD ME--
IT'S SCRAWLED ALL OVER YER FACE, YA IDJIT!
A GOOD GAME'S A GOOD GAME, AND WE'RE GONNA TELL YOU IT WAS A GOOD GAME! YOU GOT THAT?!
CLAP CLAP
EESH. EITHER OR, THE INARIZAKI CHEERING SQUAD IS STILL SCARY.
CLAP CLAP
GOOD LUCK
CLAP CLAP
LOTSA KIDS DON'T LIKE TO AGREE WITH THAT.
Y'KNOW, I GOTTA THINK KITA'S IN THE MINORITY ON THAT.
CLAP CLAP
OSAMU
ATSUMU
CLAP

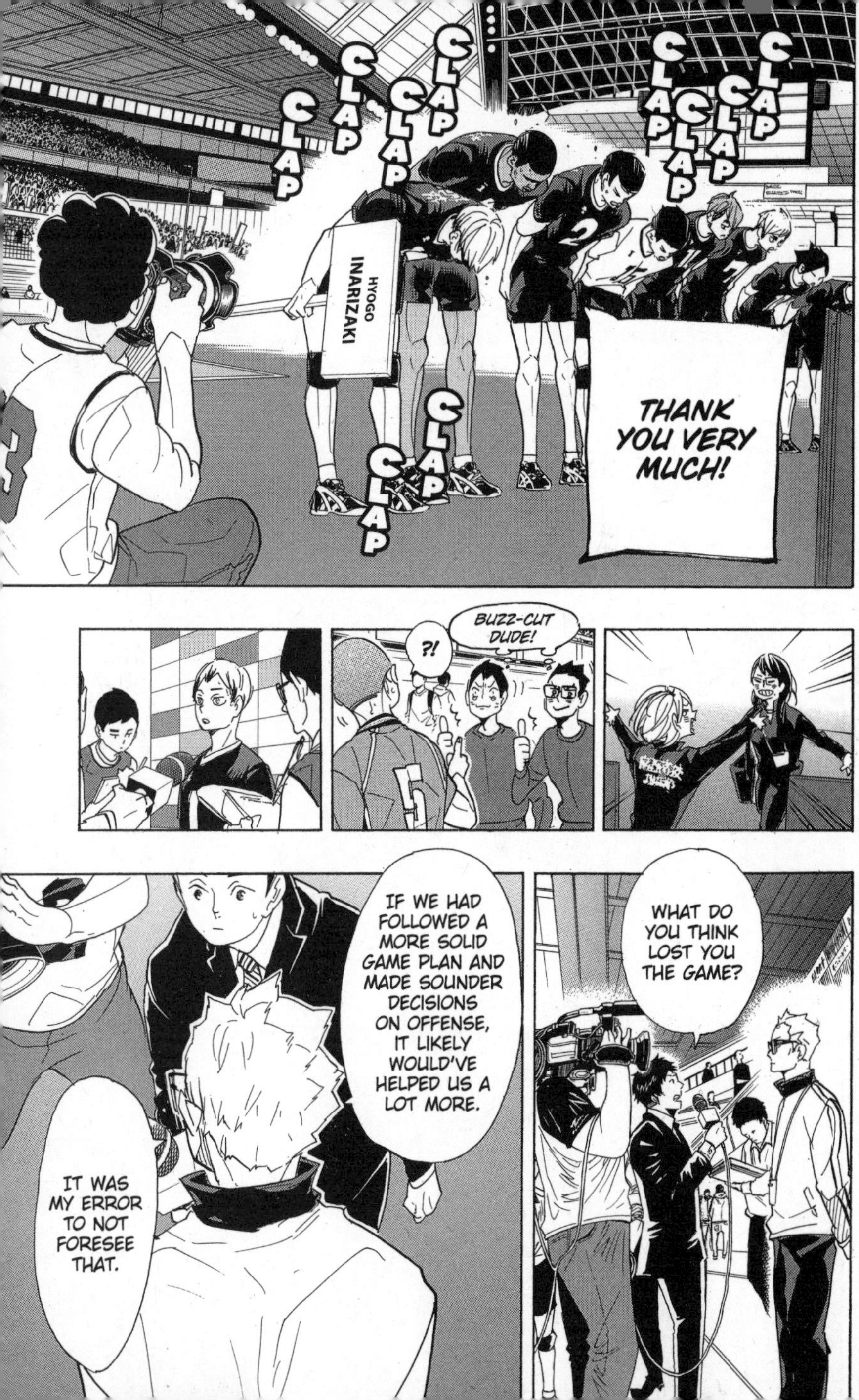
CLAP CLAP CLAP CLAP
CLAP CLAP CLAP CLAP
HYOGO INARIZAKI
CLAP CLAP
THANK YOU VERY MUCH!
BUZZ-CUT DUDE!
?!
WHAT DO YOU THINK LOST YOU THE GAME?
IF WE HAD FOLLOWED A MORE SOLID GAME PLAN AND MADE SOUNDER DECISIONS ON OFFENSE, IT LIKELY WOULD'VE HELPED US A LOT MORE.
IT WAS MY ERROR TO NOT FORESEE THAT.

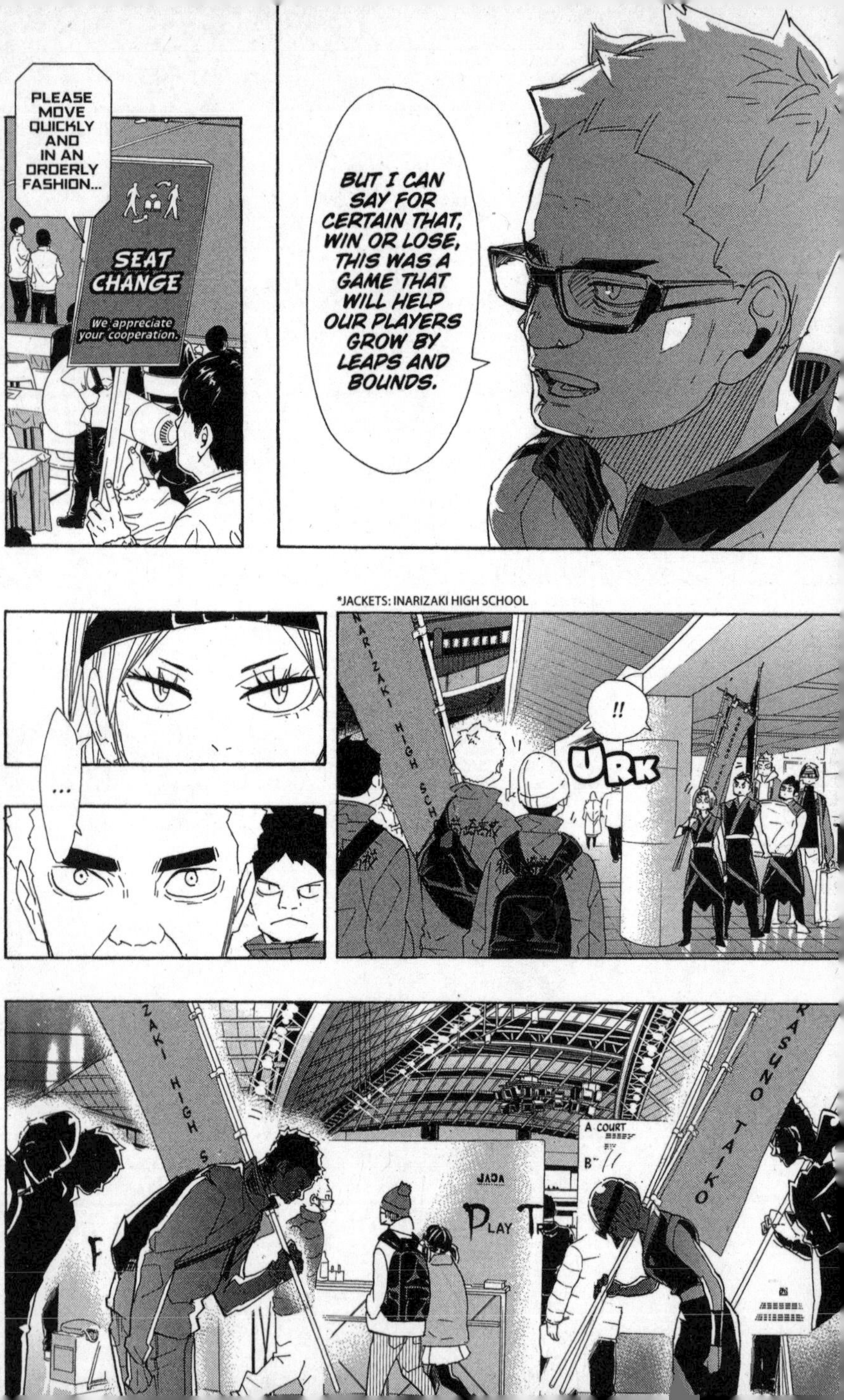
BUT I CAN SAY FOR CERTAIN THAT, WIN OR LOSE, THIS WAS A GAME THAT WILL HELP OUR PLAYERS GROW BY LEAPS AND BOUNDS.
PLEASE MOVE QUICKLY AND IN AN ORDERLY FASHION...
SEAT CHANGE
We appreciate your cooperation.
*JACKETS: INARIZAKI HIGH SCHOOL
!!
URK
...
A COURT
PLAY

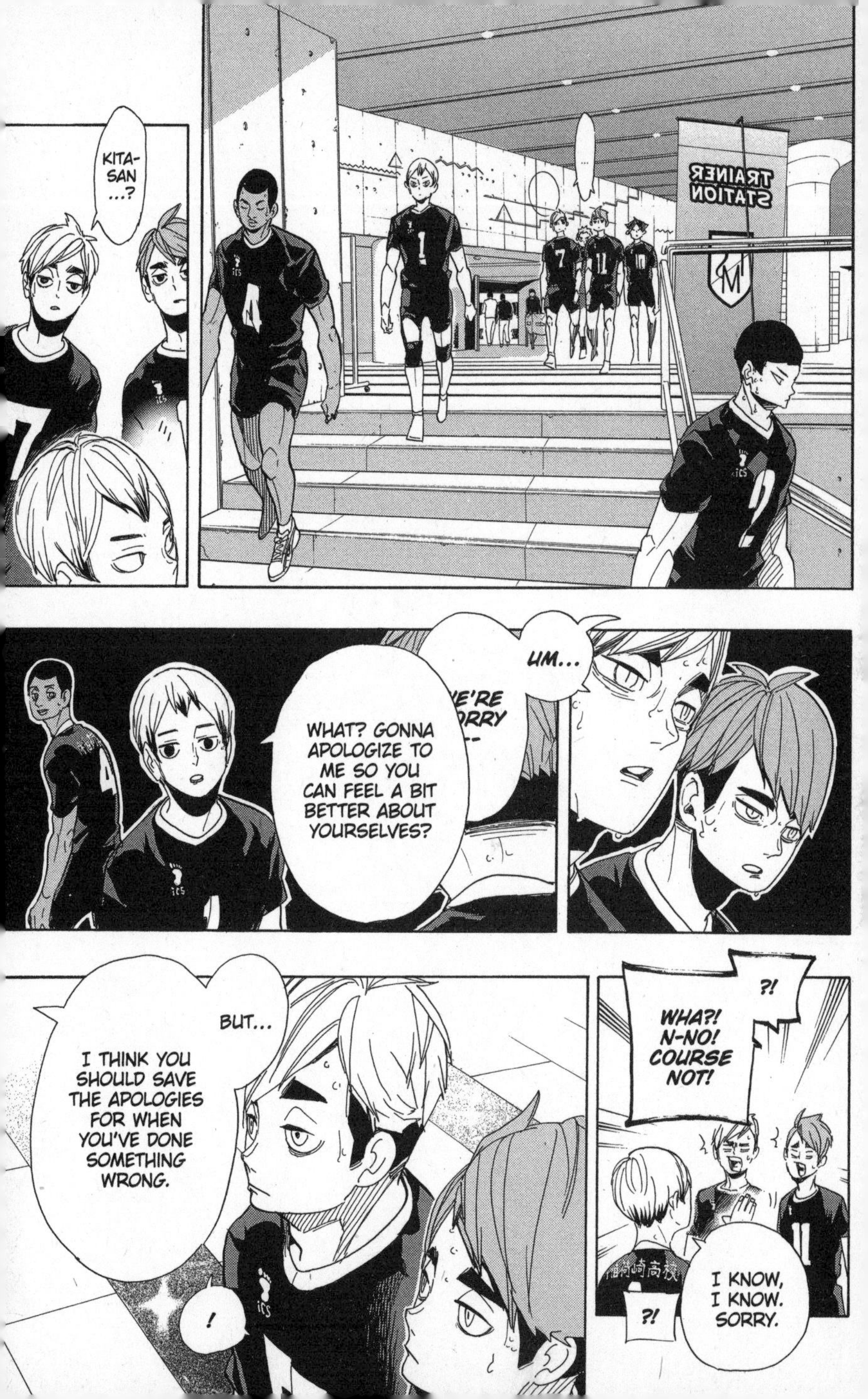
...
KITA-SAN ...?
UM...
WHAT? GONNA APOLOGIZE TO ME SO YOU CAN FEEL A BIT BETTER ABOUT YOURSELVES?
?!
WHA?! N-NO! COURSE NOT!
I KNOW, I KNOW. SORRY.
?!
BUT...
I THINK YOU SHOULD SAVE THE APOLOGIES FOR WHEN YOU'VE DONE SOMETHING WRONG.
!

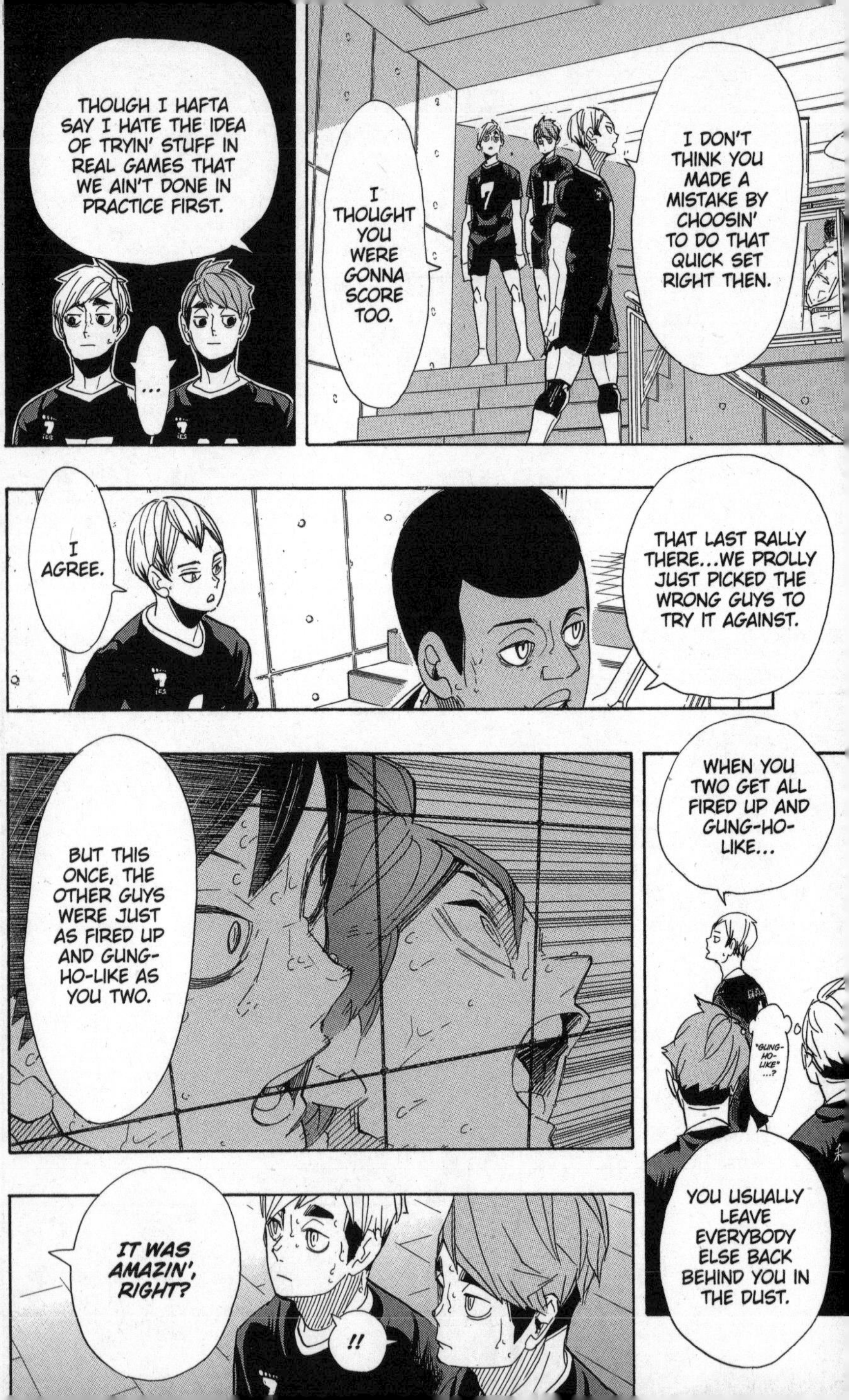
I DON'T THINK YOU MADE A MISTAKE BY CHOOSIN' TO DO THAT QUICK SET RIGHT THEN.
I THOUGHT YOU WERE GONNA SCORE TOO.
THOUGH I HAFTA SAY I HATE THE IDEA OF TRYIN' STUFF IN REAL GAMES THAT WE AIN'T DONE IN PRACTICE FIRST.
...
THAT LAST RALLY THERE...WE PROLLY JUST PICKED THE WRONG GUYS TO TRY IT AGAINST.
I AGREE.
WHEN YOU TWO GET ALL FIRED UP AND GUNG-HO-LIKE...
"GUNG-HO-LIKE" ...?
YOU USUALLY LEAVE EVERYBODY ELSE BACK BEHIND YOU IN THE DUST.
BUT THIS ONCE, THE OTHER GUYS WERE JUST AS FIRED UP AND GUNG-HO-LIKE AS YOU TWO.
IT WAS AMAZIN', RIGHT?
!!

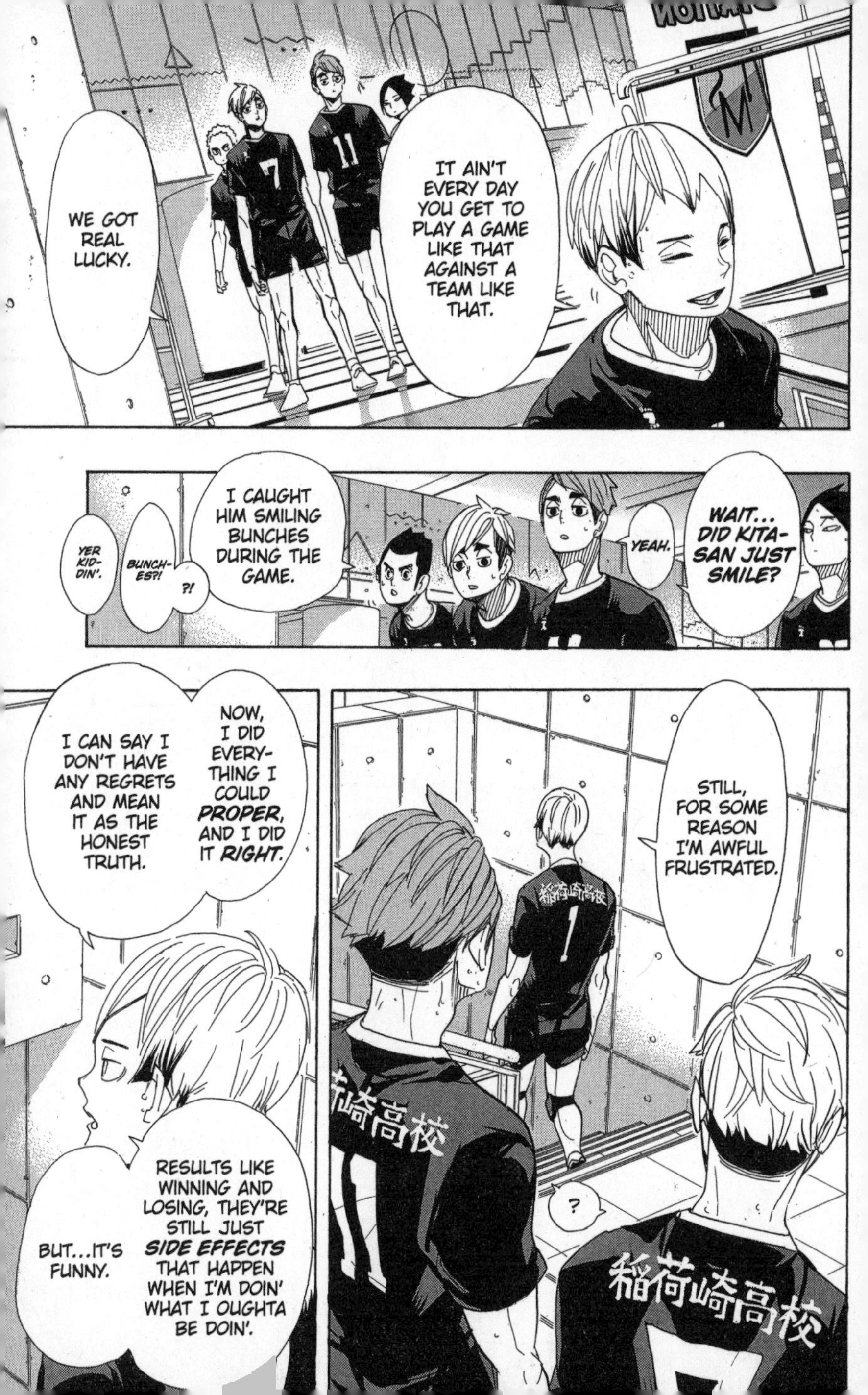
IT AIN'T EVERY DAY YOU GET TO PLAY A GAME LIKE THAT AGAINST A TEAM LIKE THAT.
WE GOT REAL LUCKY.
WAIT... DID KITA-SAN JUST SMILE?
YEAH.
I CAUGHT HIM SMILING BUNCHES DURING THE GAME.
?!
BUNCH-ES?!
YER KID-DIN'.
STILL, FOR SOME REASON I'M AWFUL FRUSTRATED.
?
NOW, I DID EVERYTHING I COULD PROPER, AND I DID IT RIGHT.
I CAN SAY I DON'T HAVE ANY REGRETS AND MEAN IT AS THE HONEST TRUTH.
RESULTS LIKE WINNING AND LOSING, THEY'RE STILL JUST SIDE EFFECTS THAT HAPPEN WHEN I'M DOIN' WHAT I OUGHTA BE DOIN'.
BUT...IT'S FUNNY.

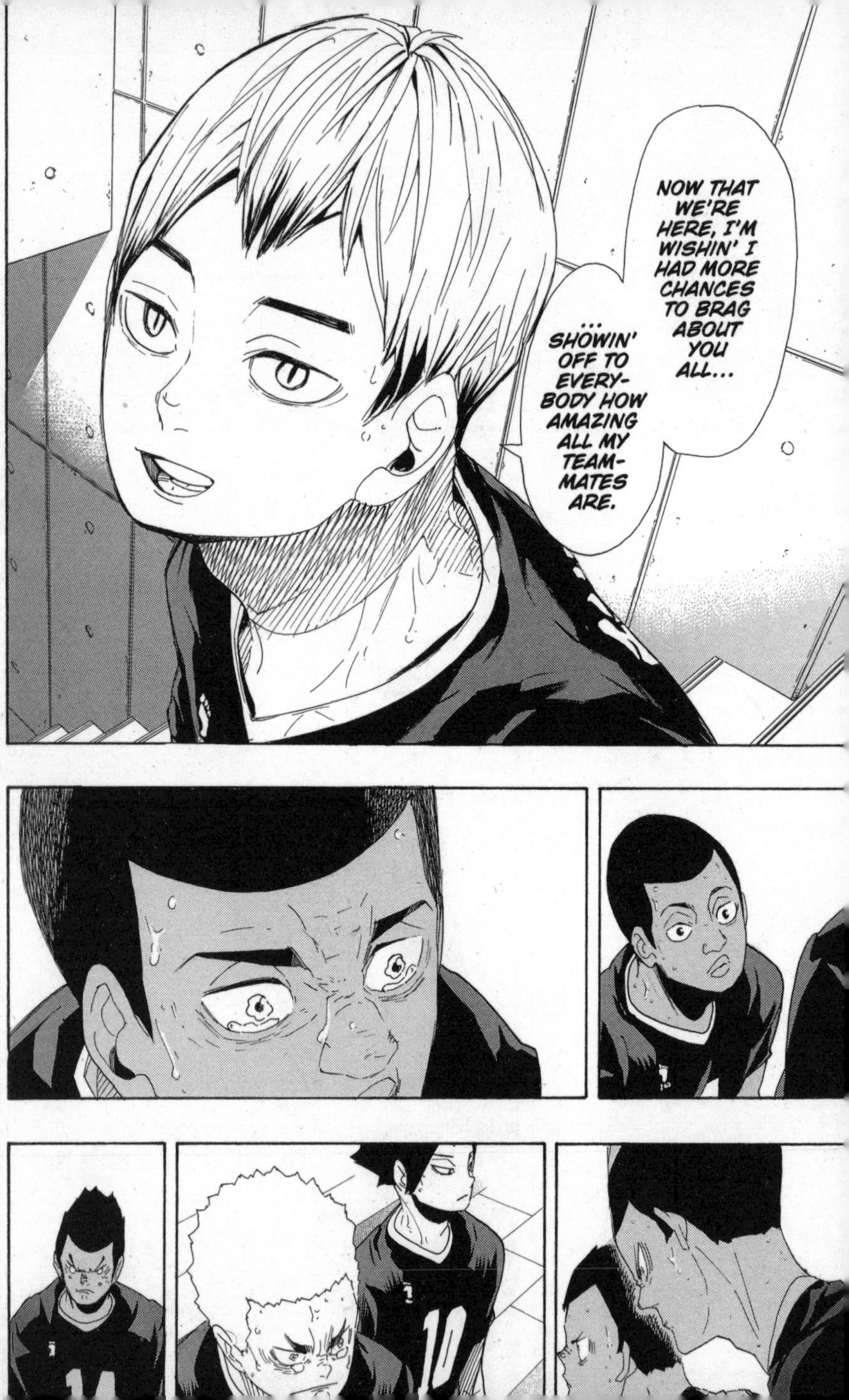
NOW THAT WE'RE HERE, I'M WISHIN' I HAD MORE CHANCES TO BRAG ABOUT YOU ALL...
...SHOWIN' OFF TO EVERY-BODY HOW AMAZING ALL MY TEAM-MATES ARE.

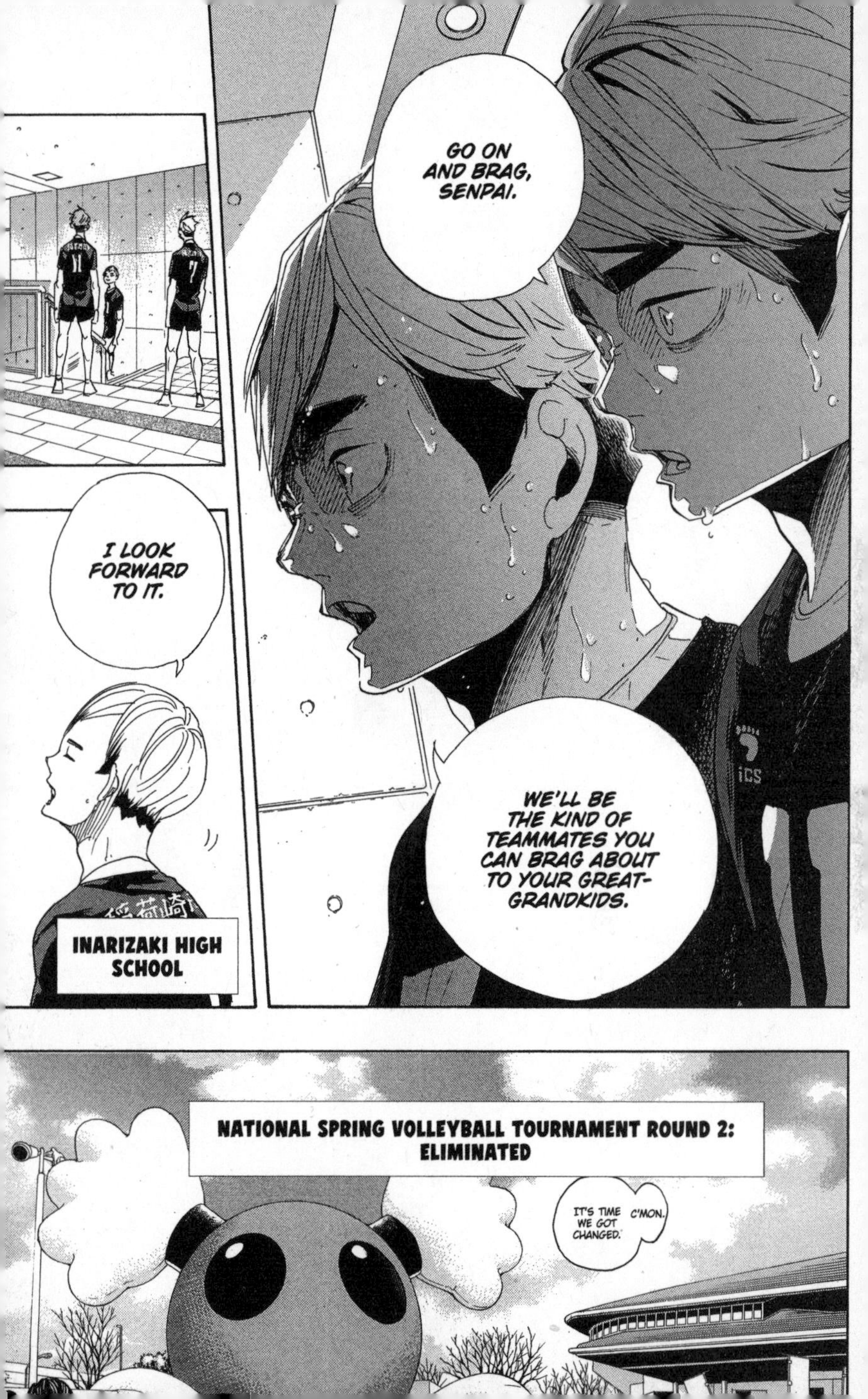
GO ON AND BRAG, SENPAI.
WE'LL BE THE KIND OF TEAMMATES YOU CAN BRAG ABOUT TO YOUR GREAT-GRANDKIDS.
I LOOK FORWARD TO IT.
INARIZAKI HIGH SCHOOL
NATIONAL SPRING VOLLEYBALL TOURNAMENT ROUND 2: ELIMINATED
C'MON.
IT'S TIME WE GOT CHANGED.

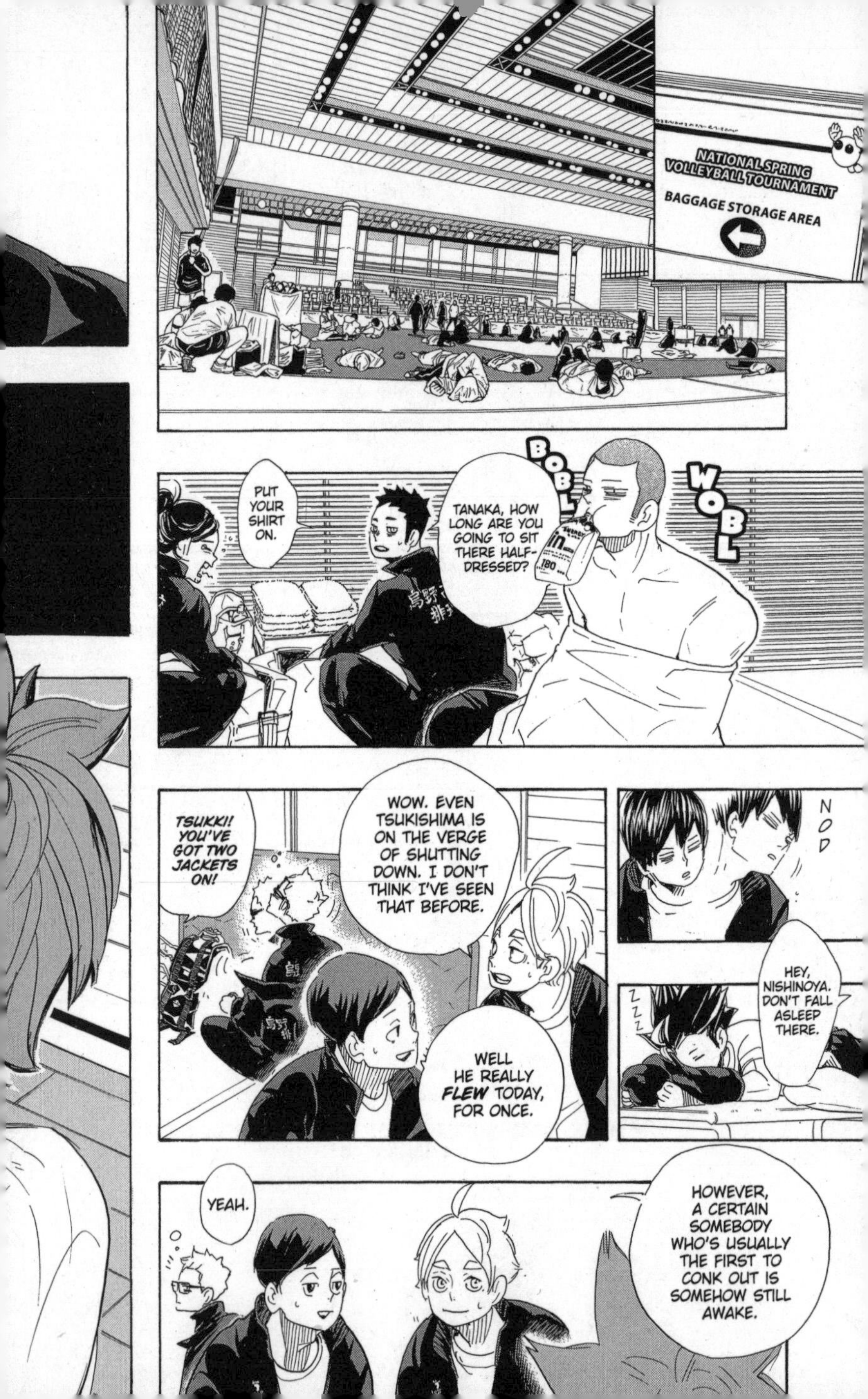
NATIONAL SPRING VOLLEYBALL TOURNAMENT
BAGGAGE STORAGE AREA
WOBL
TANAKA, HOW LONG ARE YOU GOING TO SIT THERE HALF-DRESSED?
BOBL
PUT YOUR SHIRT ON.
NOD
HEY, NISHINOYA. DON'T FALL ASLEEP THERE.
ZZZ
WOW. EVEN TSUKISHIMA IS ON THE VERGE OF SHUTTING DOWN. I DON'T THINK I'VE SEEN THAT BEFORE.
TSUKKI! YOU'VE GOT TWO JACKETS ON!
WELL HE REALLY FLEW TODAY, FOR ONCE.
HOWEVER, A CERTAIN SOMEBODY WHO'S USUALLY THE FIRST TO CONK OUT IS SOMEHOW STILL AWAKE.
YEAH.

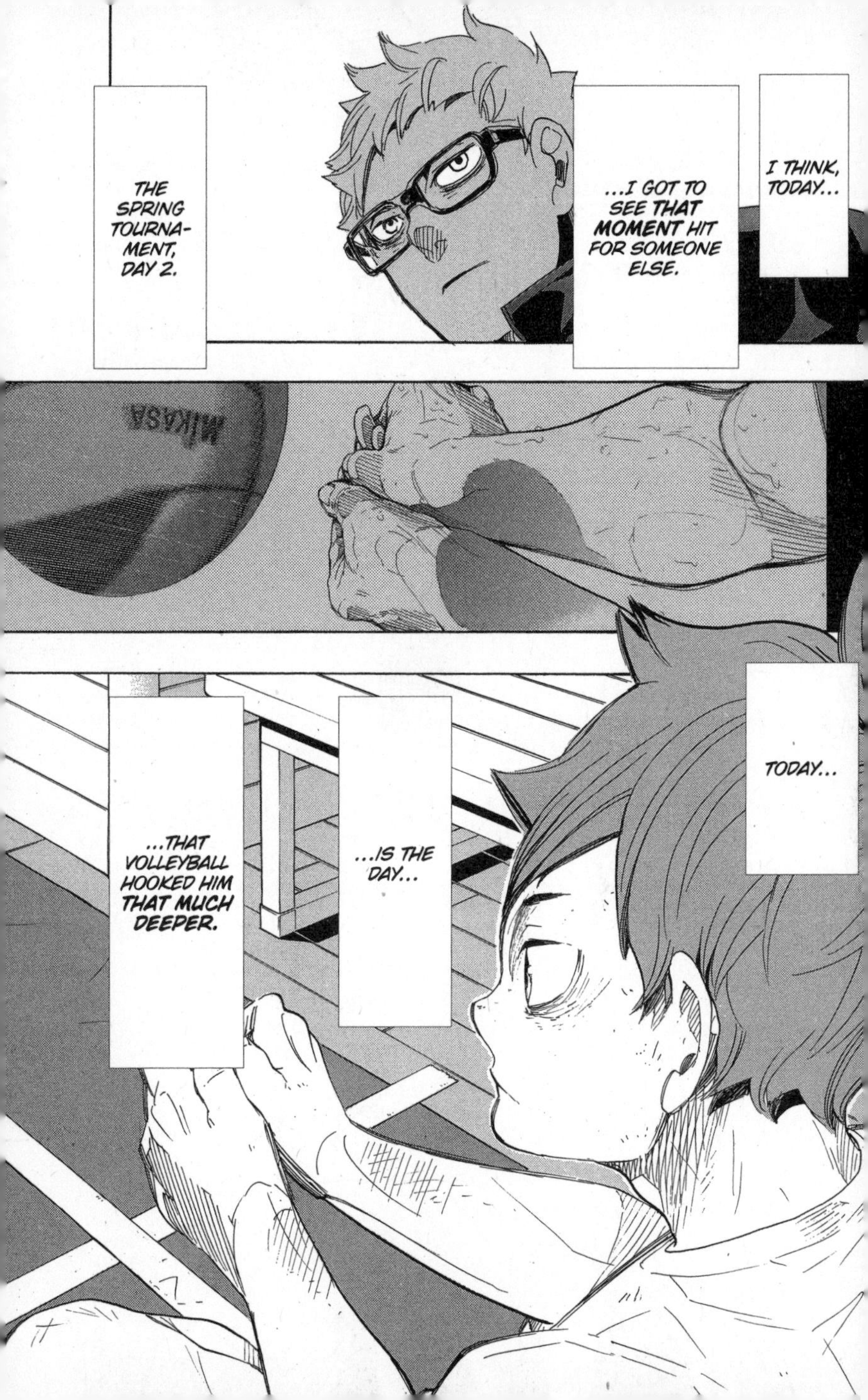
I THINK, TODAY...
...I GOT TO SEE THAT MOMENT HIT FOR SOMEONE ELSE.
THE SPRING TOURNAMENT, DAY 2.
TODAY...
...IS THE DAY...
...THAT VOLLEYBALL HOOKED HIM THAT MUCH DEEPER.

NORIMUNE KUROSU

INARIZAKI HIGH SCHOOL BOYS' VOLLEYBALL HEAD COACH

AGE: 41

CURRENT WORRY: HIS HAIRLINE DOESN'T CONCERN HIM AT ALL. NOPE. NOT ONE BIT.

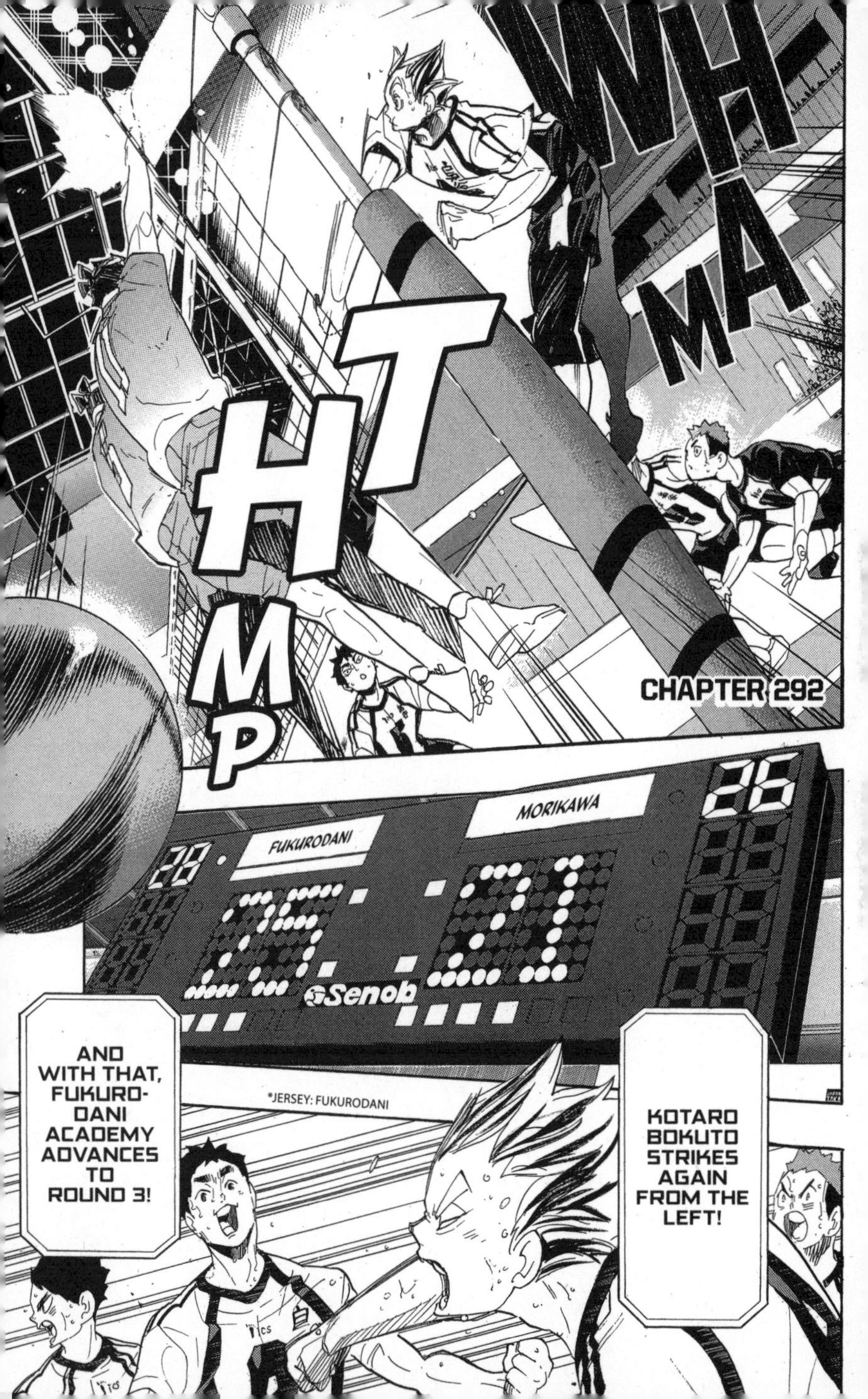
WHAM
THUMP
CHAPTER 292
MORIKAWA
FUKURODANI
26
28
25
21
Senob
KOTARO BOKUTO STRIKES AGAIN FROM THE LEFT!
AND WITH THAT, FUKURO-DANI ACADEMY ADVANCES TO ROUND 3!
*JERSEY: FUKURODANI

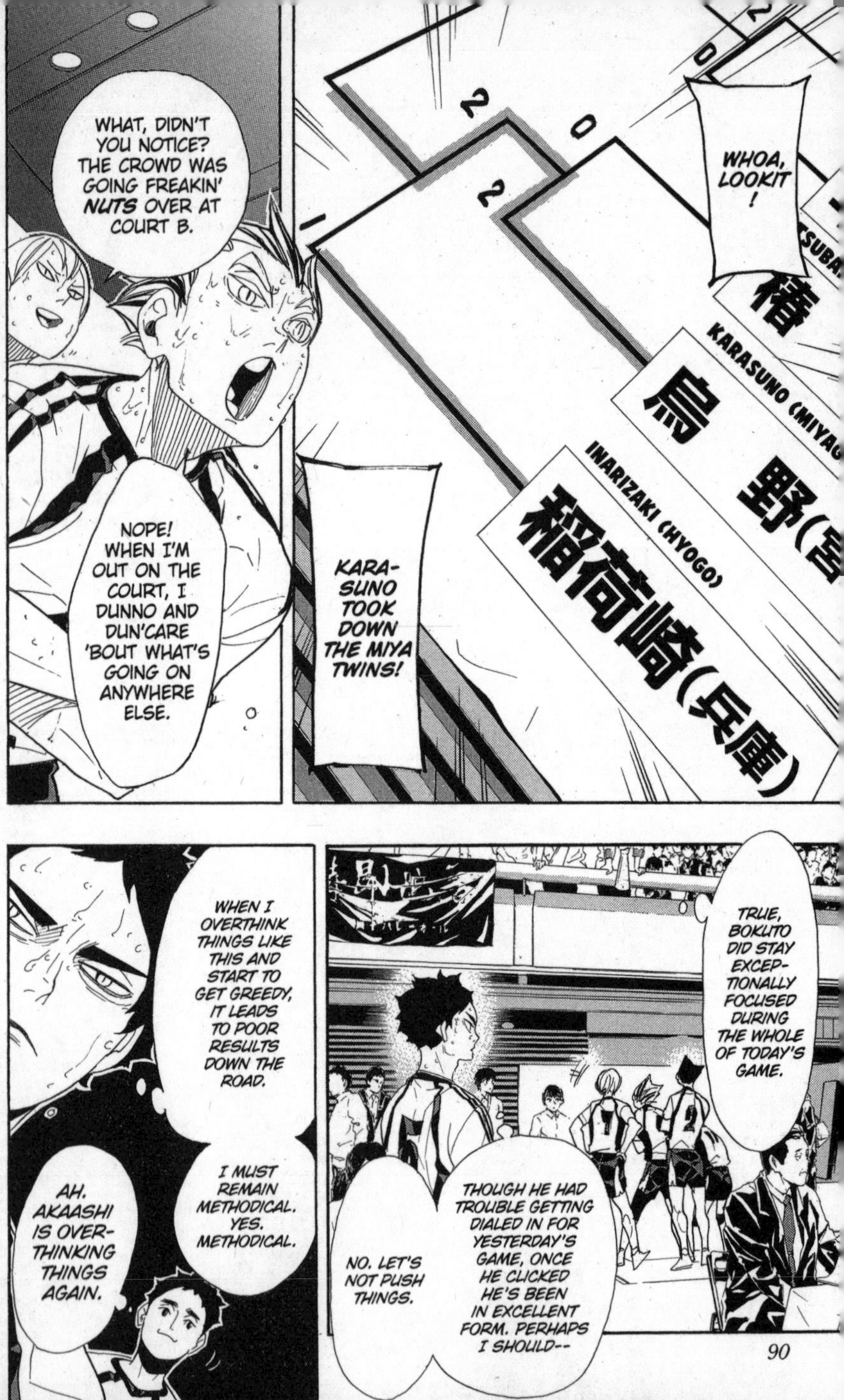
WHOA, LOOKIT!
INARIZAKI (HYOGO)
稲荷崎(兵庫)
KARA-SUNO TOOK DOWN THE MIYA TWINS!
WHAT, DIDN'T YOU NOTICE? THE CROWD WAS GOING FREAKIN' NUTS OVER AT COURT B.
NOPE! WHEN I'M OUT ON THE COURT, I DUNNO AND DUN'CARE 'BOUT WHAT'S GOING ON ANYWHERE ELSE.
TRUE, BOKUTO DID STAY EXCEP-TIONALLY FOCUSED DURING THE WHOLE OF TODAY'S GAME.
THOUGH HE HAD TROUBLE GETTING DIALED IN FOR YESTERDAY'S GAME, ONCE HE CLICKED HE'S BEEN IN EXCELLENT FORM. PERHAPS I SHOULD--
NO. LET'S NOT PUSH THINGS.
WHEN I OVERTHINK THINGS LIKE THIS AND START TO GET GREEDY, IT LEADS TO POOR RESULTS DOWN THE ROAD.
I MUST REMAIN METHODICAL. YES. METHODICAL.
AH. AKAASHI IS OVER-THINKING THINGS AGAIN.

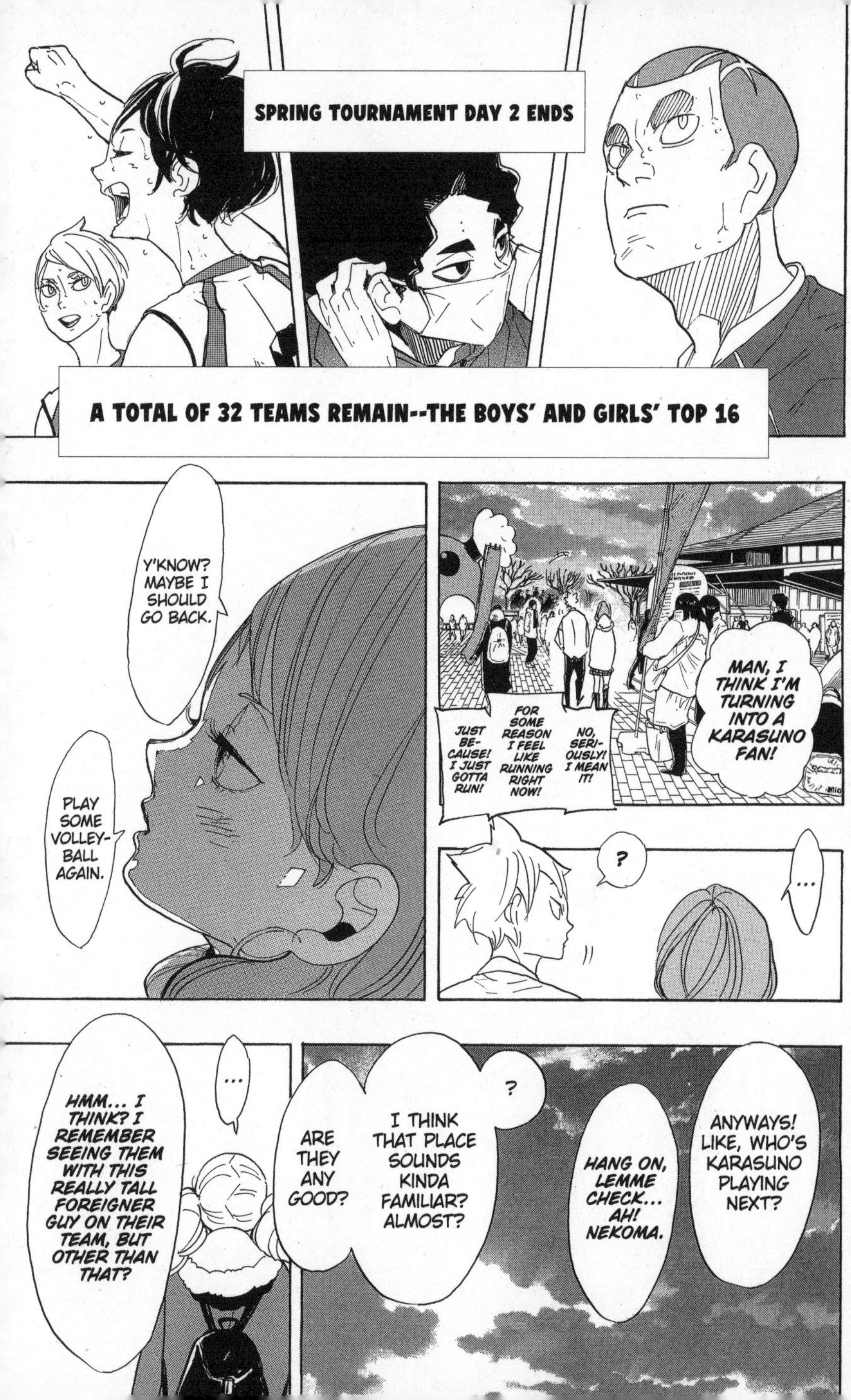
SPRING TOURNAMENT DAY 2 ENDS
A TOTAL OF 32 TEAMS REMAIN--THE BOYS' AND GIRLS' TOP 16
MAN, I THINK I'M TURNING INTO A KARASUNO FAN!
NO, SERIOUSLY! I MEAN IT!
FOR SOME REASON I FEEL LIKE RUNNING RIGHT NOW!
JUST BECAUSE! I JUST GOTTA RUN!
...
?
Y'KNOW? MAYBE I SHOULD GO BACK.
PLAY SOME VOLLEYBALL AGAIN.
ANYWAYS! LIKE, WHO'S KARASUNO PLAYING NEXT?
HANG ON, LEMME CHECK... AH! NEKOMA.
I THINK THAT PLACE SOUNDS KINDA FAMILIAR? ALMOST?
?
ARE THEY ANY GOOD?
...
HMM... I THINK? I REMEMBER SEEING THEM WITH THIS REALLY TALL FOREIGNER GUY ON THEIR TEAM, BUT OTHER THAN THAT?

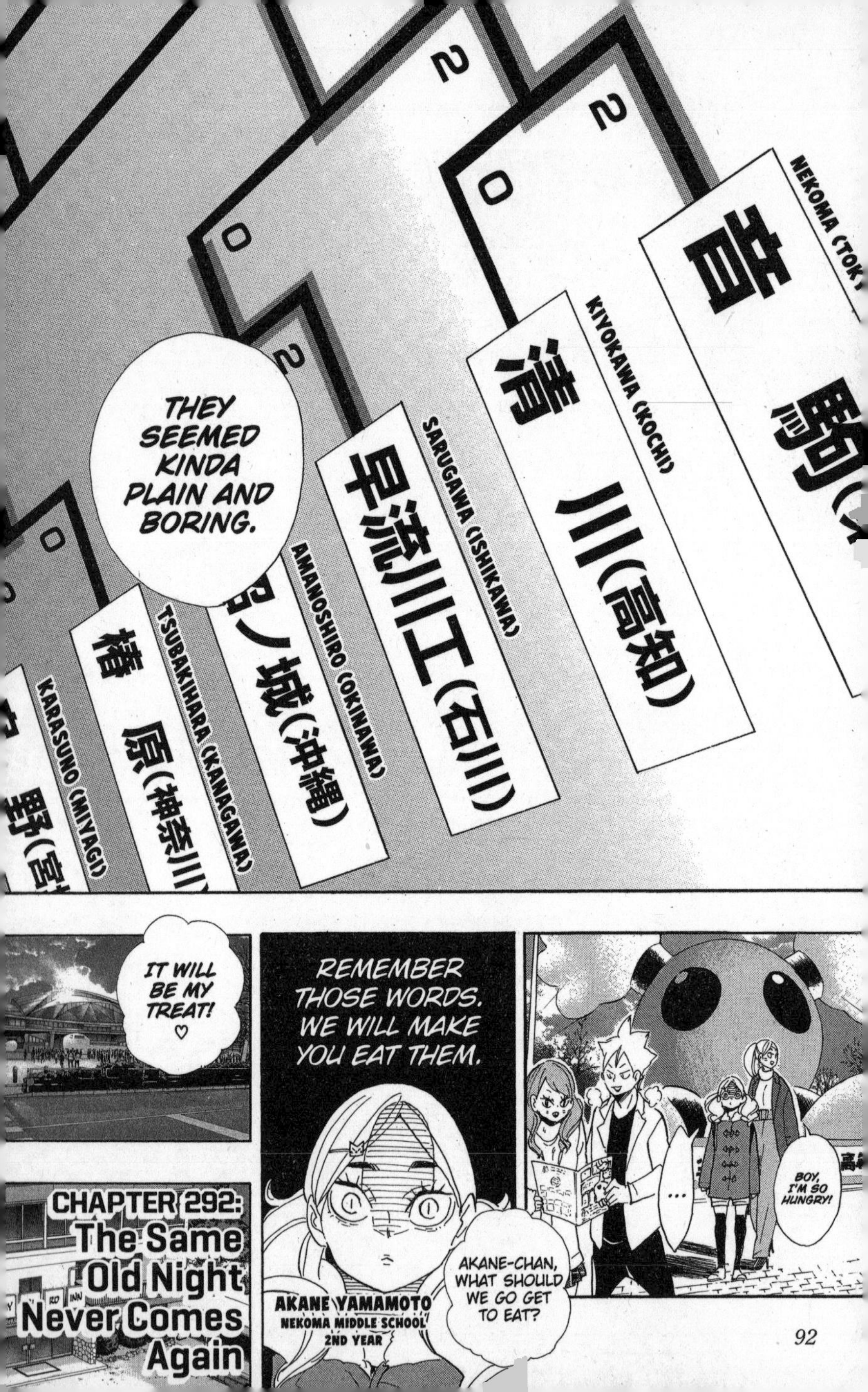
NEKOMA (TOK
KIYOKAWA (KOCHI)
清川(高知)
SARUGAWA (ISHIKAWA)
早流川工(石川)
AMANOSHIRO (OKINAWA)
ノ城(沖縄)
TSUBAKIHARA (KANAGAWA)
椿原(神奈川)
KARASUNO (MIYAGI)
THEY SEEMED KINDA PLAIN AND BORING.
BOY, I'M SO HUNGRY!
...
AKANE-CHAN, WHAT SHOULD WE GO GET TO EAT?
REMEMBER THOSE WORDS. WE WILL MAKE YOU EAT THEM.
AKANE YAMAMOTO
NEKOMA MIDDLE SCHOOL 2ND YEAR
IT WILL BE MY TREAT! ♡

CHAPTER 292: The Same Old Night Never Comes Again

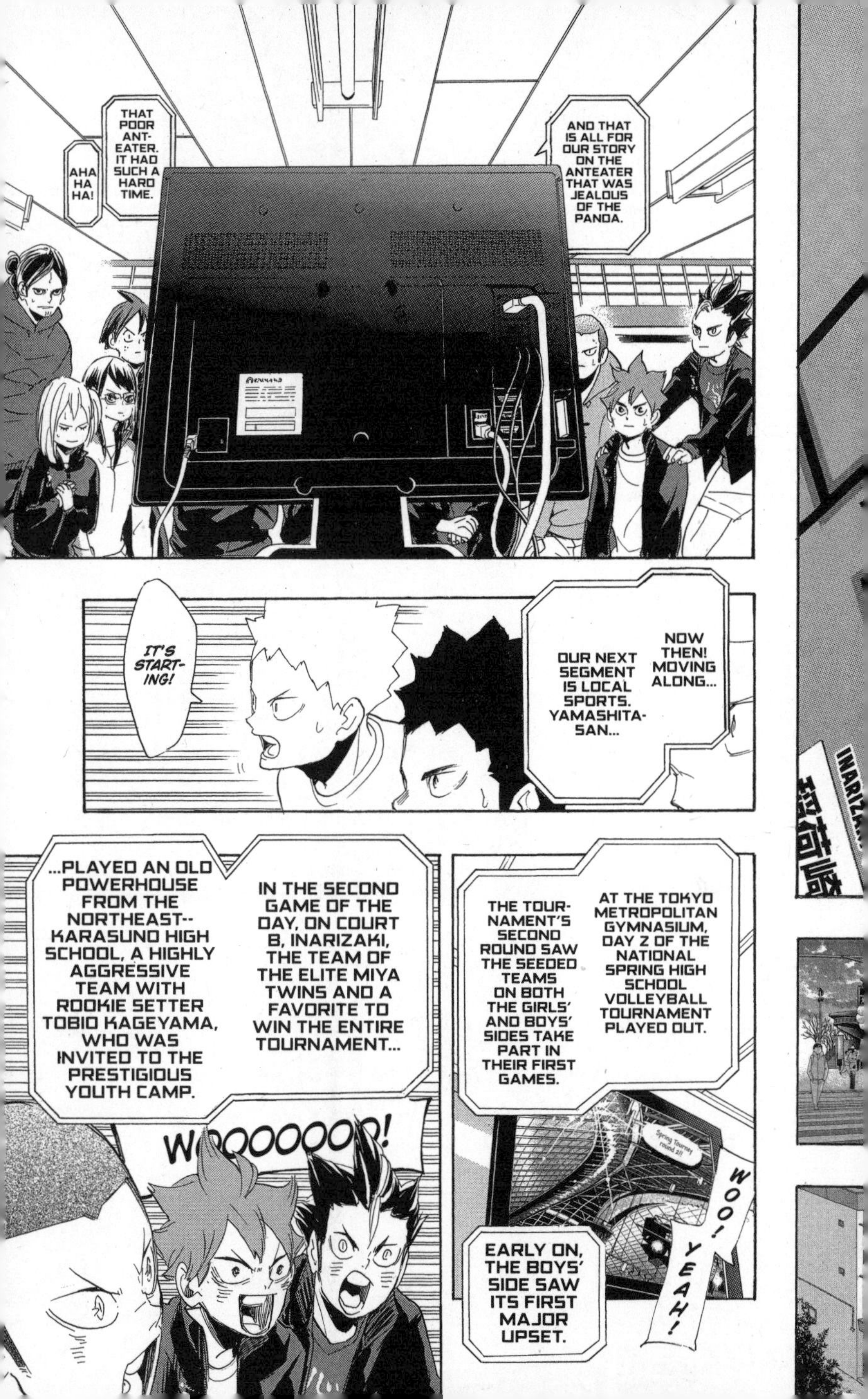
AND THAT IS ALL FOR OUR STORY ON THE ANTEATER THAT WAS JEALOUS OF THE PANDA.
THAT POOR ANT-EATER. IT HAD SUCH A HARD TIME.
AHA HA HA!
NOW THEN! MOVING ALONG...
OUR NEXT SEGMENT IS LOCAL SPORTS. YAMASHITA-SAN...
IT'S START-ING!
AT THE TOKYO METROPOLITAN GYMNASIUM, DAY 2 OF THE NATIONAL SPRING HIGH SCHOOL VOLLEYBALL TOURNAMENT PLAYED OUT.
THE TOUR-NAMENT'S SECOND ROUND SAW THE SEEDED TEAMS ON BOTH THE GIRLS' AND BOYS' SIDES TAKE PART IN THEIR FIRST GAMES.
Spring Tourney round 2!!
WOO! YEAH!
EARLY ON, THE BOYS' SIDE SAW ITS FIRST MAJOR UPSET.
IN THE SECOND GAME OF THE DAY, ON COURT B, INARIZAKI, THE TEAM OF THE ELITE MIYA TWINS AND A FAVORITE TO WIN THE ENTIRE TOURNAMENT...
...PLAYED AN OLD POWERHOUSE FROM THE NORTHEAST--KARASUNO HIGH SCHOOL, A HIGHLY AGGRESSIVE TEAM WITH ROOKIE SETTER TOBIO KAGEYAMA, WHO WAS INVITED TO THE PRESTIGIOUS YOUTH CAMP.
WOOOOOOO!

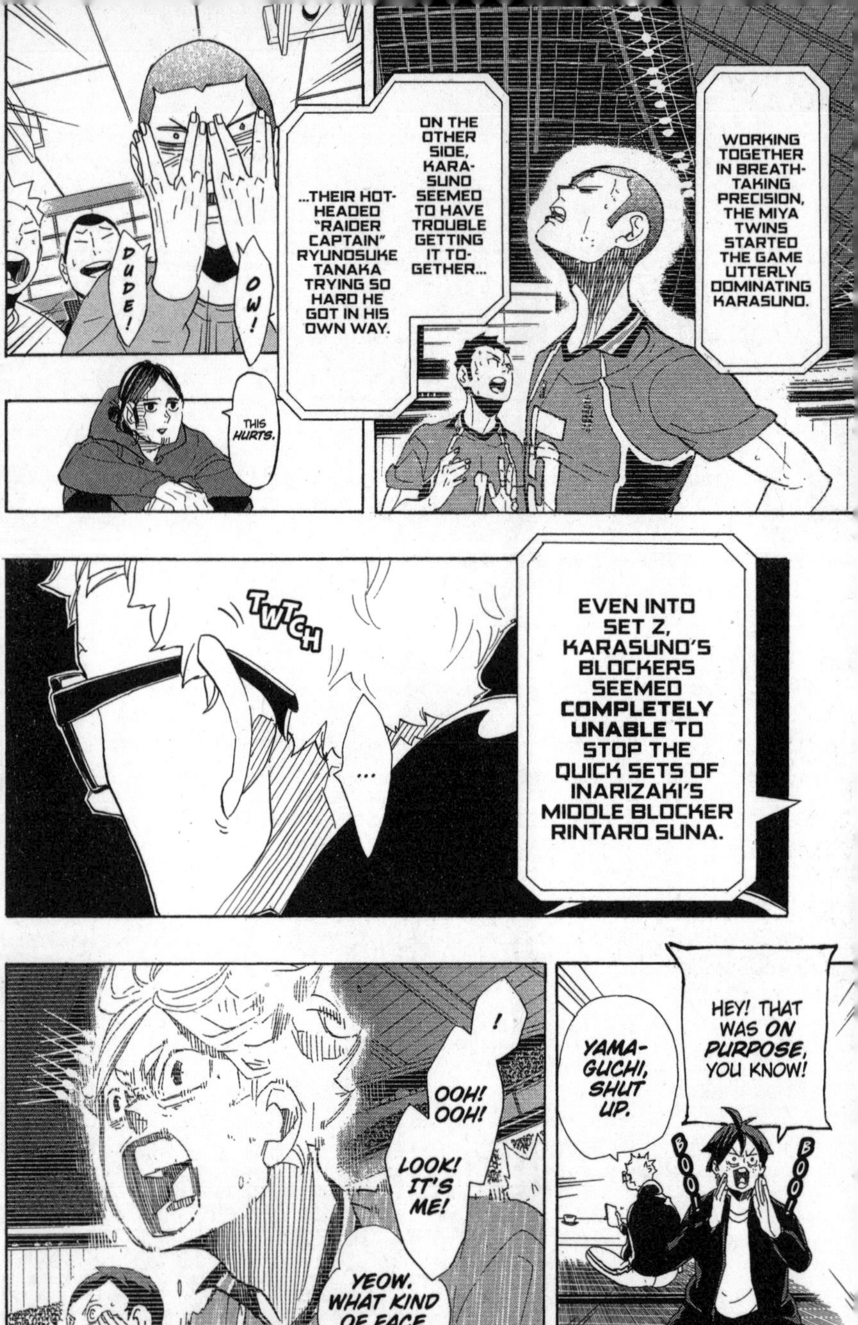
WORKING TOGETHER IN BREATH-TAKING PRECISION, THE MIYA TWINS STARTED THE GAME UTTERLY DOMINATING KARASUNO.
ON THE OTHER SIDE, KARA-SUNO SEEMED TO HAVE TROUBLE GETTING IT TO-GETHER...
...THEIR HOT-HEADED "RAIDER CAPTAIN" RYUNOSUKE TANAKA TRYING SO HARD HE GOT IN HIS OWN WAY.
OW!
DUDE!
THIS HURTS.
EVEN INTO SET 2, KARASUNO'S BLOCKERS SEEMED COMPLETELY UNABLE TO STOP THE QUICK SETS OF INARIZAKI'S MIDDLE BLOCKER RINTARO SUNA.
TWTCH
...
HEY! THAT WAS ON PURPOSE, YOU KNOW!
BOO
BOO
YAMA-GUCHI, SHUT UP.
!
OOH! OOH!
LOOK! IT'S ME!
YEOW. WHAT KIND OF FACE IS THAT, SUGA?

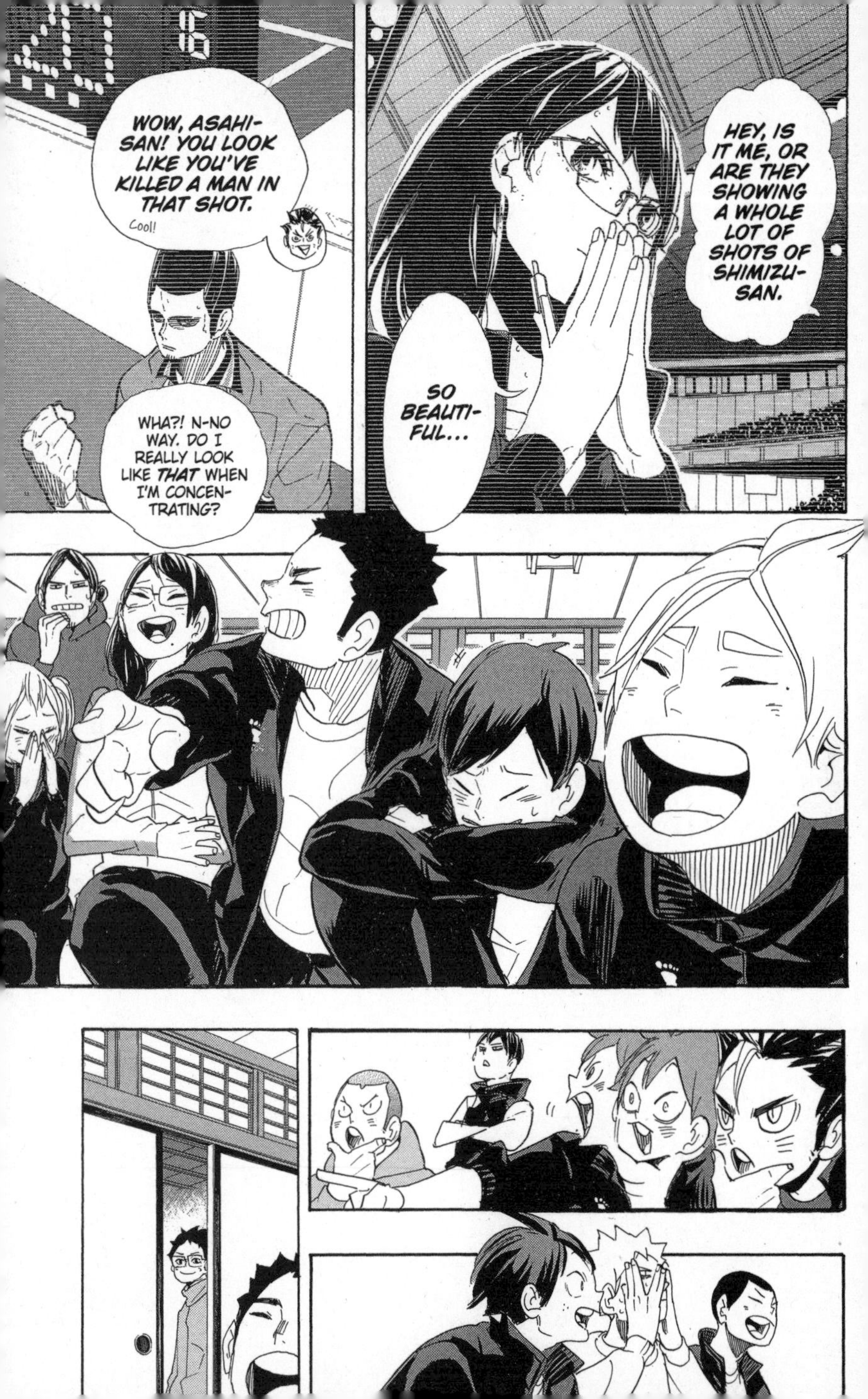
HEY, IS IT ME, OR ARE THEY SHOWING A WHOLE LOT OF SHOTS OF SHIMIZU-SAN.
SO BEAUTIFUL...
WOW, ASAHI-SAN! YOU LOOK LIKE YOU'VE KILLED A MAN IN THAT SHOT.
Cool!
WHA?! N-NO WAY. DO I REALLY LOOK LIKE THAT WHEN I'M CONCENTRATING?

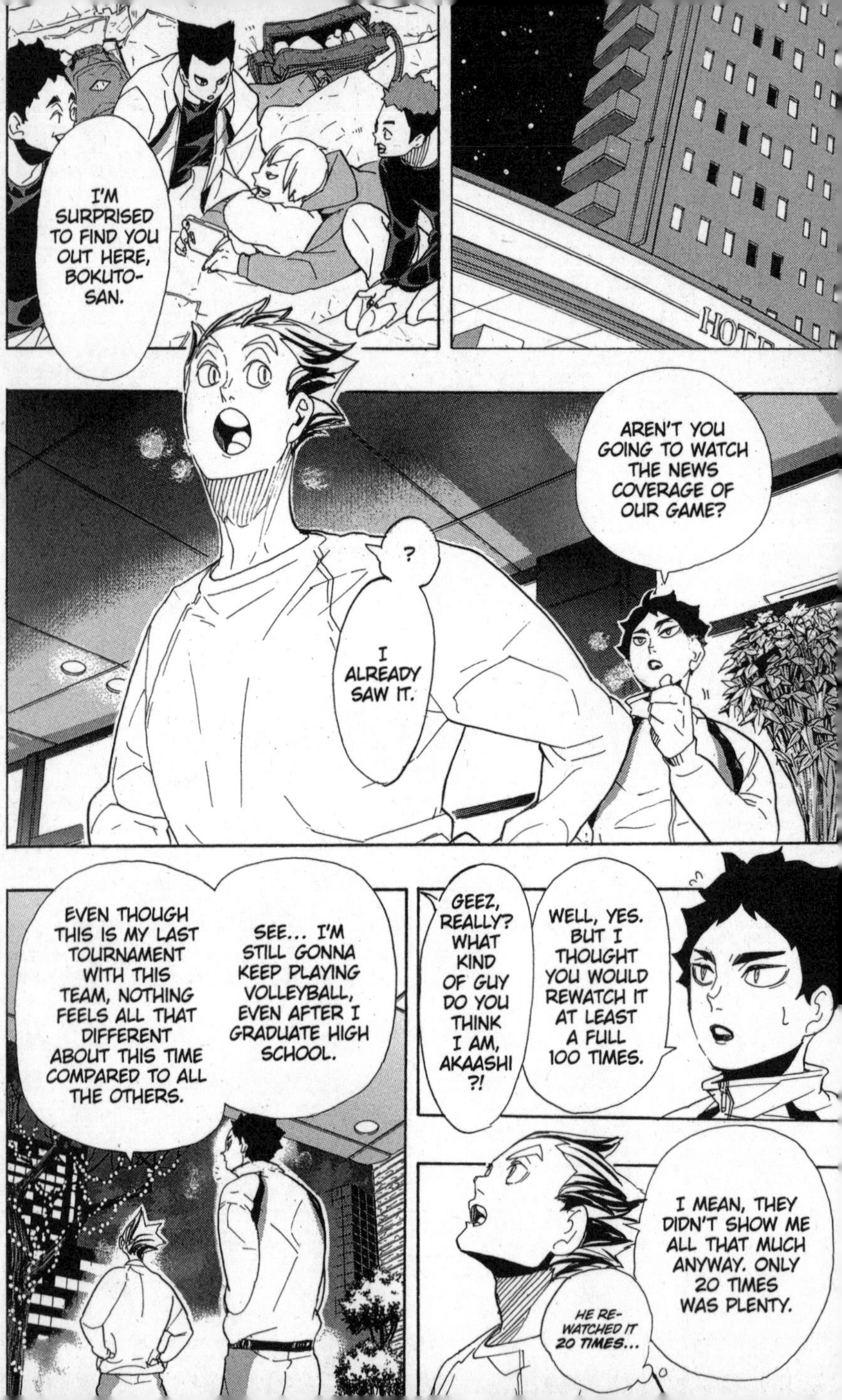
I'M SURPRISED TO FIND YOU OUT HERE, BOKUTO-SAN.
AREN'T YOU GOING TO WATCH THE NEWS COVERAGE OF OUR GAME?
?
I ALREADY SAW IT.
WELL, YES. BUT I THOUGHT YOU WOULD REWATCH IT AT LEAST A FULL 100 TIMES.
GEEZ, REALLY? WHAT KIND OF GUY DO YOU THINK I AM, AKAASHI?!
I MEAN, THEY DIDN'T SHOW ME ALL THAT MUCH ANYWAY. ONLY 20 TIMES WAS PLENTY.
HE RE-WATCHED IT 20 TIMES...
SEE... I'M STILL GONNA KEEP PLAYING VOLLEYBALL, EVEN AFTER I GRADUATE HIGH SCHOOL.
EVEN THOUGH THIS IS MY LAST TOURNAMENT WITH THIS TEAM, NOTHING FEELS ALL THAT DIFFERENT ABOUT THIS TIME COMPARED TO ALL THE OTHERS.

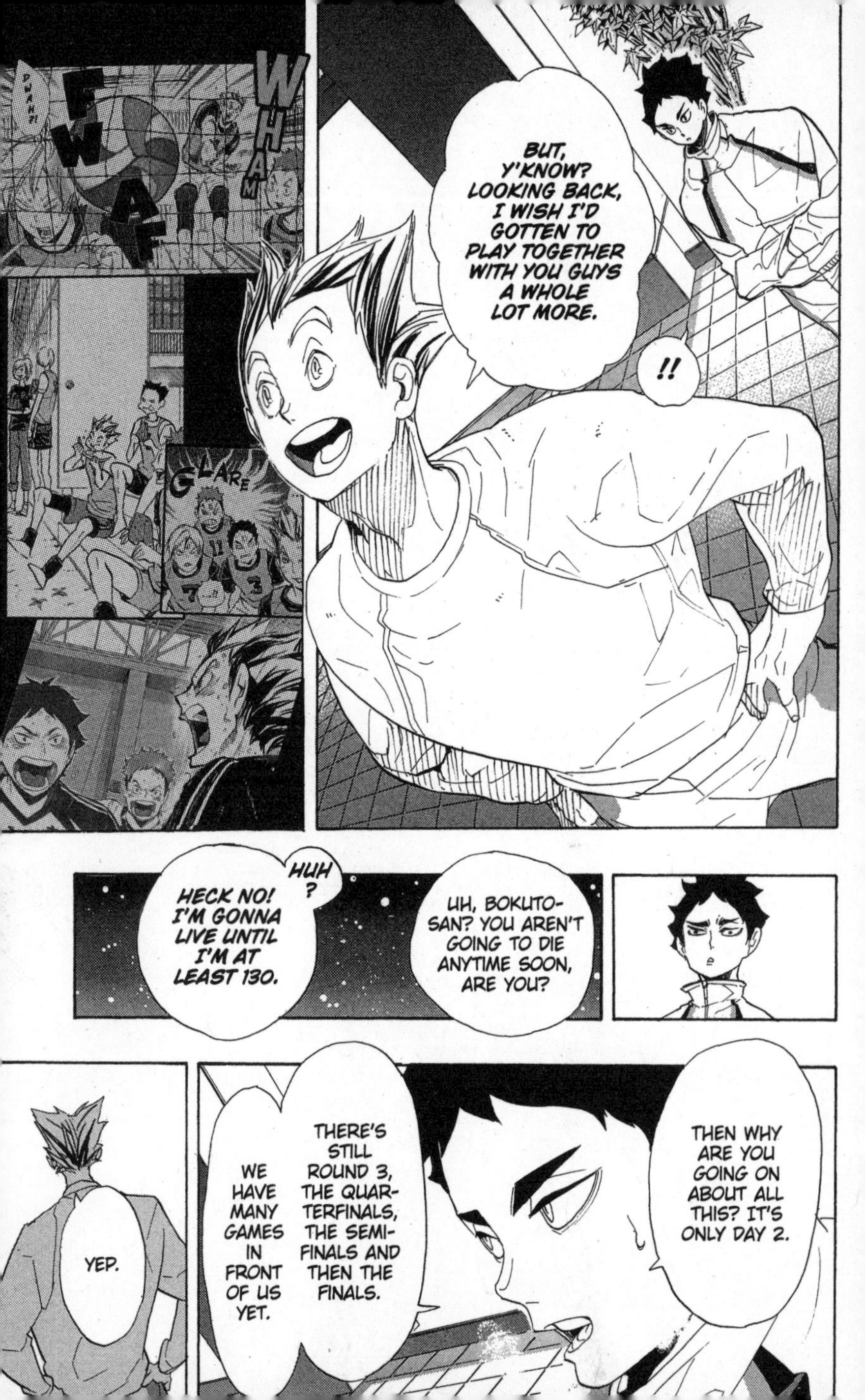
BUT, Y'KNOW? LOOKING BACK, I WISH I'D GOTTEN TO PLAY TOGETHER WITH YOU GUYS A WHOLE LOT MORE.
!!
WHAM
FWAF
GLARE
UH, BOKUTO-SAN? YOU AREN'T GOING TO DIE ANYTIME SOON, ARE YOU?
HUH?
HECK NO! I'M GONNA LIVE UNTIL I'M AT LEAST 130.
THEN WHY ARE YOU GOING ON ABOUT ALL THIS? IT'S ONLY DAY 2.
THERE'S STILL ROUND 3, THE QUARTERFINALS, THE SEMIFINALS AND THEN THE FINALS.
WE HAVE MANY GAMES IN FRONT OF US YET.
YEP.

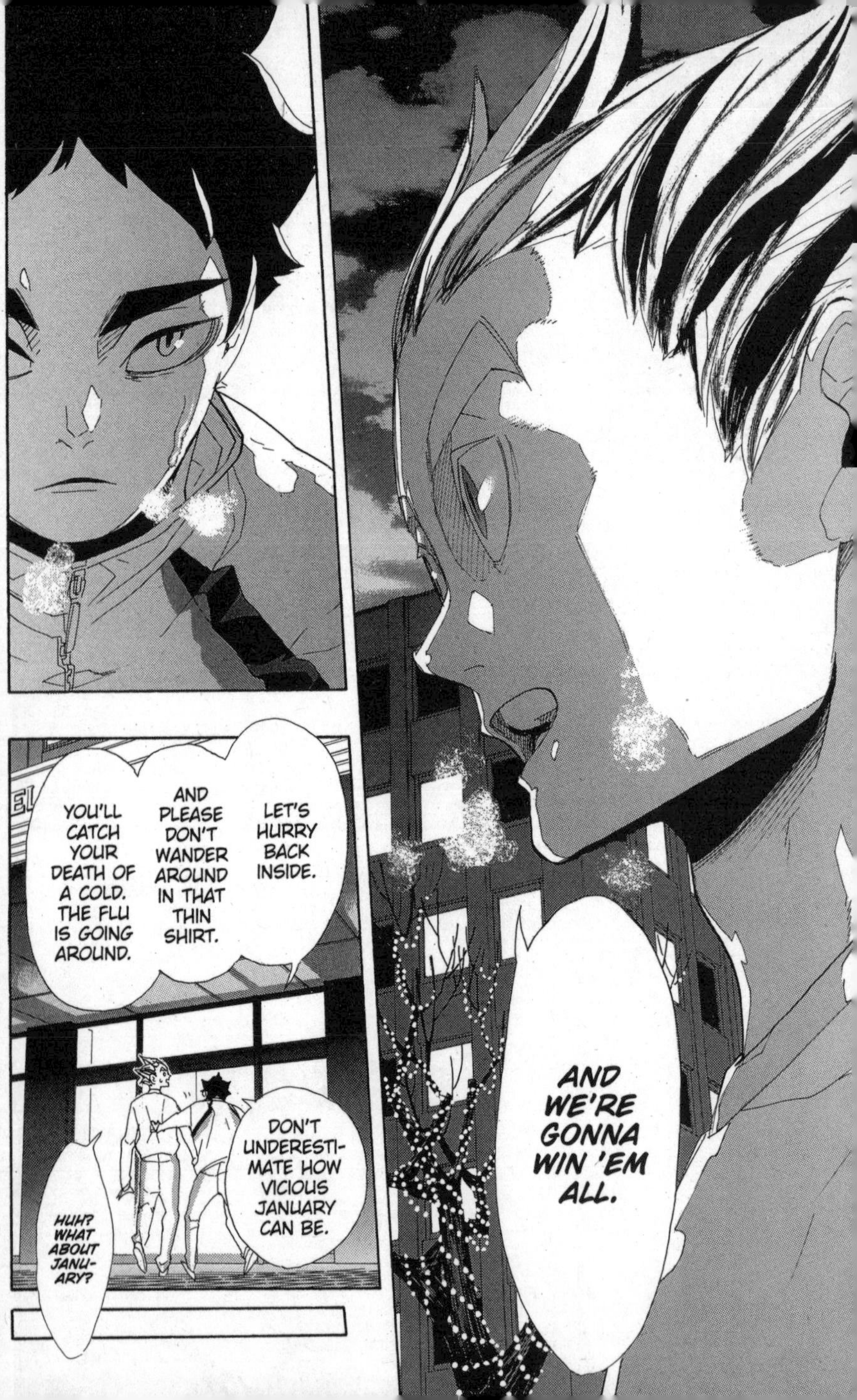
AND WE'RE GONNA WIN 'EM ALL.
LET'S HURRY BACK INSIDE.
AND PLEASE DON'T WANDER AROUND IN THAT THIN SHIRT.
YOU'LL CATCH YOUR DEATH OF A COLD. THE FLU IS GOING AROUND.
DON'T UNDERESTIMATE HOW VICIOUS JANUARY CAN BE.
HUH? WHAT ABOUT JANUARY?

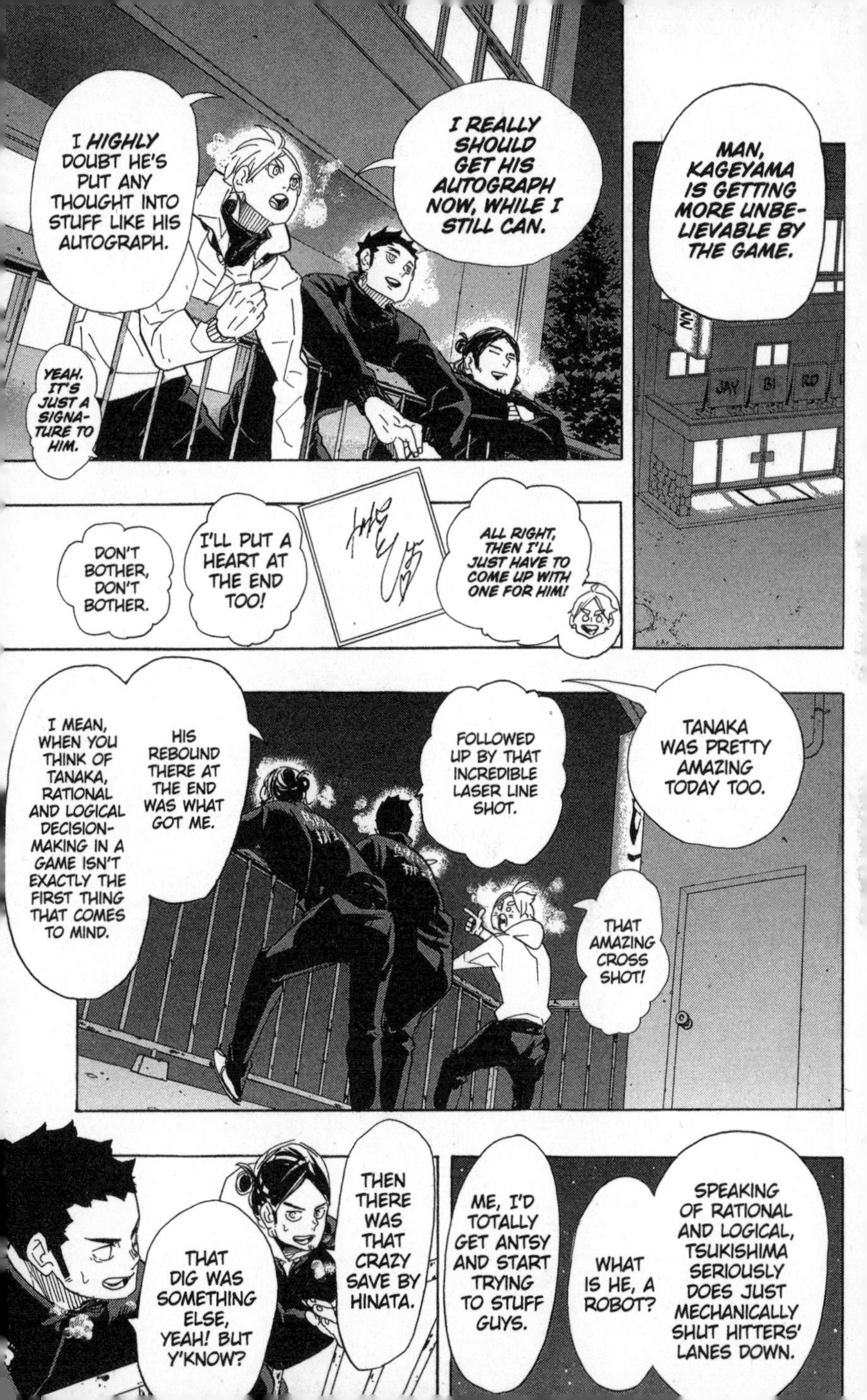
MAN, KAGEYAMA IS GETTING MORE UNBE-LIEVABLE BY THE GAME.
I REALLY SHOULD GET HIS AUTOGRAPH NOW, WHILE I STILL CAN.
I HIGHLY DOUBT HE'S PUT ANY THOUGHT INTO STUFF LIKE HIS AUTOGRAPH.
YEAH. IT'S JUST A SIGNA-TURE TO HIM.
ALL RIGHT, THEN I'LL JUST HAVE TO COME UP WITH ONE FOR HIM!
I'LL PUT A HEART AT THE END TOO!
DON'T BOTHER, DON'T BOTHER.
TANAKA WAS PRETTY AMAZING TODAY TOO.
THAT AMAZING CROSS SHOT!
FOLLOWED UP BY THAT INCREDIBLE LASER LINE SHOT.
HIS REBOUND THERE AT THE END WAS WHAT GOT ME.
I MEAN, WHEN YOU THINK OF TANAKA, RATIONAL AND LOGICAL DECISION-MAKING IN A GAME ISN'T EXACTLY THE FIRST THING THAT COMES TO MIND.
SPEAKING OF RATIONAL AND LOGICAL, TSUKISHIMA SERIOUSLY DOES JUST MECHANICALLY SHUT HITTERS' LANES DOWN.
WHAT IS HE, A ROBOT?
ME, I'D TOTALLY GET ANTSY AND START TRYING TO STUFF GUYS.
THEN THERE WAS THAT CRAZY SAVE BY HINATA.
THAT DIG WAS SOMETHING ELSE, YEAH! BUT Y'KNOW?

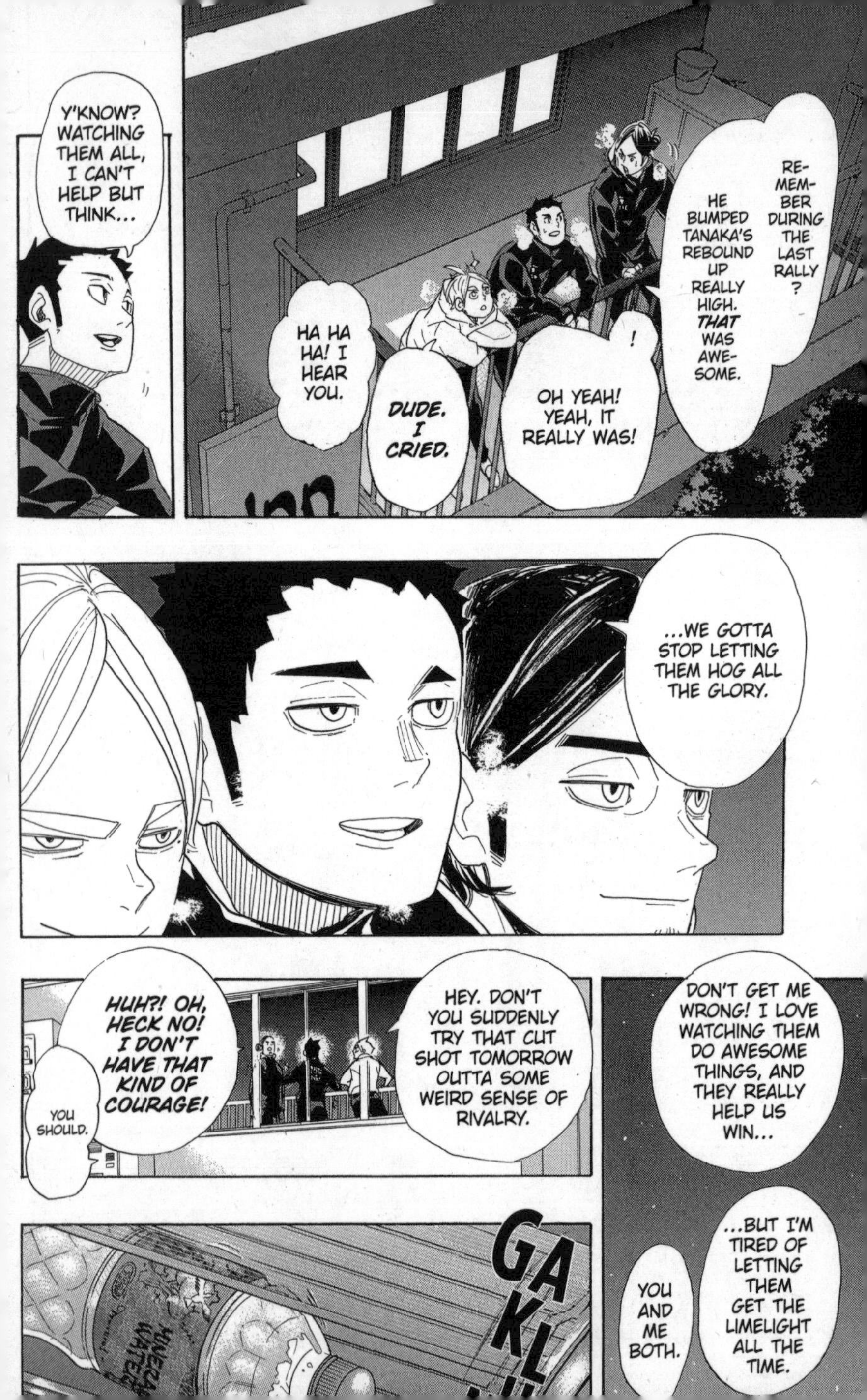
REMEMBER DURING THE LAST RALLY?
HE BUMPED TANAKA'S REBOUND UP REALLY HIGH. *THAT* WAS AWESOME.
!
OH YEAH! YEAH, IT REALLY WAS!
DUDE. I CRIED.
HA HA HA! I HEAR YOU.
Y'KNOW? WATCHING THEM ALL, I CAN'T HELP BUT THINK...
...WE GOTTA STOP LETTING THEM HOG ALL THE GLORY.
DON'T GET ME WRONG! I LOVE WATCHING THEM DO AWESOME THINGS, AND THEY REALLY HELP US WIN...
HEY. DON'T YOU SUDDENLY TRY THAT CUT SHOT TOMORROW OUTTA SOME WEIRD SENSE OF RIVALRY.
HUH?! OH, HECK NO! I DON'T HAVE THAT KIND OF COURAGE!
YOU SHOULD.
...BUT I'M TIRED OF LETTING THEM GET THE LIMELIGHT ALL THE TIME.
YOU AND ME BOTH.
GAKL

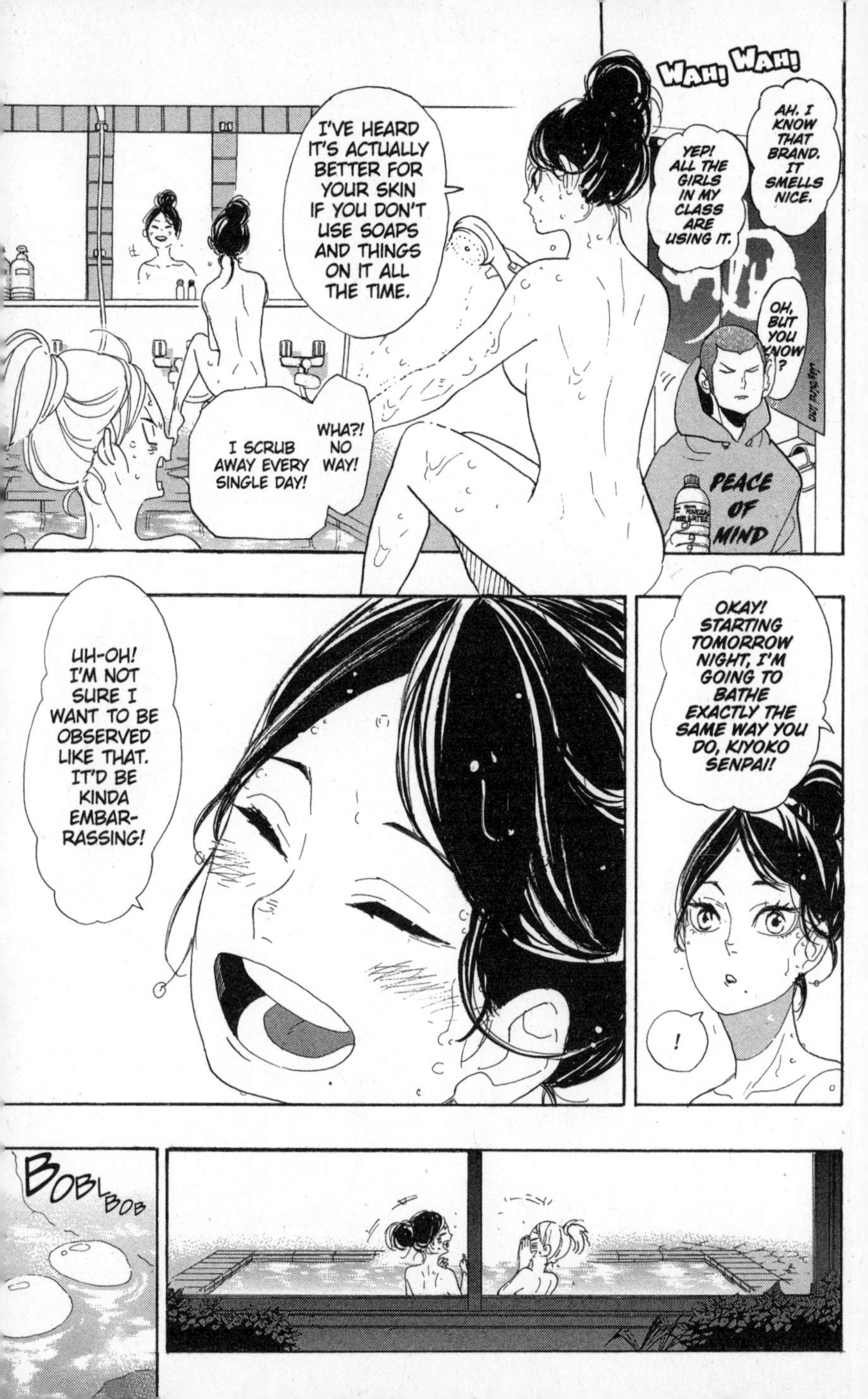
WAH! WAH!
AH. I KNOW THAT BRAND. IT SMELLS NICE.
YEP! ALL THE GIRLS IN MY CLASS ARE USING IT.
OH, BUT YOU KNOW?
PEACE OF MIND
I'VE HEARD IT'S ACTUALLY BETTER FOR YOUR SKIN IF YOU DON'T USE SOAPS AND THINGS ON IT ALL THE TIME.
WHA?! NO WAY!
I SCRUB AWAY EVERY SINGLE DAY!
OKAY! STARTING TOMORROW NIGHT, I'M GOING TO BATHE EXACTLY THE SAME WAY YOU DO, KIYOKO SENPAI!
!
UH-OH! I'M NOT SURE I WANT TO BE OBSERVED LIKE THAT. IT'D BE KINDA EMBARRASSING!
BOBLBOB

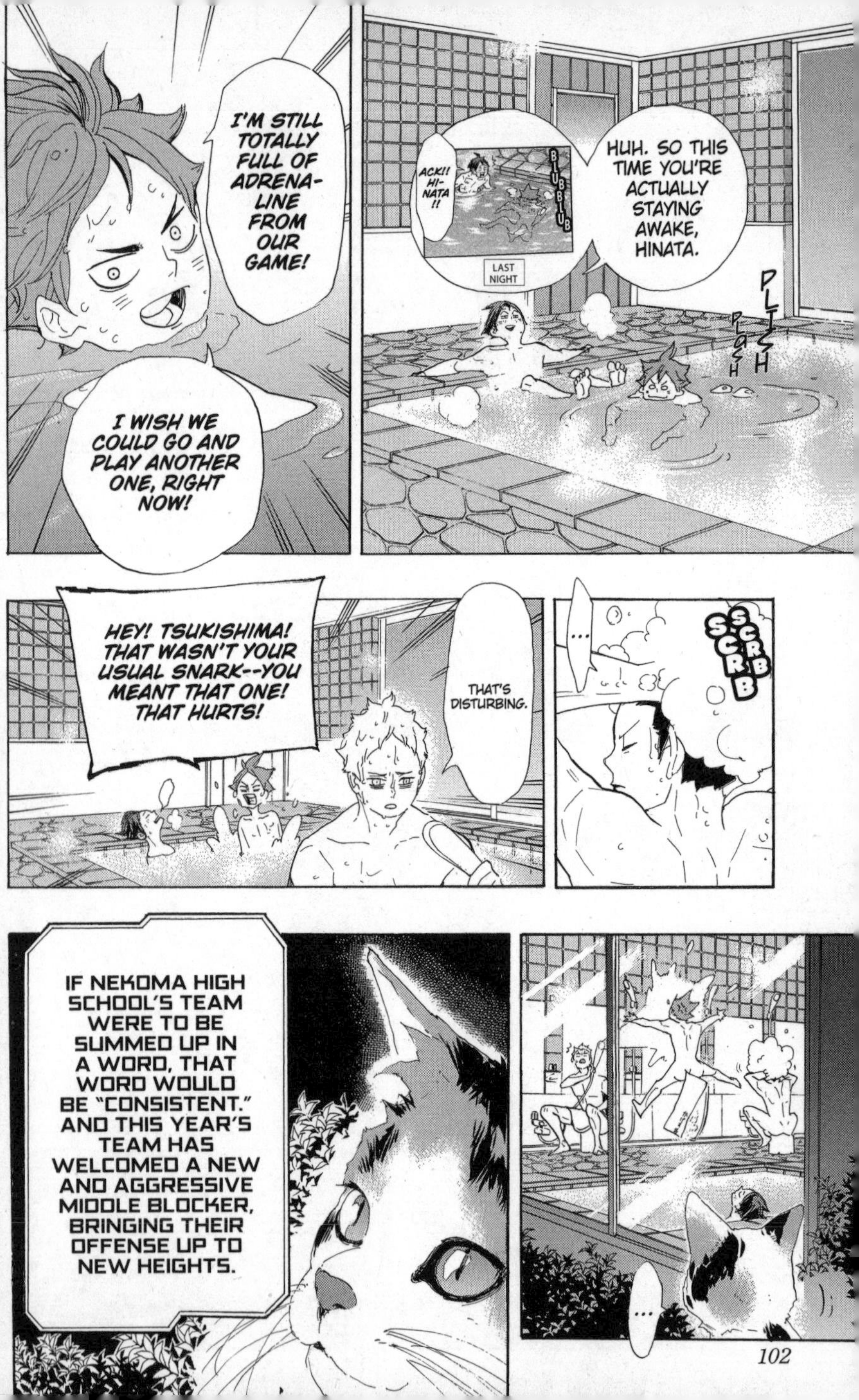
HUH. SO THIS TIME YOU'RE ACTUALLY STAYING AWAKE, HINATA.
LAST NIGHT
BLUBBLUB
ACK!! HI-NATA!!
PLISH
PLASH
I'M STILL TOTALLY FULL OF ADRENA-LINE FROM OUR GAME!
I WISH WE COULD GO AND PLAY ANOTHER ONE, RIGHT NOW!
SCRB SCRB
...
THAT'S DISTURBING.
HEY! TSUKISHIMA! THAT WASN'T YOUR USUAL SNARK--YOU MEANT THAT ONE! THAT HURTS!
...
IF NEKOMA HIGH SCHOOL'S TEAM WERE TO BE SUMMED UP IN A WORD, THAT WORD WOULD BE "CONSISTENT." AND THIS YEAR'S TEAM HAS WELCOMED A NEW AND AGGRESSIVE MIDDLE BLOCKER, BRINGING THEIR OFFENSE UP TO NEW HEIGHTS.

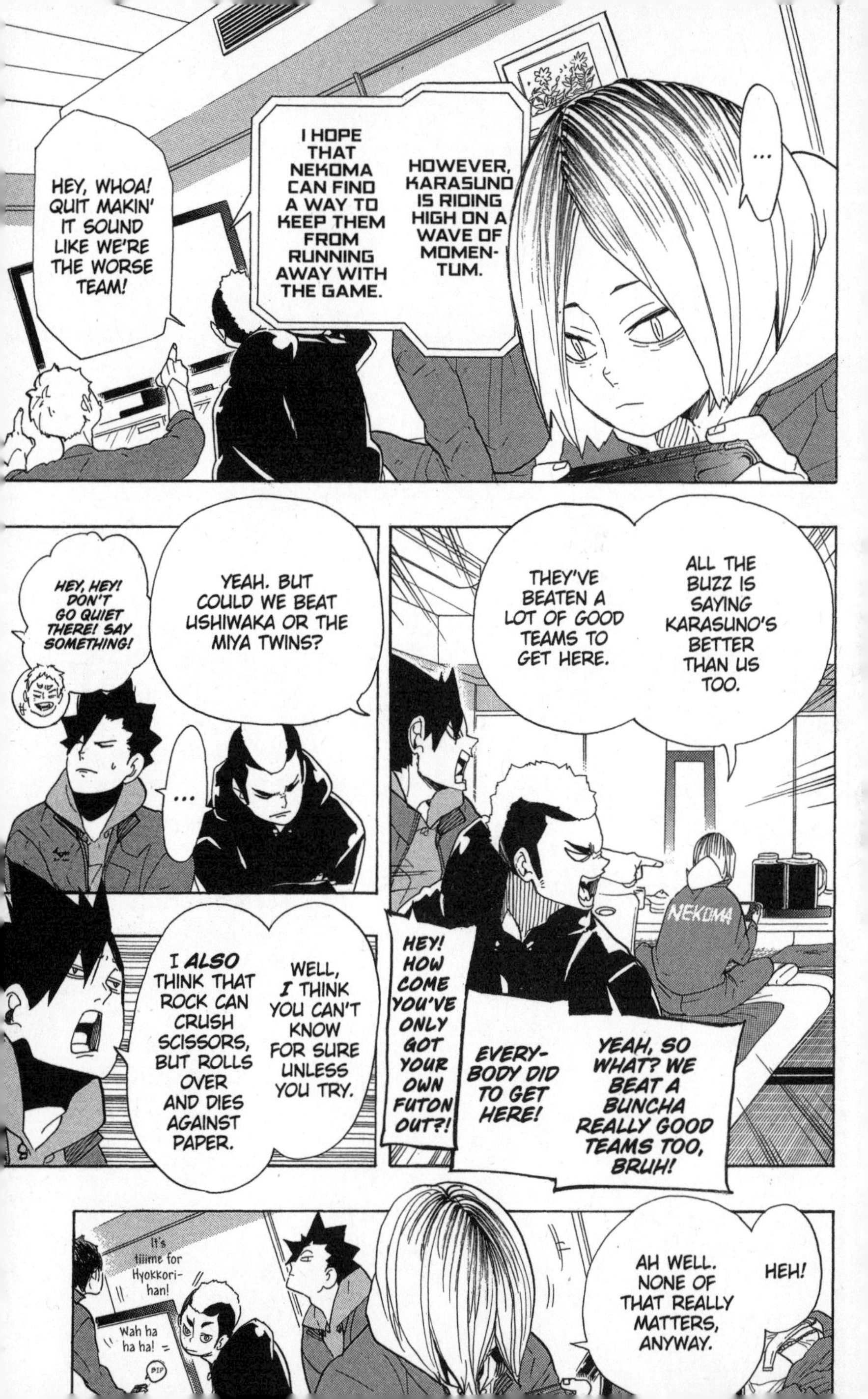
...
HOWEVER, KARASUNO IS RIDING HIGH ON A WAVE OF MOMENTUM.
I HOPE THAT NEKOMA CAN FIND A WAY TO KEEP THEM FROM RUNNING AWAY WITH THE GAME.
HEY, WHOA! QUIT MAKIN' IT SOUND LIKE WE'RE THE WORSE TEAM!
ALL THE BUZZ IS SAYING KARASUNO'S BETTER THAN US TOO.
THEY'VE BEATEN A LOT OF GOOD TEAMS TO GET HERE.
YEAH, SO WHAT? WE BEAT A BUNCHA REALLY GOOD TEAMS TOO, BRUH!
EVERY-BODY DID TO GET HERE!
HEY! HOW COME YOU'VE ONLY GOT YOUR OWN FUTON OUT?!
YEAH. BUT COULD WE BEAT USHIWAKA OR THE MIYA TWINS?
HEY, HEY! DON'T GO QUIET THERE! SAY SOMETHING!
...
WELL, I THINK YOU CAN'T KNOW FOR SURE UNLESS YOU TRY.
I ALSO THINK THAT ROCK CAN CRUSH SCISSORS, BUT ROLLS OVER AND DIES AGAINST PAPER.
HEH!
AH WELL. NONE OF THAT REALLY MATTERS, ANYWAY.
It's tiiime for Hyokkori-han!
Wah ha ha ha!

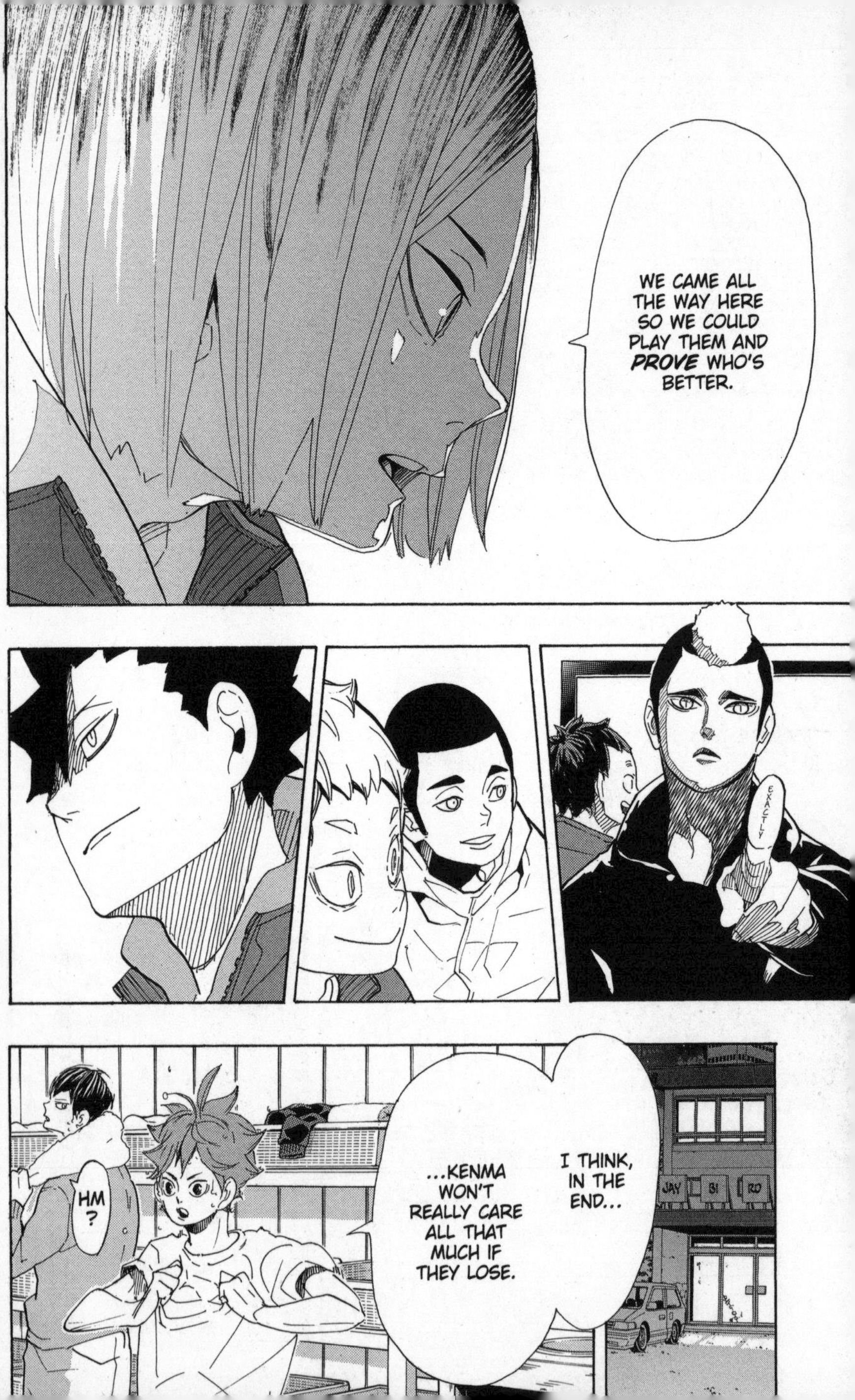
WE CAME ALL THE WAY HERE SO WE COULD PLAY THEM AND *PROVE* WHO'S BETTER.
EXACTLY
I THINK, IN THE END...
...KENMA WON'T REALLY CARE ALL THAT MUCH IF THEY LOSE.
HM?
JAY
BI
RO

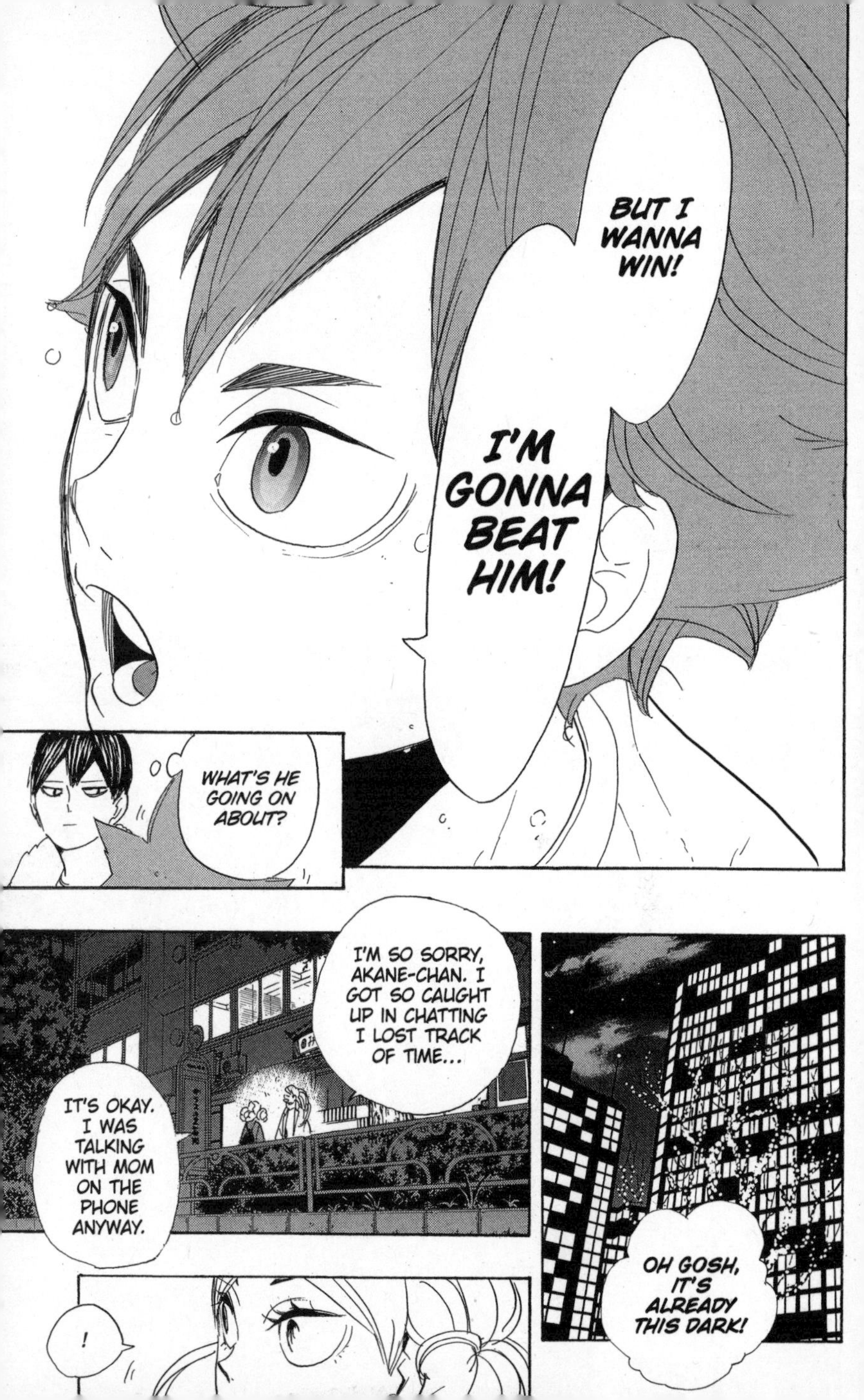
BUT I WANNA WIN!
I'M GONNA BEAT HIM!
WHAT'S HE GOING ON ABOUT?
OH GOSH, IT'S ALREADY THIS DARK!
I'M SO SORRY, AKANE-CHAN. I GOT SO CAUGHT UP IN CHATTING I LOST TRACK OF TIME...
IT'S OKAY. I WAS TALKING WITH MOM ON THE PHONE ANYWAY.
!

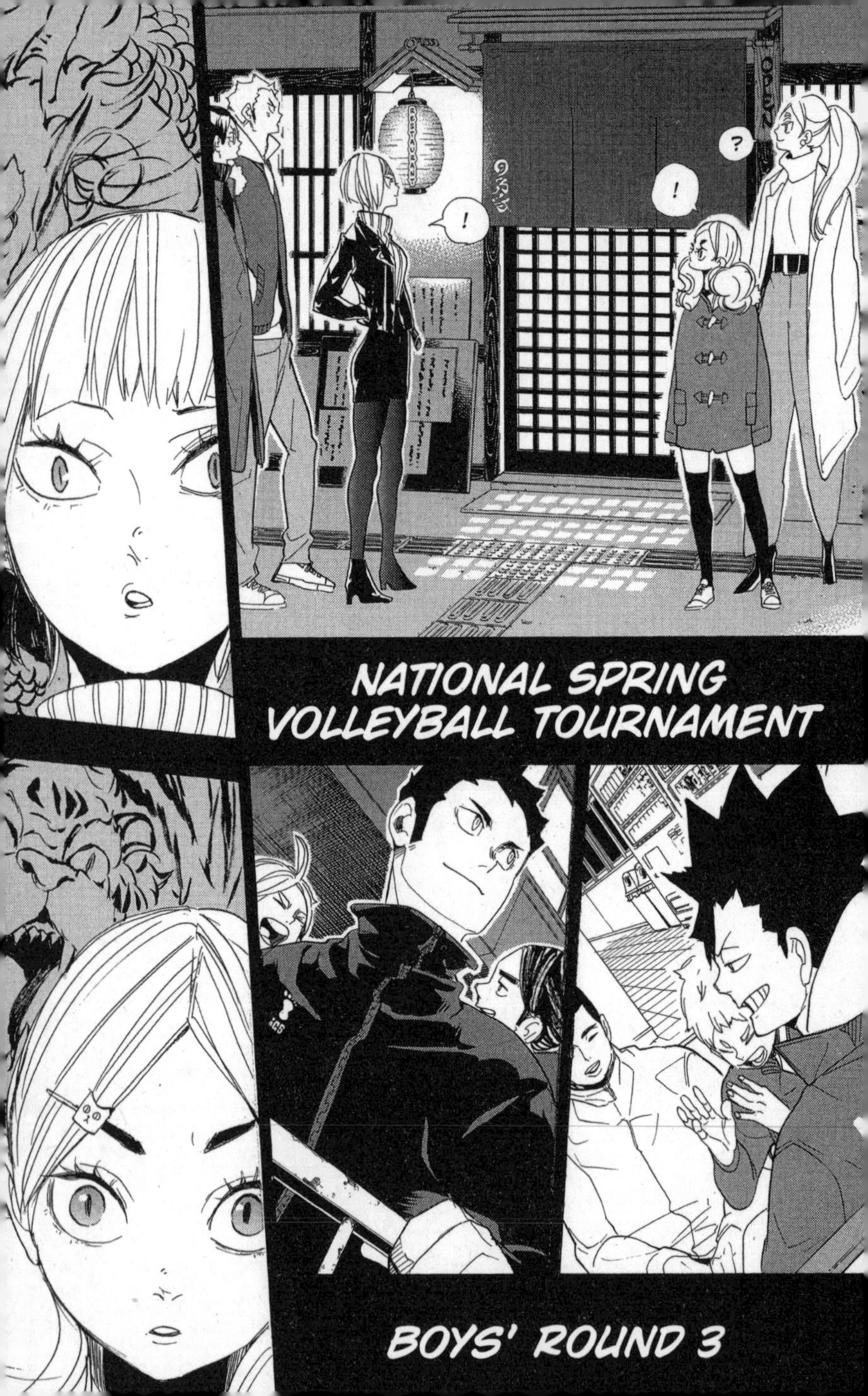
OPEN
RESTAURANT
?
!
!
NATIONAL SPRING VOLLEYBALL TOURNAMENT
BOYS' ROUND 3

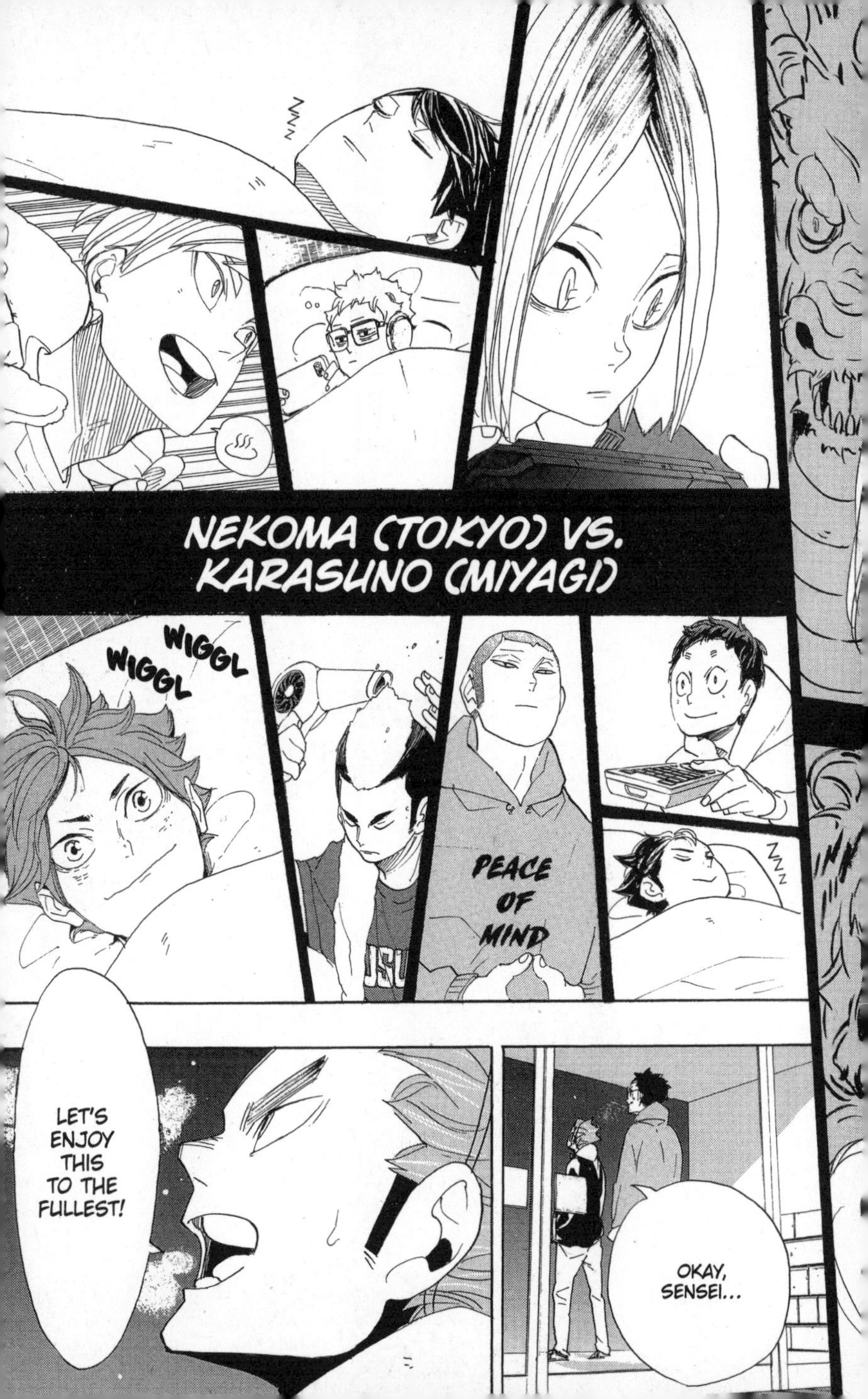
ZZZ
NEKOMA (TOKYO) VS. KARASUNO (MIYAGI)
ZZZ
PEACE OF MIND
WIGGL WIGGL
OKAY, SENSEI...
LET'S ENJOY THIS TO THE FULLEST!

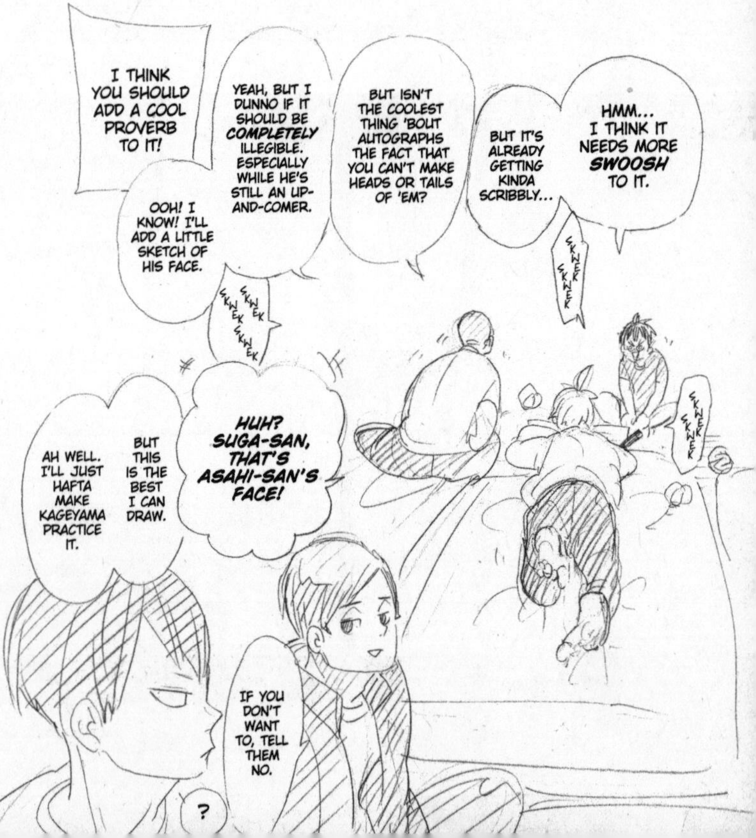

HMM... I THINK IT NEEDS MORE **SWOOSH** TO IT.
BUT IT'S ALREADY GETTING KINDA SCRIBBLY...
SKWEEK SKWEEK
BUT ISN'T THE COOLEST THING 'BOUT AUTOGRAPHS THE FACT THAT YOU CAN'T MAKE HEADS OR TAILS OF 'EM?
YEAH, BUT I DUNNO IF IT SHOULD BE **COMPLETELY** ILLEGIBLE. ESPECIALLY WHILE HE'S STILL AN UP-AND-COMER.
I THINK YOU SHOULD ADD A COOL PROVERB TO IT!
OOH! I KNOW! I'LL ADD A LITTLE SKETCH OF HIS FACE.
SKWEEK SKWEEK SKWEEK
SKWEEK SKWEEK
HUH? SUGA-SAN, THAT'S ASAHI-SAN'S FACE!
BUT THIS IS THE BEST I CAN DRAW.
AH WELL. I'LL JUST HAFTA MAKE KAGEYAMA PRACTICE IT.
IF YOU DON'T WANT TO, TELL THEM NO.
?

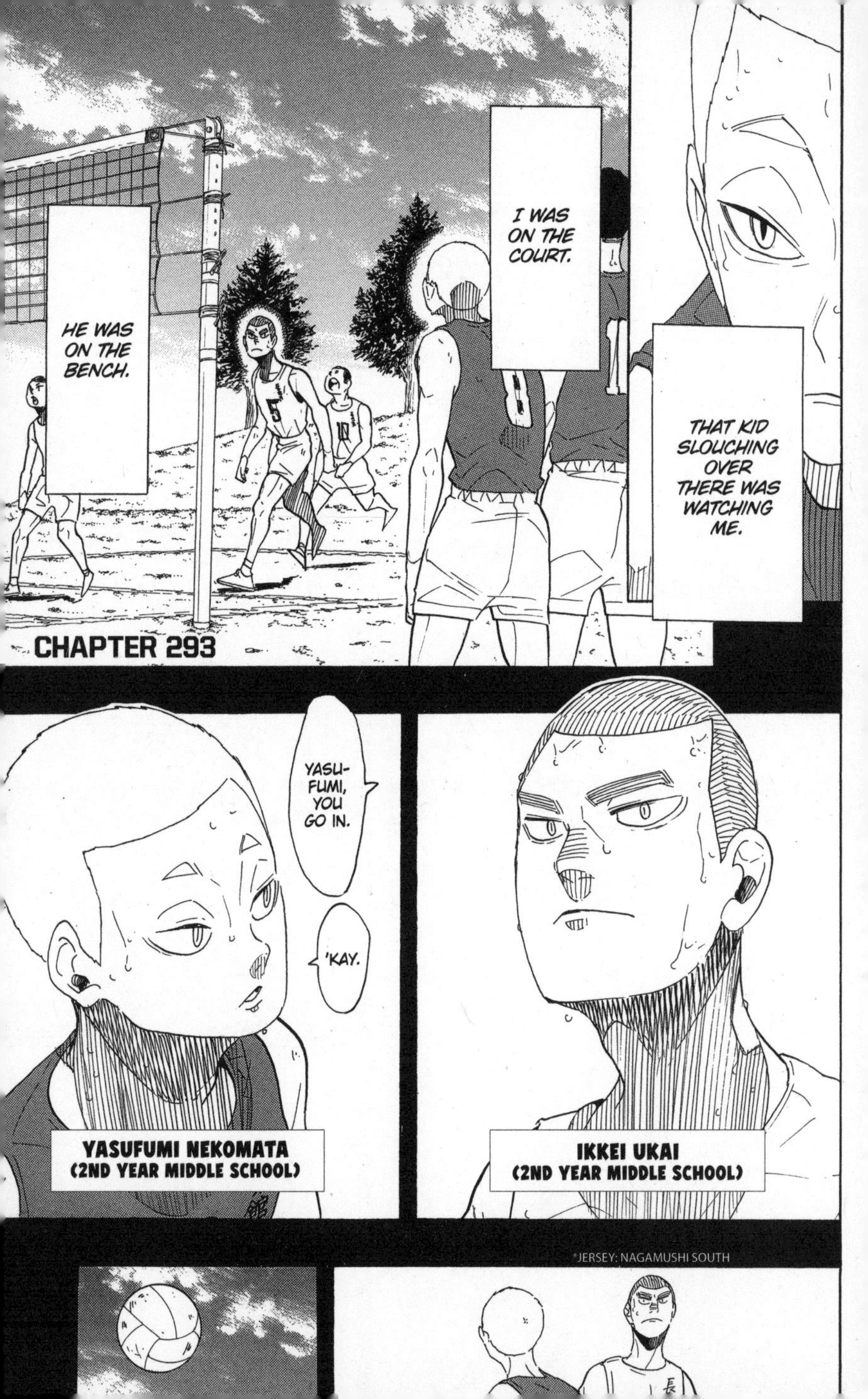
THAT KID SLOUCHING OVER THERE WAS WATCHING ME.
I WAS ON THE COURT.
HE WAS ON THE BENCH.
CHAPTER 293
IKKEI UKAI
(2ND YEAR MIDDLE SCHOOL)
YASUFUMI, YOU GO IN.
'KAY.
YASUFUMI NEKOMATA
(2ND YEAR MIDDLE SCHOOL)
*JERSEY: NAGAMUSHI SOUTH

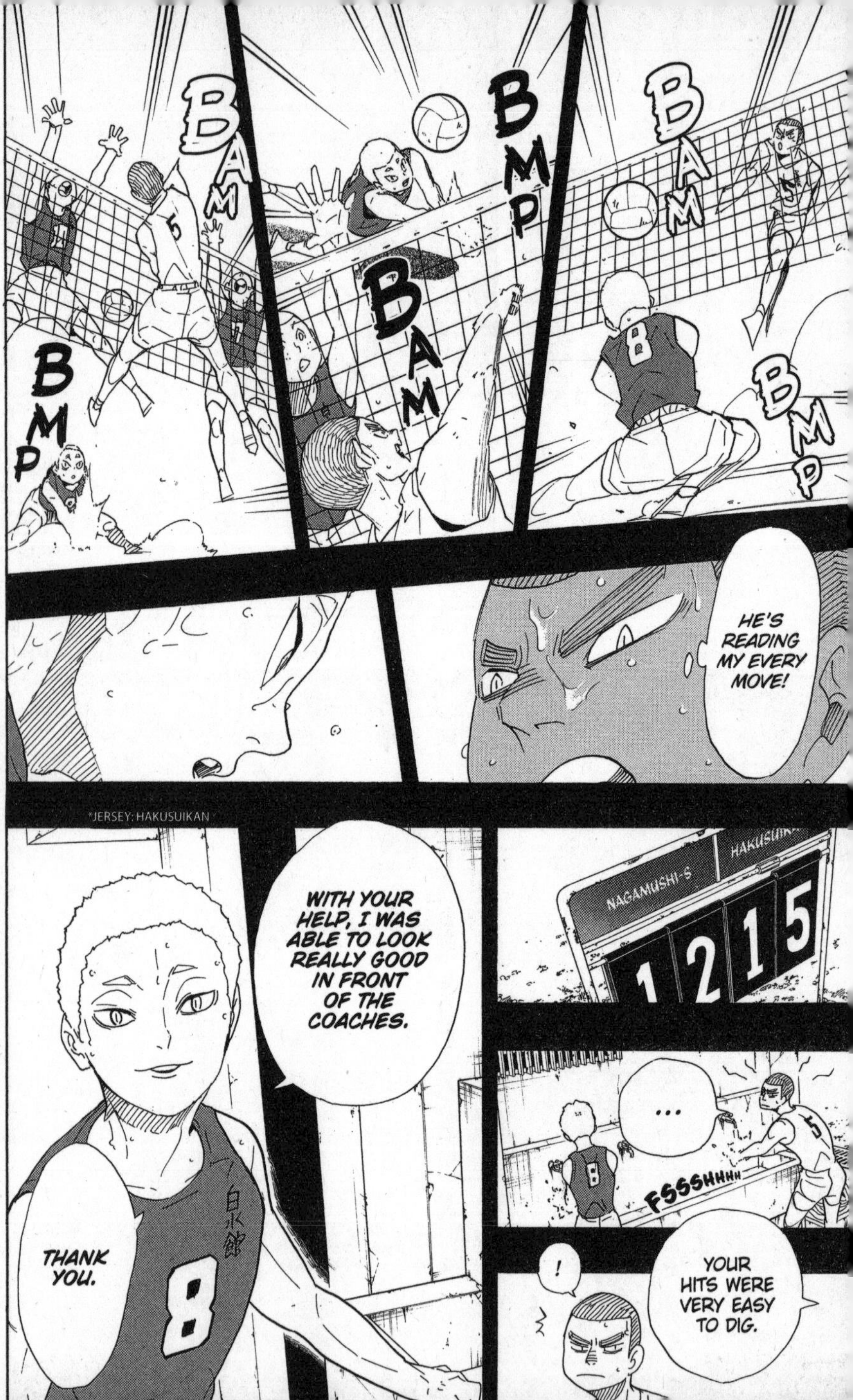
BAM
BMP
BMP
BAM
BAM
BMP
HE'S READING MY EVERY MOVE!
*JERSEY: HAKUSUIKAN
NAGAMUSHI-S
HAKUSUIKAN
12 15
...
FSSSHHHH
YOUR HITS WERE VERY EASY TO DIG.
!
WITH YOUR HELP, I WAS ABLE TO LOOK REALLY GOOD IN FRONT OF THE COACHES.
白水館
THANK YOU.

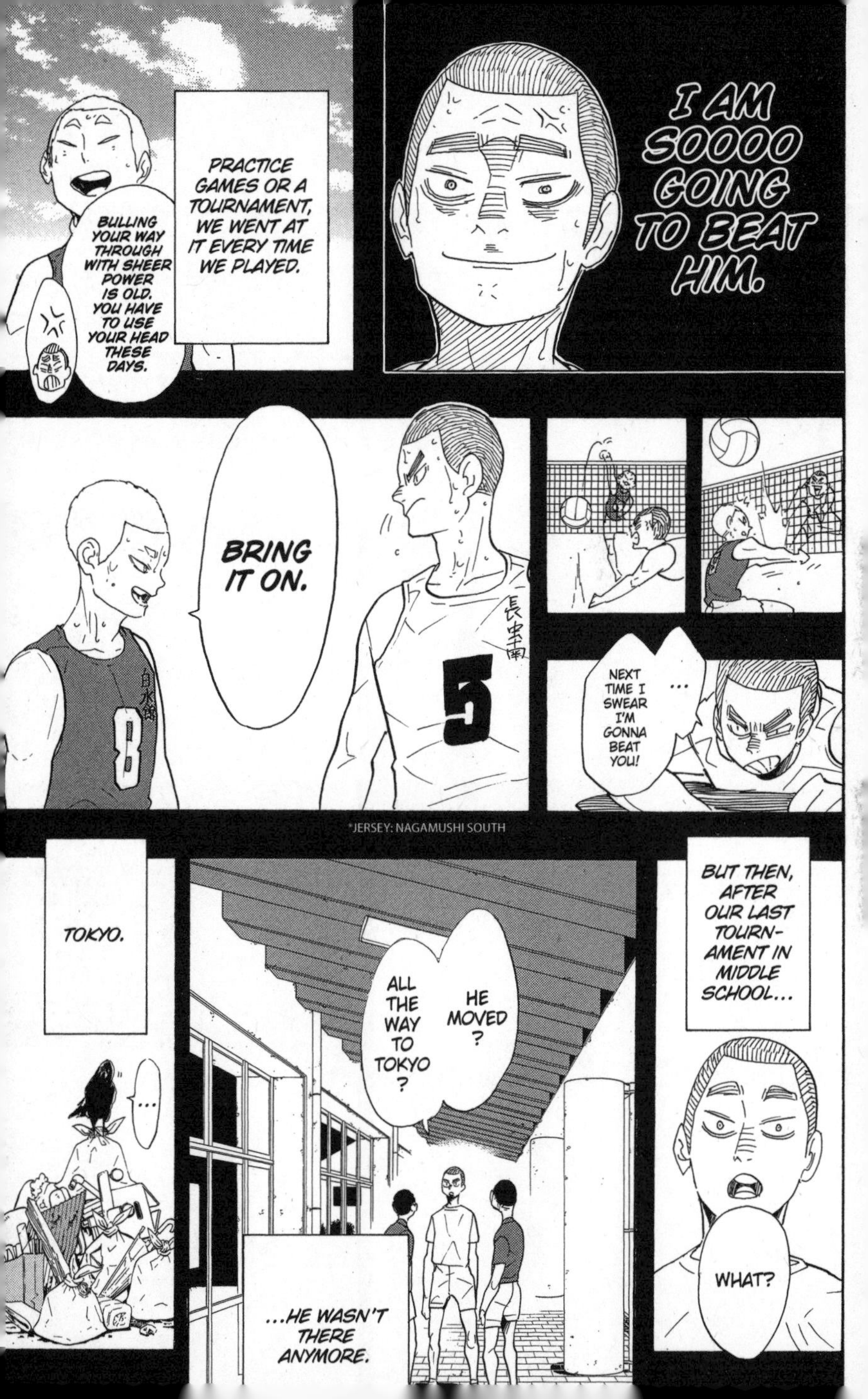
I AM SOOOO GOING TO BEAT HIM.
PRACTICE GAMES OR A TOURNAMENT, WE WENT AT IT EVERY TIME WE PLAYED.
BULLING YOUR WAY THROUGH WITH SHEER POWER IS OLD. YOU HAVE TO USE YOUR HEAD THESE DAYS.
...
NEXT TIME I SWEAR I'M GONNA BEAT YOU!
BRING IT ON.
*JERSEY: NAGAMUSHI SOUTH
BUT THEN, AFTER OUR LAST TOURNAMENT IN MIDDLE SCHOOL...
WHAT?
HE MOVED?
ALL THE WAY TO TOKYO?
...HE WASN'T THERE ANYMORE.
TOKYO.
...

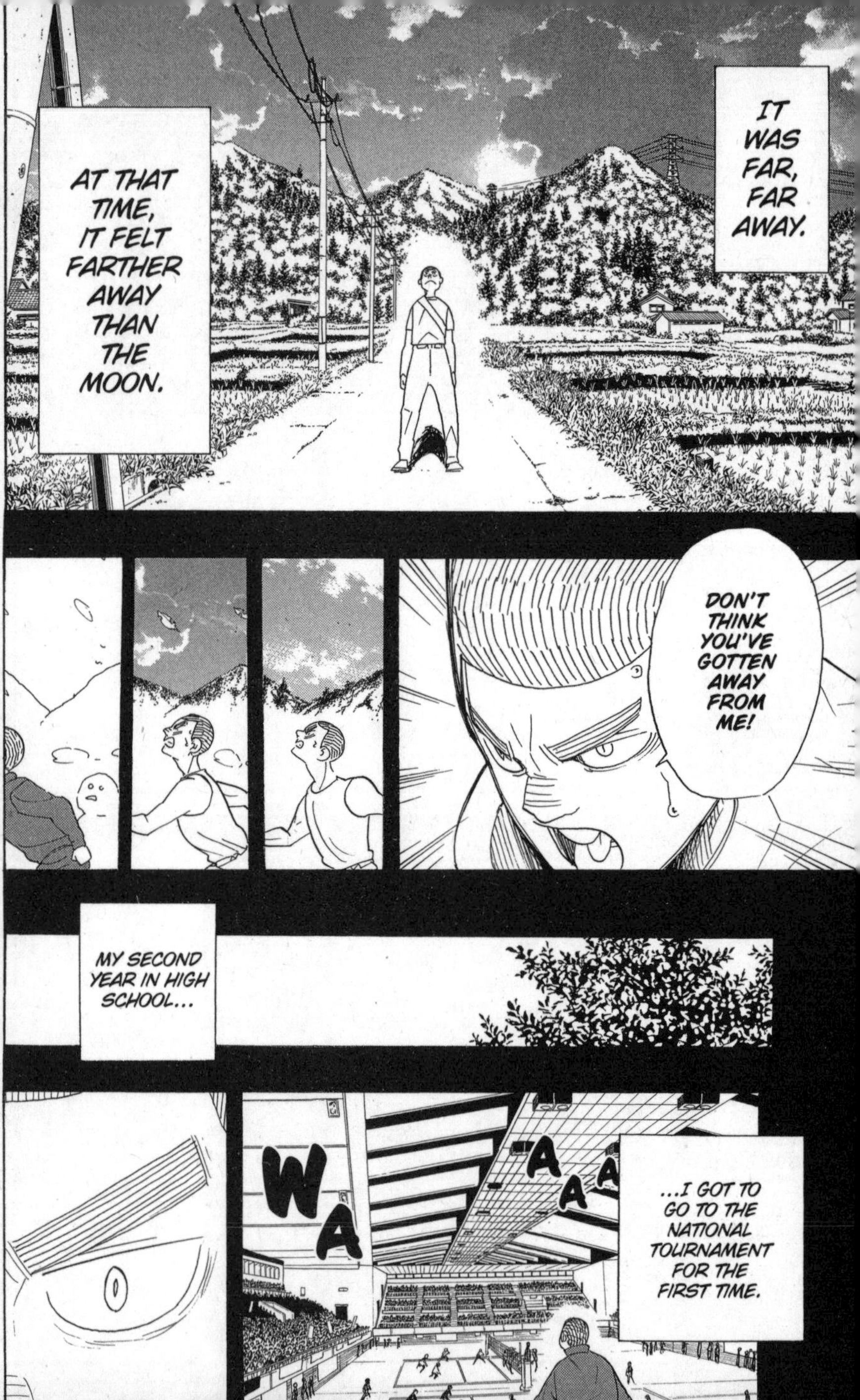
IT WAS FAR, FAR AWAY.
AT THAT TIME, IT FELT FARTHER AWAY THAN THE MOON.
DON'T THINK YOU'VE GOTTEN AWAY FROM ME!
MY SECOND YEAR IN HIGH SCHOOL...
WAAAA
...I GOT TO GO TO THE NATIONAL TOURNAMENT FOR THE FIRST TIME.

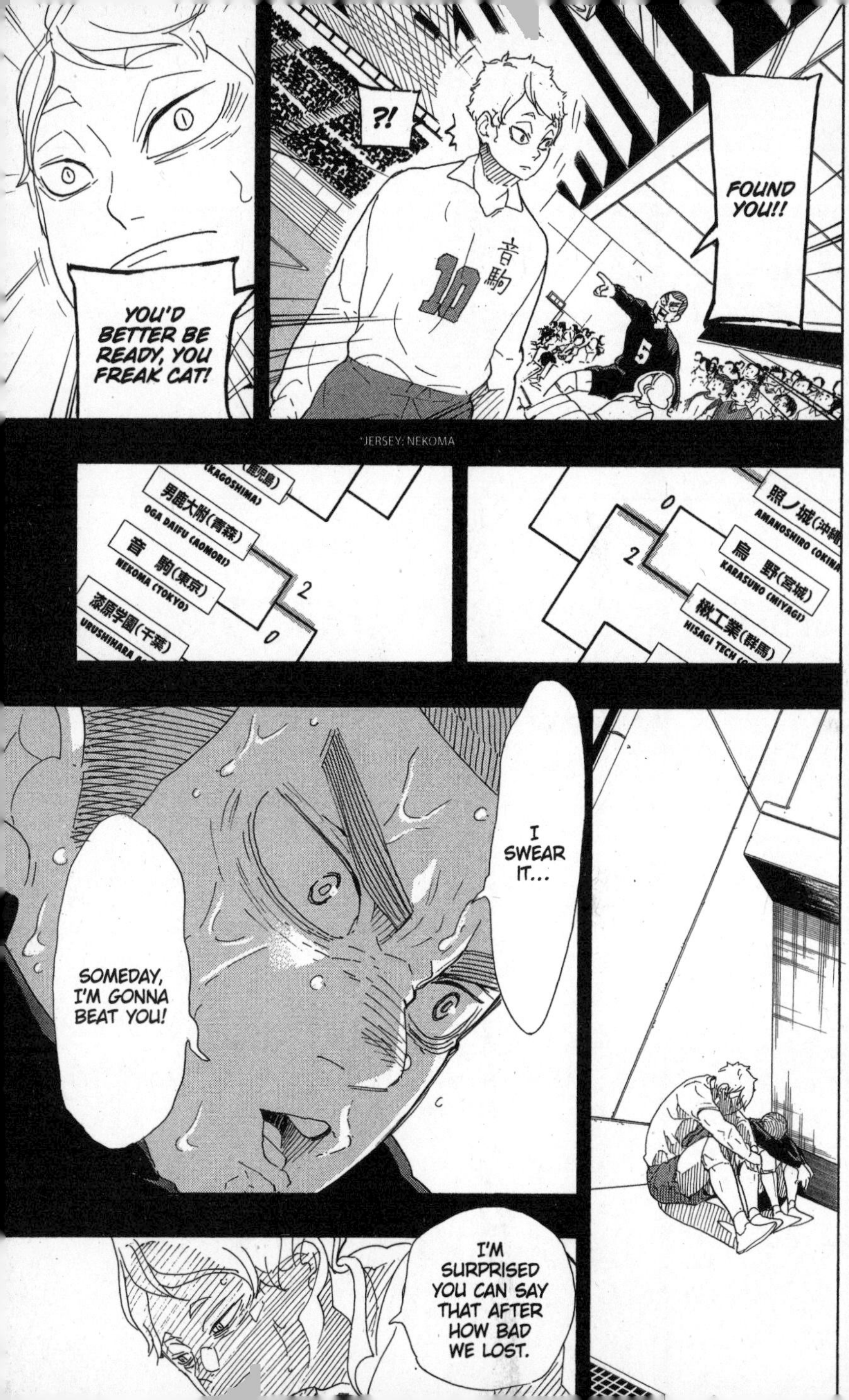
FOUND YOU!!
?!
音駒
YOU'D BETTER BE READY, YOU FREAK CAT!
*JERSEY: NEKOMA
0
照ノ城
AMANOSHIRO
2
烏 野(宮城)
KARASUNO (MIYAGI)
HISAGI TECH
(KAGOSHIMA)
男鹿大附(青森)
OGA DAIFU (AOMORI)
音 駒(東京)
NEKOMA (TOKYO)
2
0
漆原学園(千葉)
I SWEAR IT...
SOMEDAY, I'M GONNA BEAT YOU!
I'M SURPRISED YOU CAN SAY THAT AFTER HOW BAD WE LOST.

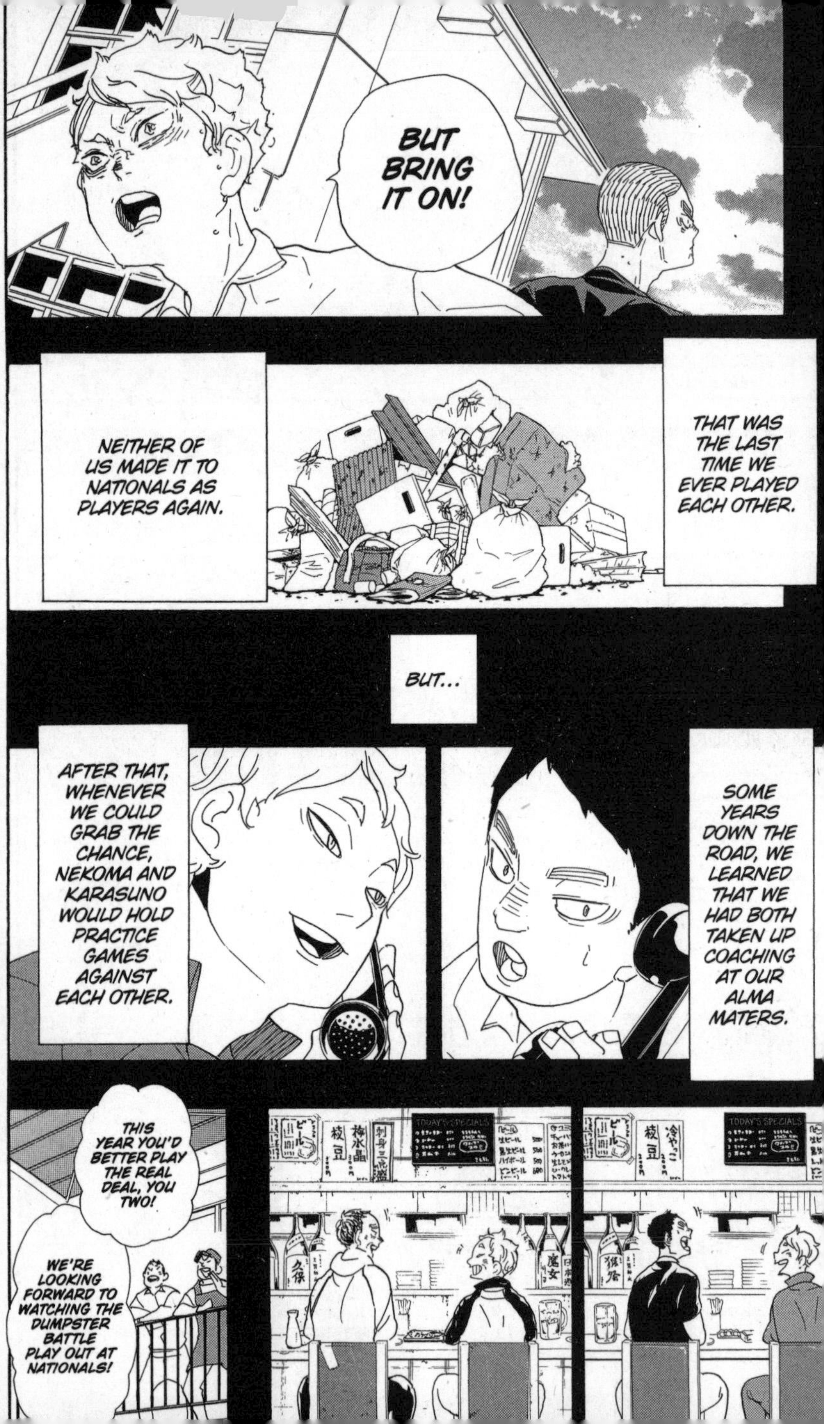
BUT BRING IT ON!
THAT WAS THE LAST TIME WE EVER PLAYED EACH OTHER.
NEITHER OF US MADE IT TO NATIONALS AS PLAYERS AGAIN.
BUT...
SOME YEARS DOWN THE ROAD, WE LEARNED THAT WE HAD BOTH TAKEN UP COACHING AT OUR ALMA MATERS.
AFTER THAT, WHENEVER WE COULD GRAB THE CHANCE, NEKOMA AND KARASUNO WOULD HOLD PRACTICE GAMES AGAINST EACH OTHER.
THIS YEAR YOU'D BETTER PLAY THE REAL DEAL, YOU TWO!
WE'RE LOOKING FORWARD TO WATCHING THE DUMPSTER BATTLE PLAY OUT AT NATIONALS!

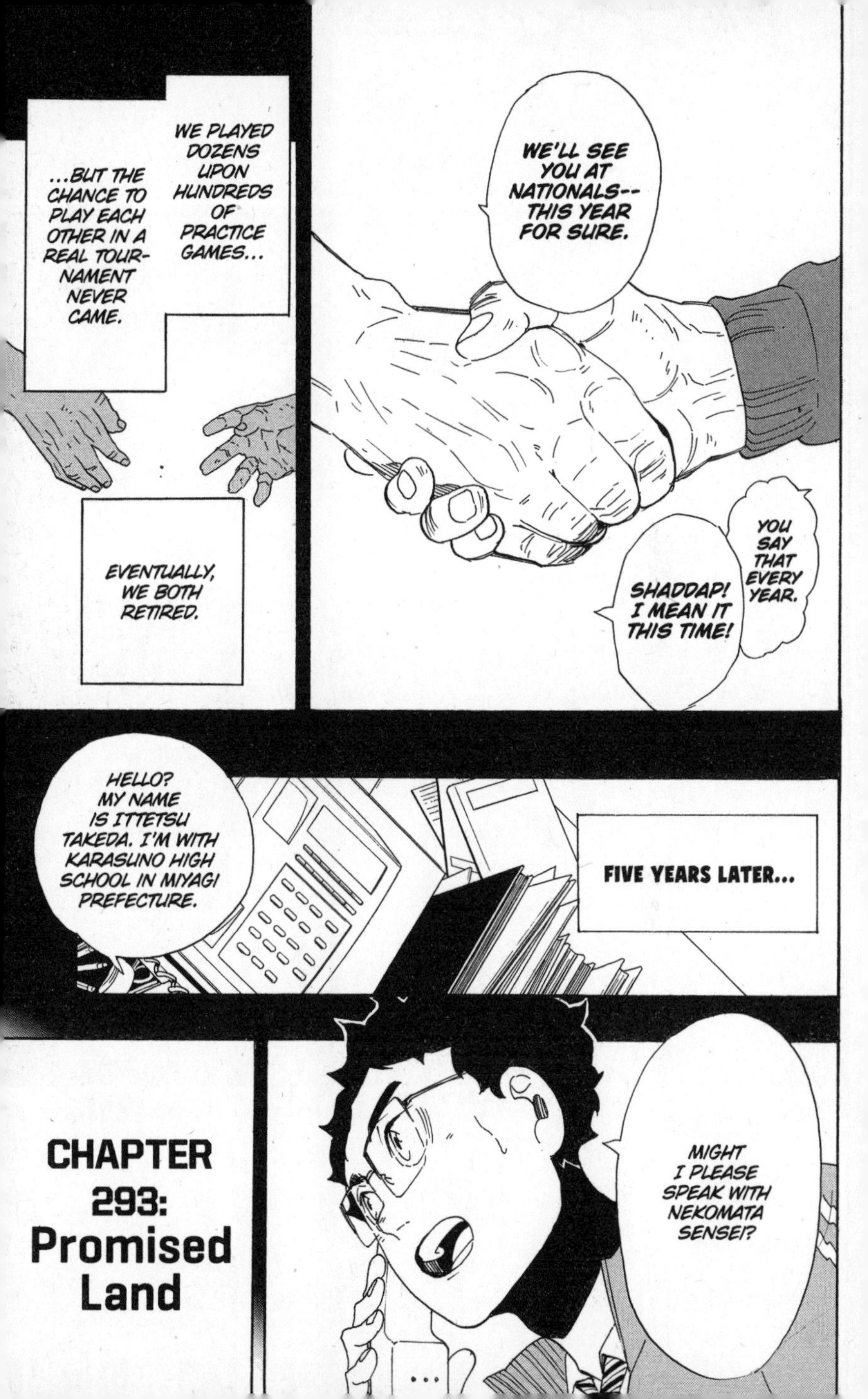
WE'LL SEE YOU AT NATIONALS-- THIS YEAR FOR SURE.
YOU SAY THAT EVERY YEAR.
SHADDAP! I MEAN IT THIS TIME!
WE PLAYED DOZENS UPON HUNDREDS OF PRACTICE GAMES...
...BUT THE CHANCE TO PLAY EACH OTHER IN A REAL TOUR-NAMENT NEVER CAME.
EVENTUALLY, WE BOTH RETIRED.
FIVE YEARS LATER...
HELLO? MY NAME IS ITTETSU TAKEDA. I'M WITH KARASUNO HIGH SCHOOL IN MIYAGI PREFECTURE.
MIGHT I PLEASE SPEAK WITH NEKOMATA SENSEI?
...
CHAPTER 293: Promised Land

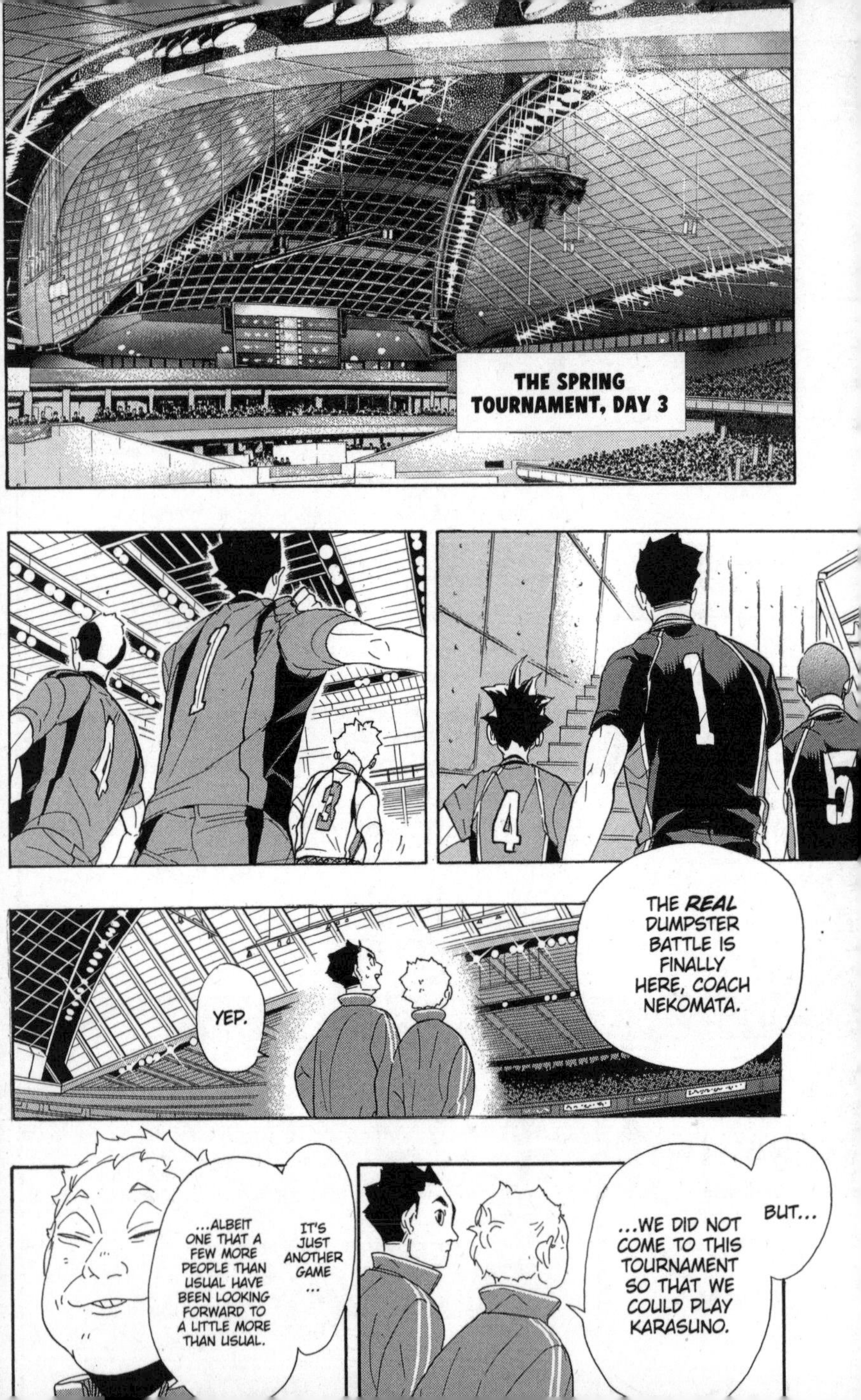
THE SPRING TOURNAMENT, DAY 3
THE *REAL* DUMPSTER BATTLE IS FINALLY HERE, COACH NEKOMATA.
YEP.
BUT...
...WE DID NOT COME TO THIS TOURNAMENT SO THAT WE COULD PLAY KARASUNO.
IT'S JUST ANOTHER GAME...
...ALBEIT ONE THAT A FEW MORE PEOPLE THAN USUAL HAVE BEEN LOOKING FORWARD TO A LITTLE MORE THAN USUAL.

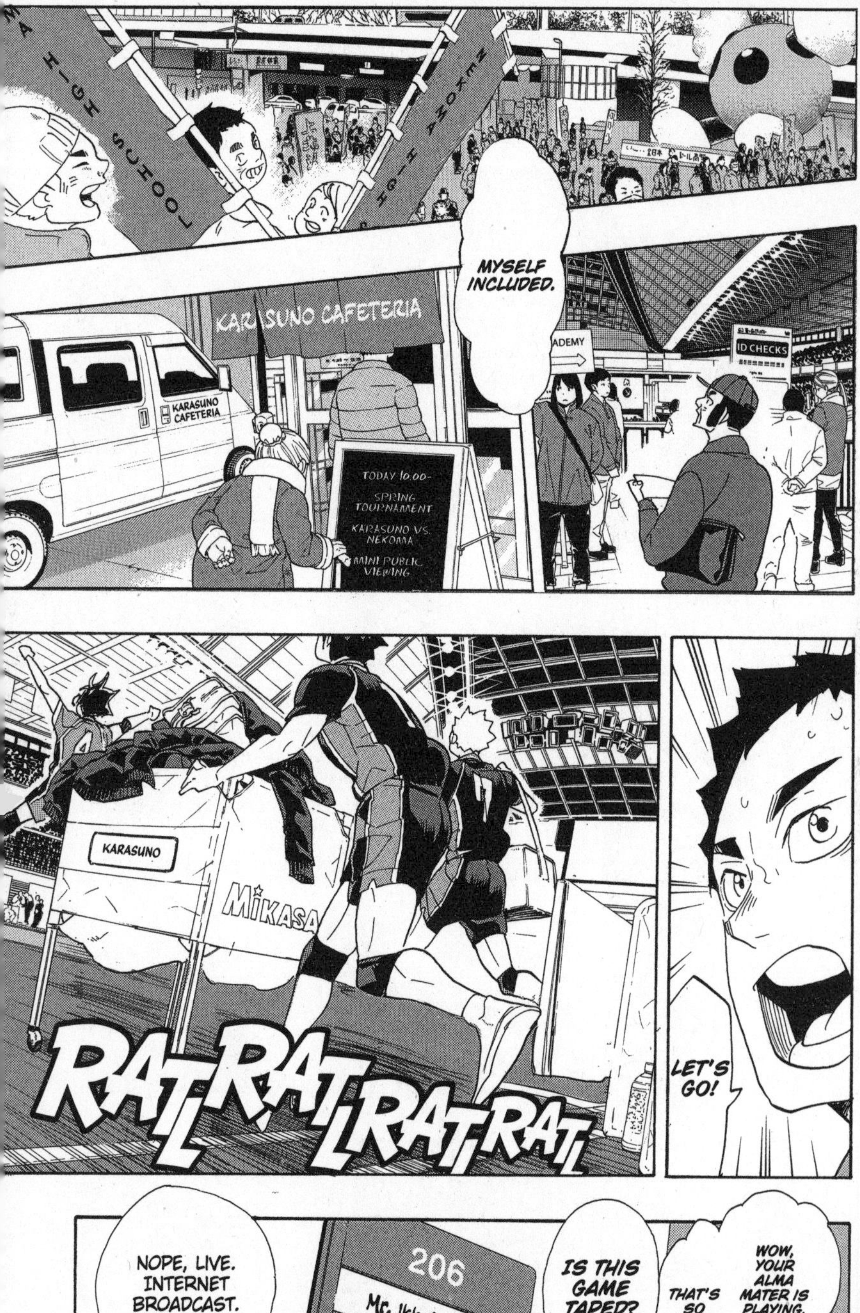
MYSELF INCLUDED.
ID CHECKS
KARASUNO CAFETERIA
KARASUNO CAFETERIA
TODAY 10:00-
SPRING TOURNAMENT
KARASUNO VS. NEKOMA
MINI PUBLIC VIEWING
LET'S GO!
KARASUNO
MIKASA
RATL RATL RATL RATL
WOW, YOUR ALMA MATER IS PLAYING, UKAI-SAN?
THAT'S SO NEAT!
IS THIS GAME TAPED?
206
Mr. Ikkei Ukai
NOPE, LIVE. INTERNET BROADCAST.

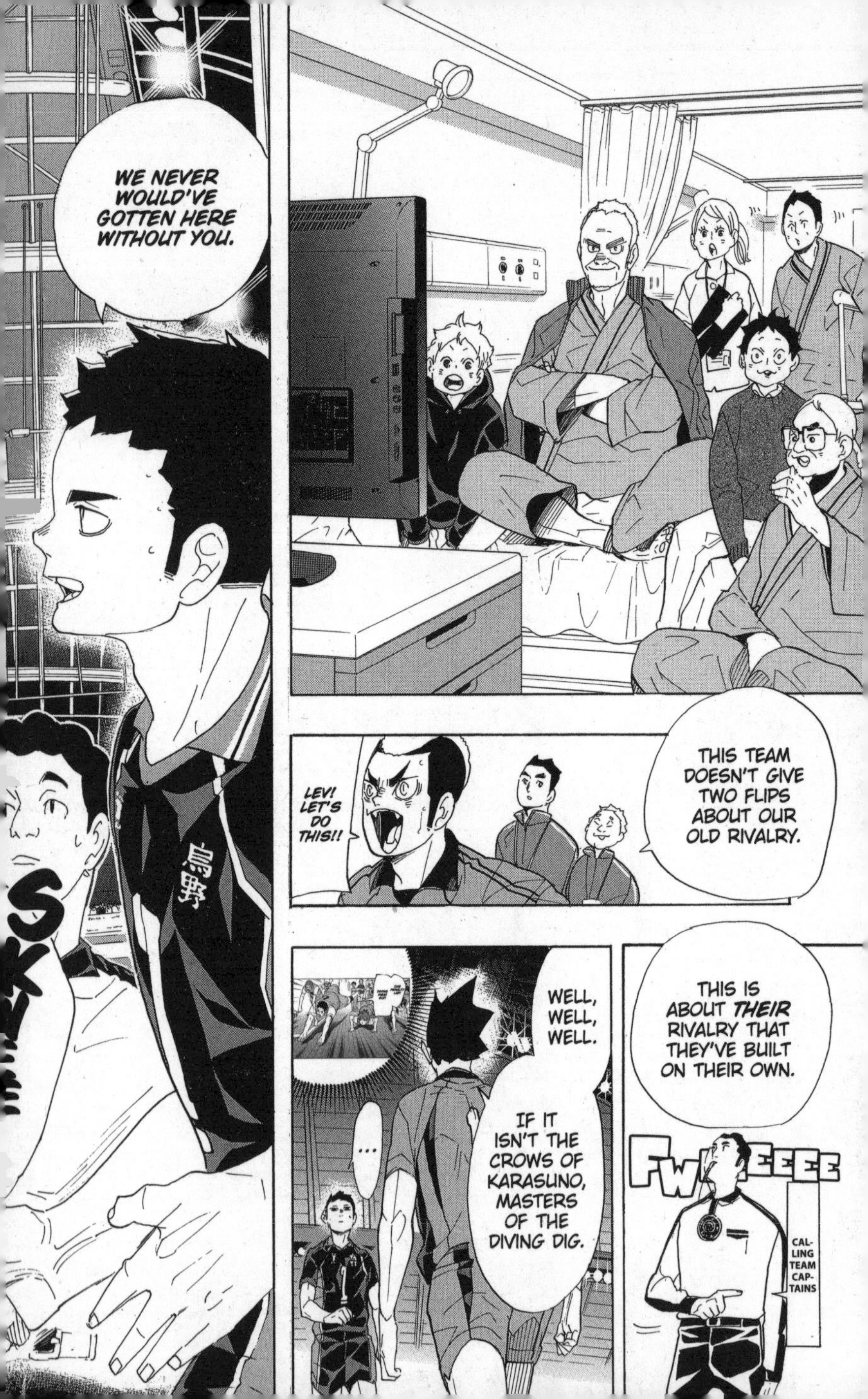
THIS TEAM DOESN'T GIVE TWO FLIPS ABOUT OUR OLD RIVALRY.
LEV! LET'S DO THIS!!
THIS IS ABOUT *THEIR* RIVALRY THAT THEY'VE BUILT ON THEIR OWN.
FWEEEE
CALLING TEAM CAPTAINS
WELL, WELL, WELL.
IF IT ISN'T THE CROWS OF KARASUNO, MASTERS OF THE DIVING DIG.
...
WE NEVER WOULD'VE GOTTEN HERE WITHOUT YOU.

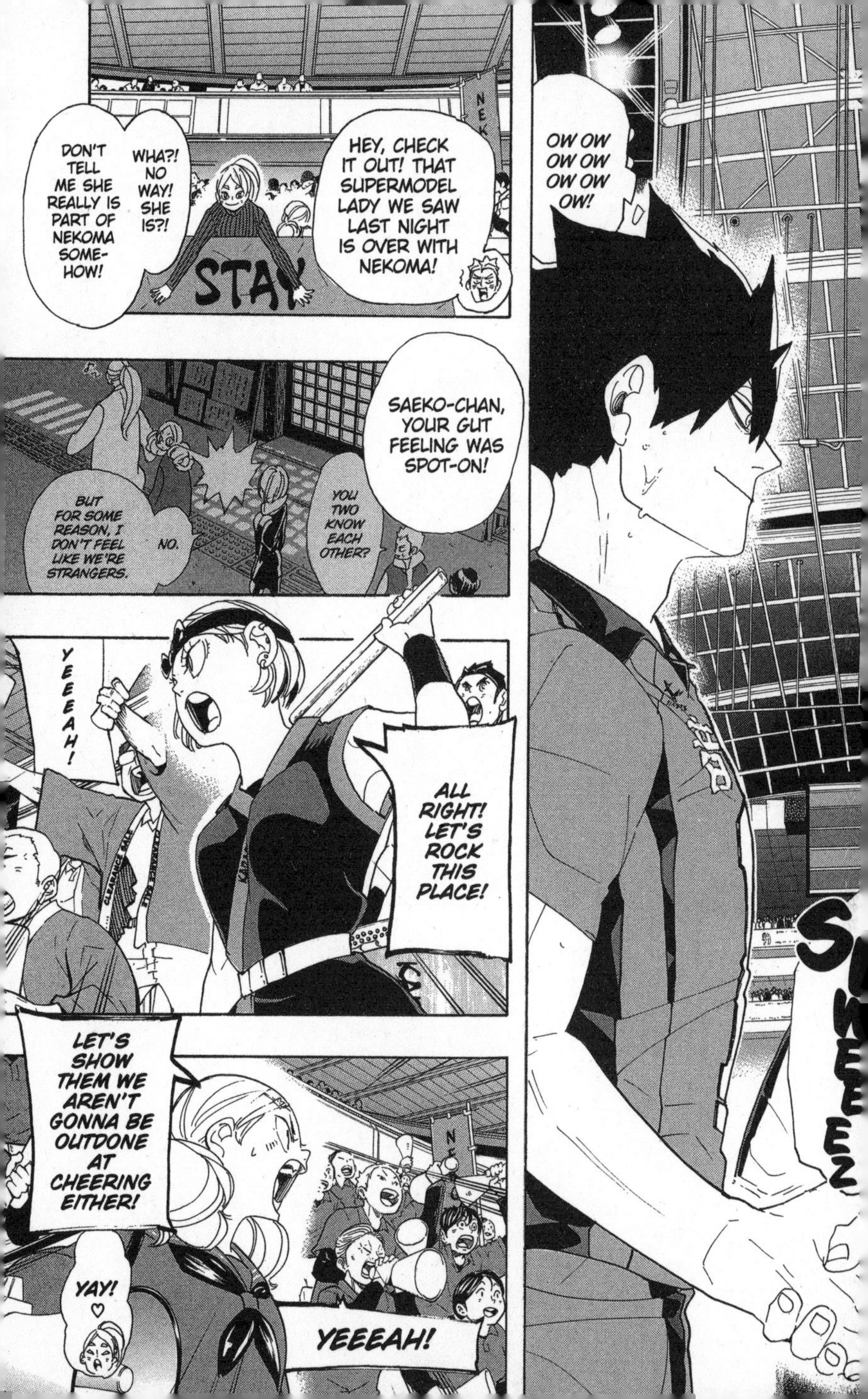
OW OW OW OW OW OW OW!
HEY, CHECK IT OUT! THAT SUPERMODEL LADY WE SAW LAST NIGHT IS OVER WITH NEKOMA!
STAY
WHA?! NO WAY! SHE IS?!
DON'T TELL ME SHE REALLY IS PART OF NEKOMA SOMEHOW!
SAEKO-CHAN, YOUR GUT FEELING WAS SPOT-ON!
YOU TWO KNOW EACH OTHER?
NO.
BUT FOR SOME REASON, I DON'T FEEL LIKE WE'RE STRANGERS.
ALL RIGHT! LET'S ROCK THIS PLACE!
YEEEEAH!
LET'S SHOW THEM WE AREN'T GONNA BE OUTDONE AT CHEERING EITHER!
YEEEAH!
YAY! ♡

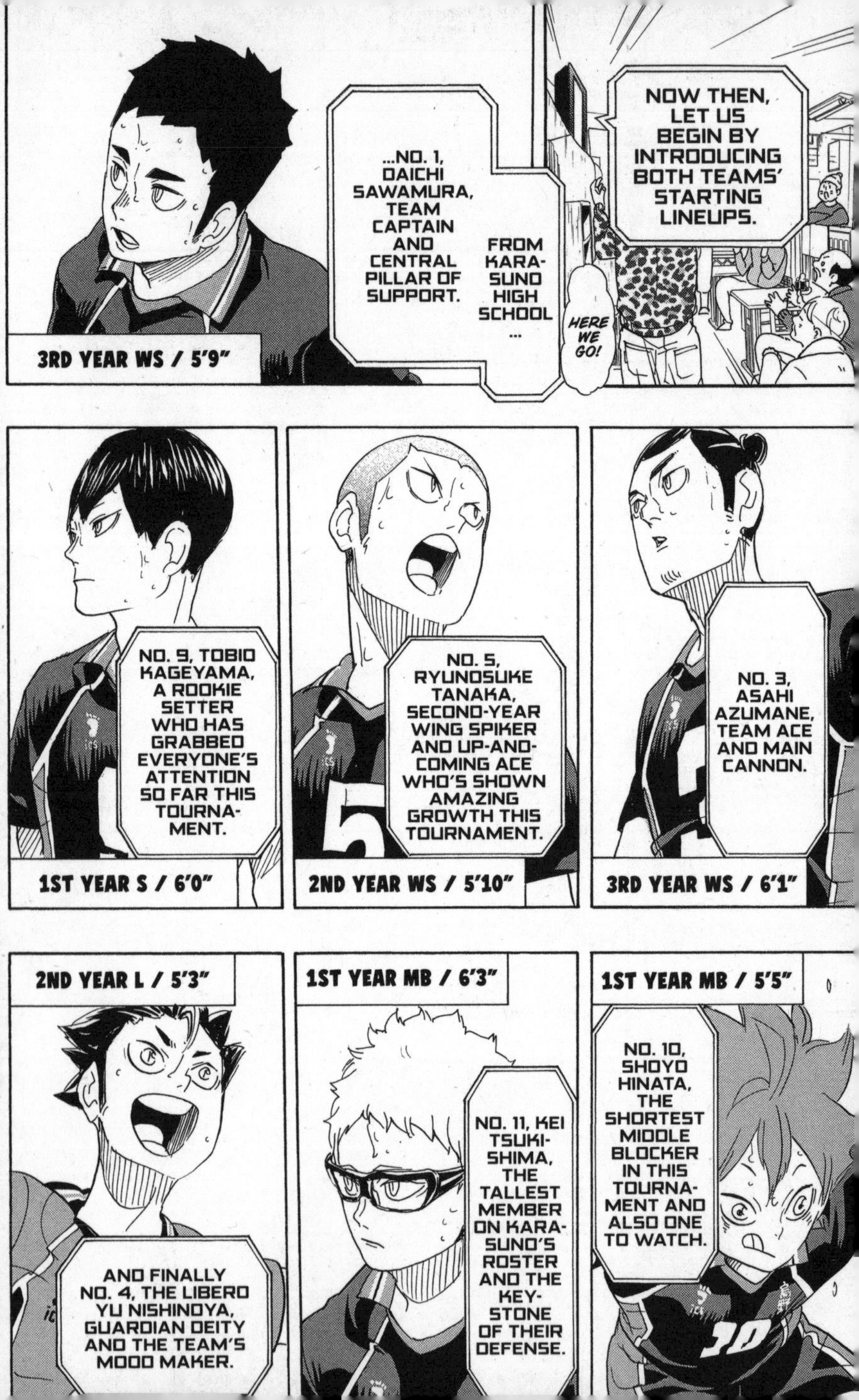
NOW THEN, LET US BEGIN BY INTRODUCING BOTH TEAMS' STARTING LINEUPS.
HERE WE GO!
FROM KARA-SUNO HIGH SCHOOL ...
...NO. 1, DAICHI SAWAMURA, TEAM CAPTAIN AND CENTRAL PILLAR OF SUPPORT.
3RD YEAR WS / 5'9"
3RD YEAR WS / 6'1"
NO. 3, ASAHI AZUMANE, TEAM ACE AND MAIN CANNON.
2ND YEAR WS / 5'10"
NO. 5, RYUNOSUKE TANAKA, SECOND-YEAR WING SPIKER AND UP-AND-COMING ACE WHO'S SHOWN AMAZING GROWTH THIS TOURNAMENT.
1ST YEAR S / 6'0"
NO. 9, TOBIO KAGEYAMA, A ROOKIE SETTER WHO HAS GRABBED EVERYONE'S ATTENTION SO FAR THIS TOURNA-MENT.
1ST YEAR MB / 5'5"
NO. 10, SHOYO HINATA, THE SHORTEST MIDDLE BLOCKER IN THIS TOURNA-MENT AND ALSO ONE TO WATCH.
1ST YEAR MB / 6'3"
NO. 11, KEI TSUKI-SHIMA, THE TALLEST MEMBER ON KARA-SUNO'S ROSTER AND THE KEY-STONE OF THEIR DEFENSE.
2ND YEAR L / 5'3"
AND FINALLY NO. 4, THE LIBERO YU NISHINOYA, GUARDIAN DEITY AND THE TEAM'S MOOD MAKER.

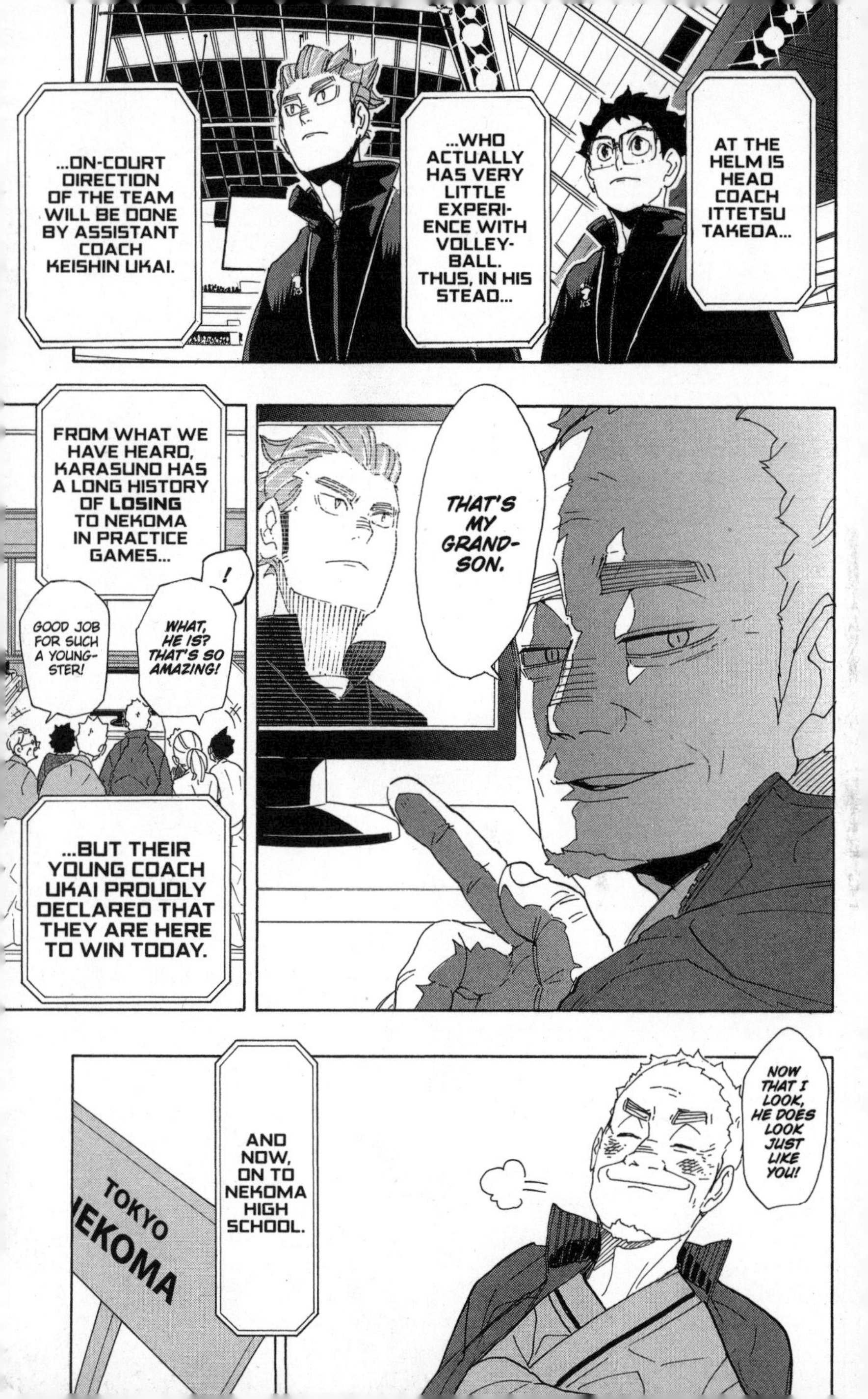
AT THE HELM IS HEAD COACH ITTETSU TAKEDA...
...WHO ACTUALLY HAS VERY LITTLE EXPERIENCE WITH VOLLEYBALL. THUS, IN HIS STEAD...
...ON-COURT DIRECTION OF THE TEAM WILL BE DONE BY ASSISTANT COACH KEISHIN UKAI.
THAT'S MY GRANDSON.
FROM WHAT WE HAVE HEARD, KARASUNO HAS A LONG HISTORY OF LOSING TO NEKOMA IN PRACTICE GAMES...
!
WHAT, HE IS? THAT'S SO AMAZING!
GOOD JOB FOR SUCH A YOUNGSTER!
...BUT THEIR YOUNG COACH UKAI PROUDLY DECLARED THAT THEY ARE HERE TO WIN TODAY.
NOW THAT I LOOK, HE DOES LOOK JUST LIKE YOU!
AND NOW, ON TO NEKOMA HIGH SCHOOL.
TOKYO
EKOMA

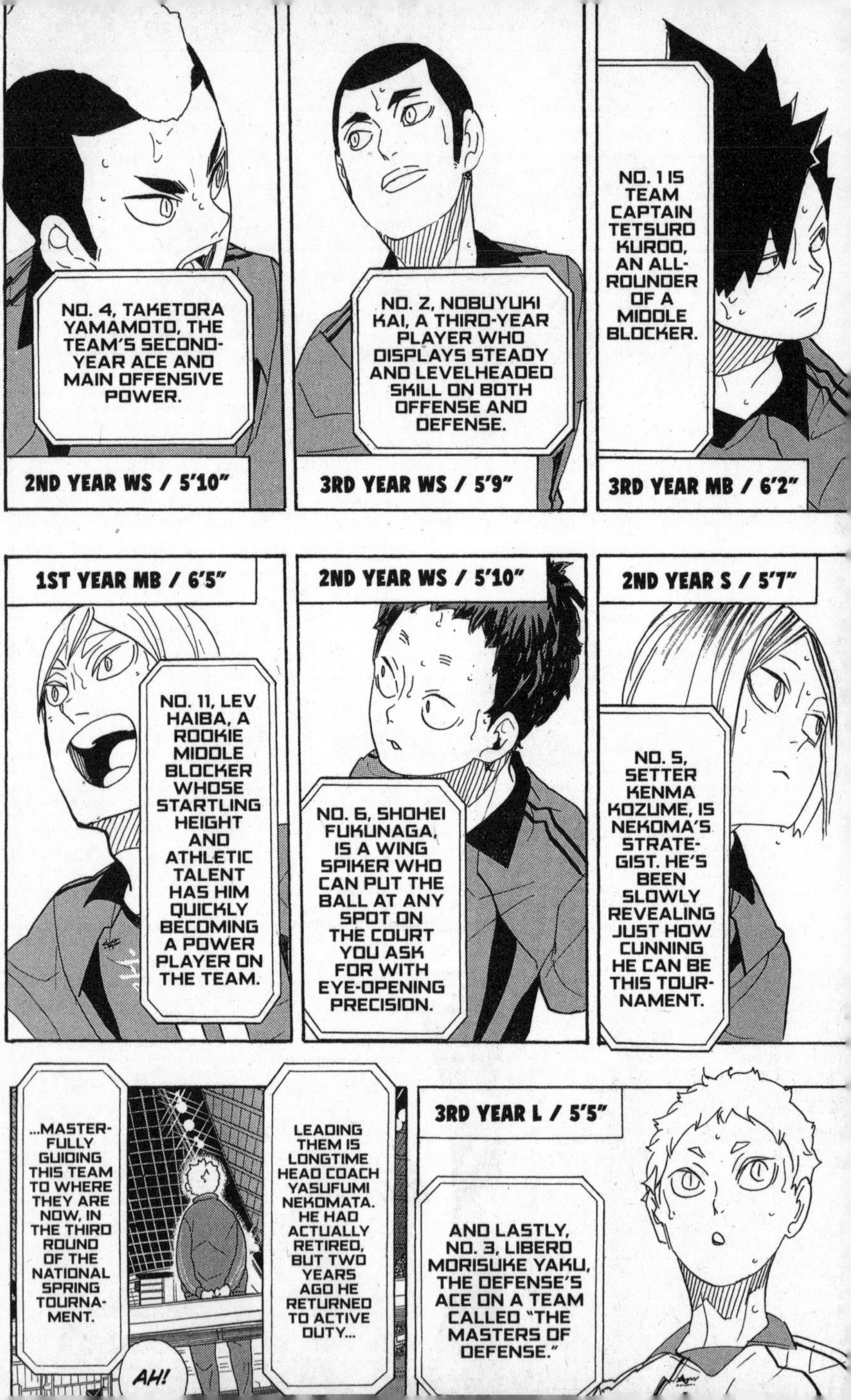
NO. 1 IS TEAM CAPTAIN TETSURO KUROO, AN ALL-ROUNDER OF A MIDDLE BLOCKER.
3RD YEAR MB / 6'2"
NO. 2, NOBUYUKI KAI, A THIRD-YEAR PLAYER WHO DISPLAYS STEADY AND LEVELHEADED SKILL ON BOTH OFFENSE AND DEFENSE.
3RD YEAR WS / 5'9"
NO. 4, TAKETORA YAMAMOTO, THE TEAM'S SECOND-YEAR ACE AND MAIN OFFENSIVE POWER.
2ND YEAR WS / 5'10"
2ND YEAR S / 5'7"
NO. 5, SETTER KENMA KOZUME, IS NEKOMA'S STRATEGIST. HE'S BEEN SLOWLY REVEALING JUST HOW CUNNING HE CAN BE THIS TOURNAMENT.
2ND YEAR WS / 5'10"
NO. 6, SHOHEI FUKUNAGA, IS A WING SPIKER WHO CAN PUT THE BALL AT ANY SPOT ON THE COURT YOU ASK FOR WITH EYE-OPENING PRECISION.
1ST YEAR MB / 6'5"
NO. 11, LEV HAIBA, A ROOKIE MIDDLE BLOCKER WHOSE STARTLING HEIGHT AND ATHLETIC TALENT HAS HIM QUICKLY BECOMING A POWER PLAYER ON THE TEAM.
3RD YEAR L / 5'5"
AND LASTLY, NO. 3, LIBERO MORISUKE YAKU, THE DEFENSE'S ACE ON A TEAM CALLED "THE MASTERS OF DEFENSE."
LEADING THEM IS LONGTIME HEAD COACH YASUFUMI NEKOMATA. HE HAD ACTUALLY RETIRED, BUT TWO YEARS AGO HE RETURNED TO ACTIVE DUTY...
...MASTERFULLY GUIDING THIS TEAM TO WHERE THEY ARE NOW, IN THE THIRD ROUND OF THE NATIONAL SPRING TOURNAMENT.
AH!

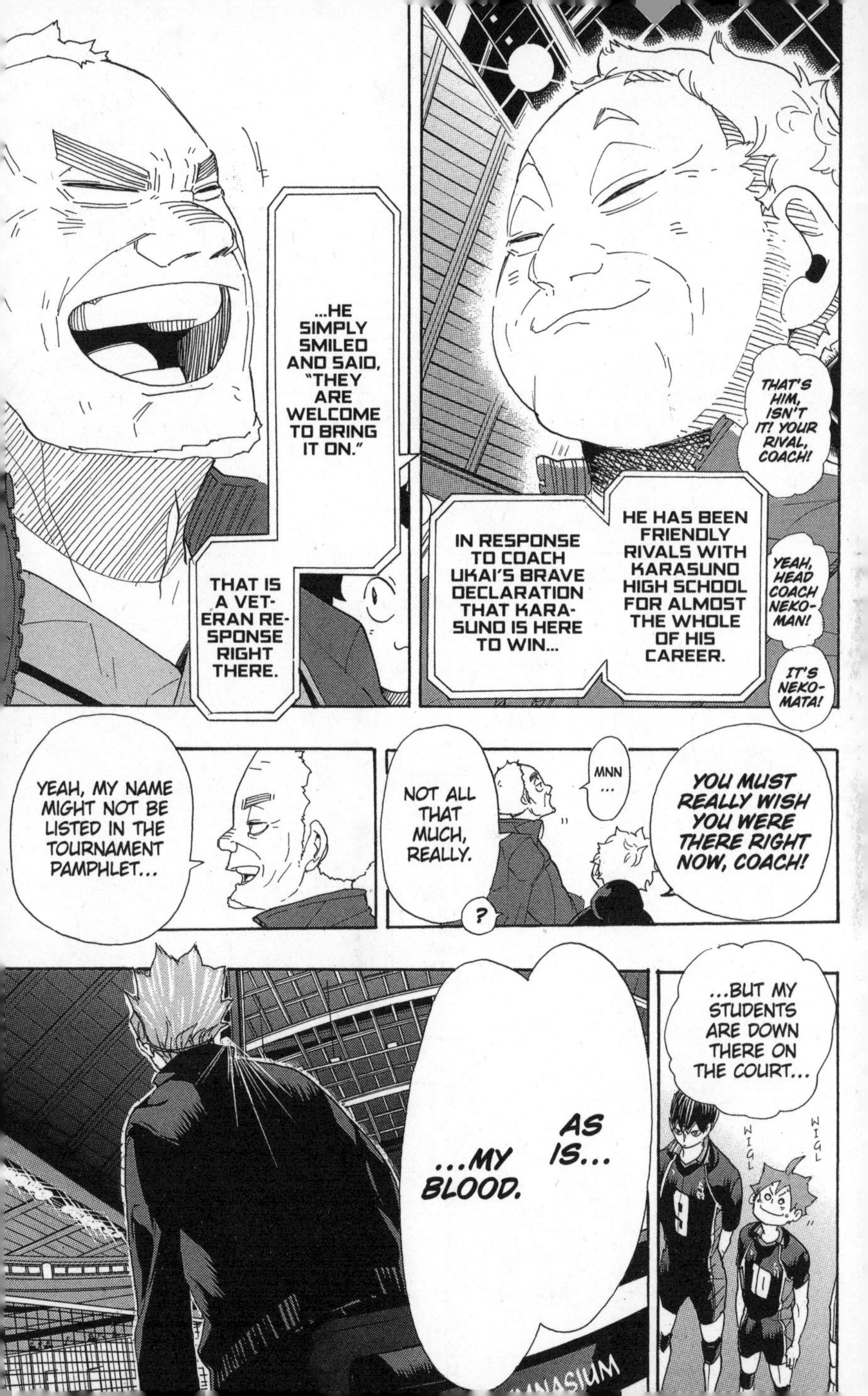
THAT'S HIM, ISN'T IT! YOUR RIVAL, COACH!
YEAH, HEAD COACH NEKO-MAN!
IT'S NEKO-MATA!
HE HAS BEEN FRIENDLY RIVALS WITH KARASUNO HIGH SCHOOL FOR ALMOST THE WHOLE OF HIS CAREER.
IN RESPONSE TO COACH UKAI'S BRAVE DECLARATION THAT KARA-SUNO IS HERE TO WIN...
...HE SIMPLY SMILED AND SAID, "THEY ARE WELCOME TO BRING IT ON."
THAT IS A VET-ERAN RE-SPONSE RIGHT THERE.
YOU MUST REALLY WISH YOU WERE THERE RIGHT NOW, COACH!
MNN...
NOT ALL THAT MUCH, REALLY.
?
YEAH, MY NAME MIGHT NOT BE LISTED IN THE TOURNAMENT PAMPHLET...
...BUT MY STUDENTS ARE DOWN THERE ON THE COURT...
WIGL
WIGL
AS IS...
...MY BLOOD.

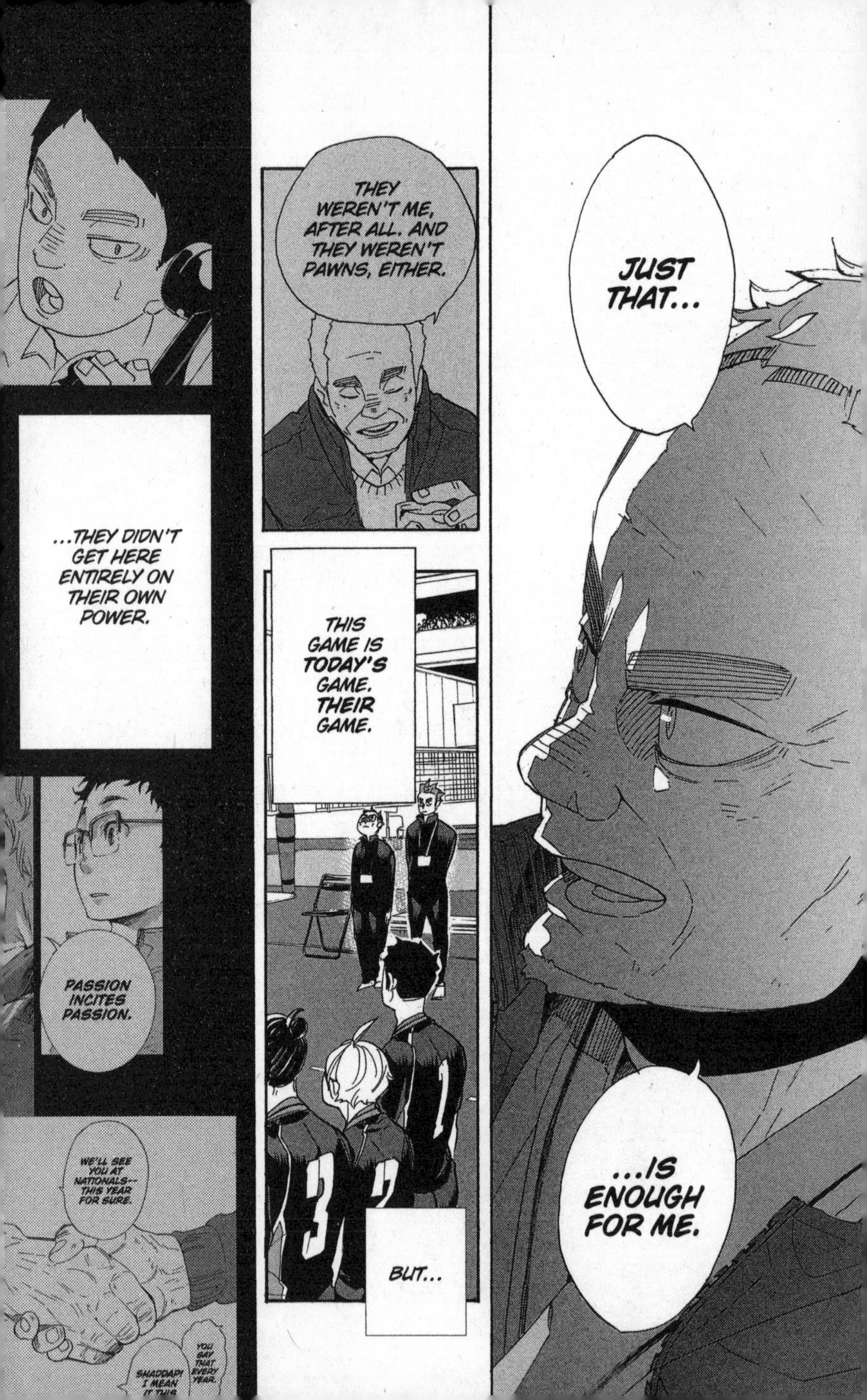
JUST THAT...
...IS ENOUGH FOR ME.
THEY WEREN'T ME, AFTER ALL. AND THEY WEREN'T PAWNS, EITHER.
THIS GAME IS TODAY'S GAME. THEIR GAME.
BUT...
...THEY DIDN'T GET HERE ENTIRELY ON THEIR OWN POWER.
PASSION INCITES PASSION.
WE'LL SEE YOU AT NATIONALS-- THIS YEAR FOR SURE.
YOU SAY THAT EVERY YEAR.
SHADDAP! I MEAN

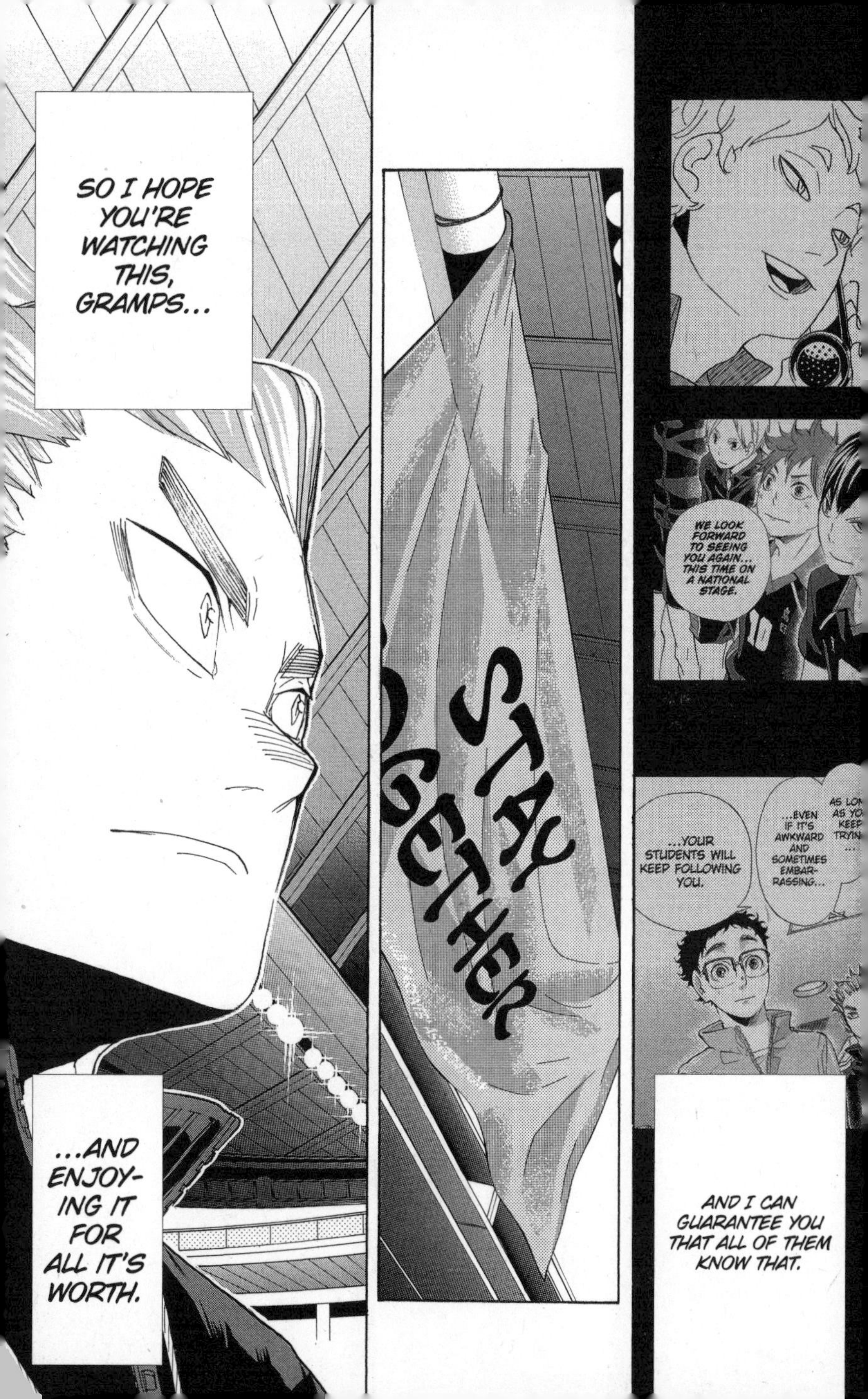
WE LOOK FORWARD TO SEEING YOU AGAIN... THIS TIME ON A NATIONAL STAGE.
AS LON AS YO KEEP TRYIN...
...EVEN IF IT'S AWKWARD AND SOMETIMES EMBAR-RASSING...
...YOUR STUDENTS WILL KEEP FOLLOWING YOU.
AND I CAN GUARANTEE YOU THAT ALL OF THEM KNOW THAT.
STAY
GETHER
SO I HOPE YOU'RE WATCHING THIS, GRAMPS...
...AND ENJOY-ING IT FOR ALL IT'S WORTH.

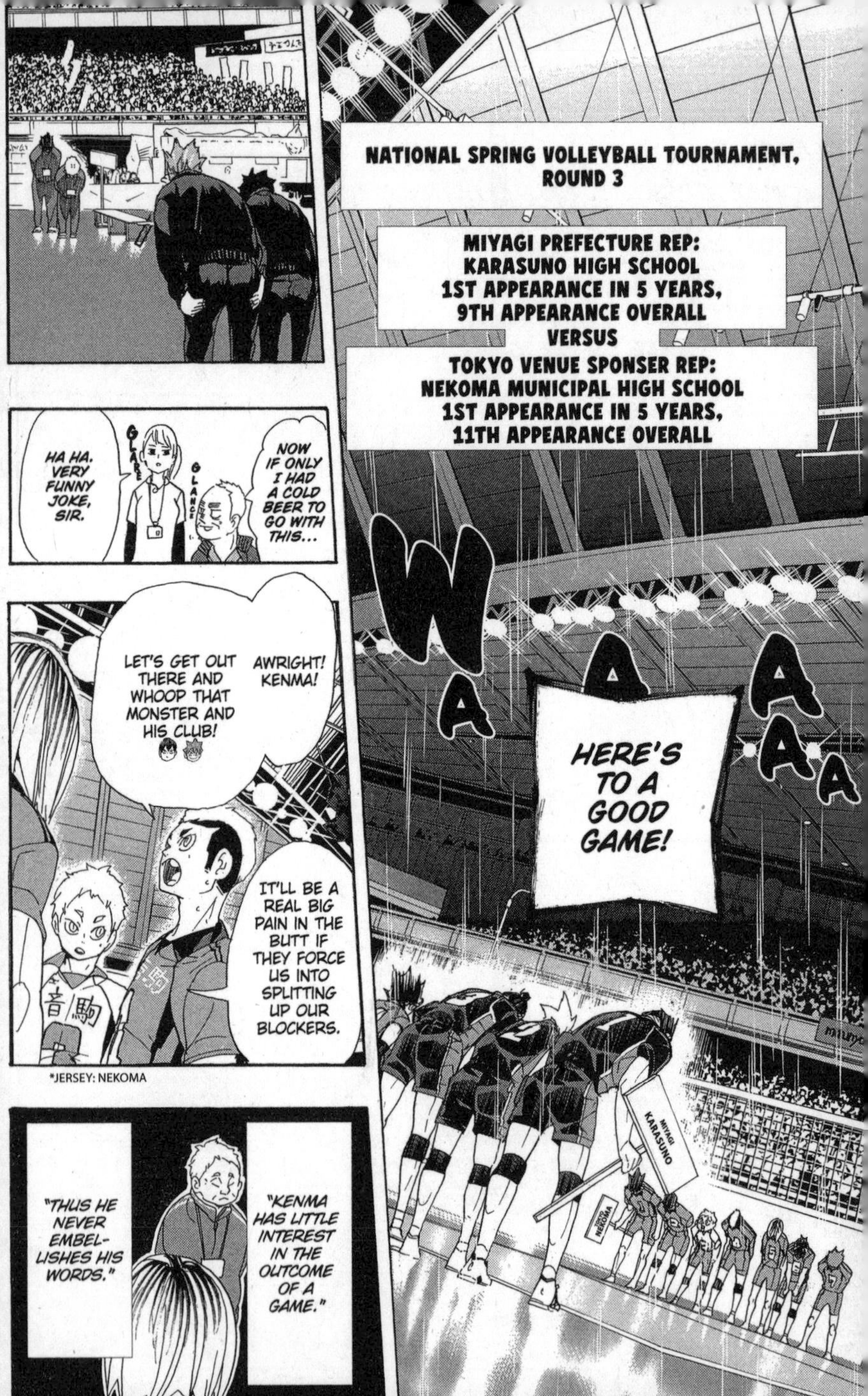
NATIONAL SPRING VOLLEYBALL TOURNAMENT, ROUND 3
MIYAGI PREFECTURE REP: KARASUNO HIGH SCHOOL 1ST APPEARANCE IN 5 YEARS, 9TH APPEARANCE OVERALL
VERSUS
TOKYO VENUE SPONSER REP: NEKOMA MUNICIPAL HIGH SCHOOL 1ST APPEARANCE IN 5 YEARS, 11TH APPEARANCE OVERALL
WAAAAAA
HERE'S TO A GOOD GAME!
MIYAGI KARASUNO
NEKOMA
NOW IF ONLY I HAD A COLD BEER TO GO WITH THIS...
GLANCE
GLARE
HA HA. VERY FUNNY JOKE, SIR.
AWRIGHT! KENMA!
LET'S GET OUT THERE AND WHOOP THAT MONSTER AND HIS CLUB!
IT'LL BE A REAL BIG PAIN IN THE BUTT IF THEY FORCE US INTO SPLITTING UP OUR BLOCKERS.
音駒
"KENMA HAS LITTLE INTEREST IN THE OUTCOME OF A GAME."
"THUS HE NEVER EMBELLISHES HIS WORDS."
*JERSEY: NEKOMA

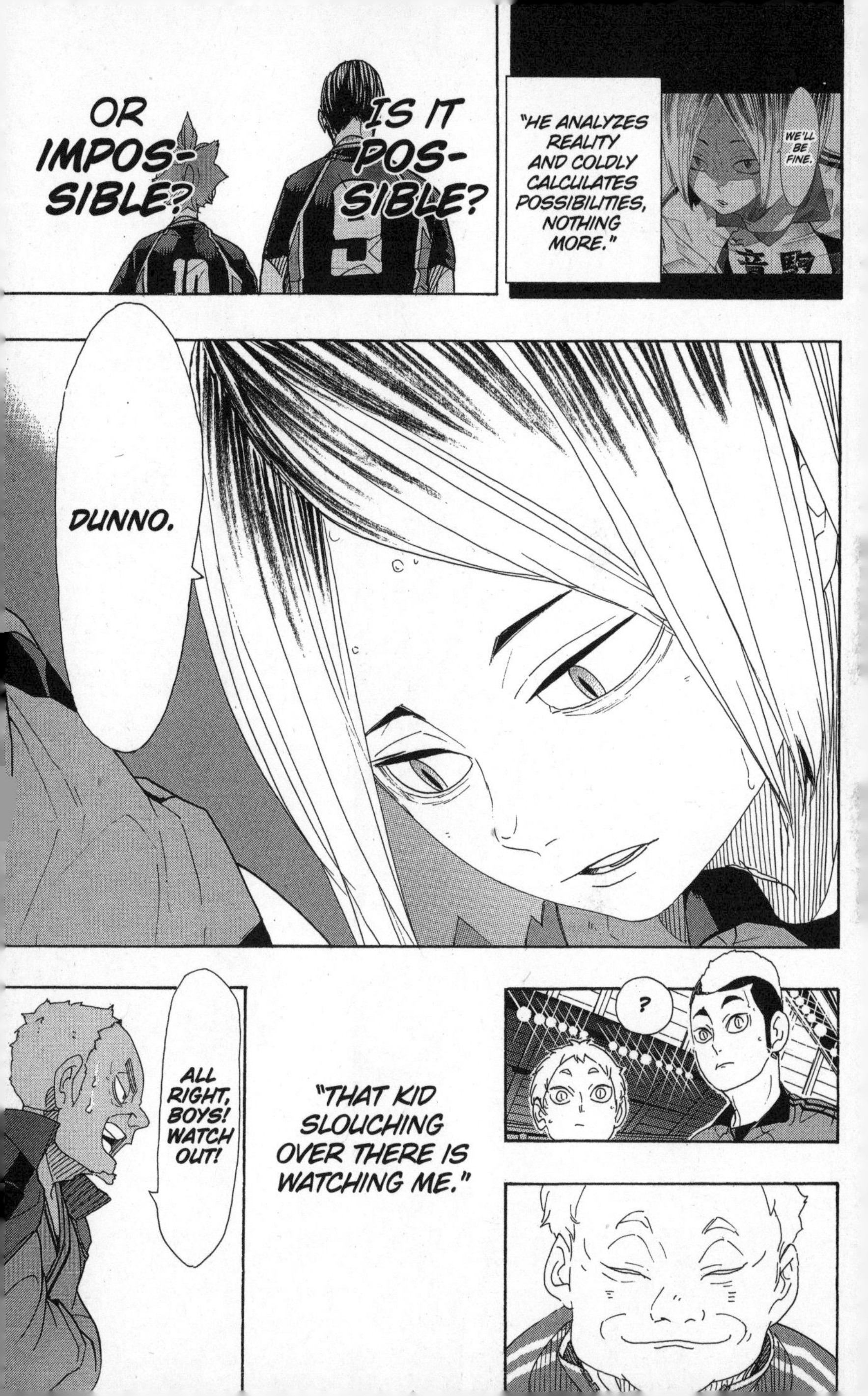
WE'LL BE FINE.
"HE ANALYZES REALITY AND COLDLY CALCULATES POSSIBILITIES, NOTHING MORE."
IS IT POS-SIBLE?
OR IMPOS-SIBLE?
DUNNO.
?
"THAT KID SLOUCHING OVER THERE IS WATCHING ME."
ALL RIGHT, BOYS! WATCH OUT!

ASSISTANTS DREW A LLUSTRATION FOR ME FOR MY BIRTHDAY!
THANK YOU SO MUCH FOR EVERYTHING YOU DO!

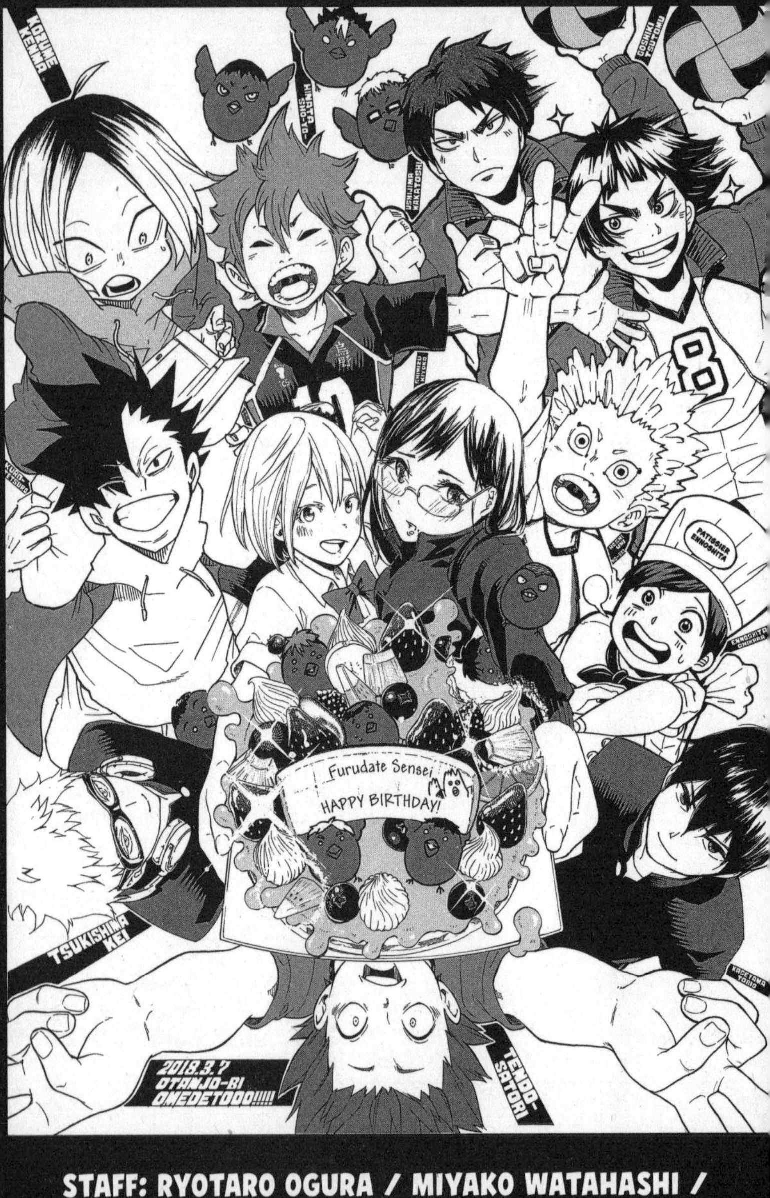
KOZUME KENMA
HINATA SHO-YO
USHIJIMA WAKATOSHI
GOSHIKI TSUTOMU
SHIMIZU KIYOKO
PATISSIER ENNOSHITA
ENNOSHITA CHIKARA
Furudate Sensei
HAPPY BIRTHDAY!
TSUKISHIMA KEI
KAGEYAMA TOBIO
TENDO SATORI
2018.3.7
OTANJO-BI
OMEDETOOO!!!!!

STAFF: RYOTARO OGURA / MIYAKO WATAHASHI /
SAKUJI KOIZUMI / YU AOKI / DAI HOSHIKAWA /

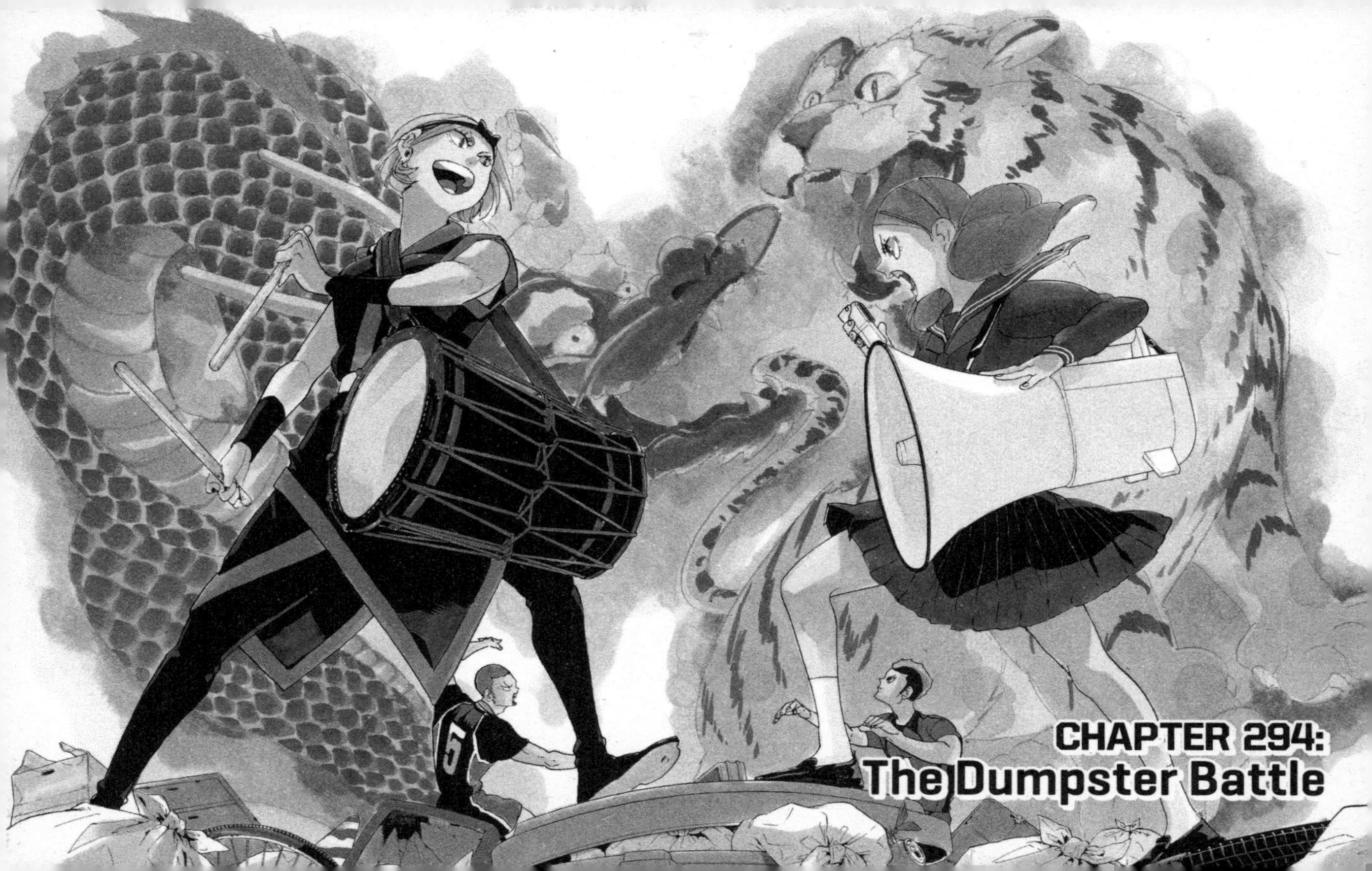
CHAPTER 294:
The Dumpster Battle

HAIKYU!!

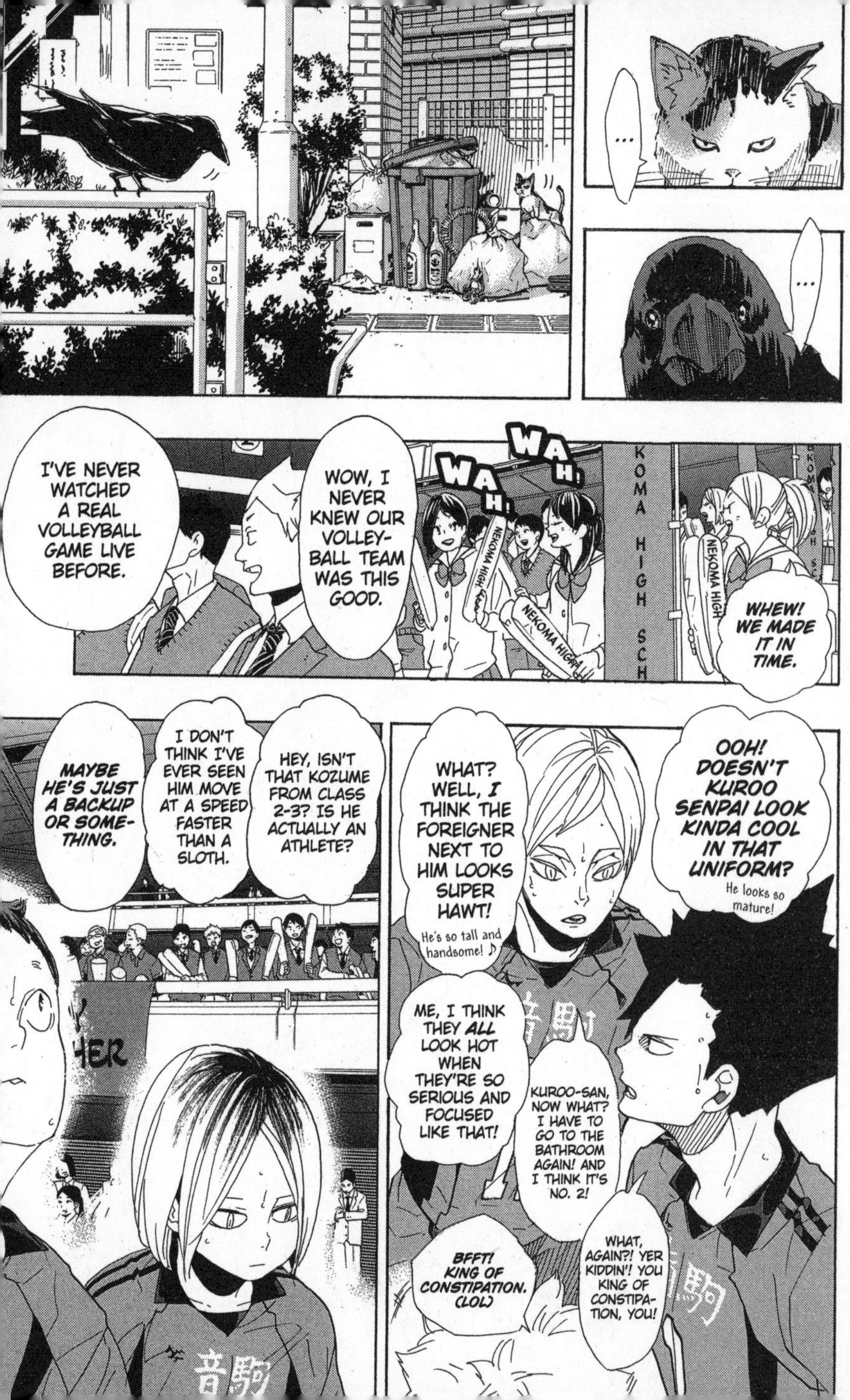
...
...
WHEW! WE MADE IT IN TIME.
WAH!
WAH!
NEKOMA HIGH
NEKOMA HIGH
NEKOMA HIGH
WOW, I NEVER KNEW OUR VOLLEY-BALL TEAM WAS THIS GOOD.
I'VE NEVER WATCHED A REAL VOLLEYBALL GAME LIVE BEFORE.
OOH! DOESN'T KUROO SENPAI LOOK KINDA COOL IN THAT UNIFORM?
He looks so mature!
WHAT? WELL, I THINK THE FOREIGNER NEXT TO HIM LOOKS SUPER HAWT!
He's so tall and handsome! ♪
ME, I THINK THEY ALL LOOK HOT WHEN THEY'RE SO SERIOUS AND FOCUSED LIKE THAT!
KUROO-SAN, NOW WHAT? I HAVE TO GO TO THE BATHROOM AGAIN! AND I THINK IT'S NO. 2!
WHAT, AGAIN?! YER KIDDIN'! YOU KING OF CONSTIPA-TION, YOU!
BFFT! KING OF CONSTIPATION. (LOL)
HEY, ISN'T THAT KOZUME FROM CLASS 2-3? IS HE ACTUALLY AN ATHLETE?
I DON'T THINK I'VE EVER SEEN HIM MOVE AT A SPEED FASTER THAN A SLOTH.
MAYBE HE'S JUST A BACKUP OR SOME-THING.

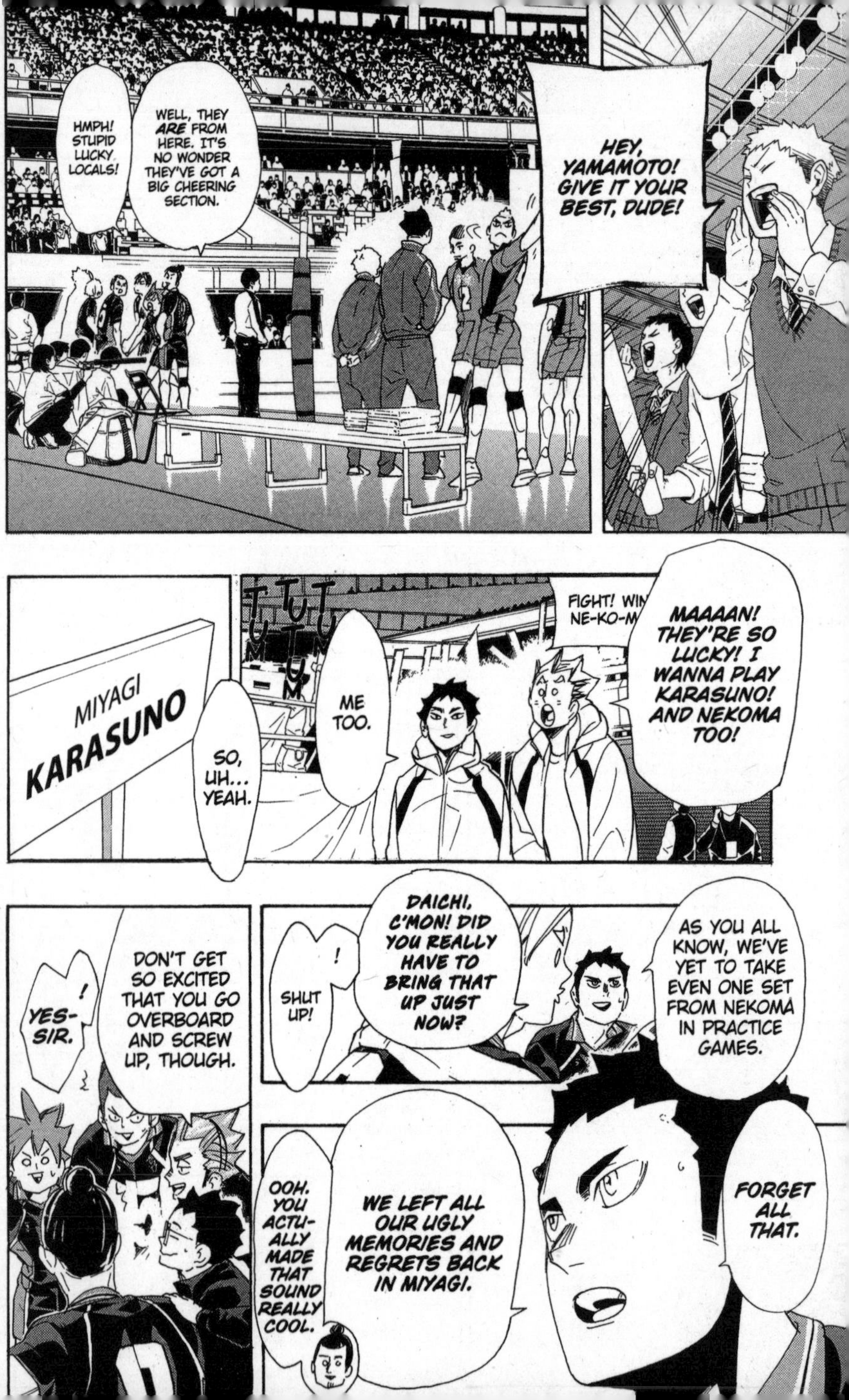
HEY, YAMAMOTO! GIVE IT YOUR BEST, DUDE!
WELL, THEY ARE FROM HERE. IT'S NO WONDER THEY'VE GOT A BIG CHEERING SECTION.
HMPH! STUPID LUCKY LOCALS!
MAAAAN! THEY'RE SO LUCKY! I WANNA PLAY KARASUNO! AND NEKOMA TOO!
FIGHT! WIN
NE-KO-M
ME TOO.
SO, UH... YEAH.
MIYAGI
KARASUNO
AS YOU ALL KNOW, WE'VE YET TO TAKE EVEN ONE SET FROM NEKOMA IN PRACTICE GAMES.
DAICHI, C'MON! DID YOU REALLY HAVE TO BRING THAT UP JUST NOW?
!
SHUT UP!
FORGET ALL THAT.
WE LEFT ALL OUR UGLY MEMORIES AND REGRETS BACK IN MIYAGI.
OOH. YOU ACTUALLY MADE THAT SOUND REALLY COOL.
DON'T GET SO EXCITED THAT YOU GO OVERBOARD AND SCREW UP, THOUGH.
!
YES-SIR.

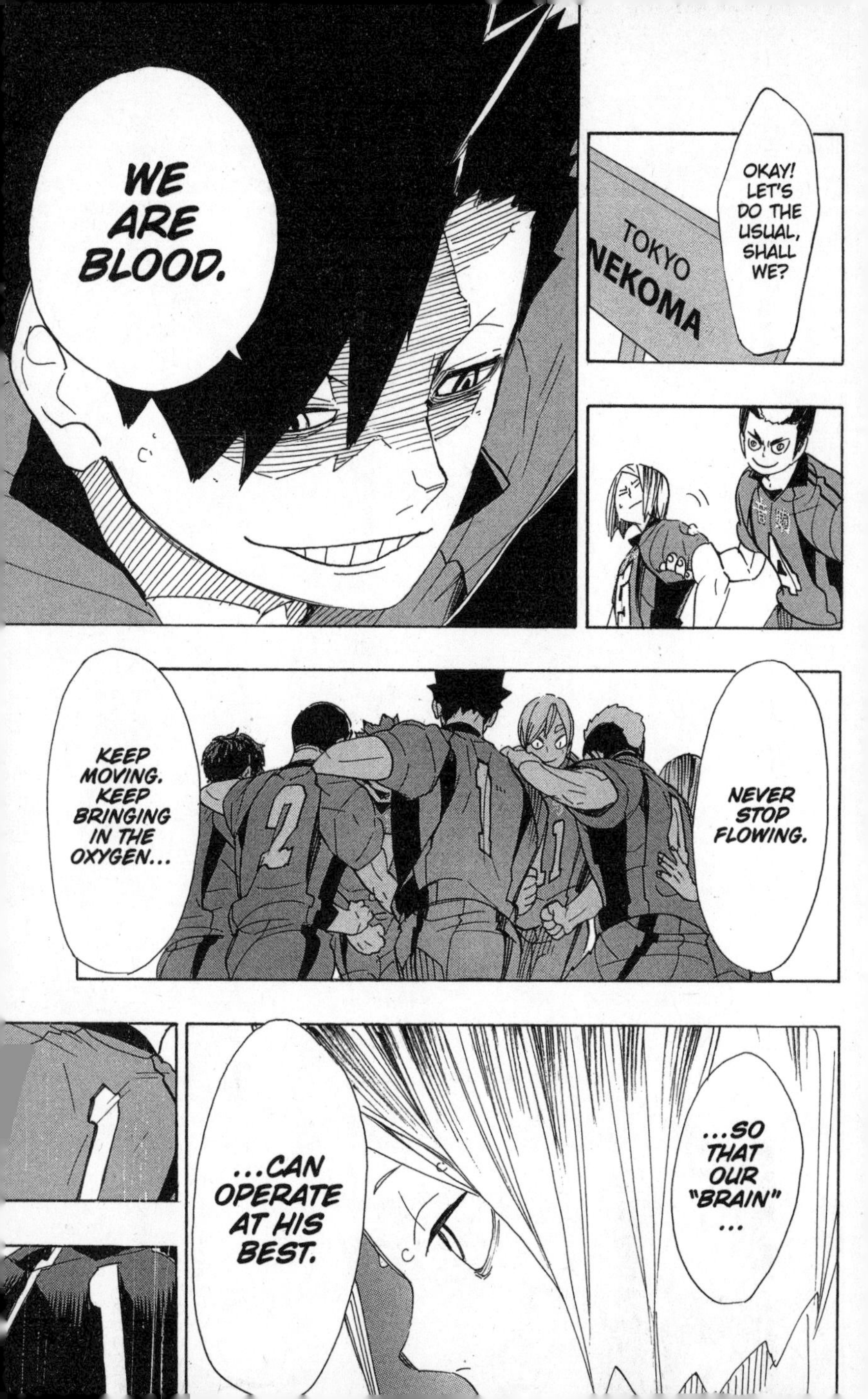
OKAY! LET'S DO THE USUAL, SHALL WE?
TOKYO NEKOMA
WE ARE BLOOD.
NEVER STOP FLOWING.
KEEP MOVING. KEEP BRINGING IN THE OXYGEN...
...SO THAT OUR "BRAIN"...
...CAN OPERATE AT HIS BEST.

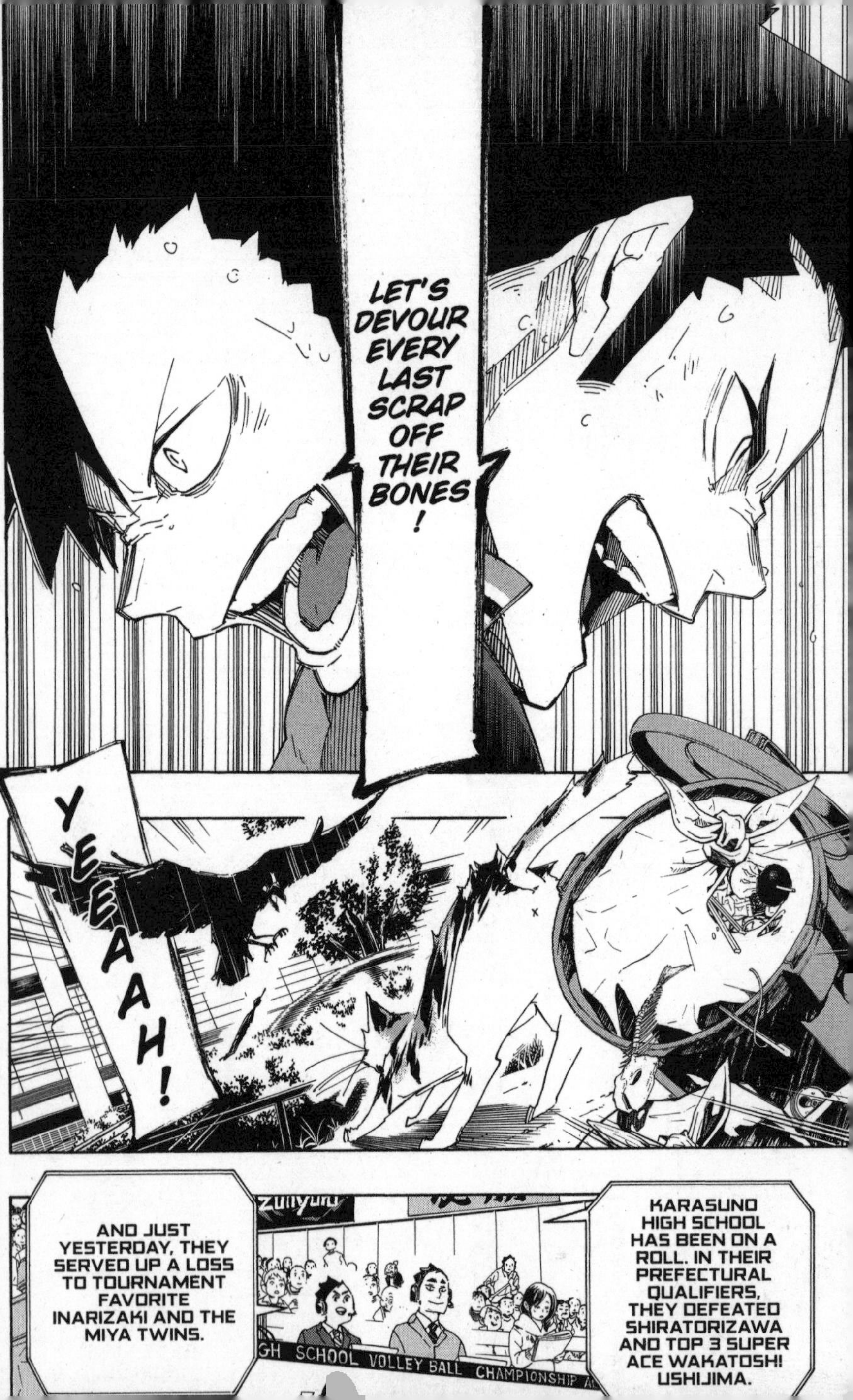
LET'S DEVOUR EVERY LAST SCRAP OFF THEIR BONES!
YEEAAH!
KARASUNO HIGH SCHOOL HAS BEEN ON A ROLL. IN THEIR PREFECTURAL QUALIFIERS, THEY DEFEATED SHIRATORIZAWA AND TOP 3 SUPER ACE WAKATOSHI USHIJIMA.
AND JUST YESTERDAY, THEY SERVED UP A LOSS TO TOURNAMENT FAVORITE INARIZAKI AND THE MIYA TWINS.
SCHOOL VOLLEY BALL CHAMPIONSHIP

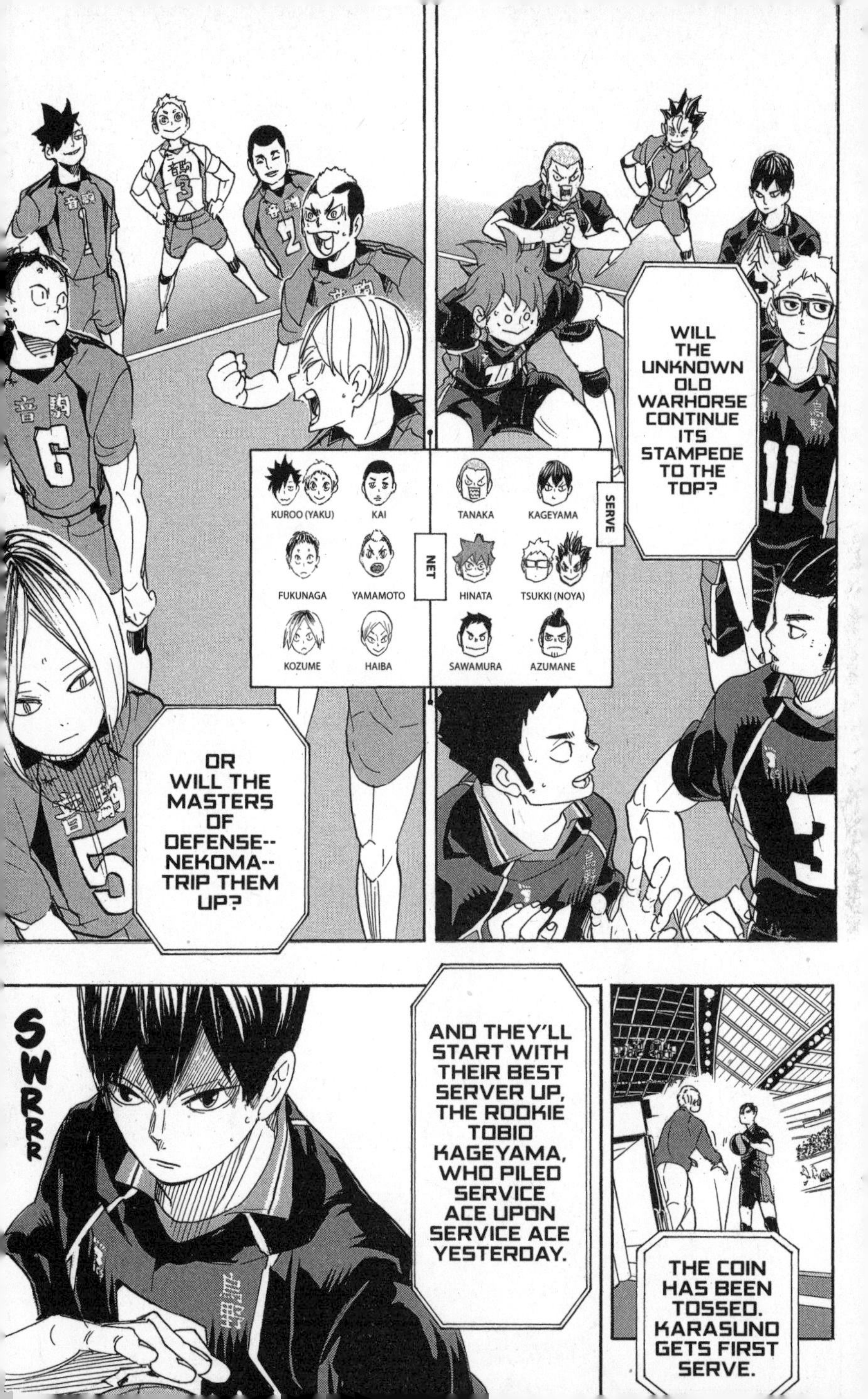
WILL THE UNKNOWN OLD WARHORSE CONTINUE ITS STAMPEDE TO THE TOP?
OR WILL THE MASTERS OF DEFENSE--NEKOMA--TRIP THEM UP?
SERVE
TANAKA
KAGEYAMA
HINATA
TSUKKI (NOYA)
SAWAMURA
AZUMANE
NET
KUROO (YAKU)
KAI
FUKUNAGA
YAMAMOTO
KOZUME
HAIBA
THE COIN HAS BEEN TOSSED. KARASUNO GETS FIRST SERVE.
AND THEY'LL START WITH THEIR BEST SERVER UP, THE ROOKIE TOBIO KAGEYAMA, WHO PILED SERVICE ACE UPON SERVICE ACE YESTERDAY.
SWRRR

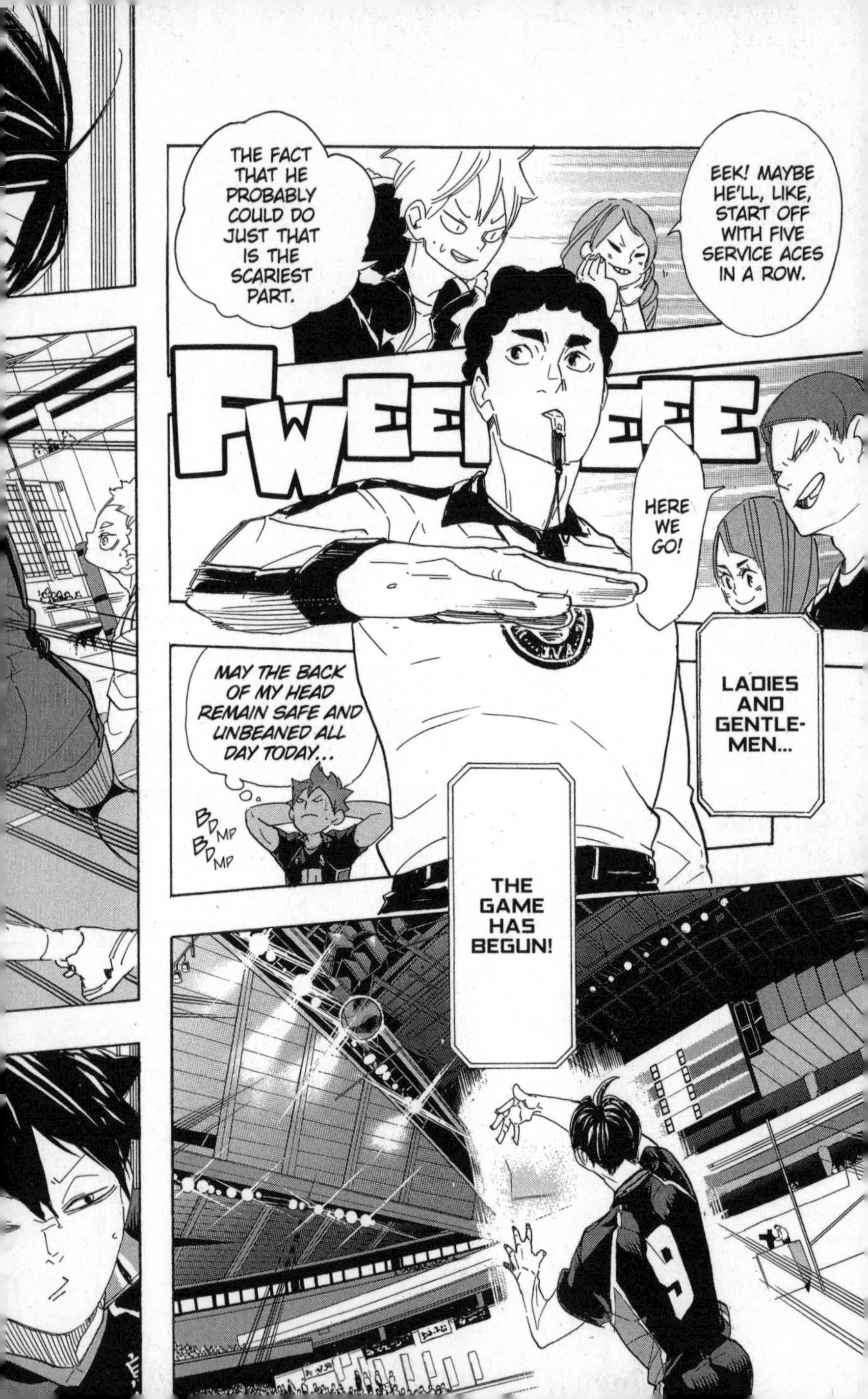
EEK! MAYBE HE'LL, LIKE, START OFF WITH FIVE SERVICE ACES IN A ROW.
THE FACT THAT HE PROBABLY COULD DO JUST THAT IS THE SCARIEST PART.
FWEEEEEE
HERE WE GO!
LADIES AND GENTLE-MEN...
MAY THE BACK OF MY HEAD REMAIN SAFE AND UNBEANED ALL DAY TODAY...
BDMP BDMP
THE GAME HAS BEGUN!

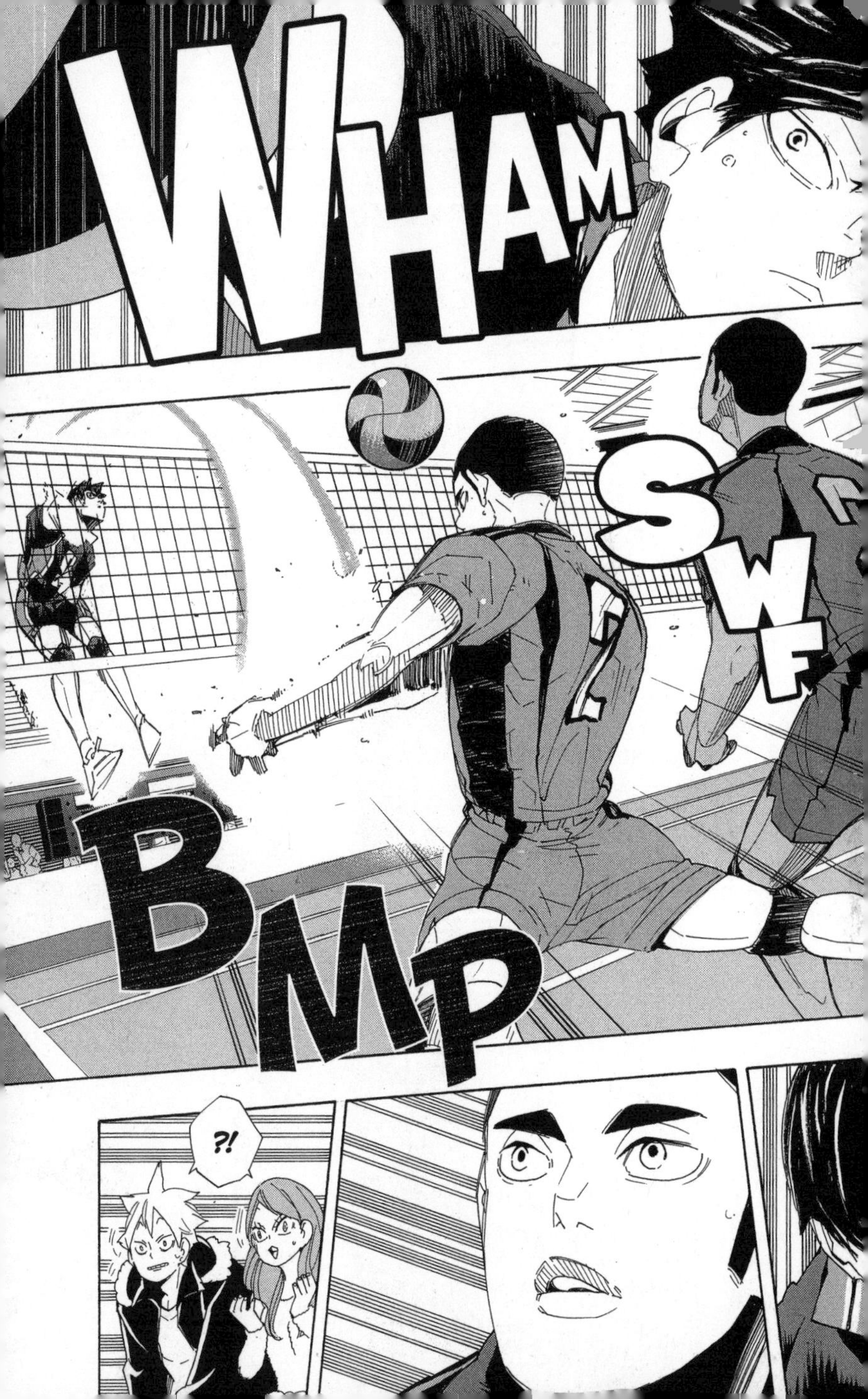
WHAM
SWF
BMP
?!

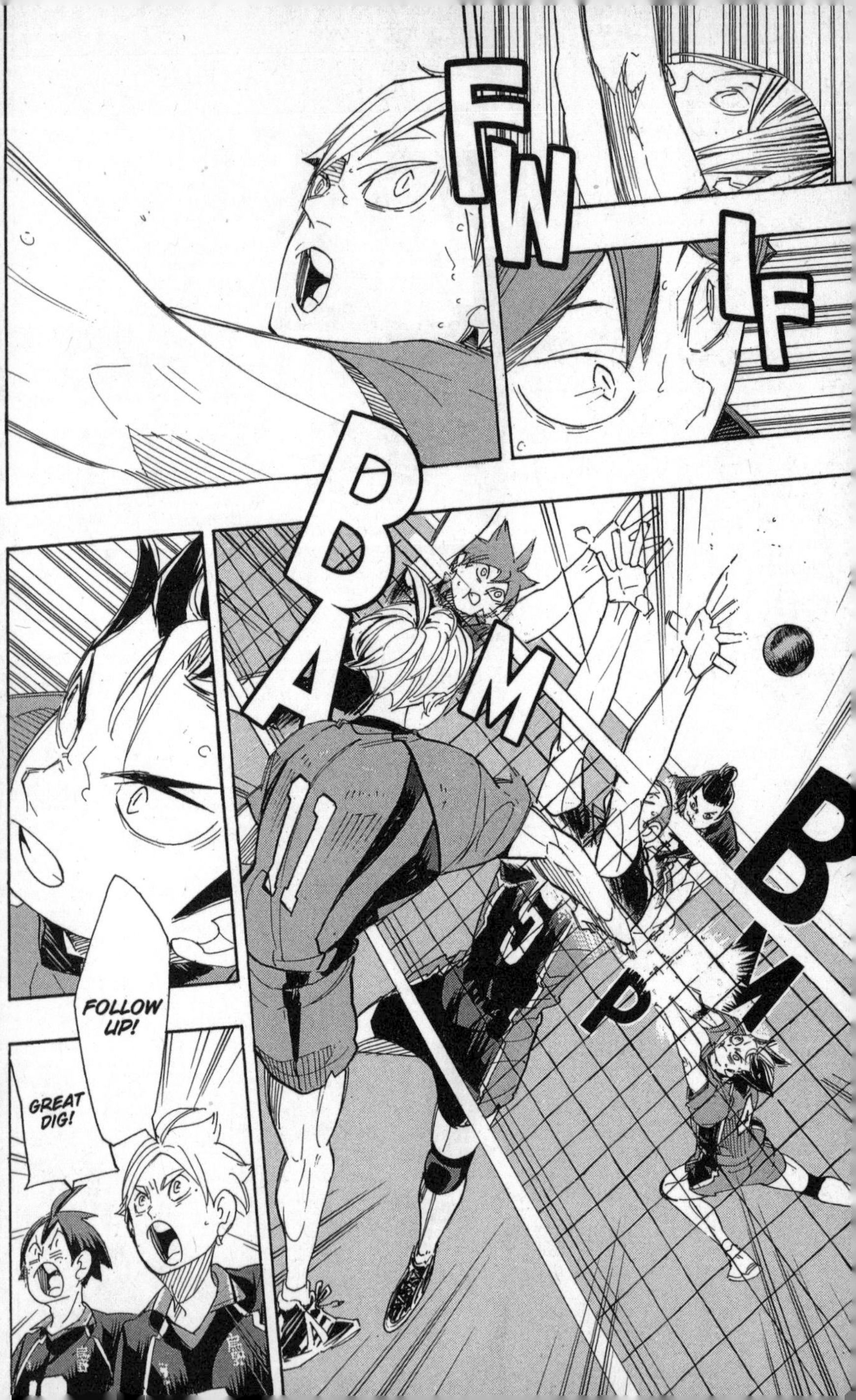
FWIF
BAM
BAMP
FOLLOW UP!
GREAT DIG!

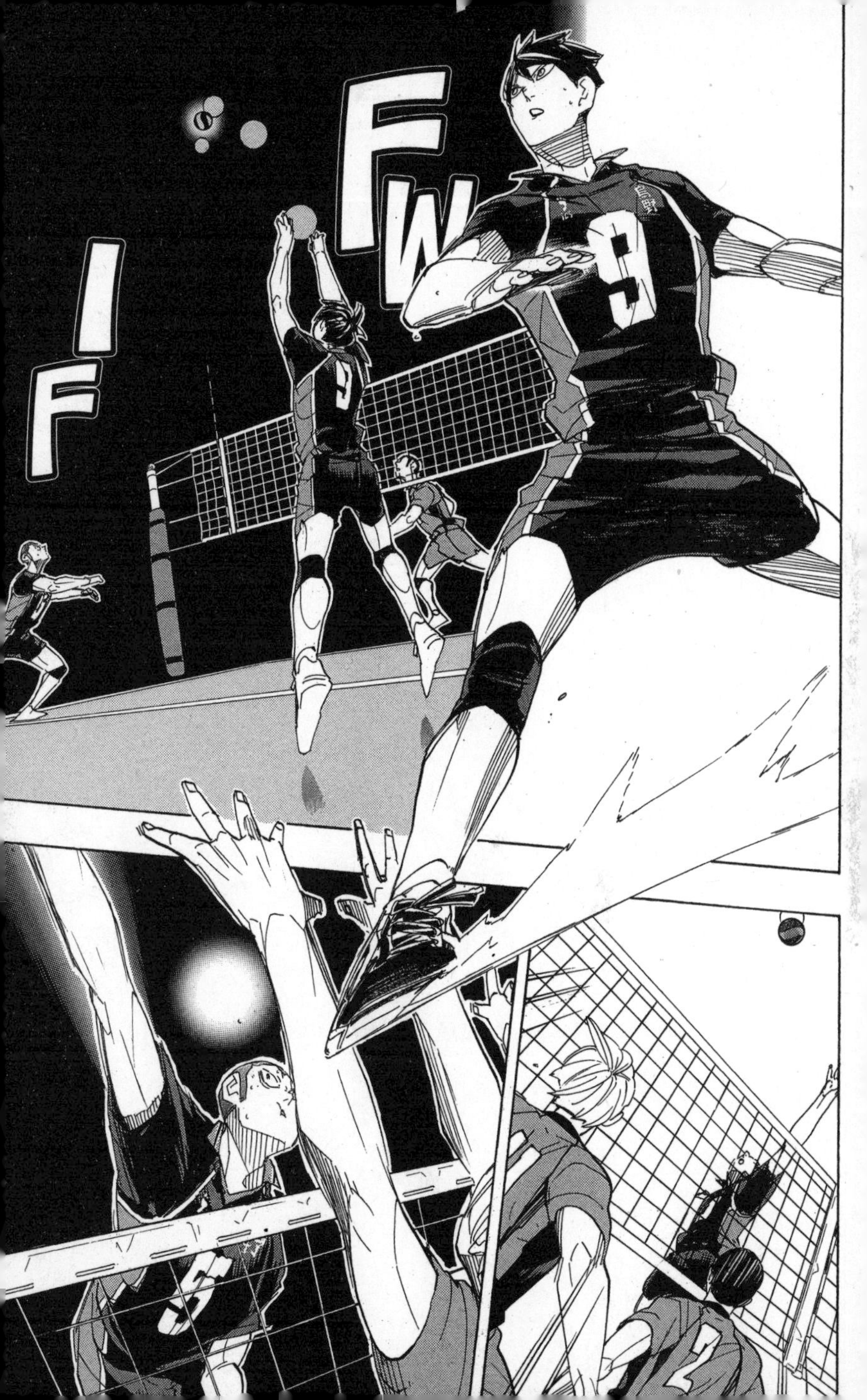
FW
IF

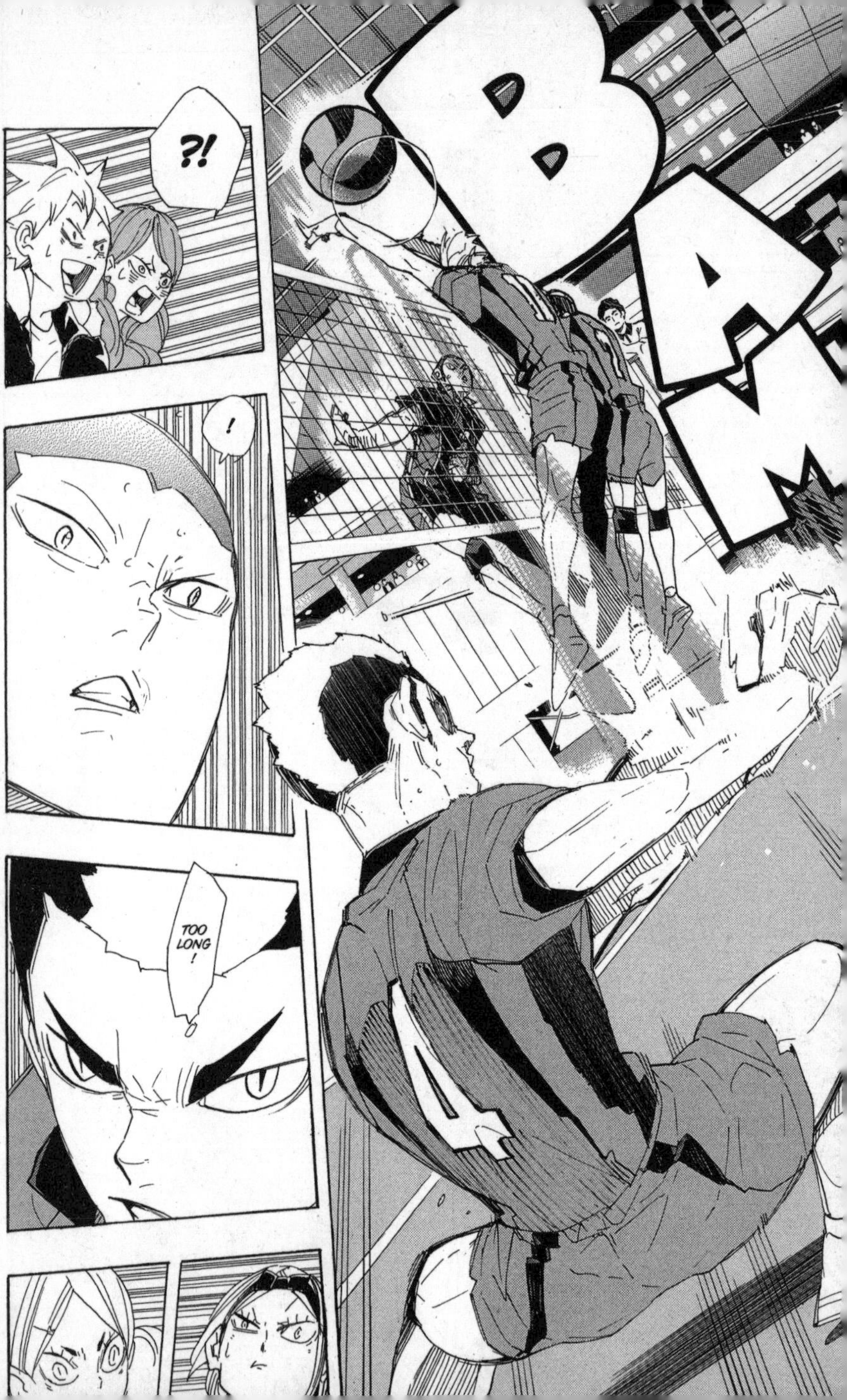
BAM
?!
!
TOO LONG!

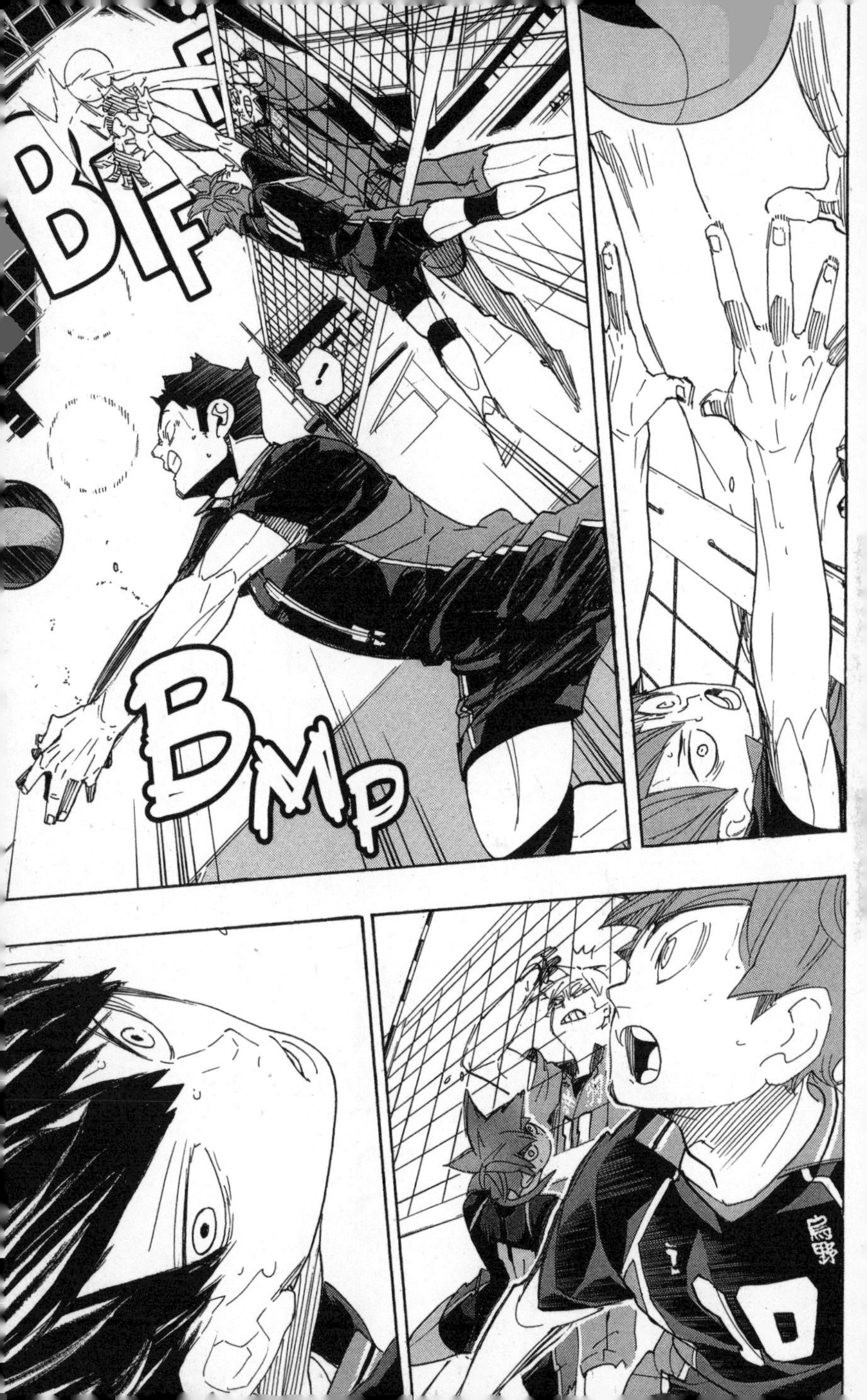
BIF
!
BMP

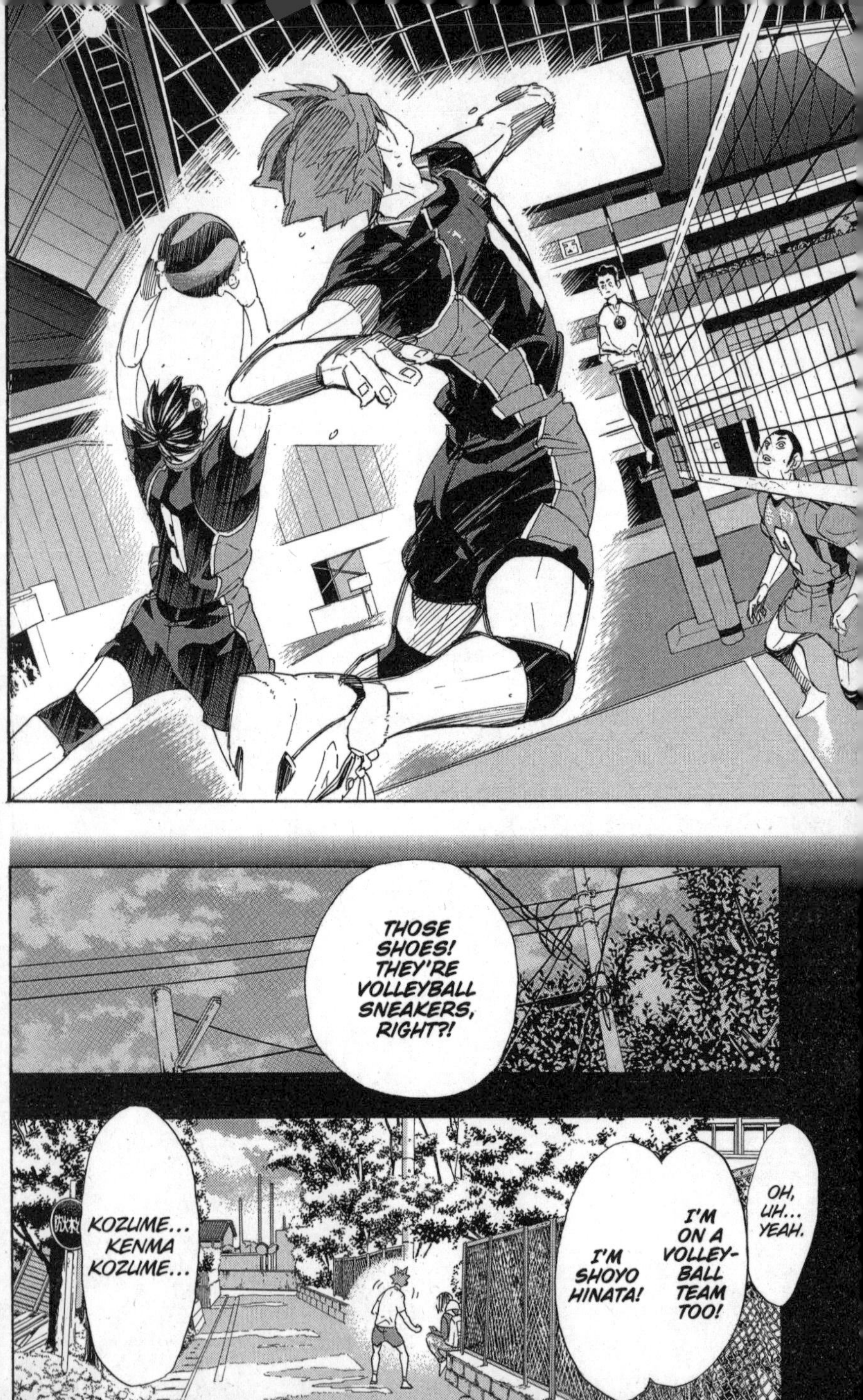
THOSE SHOES! THEY'RE VOLLEYBALL SNEAKERS, RIGHT?!
OH, UH... YEAH.
I'M ON A VOLLEY-BALL TEAM TOO!
I'M SHOYO HINATA!
KOZUME... KENMA KOZUME...

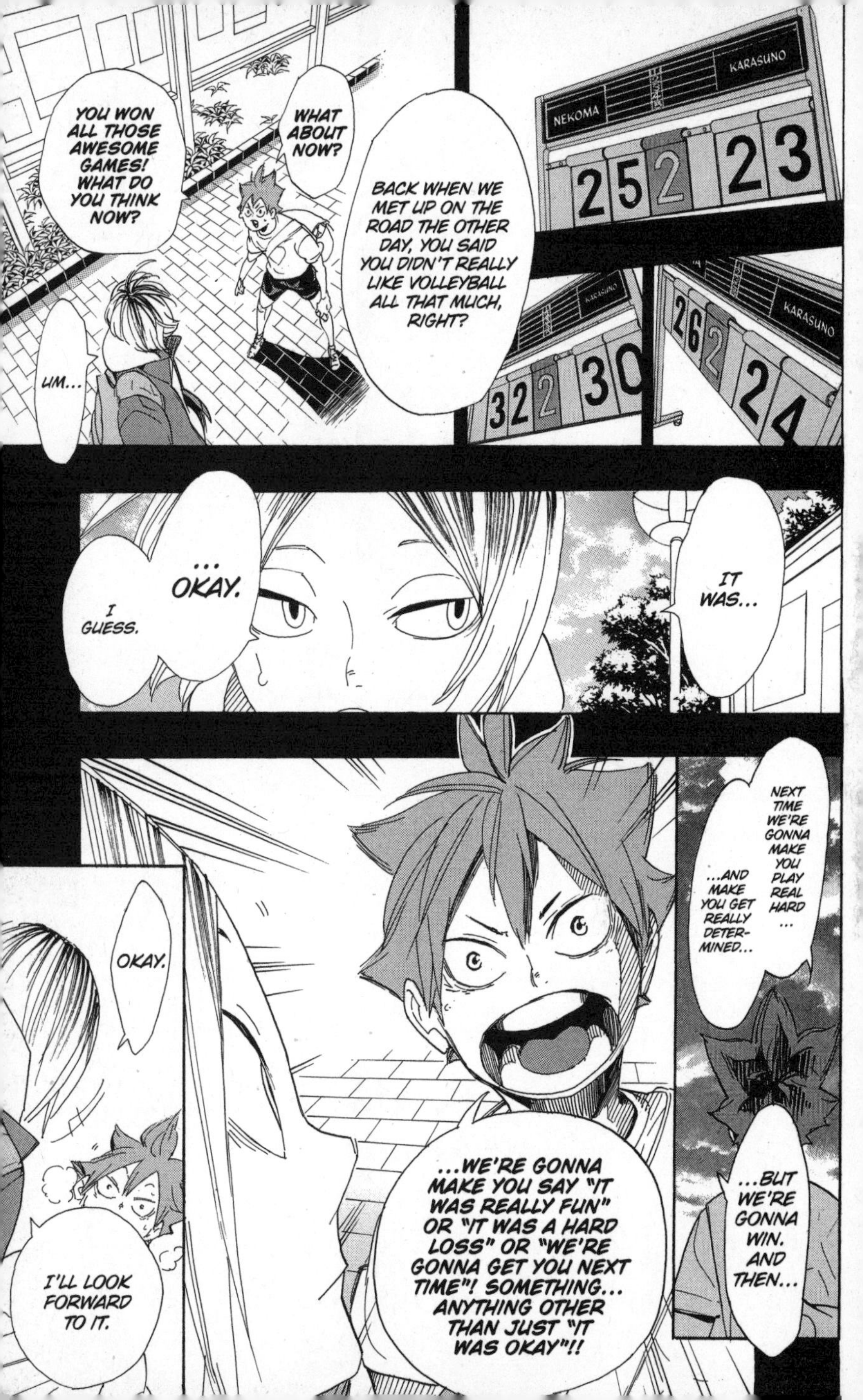
NEKOMA
KARASUNO
25 2 23
32 2 30
26 2 24
BACK WHEN WE MET UP ON THE ROAD THE OTHER DAY, YOU SAID YOU DIDN'T REALLY LIKE VOLLEYBALL ALL THAT MUCH, RIGHT?
WHAT ABOUT NOW?
YOU WON ALL THOSE AWESOME GAMES! WHAT DO YOU THINK NOW?
UM...
IT WAS...
... OKAY.
I GUESS.
NEXT TIME WE'RE GONNA MAKE YOU PLAY REAL HARD...
...AND MAKE YOU GET REALLY DETERMINED...
...BUT WE'RE GONNA WIN. AND THEN...
...WE'RE GONNA MAKE YOU SAY "IT WAS REALLY FUN" OR "IT WAS A HARD LOSS" OR "WE'RE GONNA GET YOU NEXT TIME"! SOMETHING... ANYTHING OTHER THAN JUST "IT WAS OKAY"!!
OKAY.
I'LL LOOK FORWARD TO IT.

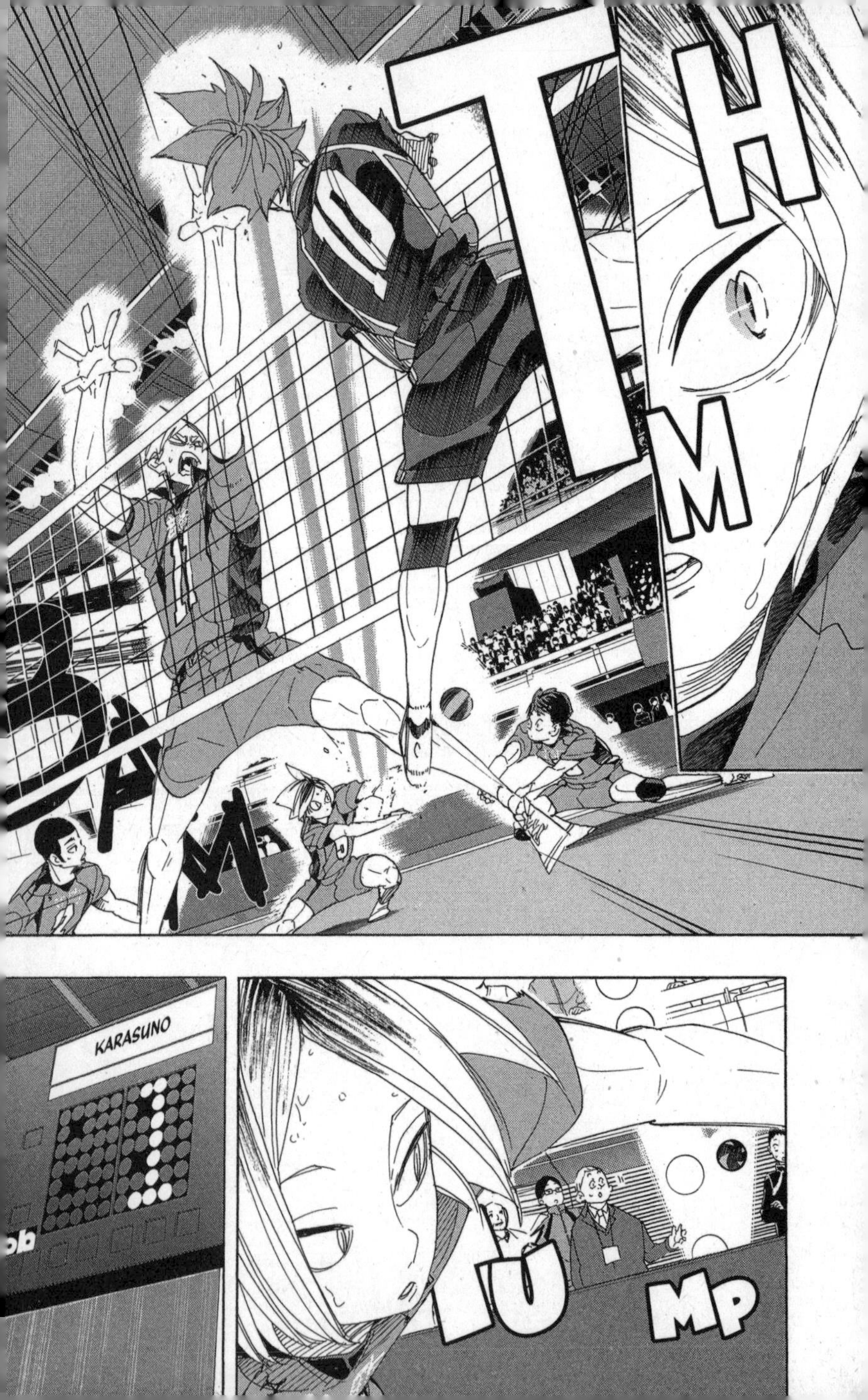
THM
BAM
KARASUNO

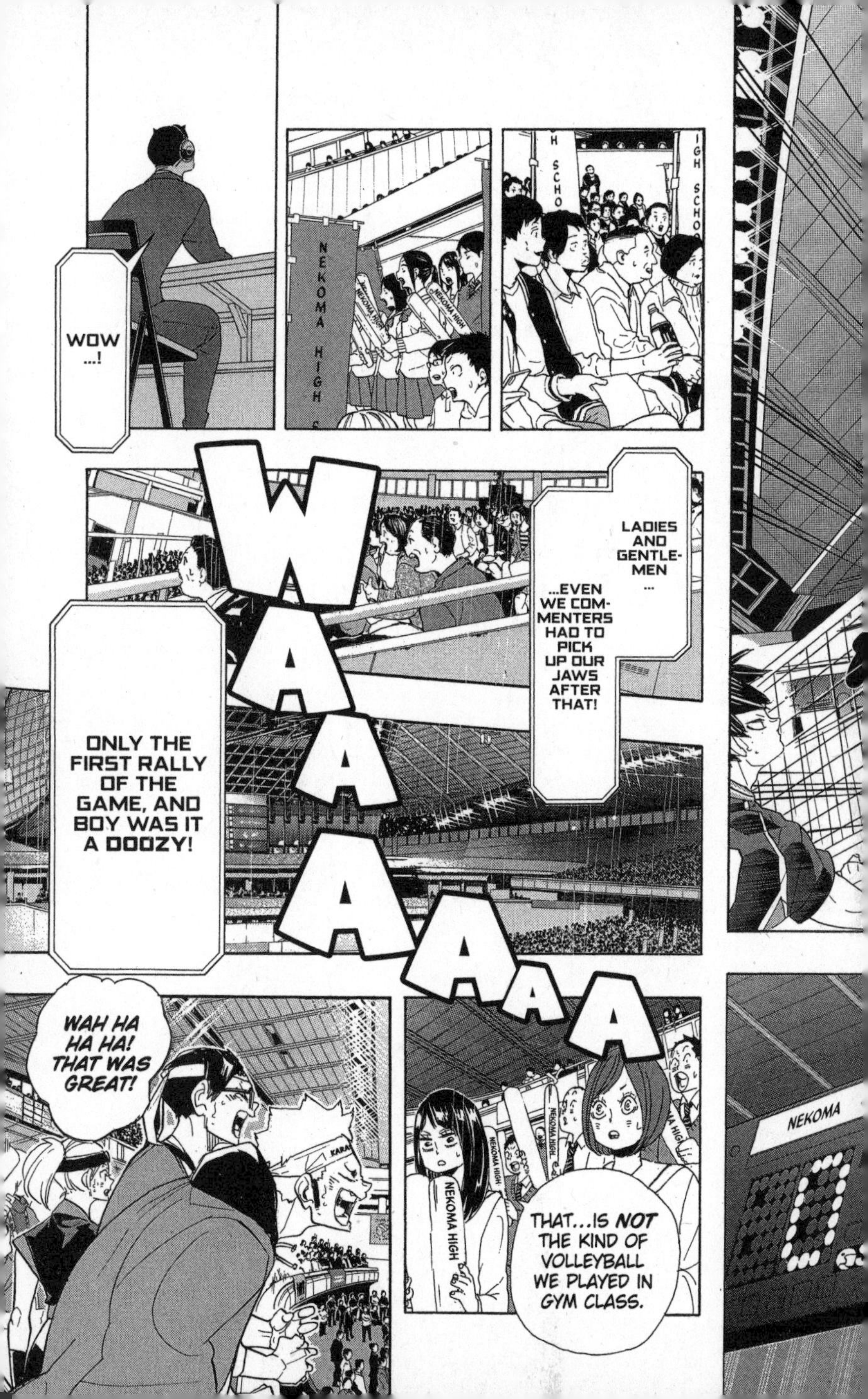
WOW ...!
WAAAAAAA
LADIES AND GENTLEMEN ...
...EVEN WE COMMENTERS HAD TO PICK UP OUR JAWS AFTER THAT!
ONLY THE FIRST RALLY OF THE GAME, AND BOY WAS IT A DOOZY!
NEKOMA
THAT...IS NOT THE KIND OF VOLLEYBALL WE PLAYED IN GYM CLASS.
WAH HA HA HA! THAT WAS GREAT!

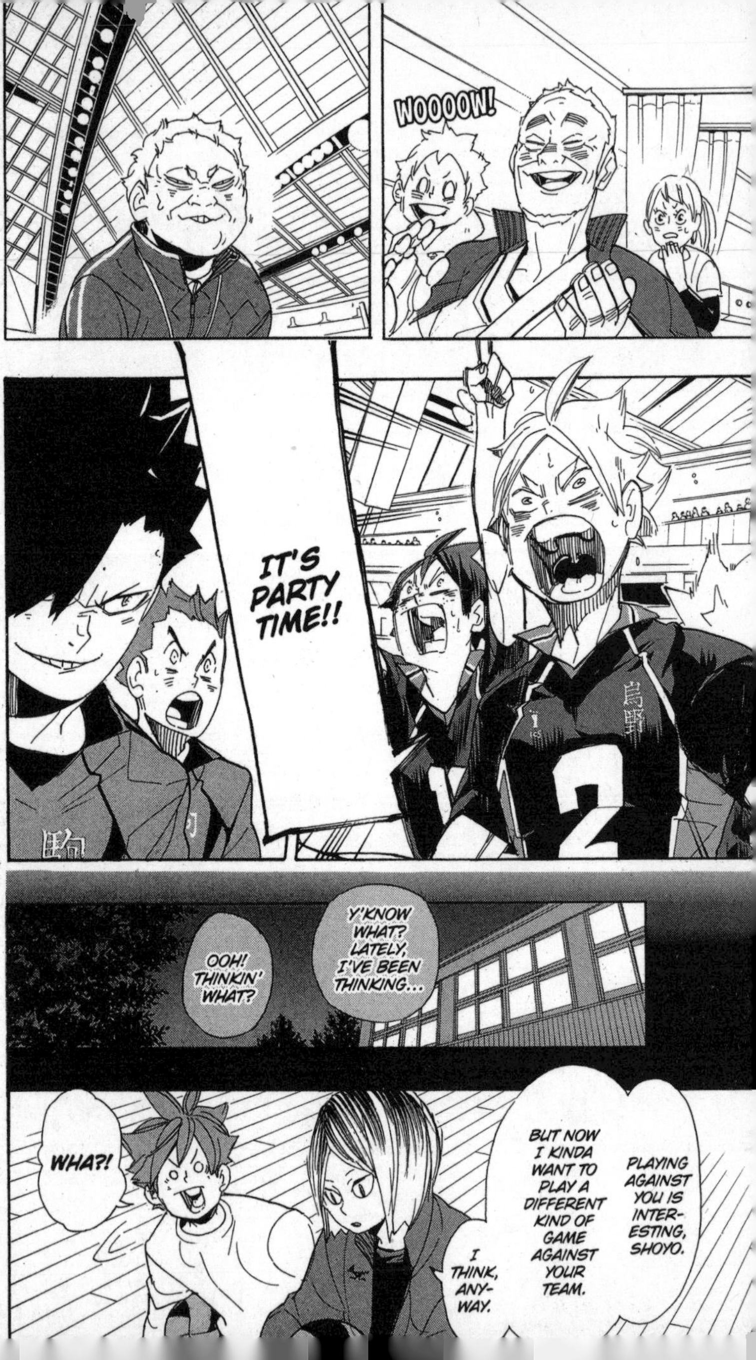
WOOOOW!
IT'S PARTY TIME!!
Y'KNOW WHAT? LATELY, I'VE BEEN THINKING...
OOH! THINKIN' WHAT?
PLAYING AGAINST YOU IS INTER-ESTING, SHOYO.
BUT NOW I KINDA WANT TO PLAY A DIFFERENT KIND OF GAME AGAINST YOUR TEAM.
I THINK, ANY-WAY.
WHA?!

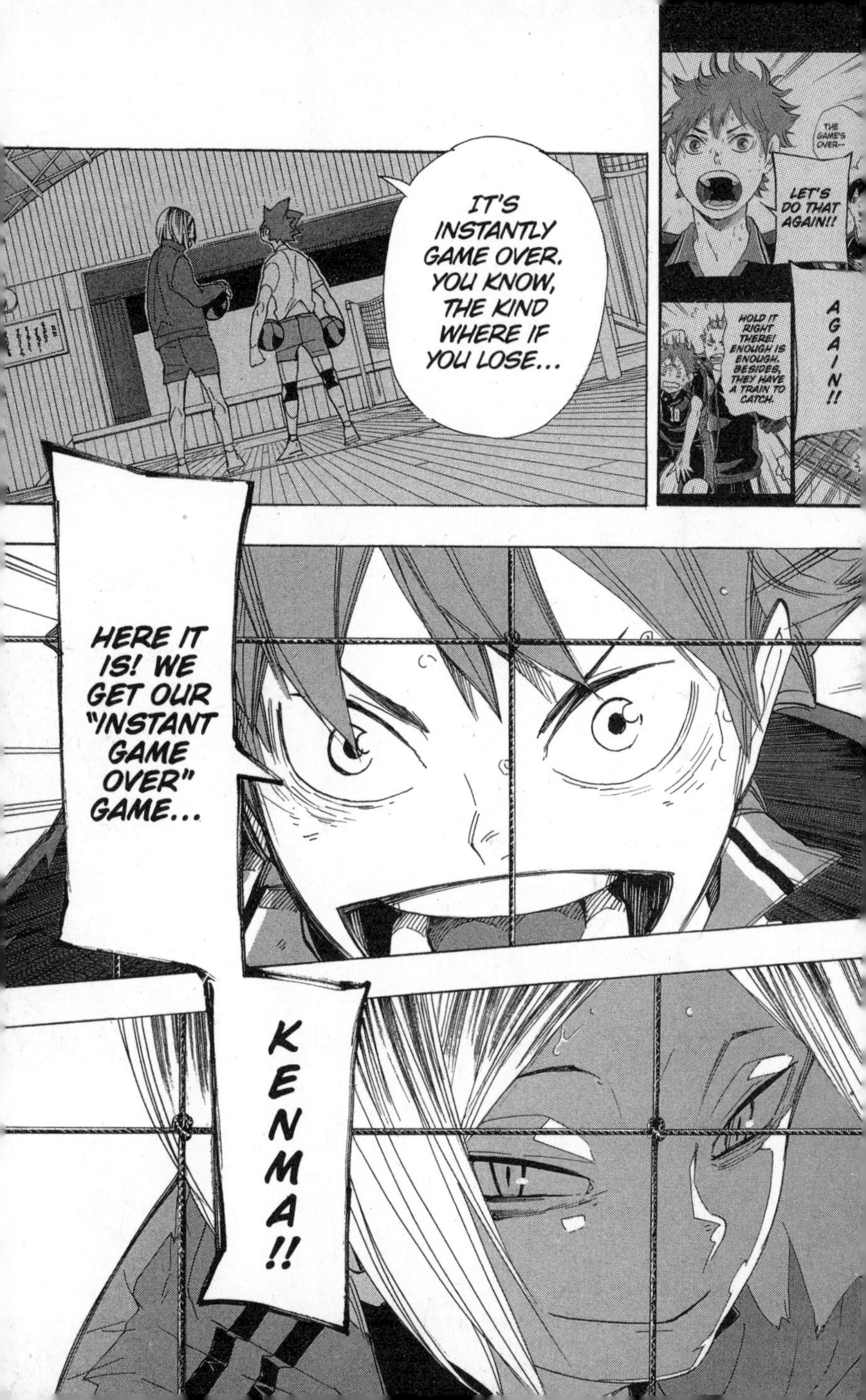
THE GAME'S OVER—
LET'S DO THAT AGAIN!!
AGAIN!!
HOLD IT RIGHT THERE! ENOUGH IS ENOUGH. BESIDES, THEY HAVE A TRAIN TO CATCH.
IT'S INSTANTLY GAME OVER. YOU KNOW, THE KIND WHERE IF YOU LOSE...
HERE IT IS! WE GET OUR "INSTANT GAME OVER" GAME...
KENMA!!

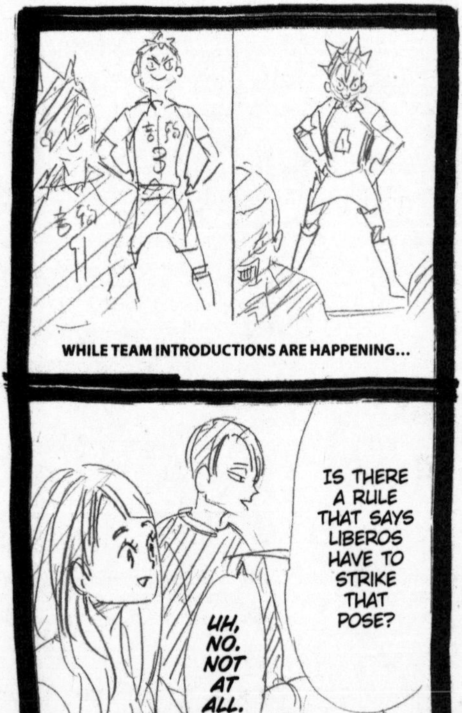
WHILE TEAM INTRODUCTIONS ARE HAPPENING...
IS THERE A RULE THAT SAYS LIBEROS HAVE TO STRIKE THAT POSE?
UH, NO. NOT AT ALL.

CHAPTER 295: The Monster Crows

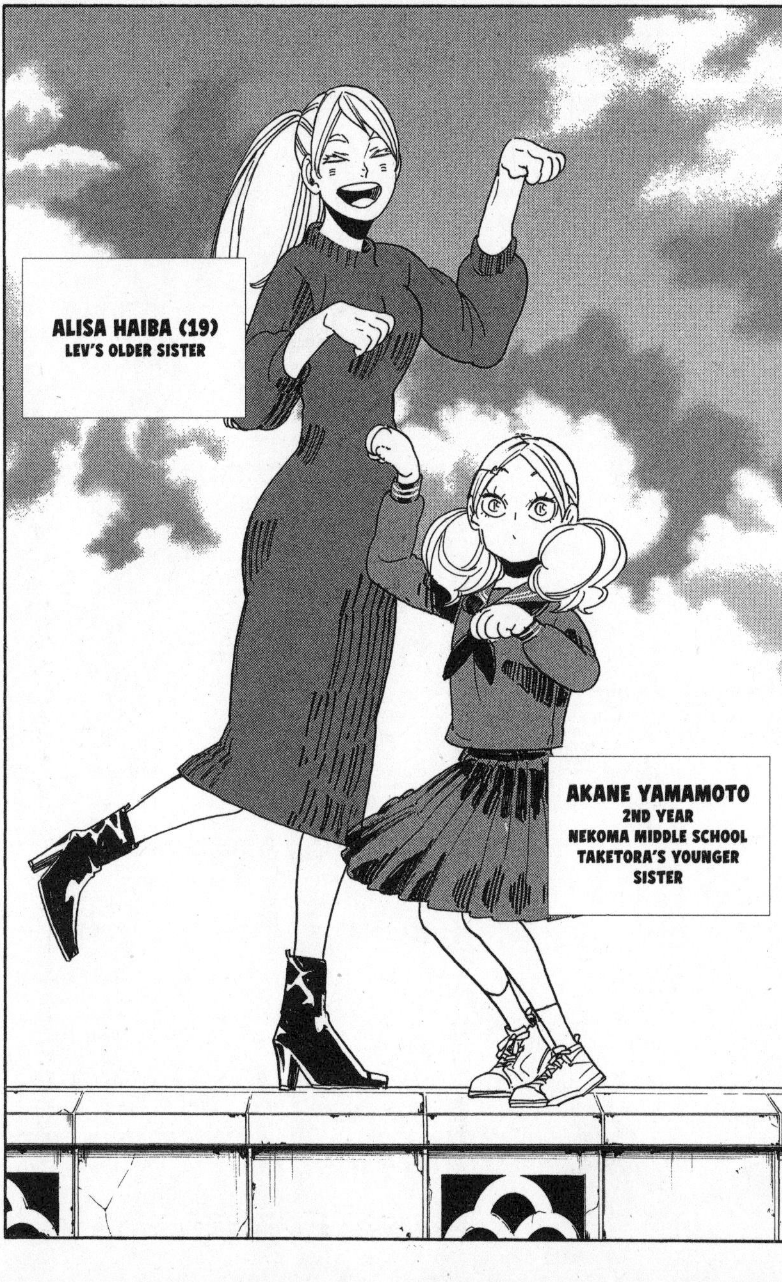
ALISA HAIBA (19)
LEV'S OLDER SISTER
AKANE YAMAMOTO
2ND YEAR
NEKOMA MIDDLE SCHOOL
TAKETORA'S YOUNGER
SISTER

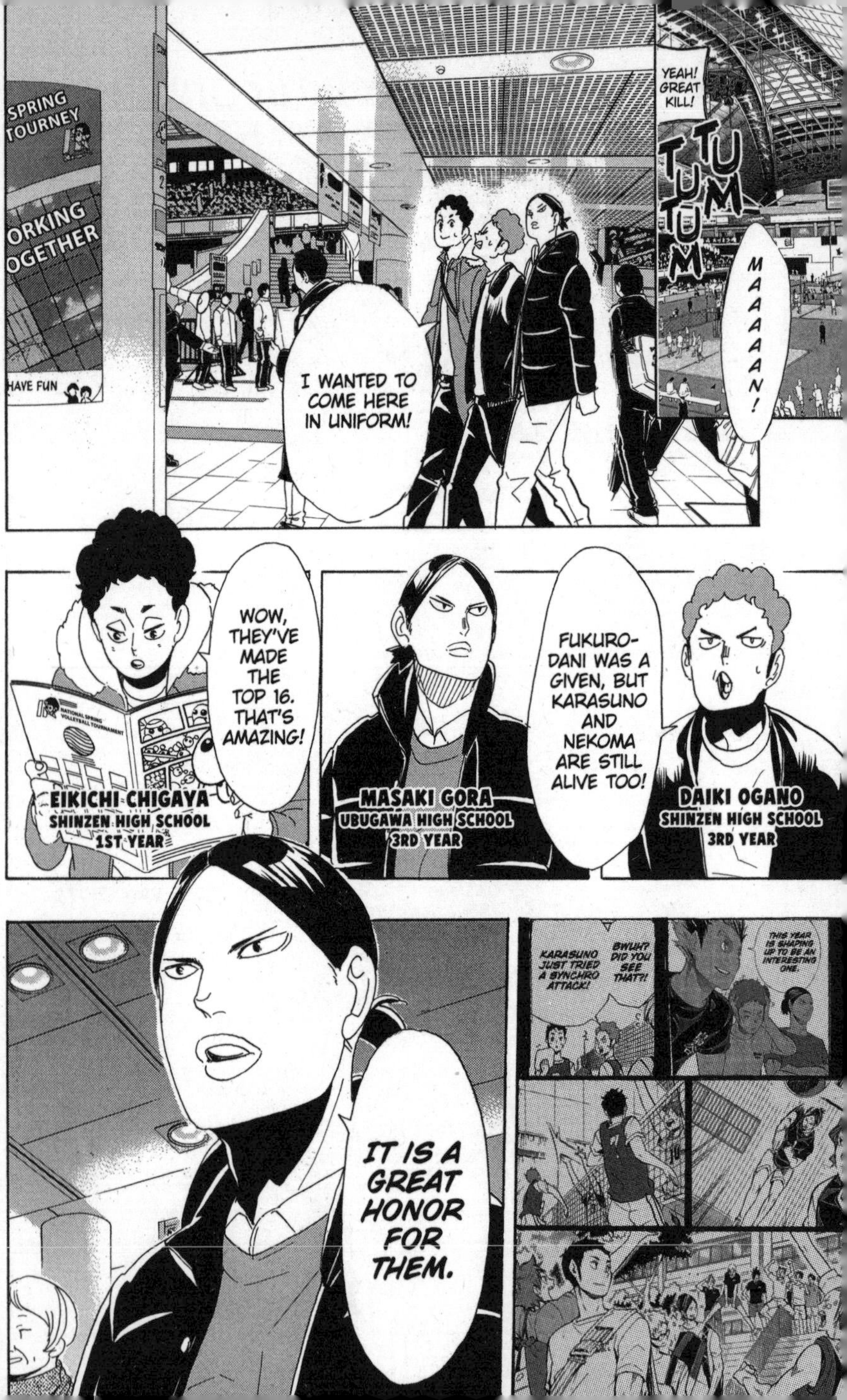

YEAH! GREAT KILL!
TUM TUM TUM TUM
MAAAAAN!
SPRING TOURNEY
ORKING OGETHER
HAVE FUN
I WANTED TO COME HERE IN UNIFORM!
FUKURO-DANI WAS A GIVEN, BUT KARASUNO AND NEKOMA ARE STILL ALIVE TOO!
DAIKI OGANO SHINZEN HIGH SCHOOL 3RD YEAR
MASAKI GORA UBUGAWA HIGH SCHOOL 3RD YEAR
WOW, THEY'VE MADE THE TOP 16. THAT'S AMAZING!
EIKICHI CHIGAYA SHINZEN HIGH SCHOOL 1ST YEAR
THIS YEAR IS SHAPING UP TO BE AN INTERESTING ONE.
BWUH? DID YOU SEE THAT?!
KARASUNO JUST TRIED A SYNCHRO ATTACK!
IT IS A GREAT HONOR FOR THEM.

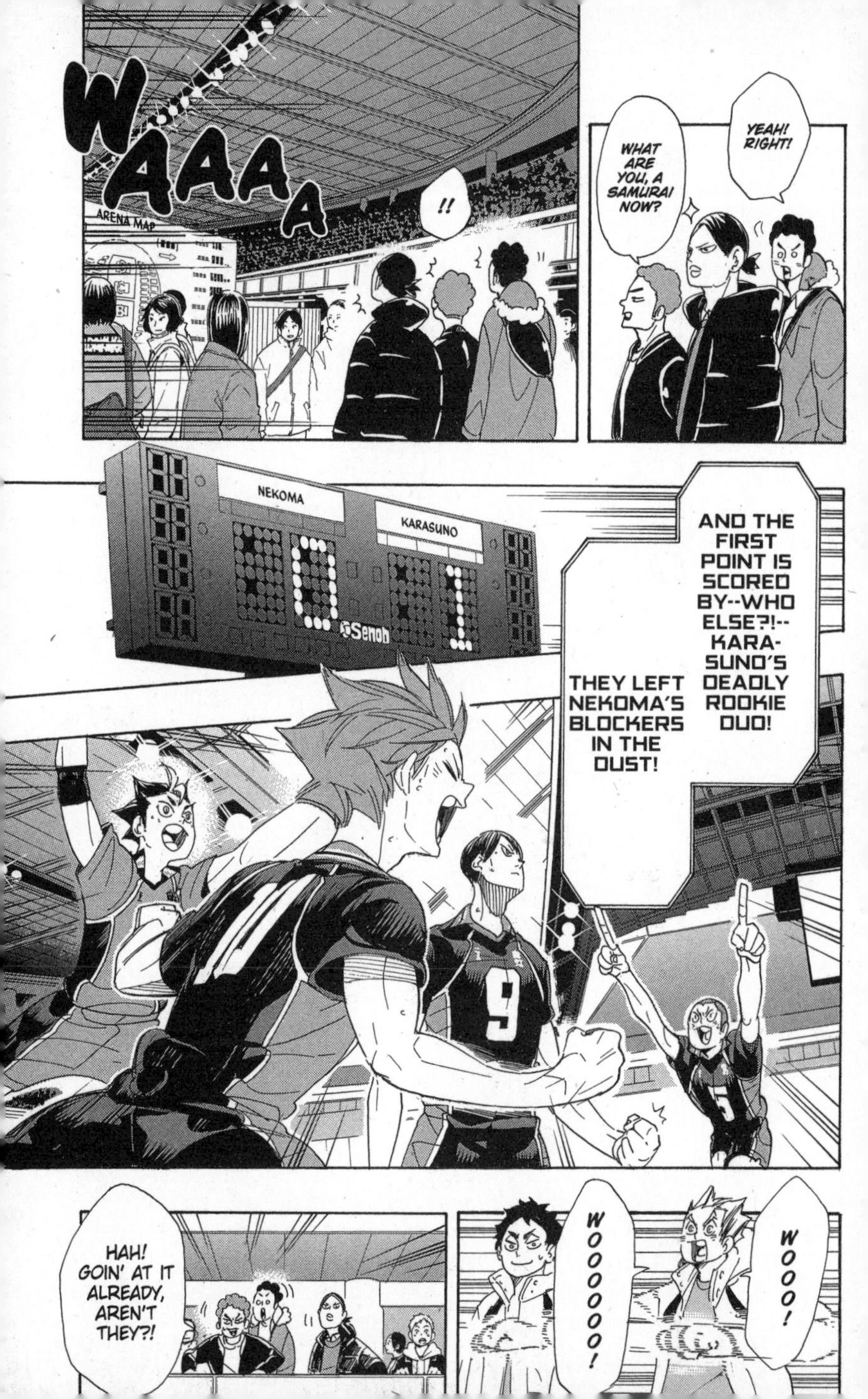
WHAT ARE YOU, A SAMURAI NOW?
YEAH! RIGHT!
WAAAAA
ARENA MAP
!!
NEKOMA
KARASUNO
0
1
Senoh
AND THE FIRST POINT IS SCORED BY--WHO ELSE?!--KARASUNO'S DEADLY ROOKIE DUO!
THEY LEFT NEKOMA'S BLOCKERS IN THE DUST!
WOOO!
WOOOOOOO!
HAH! GOIN' AT IT ALREADY, AREN'T THEY?!

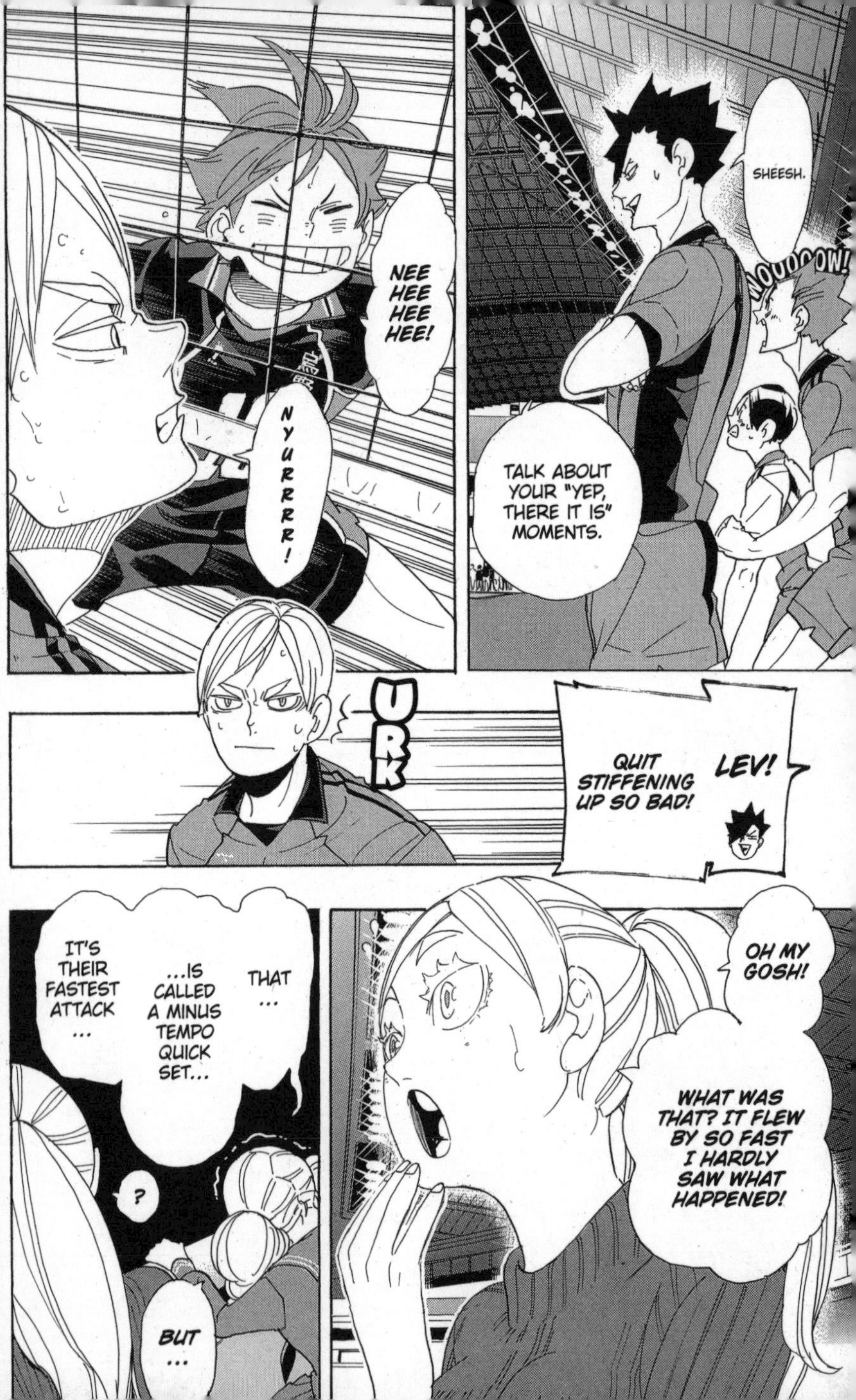
SHEESH.
WOOOOOW!
TALK ABOUT YOUR "YEP, THERE IT IS" MOMENTS.
NEE HEE HEE HEE!
NYURRRR!
LEV!
QUIT STIFFENING UP SO BAD!
URK
OH MY GOSH!
WHAT WAS THAT? IT FLEW BY SO FAST I HARDLY SAW WHAT HAPPENED!
THAT ...
...IS CALLED A MINUS TEMPO QUICK SET...
IT'S THEIR FASTEST ATTACK ...
?
BUT ...

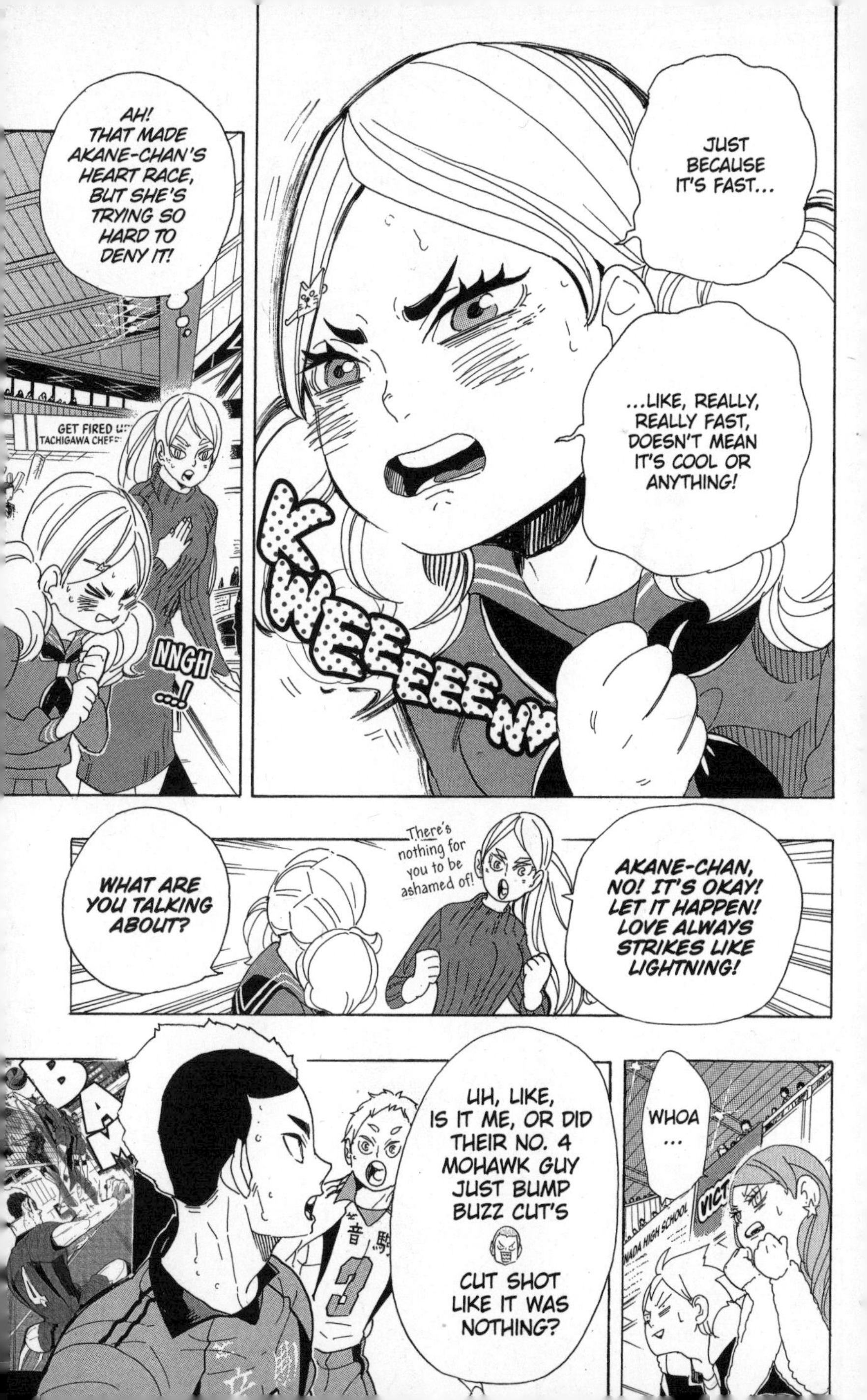
JUST BECAUSE IT'S FAST...
...LIKE, REALLY, REALLY FAST, DOESN'T MEAN IT'S COOL OR ANYTHING!
KWEEEEEN
AH! THAT MADE AKANE-CHAN'S HEART RACE, BUT SHE'S TRYING SO HARD TO DENY IT!
GET FIRED
TACHIGAWA
NNGH ...!
AKANE-CHAN, NO! IT'S OKAY! LET IT HAPPEN! LOVE ALWAYS STRIKES LIKE LIGHTNING!
There's nothing for you to be ashamed of!
WHAT ARE YOU TALKING ABOUT?
WHOA ...
NADA HIGH SCHOOL
VICT
UH, LIKE, IS IT ME, OR DID THEIR NO. 4 MOHAWK GUY JUST BUMP BUZZ CUT'S CUT SHOT LIKE IT WAS NOTHING?
BAM

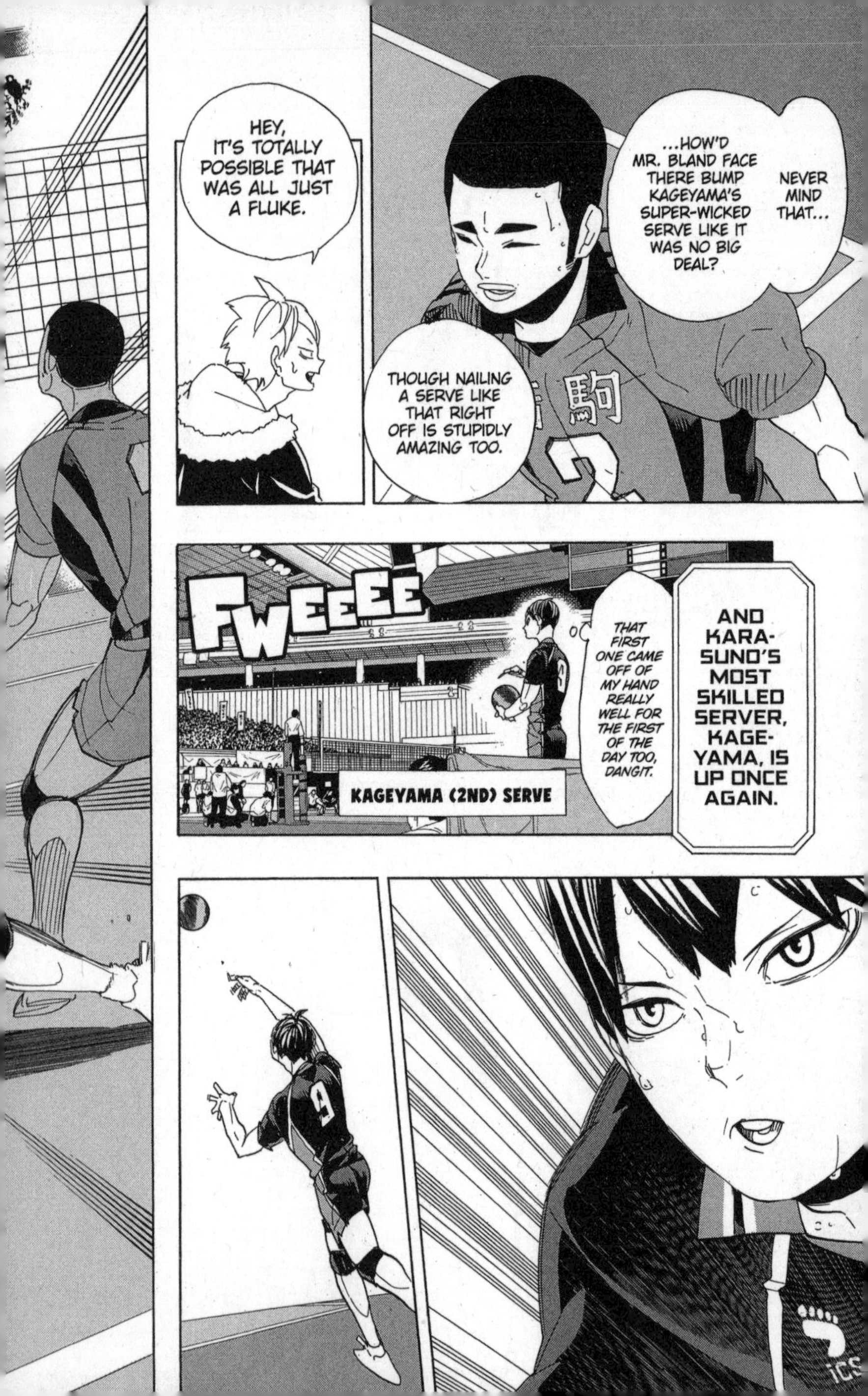
NEVER MIND THAT...
...HOW'D MR. BLAND FACE THERE BUMP KAGEYAMA'S SUPER-WICKED SERVE LIKE IT WAS NO BIG DEAL?
THOUGH NAILING A SERVE LIKE THAT RIGHT OFF IS STUPIDLY AMAZING TOO.
HEY, IT'S TOTALLY POSSIBLE THAT WAS ALL JUST A FLUKE.
AND KARASUNO'S MOST SKILLED SERVER, KAGEYAMA, IS UP ONCE AGAIN.
THAT FIRST ONE CAME OFF OF MY HAND REALLY WELL FOR THE FIRST OF THE DAY TOO, DANGIT.
FWEEEE
KAGEYAMA (2ND) SERVE

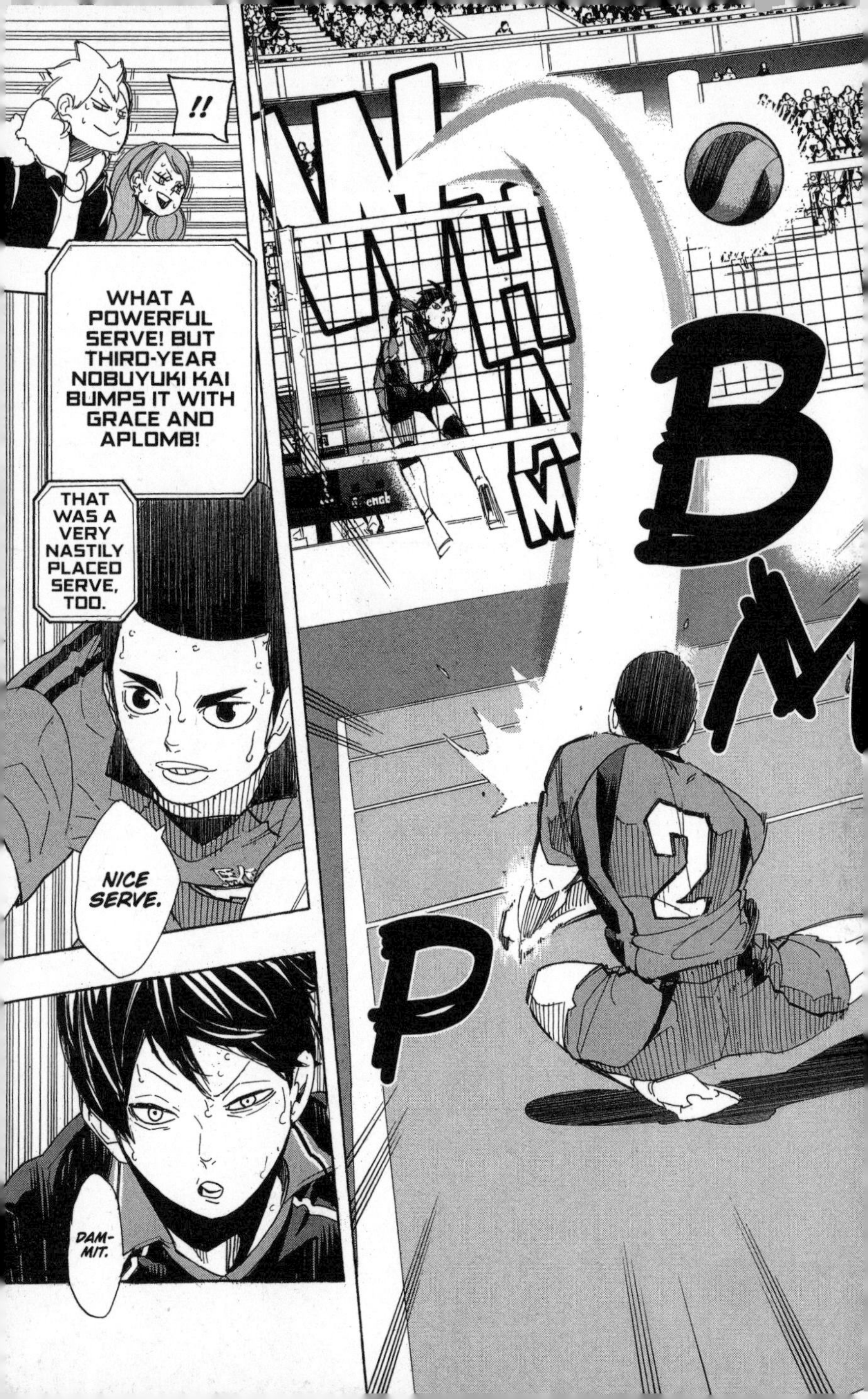
WHAM
!!
WHAT A POWERFUL SERVE! BUT THIRD-YEAR NOBUYUKI KAI BUMPS IT WITH GRACE AND APLOMB!
THAT WAS A VERY NASTILY PLACED SERVE, TOO.
NICE SERVE.
DAM-MIT.

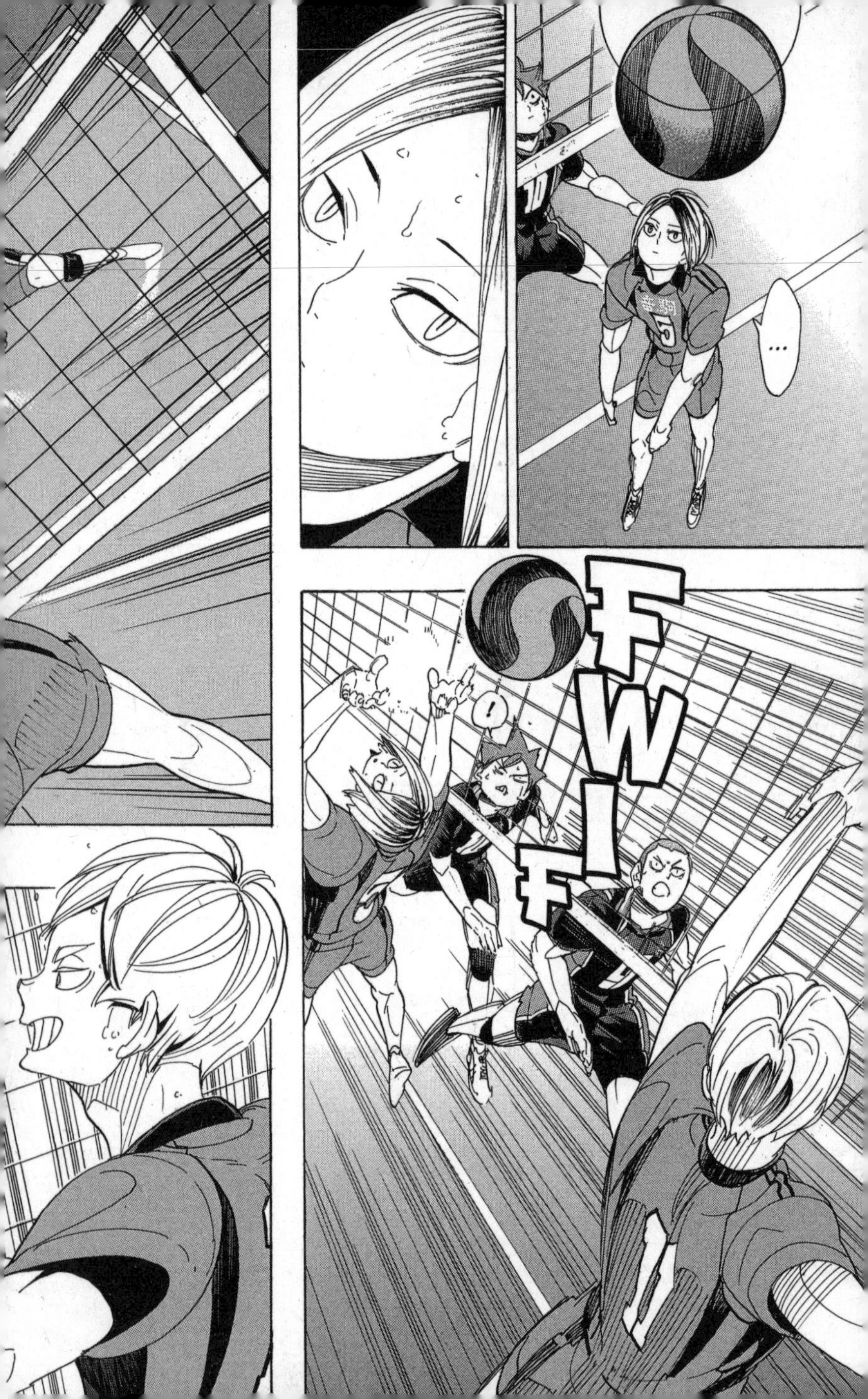
...
!
FWIF

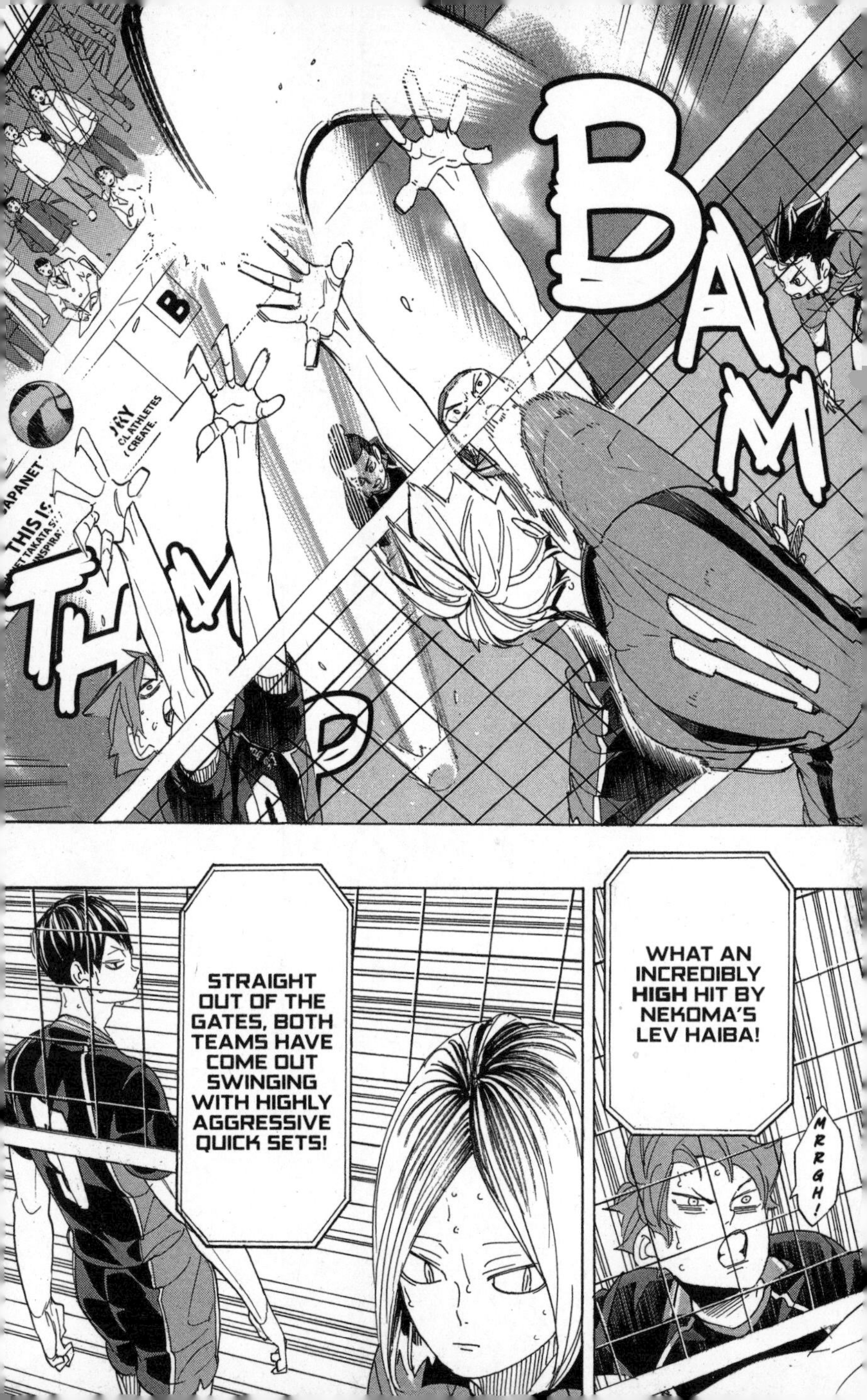
BAM
THUMP
WHAT AN INCREDIBLY HIGH HIT BY NEKOMA'S LEV HAIBA!
MRRGH!
STRAIGHT OUT OF THE GATES, BOTH TEAMS HAVE COME OUT SWINGING WITH HIGHLY AGGRESSIVE QUICK SETS!

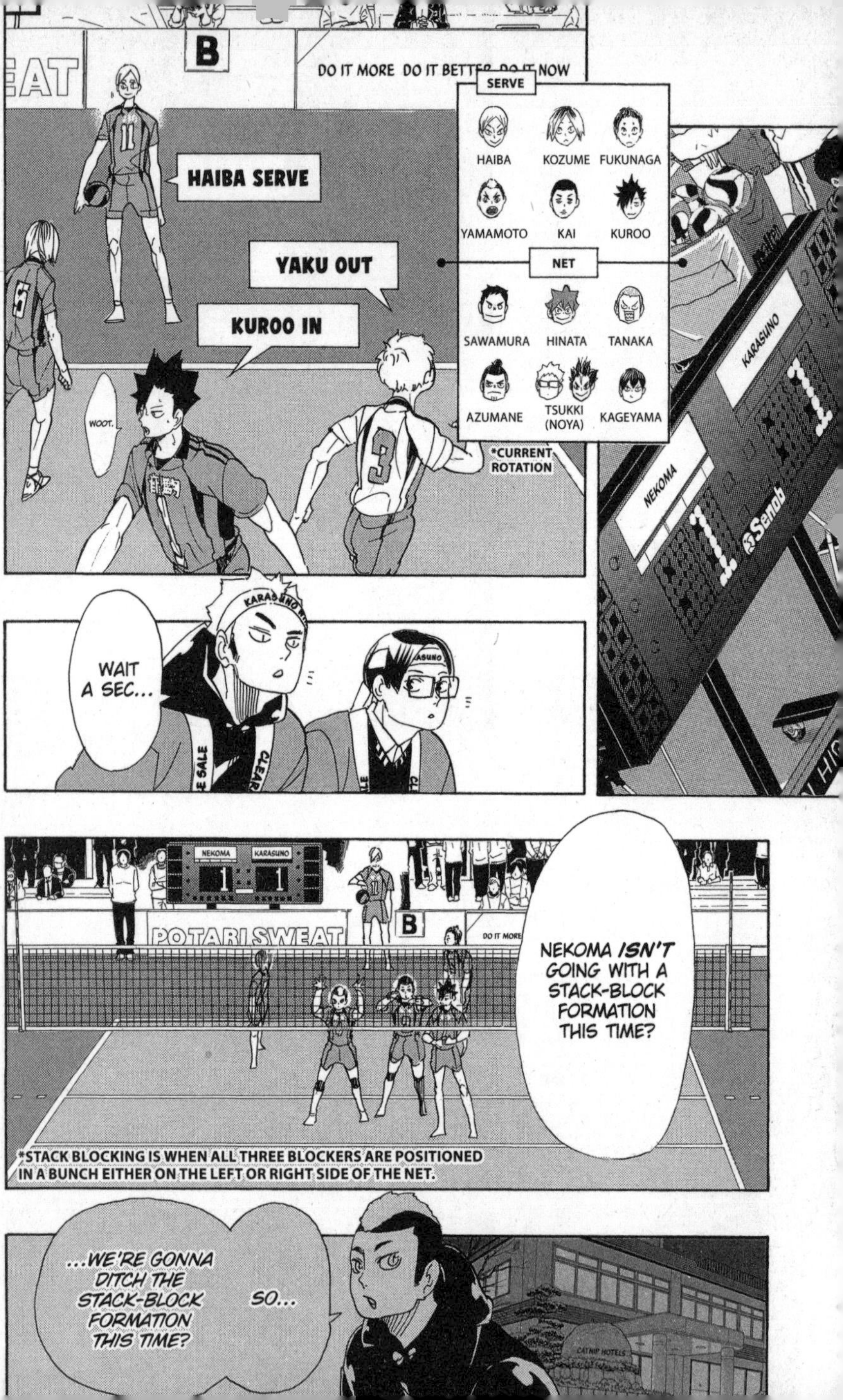

KARASUNO
NEKOMA
Senob
B
DO IT MORE DO IT BETTER DO IT NOW
SERVE
HAIBA
KOZUME
FUKUNAGA
YAMAMOTO
KAI
KUROO
NET
SAWAMURA
HINATA
TANAKA
AZUMANE
TSUKKI (NOYA)
KAGEYAMA
*CURRENT ROTATION
HAIBA SERVE
YAKU OUT
KUROO IN
WOOT.
WAIT A SEC...
NEKOMA
KARASUNO
POTARI SWEAT
B
DO IT MORE
NEKOMA *ISN'T* GOING WITH A STACK-BLOCK FORMATION THIS TIME?
*STACK BLOCKING IS WHEN ALL THREE BLOCKERS ARE POSITIONED IN A BUNCH EITHER ON THE LEFT OR RIGHT SIDE OF THE NET.
SO...
...WE'RE GONNA DITCH THE STACK-BLOCK FORMATION THIS TIME?
CATNIP HOTELS

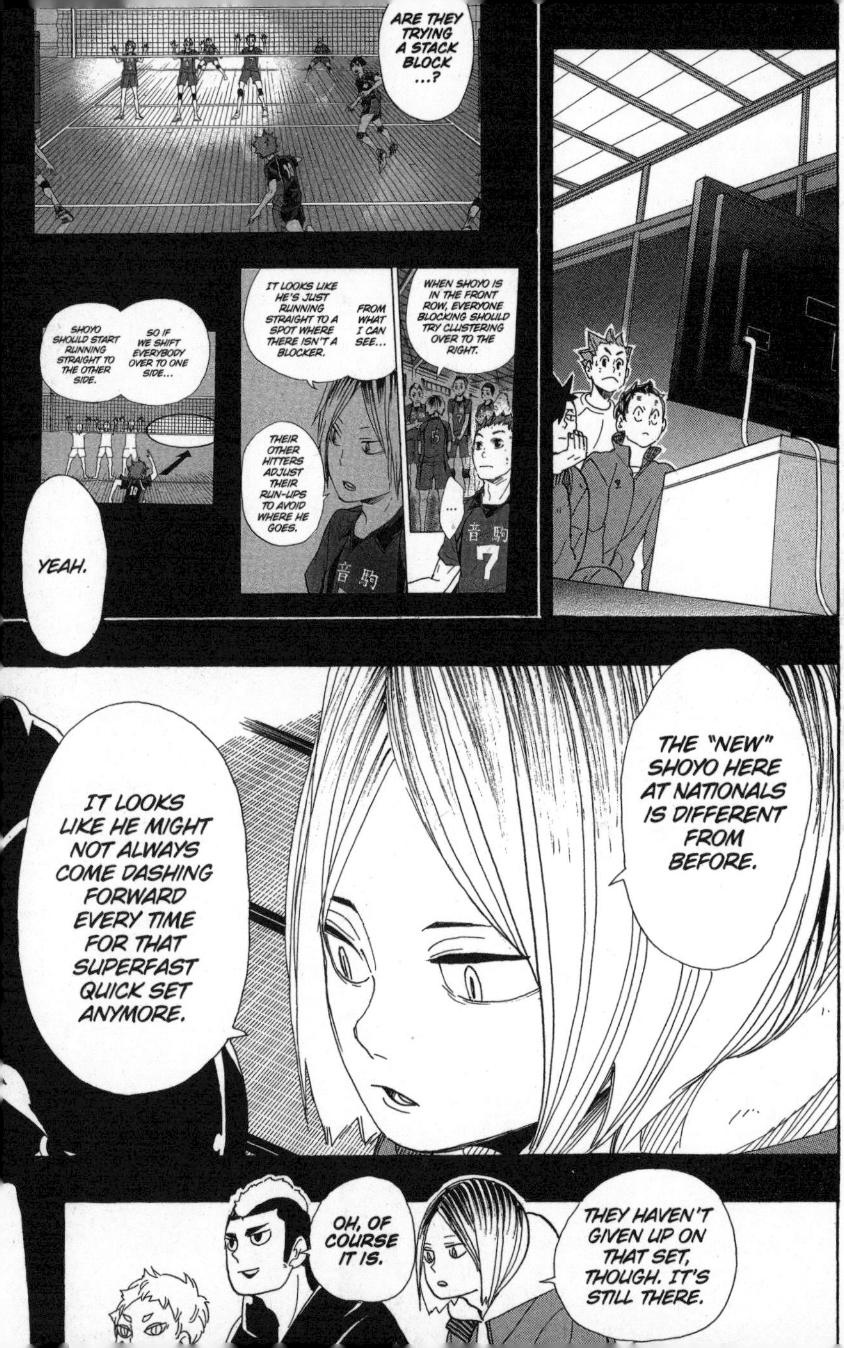
ARE THEY TRYING A STACK BLOCK ...?
WHEN SHOYO IS IN THE FRONT ROW, EVERYONE BLOCKING SHOULD TRY CLUSTERING OVER TO THE RIGHT.
...
FROM WHAT I CAN SEE...
IT LOOKS LIKE HE'S JUST RUNNING STRAIGHT TO A SPOT WHERE THERE ISN'T A BLOCKER.
THEIR OTHER HITTERS ADJUST THEIR RUN-UPS TO AVOID WHERE HE GOES.
SO IF WE SHIFT EVERYBODY OVER TO ONE SIDE...
SHOYO SHOULD START RUNNING STRAIGHT TO THE OTHER SIDE.
YEAH.
THE "NEW" SHOYO HERE AT NATIONALS IS DIFFERENT FROM BEFORE.
IT LOOKS LIKE HE MIGHT NOT ALWAYS COME DASHING FORWARD EVERY TIME FOR THAT SUPERFAST QUICK SET ANYMORE.
THEY HAVEN'T GIVEN UP ON THAT SET, THOUGH. IT'S STILL THERE.
OH, OF COURSE IT IS.

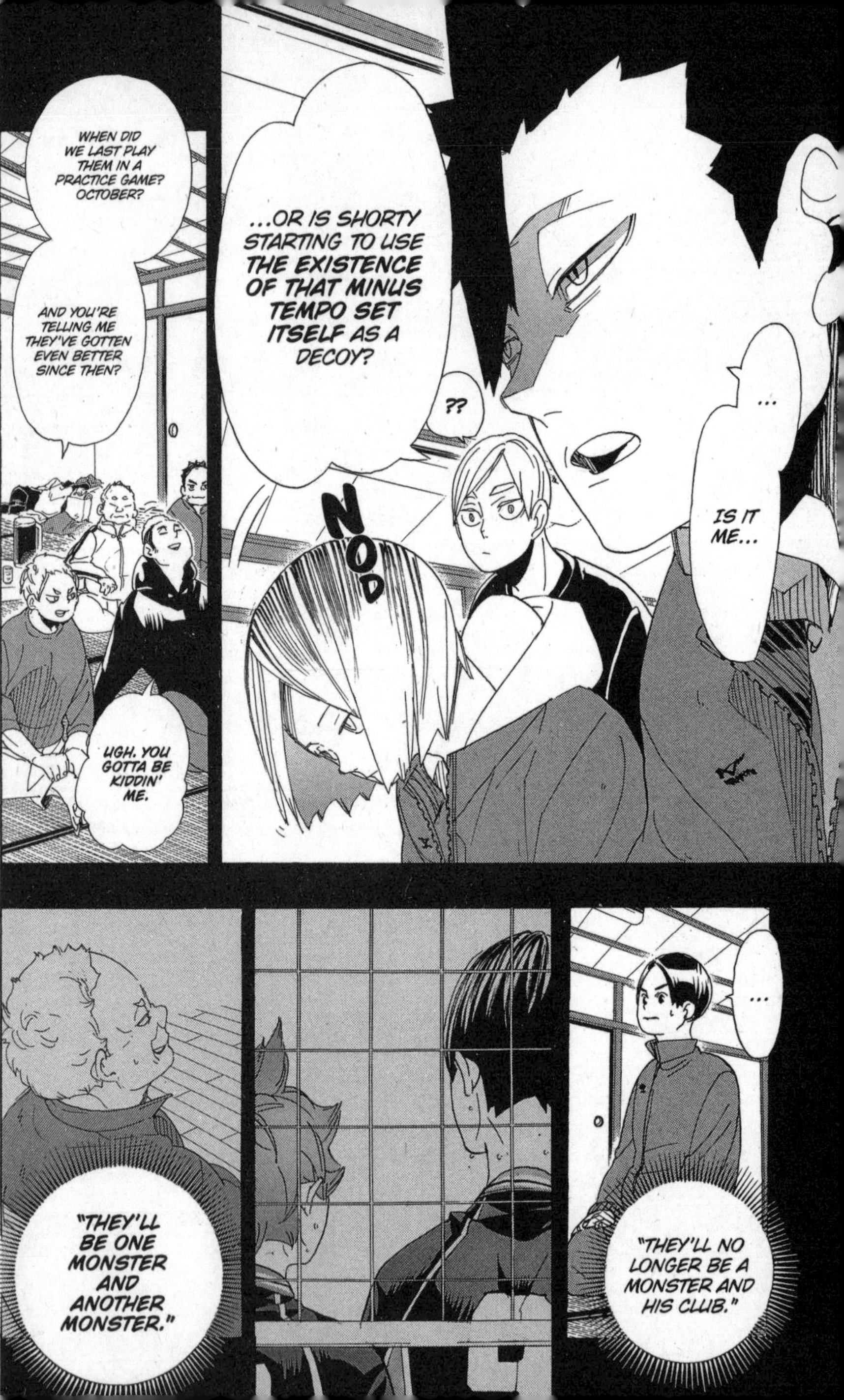
...
IS IT ME...
...OR IS SHORTY STARTING TO USE THE EXISTENCE OF THAT MINUS TEMPO SET ITSELF AS A DECOY?
??
NOD
WHEN DID WE LAST PLAY THEM IN A PRACTICE GAME? OCTOBER?
AND YOU'RE TELLING ME THEY'VE GOTTEN EVEN BETTER SINCE THEN?
UGH. YOU GOTTA BE KIDDIN' ME.
...
"THEY'LL NO LONGER BE A MONSTER AND HIS CLUB."
"THEY'LL BE ONE MONSTER AND ANOTHER MONSTER."

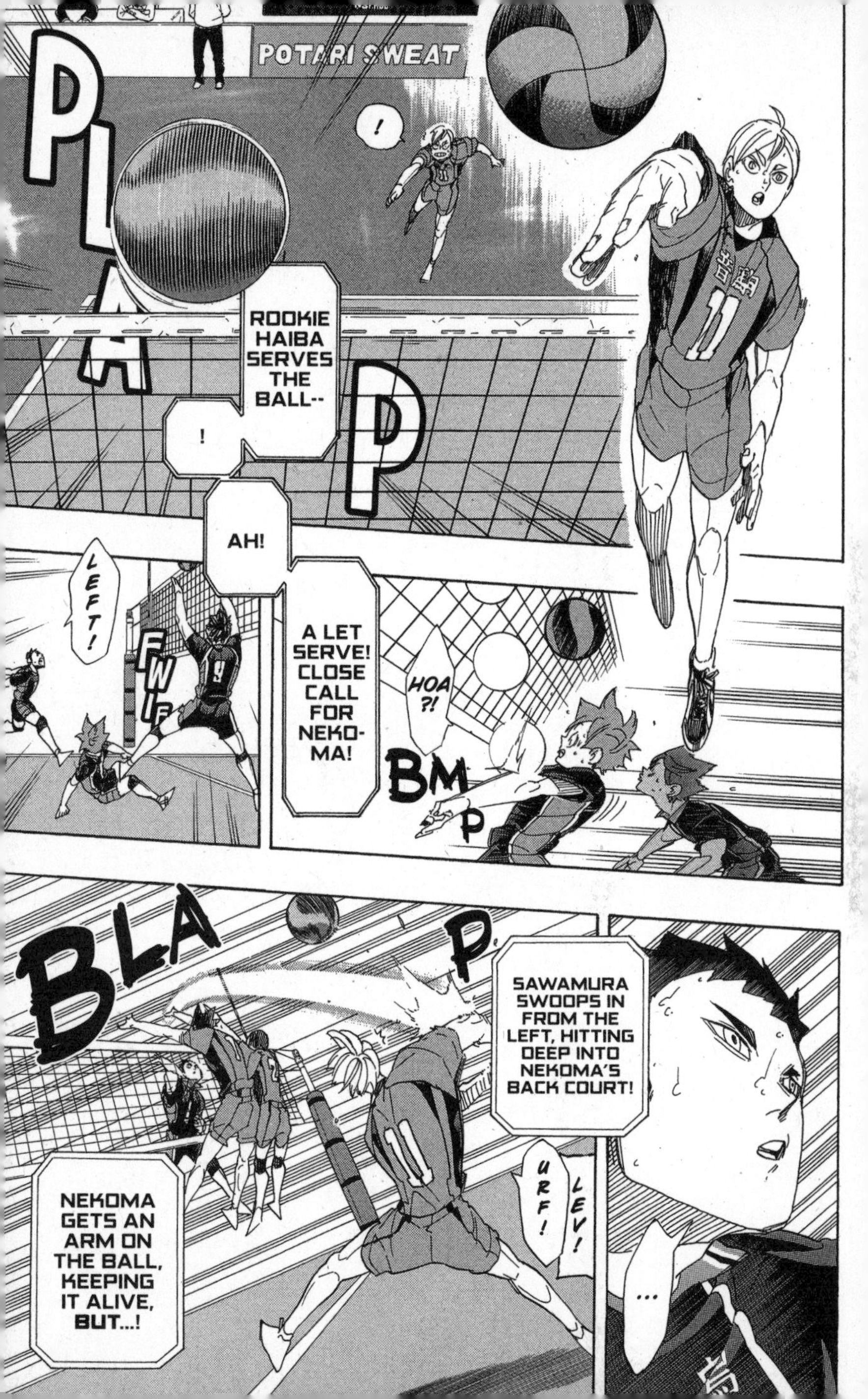
POTARI SWEAT
!
ROOKIE HAIBA SERVES THE BALL--
!
PLAP
AH!
A LET SERVE! CLOSE CALL FOR NEKO-MA!
HOA?!
BMP
LEFT!
FWIP
SAWAMURA SWOOPS IN FROM THE LEFT, HITTING DEEP INTO NEKOMA'S BACK COURT!
LEV!
URF!
...
BLAP
NEKOMA GETS AN ARM ON THE BALL, KEEPING IT ALIVE, BUT...!

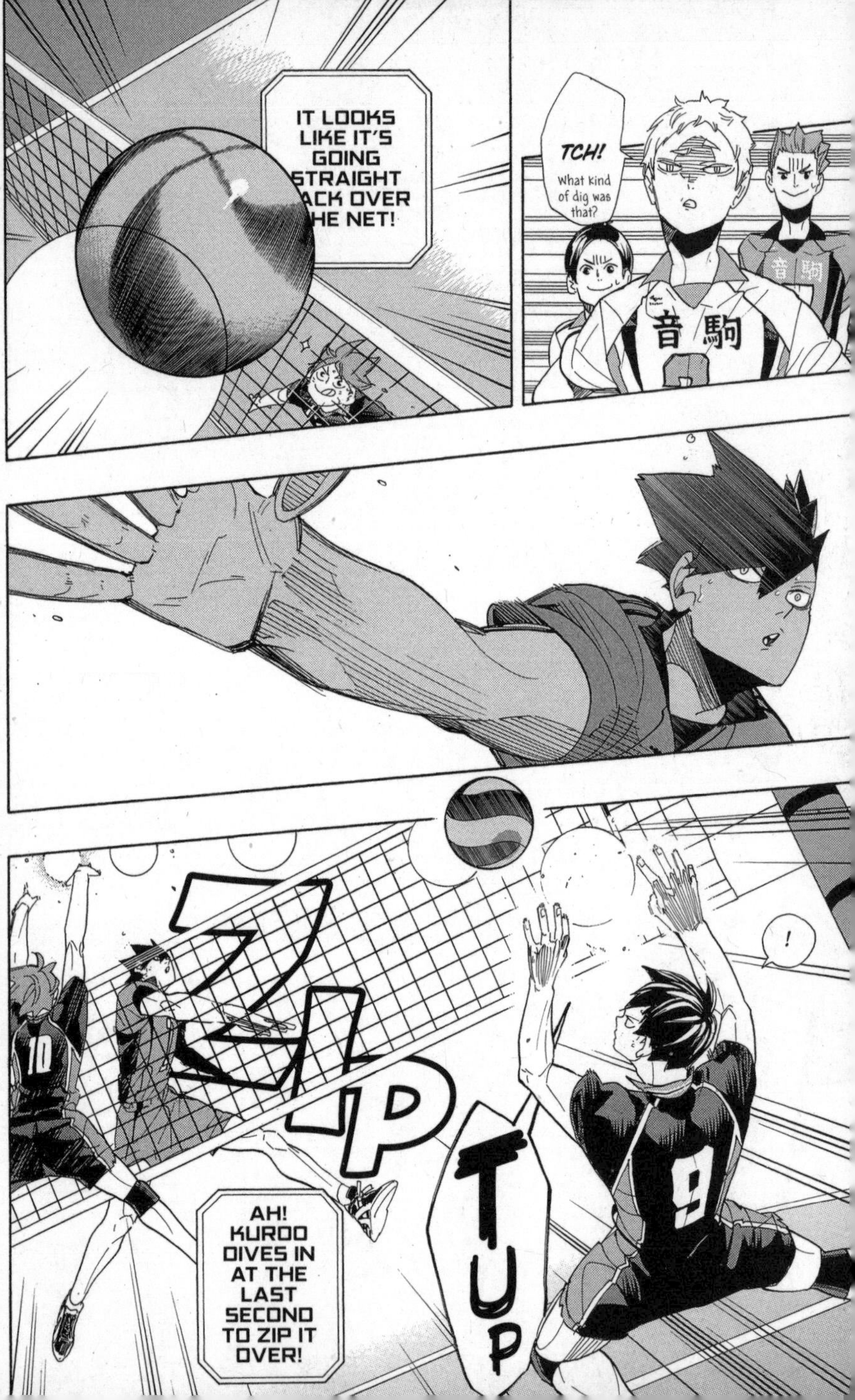
TCH!
What kind of dig was that?
音駒
IT LOOKS LIKE IT'S GOING STRAIGHT ACK OVER HE NET!
!
ZIP
TUP
AH! KUROO DIVES IN AT THE LAST SECOND TO ZIP IT OVER!

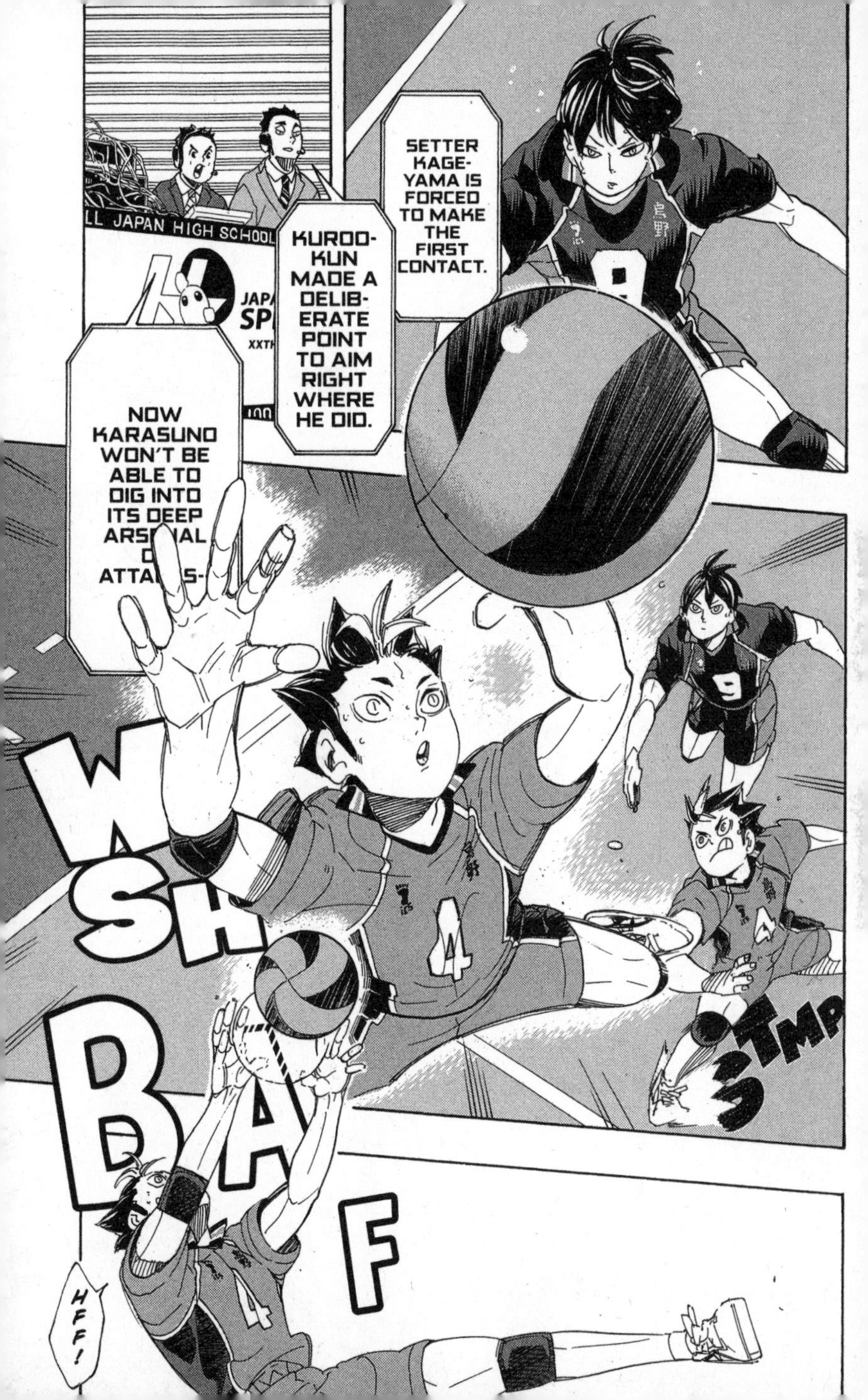
LL JAPAN HIGH SCHOOL
SETTER KAGE-YAMA IS FORCED TO MAKE THE FIRST CONTACT.
KUROO-KUN MADE A DELIB-ERATE POINT TO AIM RIGHT WHERE HE DID.
NOW KARASUNO WON'T BE ABLE TO DIG INTO ITS DEEP ARSENAL OF ATTACKS-
STMP
BAF
HFF!

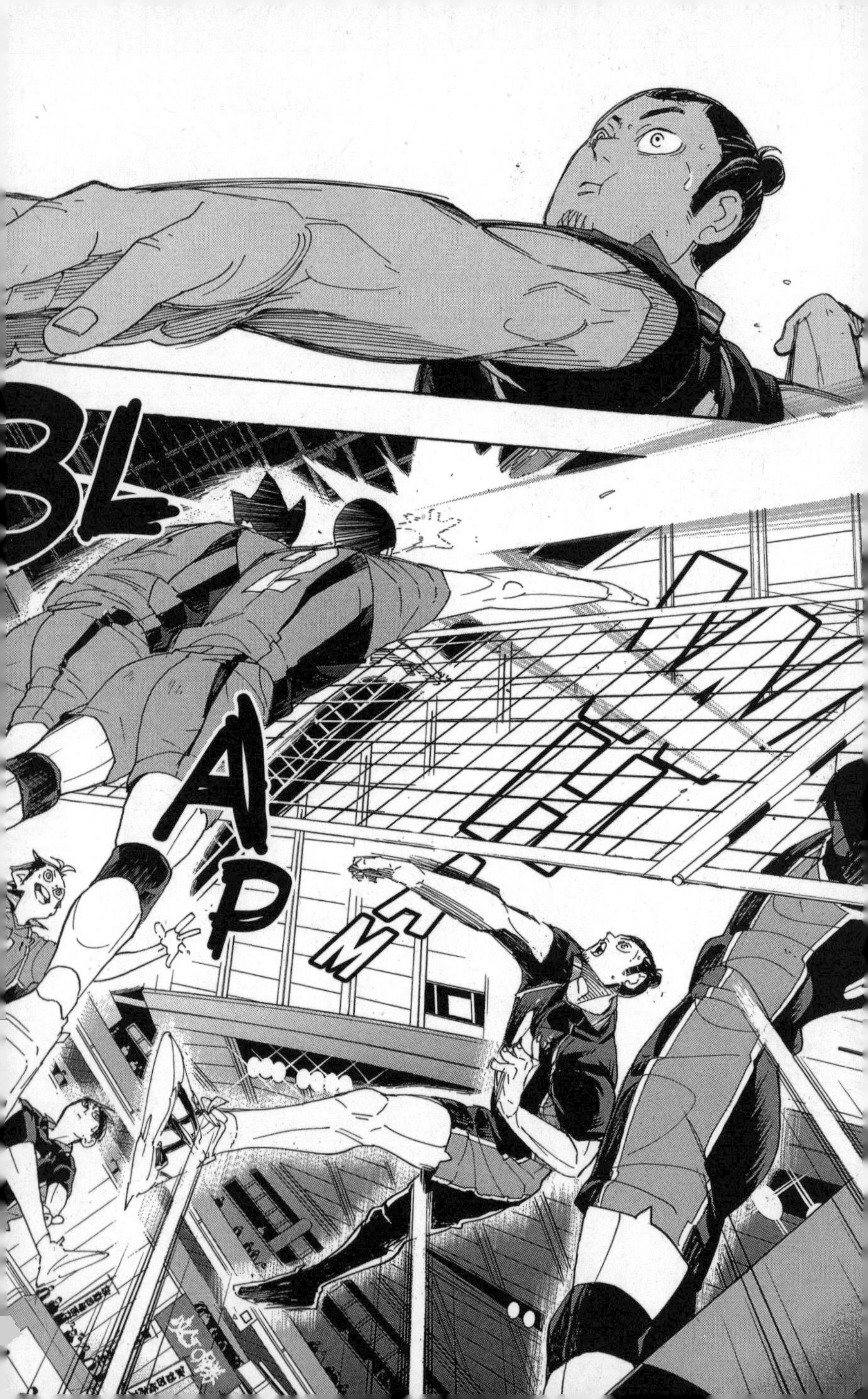
BLAP
WHAM

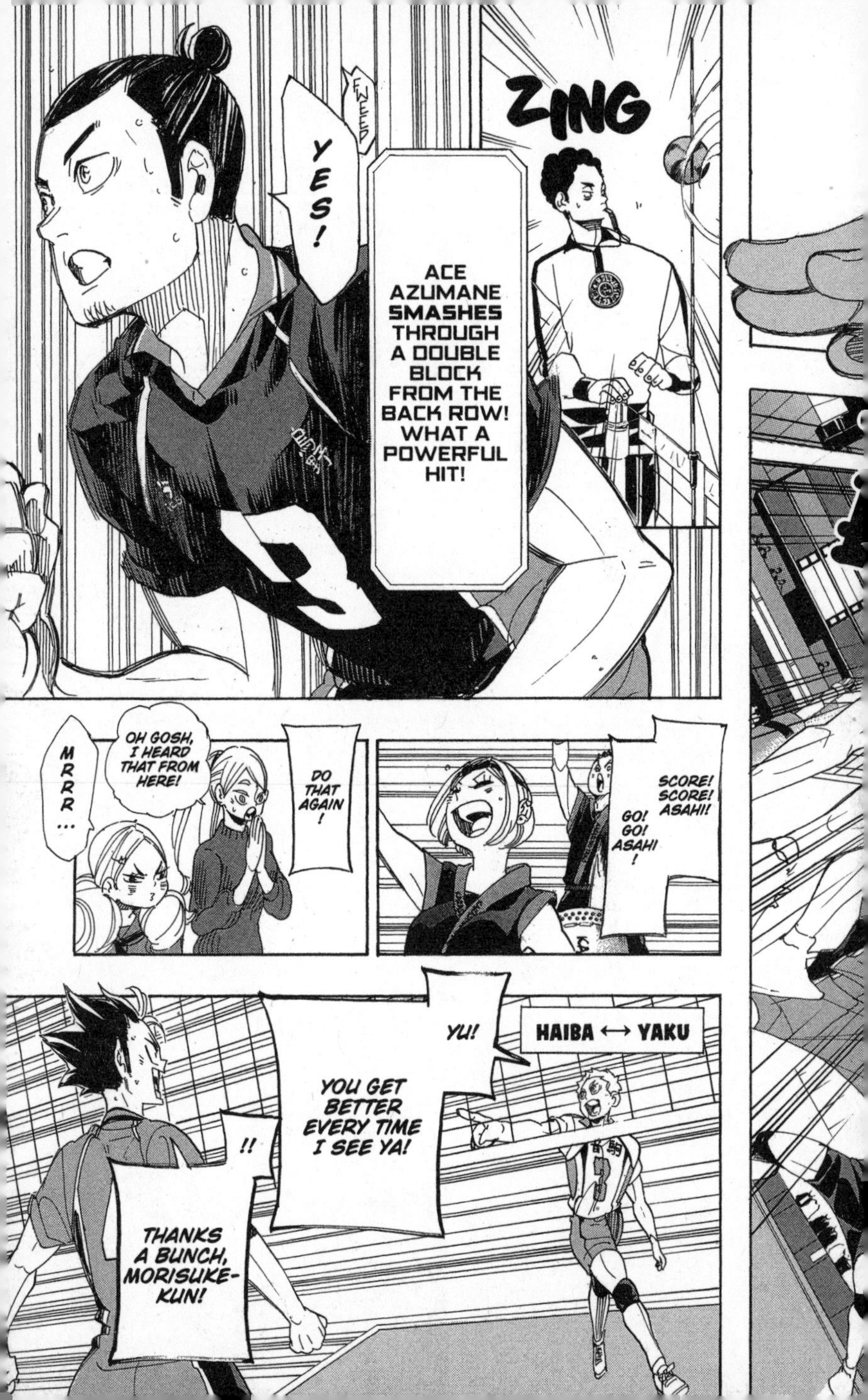
ZING
ACE AZUMANE SMASHES THROUGH A DOUBLE BLOCK FROM THE BACK ROW! WHAT A POWERFUL HIT!
FWEEP
YES!
SCORE! SCORE! ASAHI!
GO! GO! ASAHI!
DO THAT AGAIN!
OH GOSH, I HEARD THAT FROM HERE!
MRRR...
HAIBA ⟷ YAKU
YU!
YOU GET BETTER EVERY TIME I SEE YA!
!!
THANKS A BUNCH, MORISUKE-KUN!

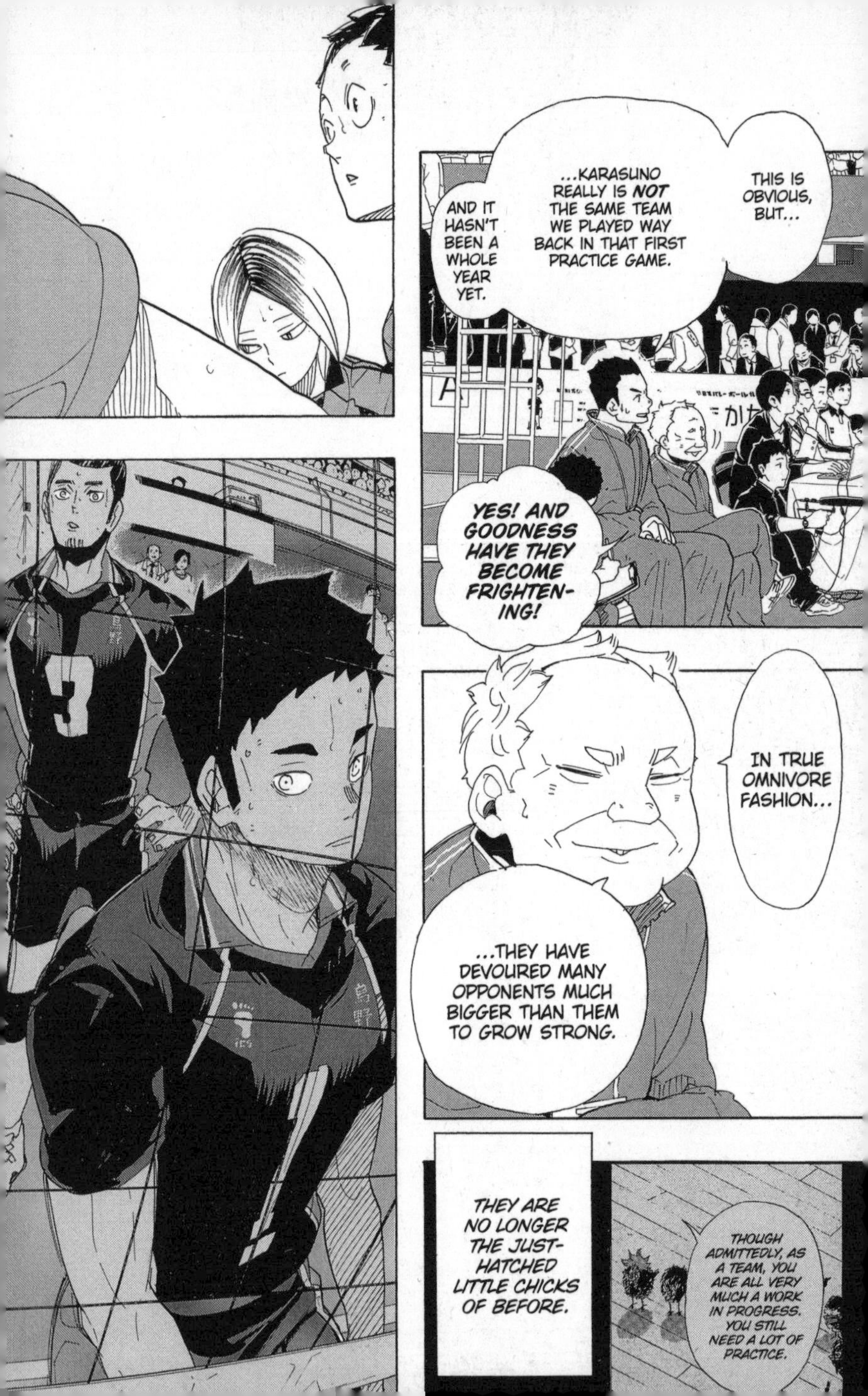
THIS IS OBVIOUS, BUT...
...KARASUNO REALLY IS **NOT** THE SAME TEAM WE PLAYED WAY BACK IN THAT FIRST PRACTICE GAME.
AND IT HASN'T BEEN A WHOLE YEAR YET.
YES! AND GOODNESS HAVE THEY BECOME FRIGHTEN-ING!
IN TRUE OMNIVORE FASHION...
...THEY HAVE DEVOURED MANY OPPONENTS MUCH BIGGER THAN THEM TO GROW STRONG.
THOUGH ADMITTEDLY, AS A TEAM, YOU ARE ALL VERY MUCH A WORK IN PROGRESS. YOU STILL NEED A LOT OF PRACTICE.
THEY ARE NO LONGER THE JUST-HATCHED LITTLE CHICKS OF BEFORE.

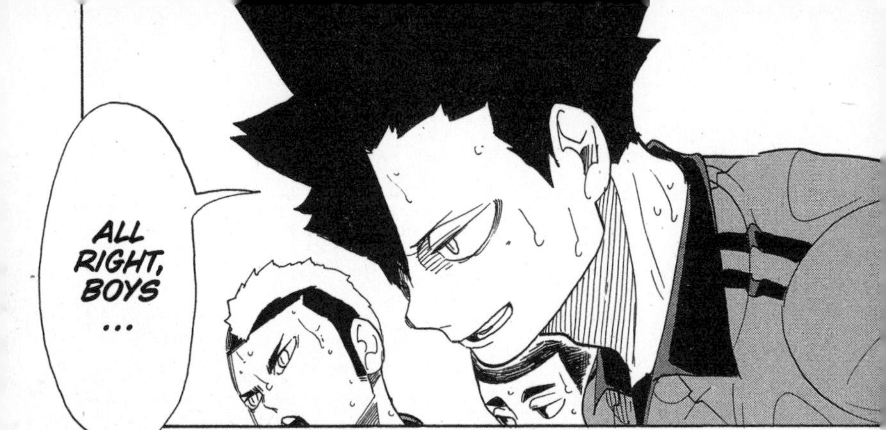
ALL RIGHT, BOYS...

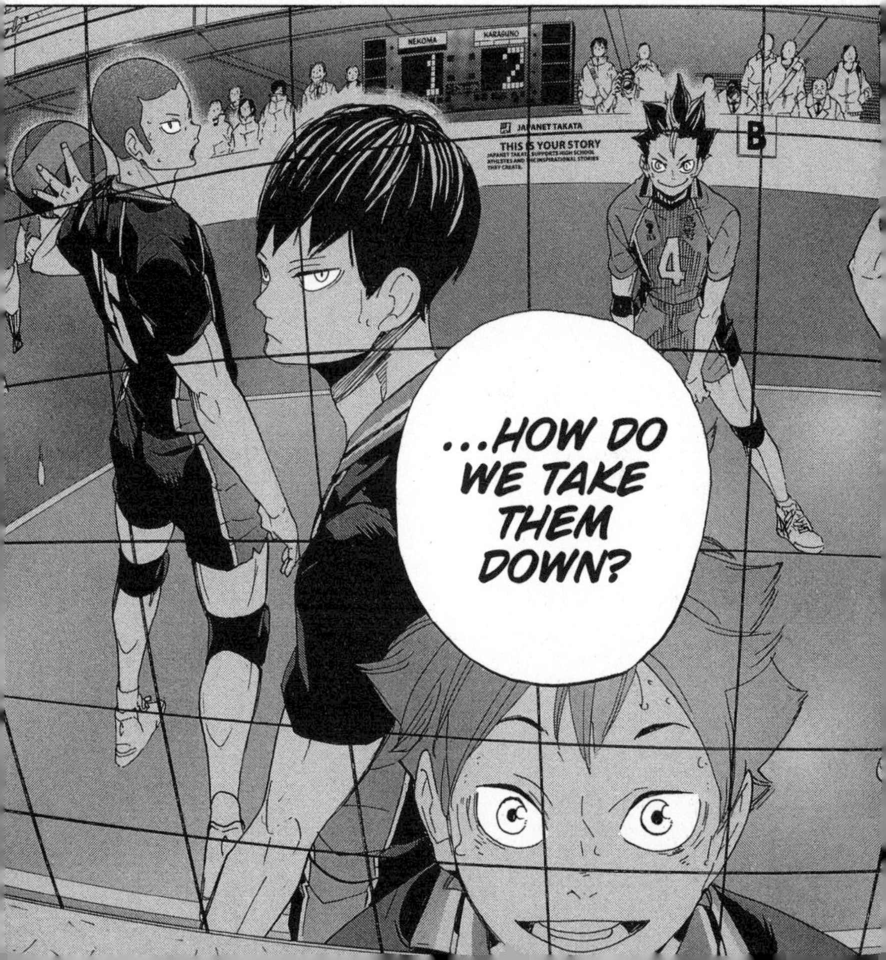
NEKOMA
KARASUNO
JAPANET TAKATA
THIS IS YOUR STORY
B
...HOW DO WE TAKE THEM DOWN?

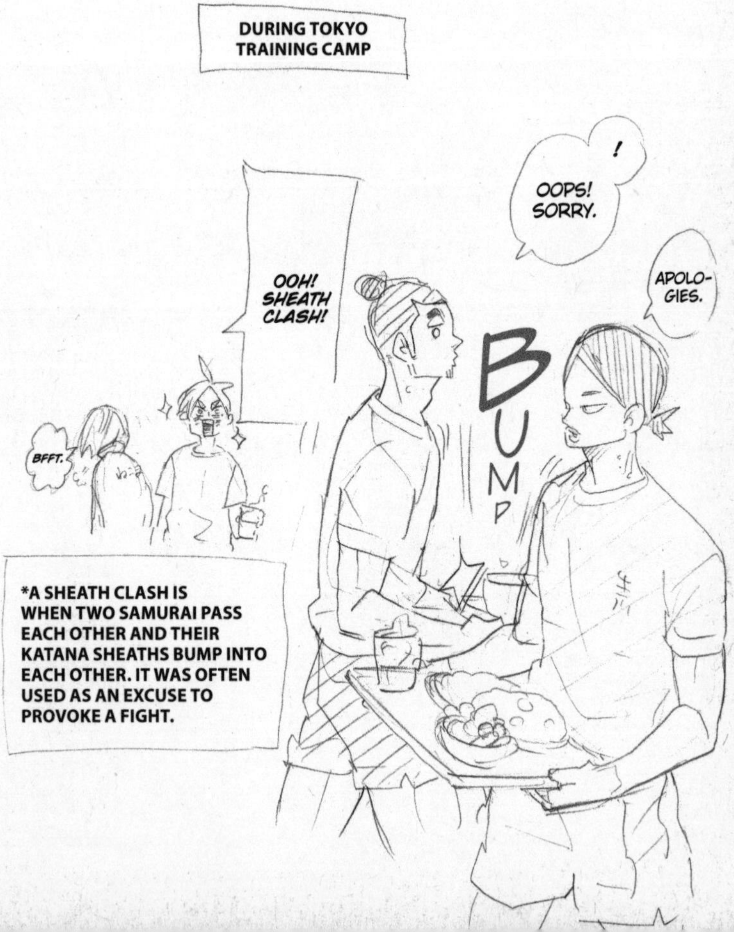
DURING TOKYO TRAINING CAMP
!
OOPS! SORRY.
APOLOGIES.
BUMP
OOH! SHEATH CLASH!
BFFT.
*A SHEATH CLASH IS WHEN TWO SAMURAI PASS EACH OTHER AND THEIR KATANA SHEATHS BUMP INTO EACH OTHER. IT WAS OFTEN USED AS AN EXCUSE TO PROVOKE A FIGHT.

CHAPTER 258: Running in Parallel

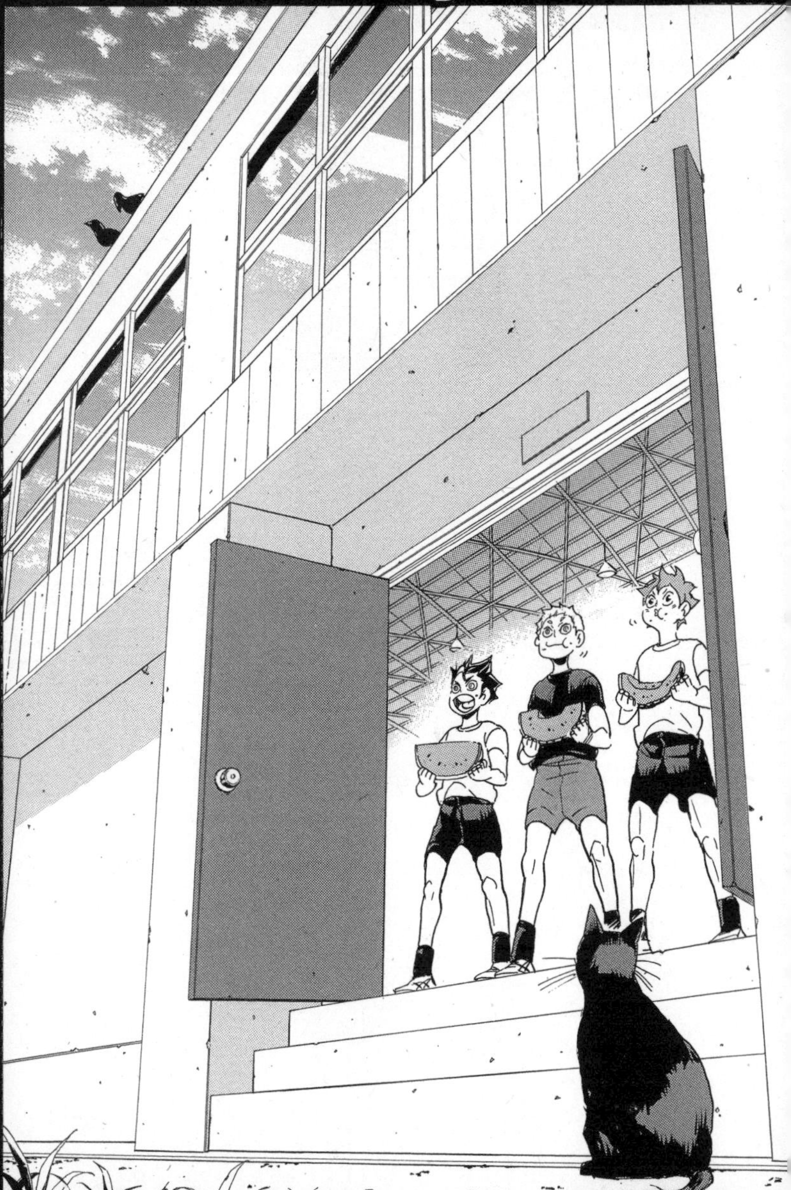

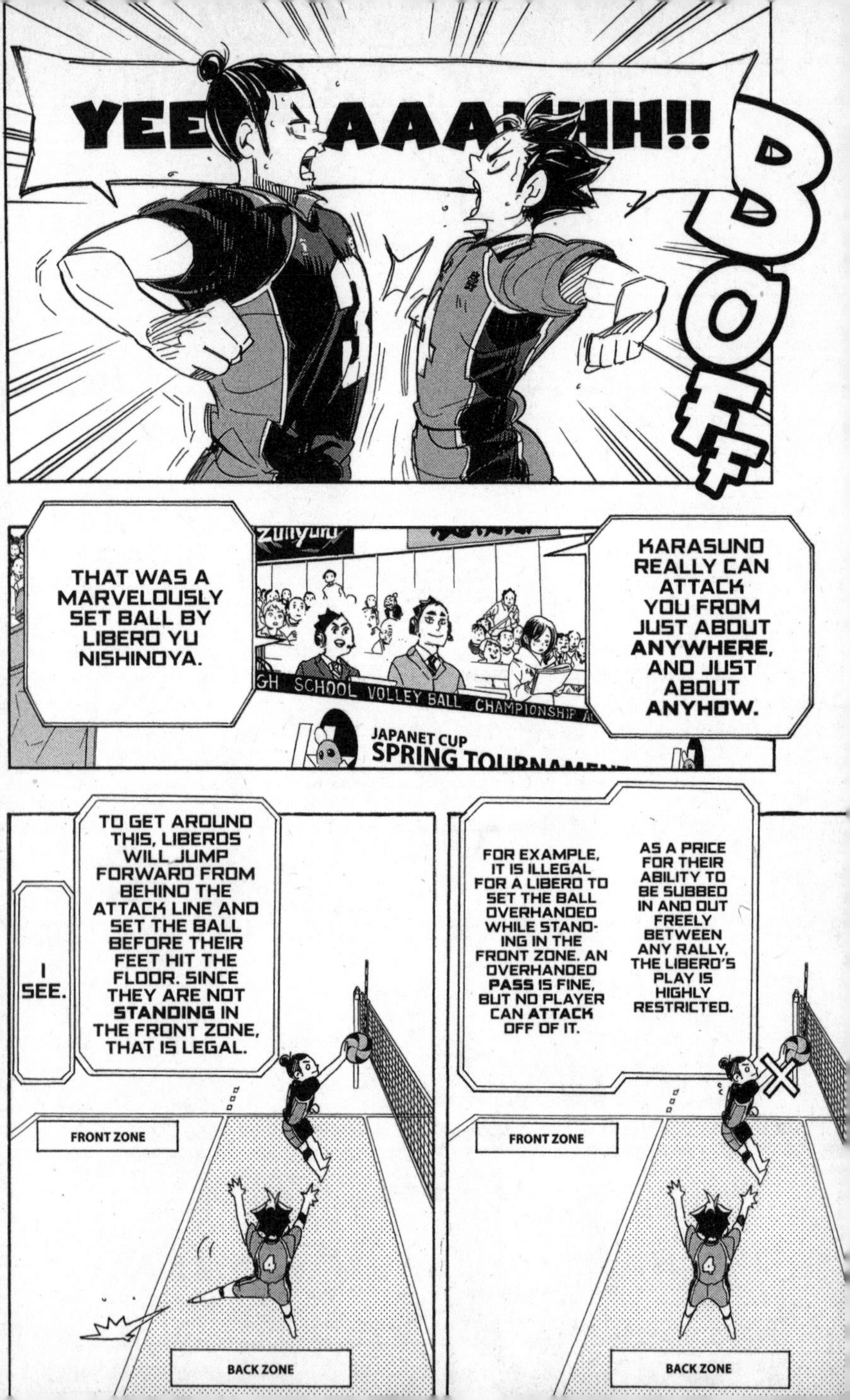
YEE AAAA HH!!
BOFF
KARASUNO REALLY CAN ATTACK YOU FROM JUST ABOUT ANYWHERE, AND JUST ABOUT ANYHOW.
THAT WAS A MARVELOUSLY SET BALL BY LIBERO YU NISHINOYA.
SCHOOL VOLLEY BALL CHAMPIONSHIP
JAPANET CUP
SPRING TOURNAM
AS A PRICE FOR THEIR ABILITY TO BE SUBBED IN AND OUT FREELY BETWEEN ANY RALLY, THE LIBERO'S PLAY IS HIGHLY RESTRICTED.
FOR EXAMPLE, IT IS ILLEGAL FOR A LIBERO TO SET THE BALL OVERHANDED WHILE STANDING IN THE FRONT ZONE. AN OVERHANDED PASS IS FINE, BUT NO PLAYER CAN ATTACK OFF OF IT.
FRONT ZONE
BACK ZONE
TO GET AROUND THIS, LIBEROS WILL JUMP FORWARD FROM BEHIND THE ATTACK LINE AND SET THE BALL BEFORE THEIR FEET HIT THE FLOOR. SINCE THEY ARE NOT STANDING IN THE FRONT ZONE, THAT IS LEGAL.
I SEE.
FRONT ZONE
BACK ZONE

EXACTLY. IT'S THE PLAYERS WHO CAN PERFORM WELL INSIDE **AND OUTSIDE** OF THEIR AREA OF EXPERTISE WHO MAKE IT FURTHER IN THIS SPORT.

...BUT THE HIGHER UP IN THE GAME YOU GO, THE MORE THEY ARE ASKED TO PERFORM TASKS **NOT** DEFENSE RELATED.

MANY PEOPLE ASSUME LIBEROS WILL **ONLY** PLAY DEFENSE...

THIS FROM THE GUY WHO WAS HITTING THE GROUND AT THE SAME TIME AS THE BALL ONLY A FEW MONTHS AGO.

FWEEE

TUMP Dotto!

SERVE	*CURRENT ROTATION		
TANAKA	KAGEYAMA	TSUKKI (NOYA)	
HINATA	SAWAMURA	AZUMANE	

NET		
KUROO	KAI	YAMAMOTO
FUKUNAGA	KOZUME	HAIBA (YAKU)

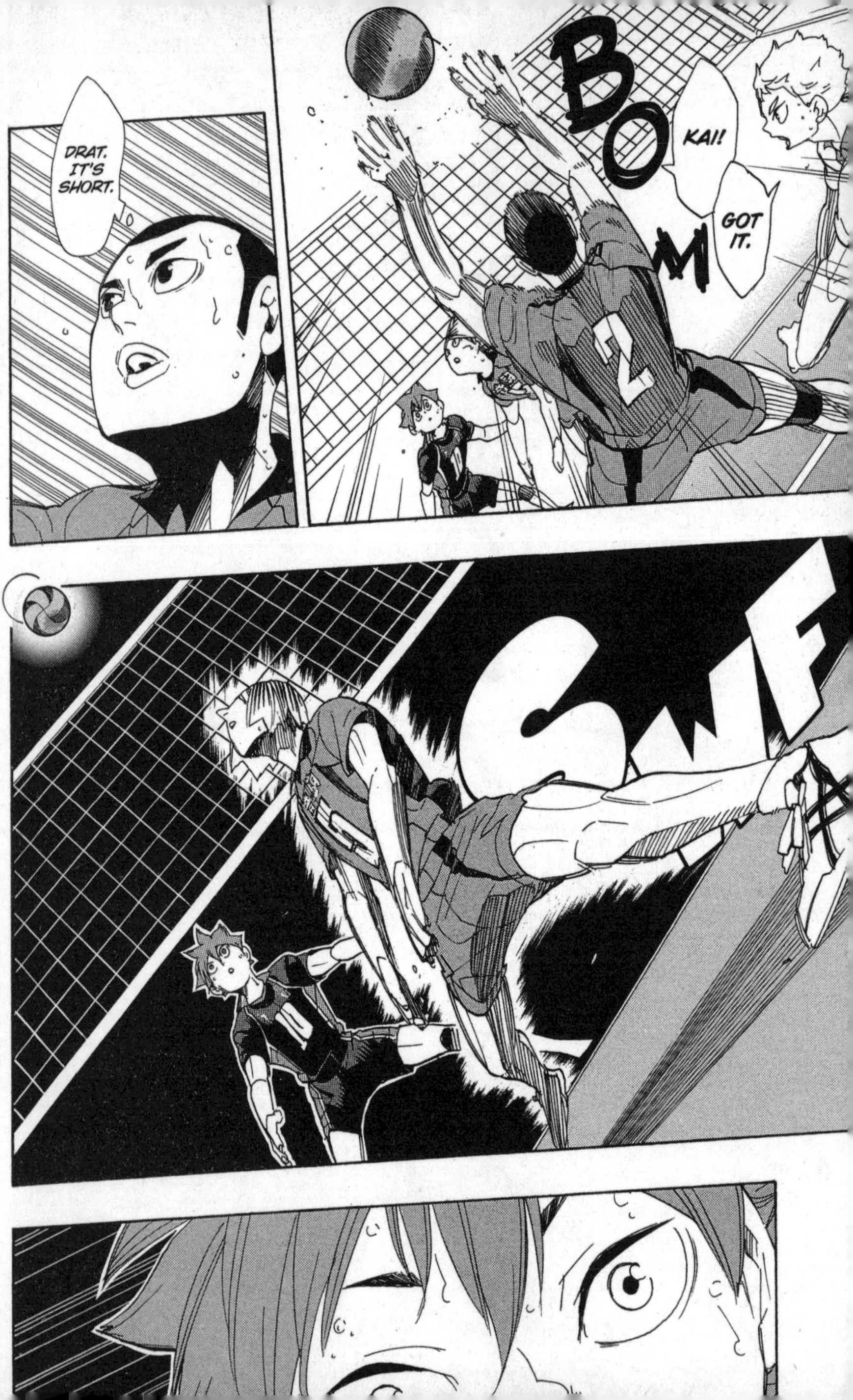
BOOM
KAI!
GOT IT.
DRAT. IT'S SHORT.

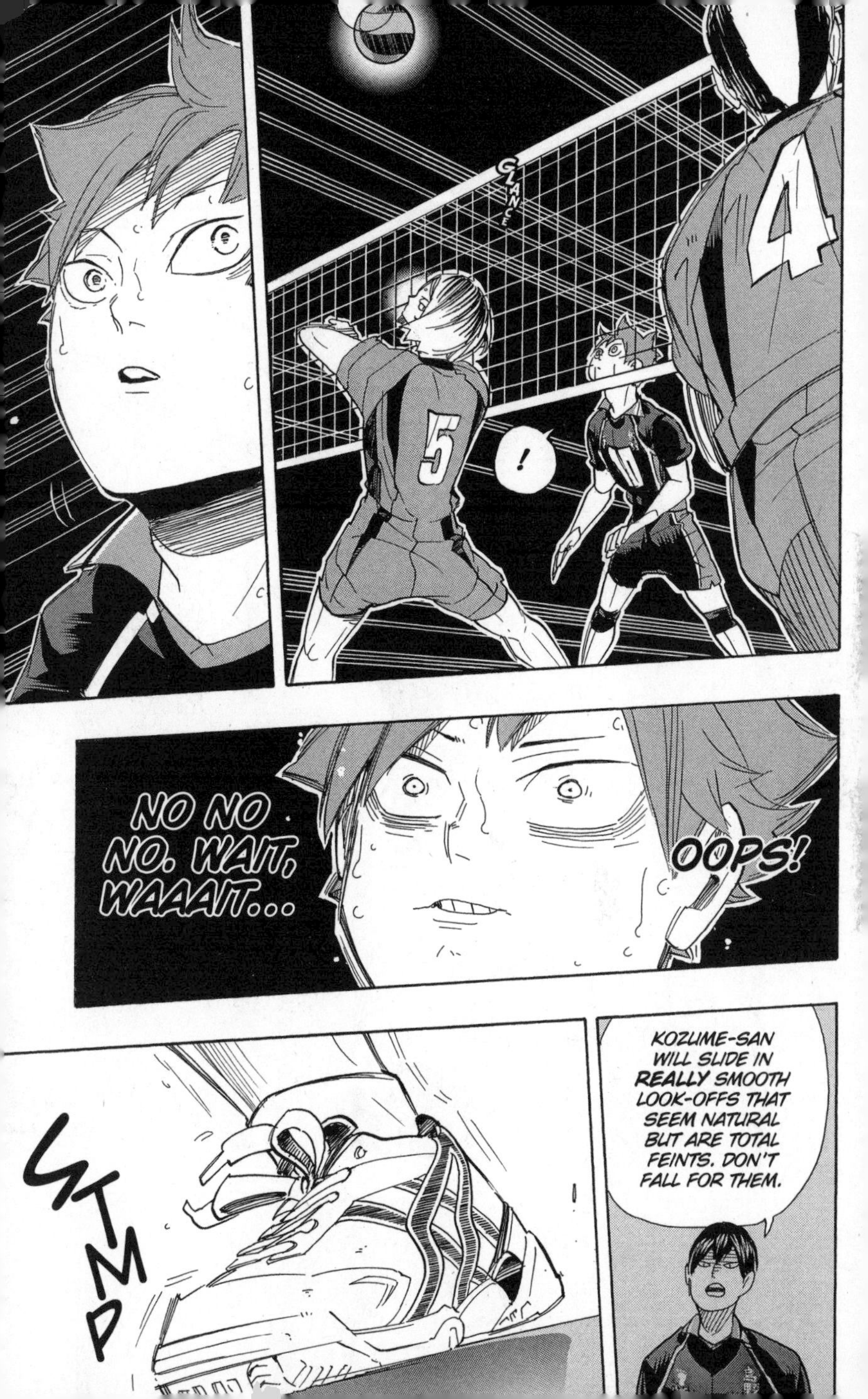
GLANCE
!
OOPS!
NO NO NO. WAIT, WAAAIT...
KOZUME-SAN WILL SLIDE IN REALLY SMOOTH LOOK-OFFS THAT SEEM NATURAL BUT ARE TOTAL FEINTS. DON'T FALL FOR THEM.
STMP

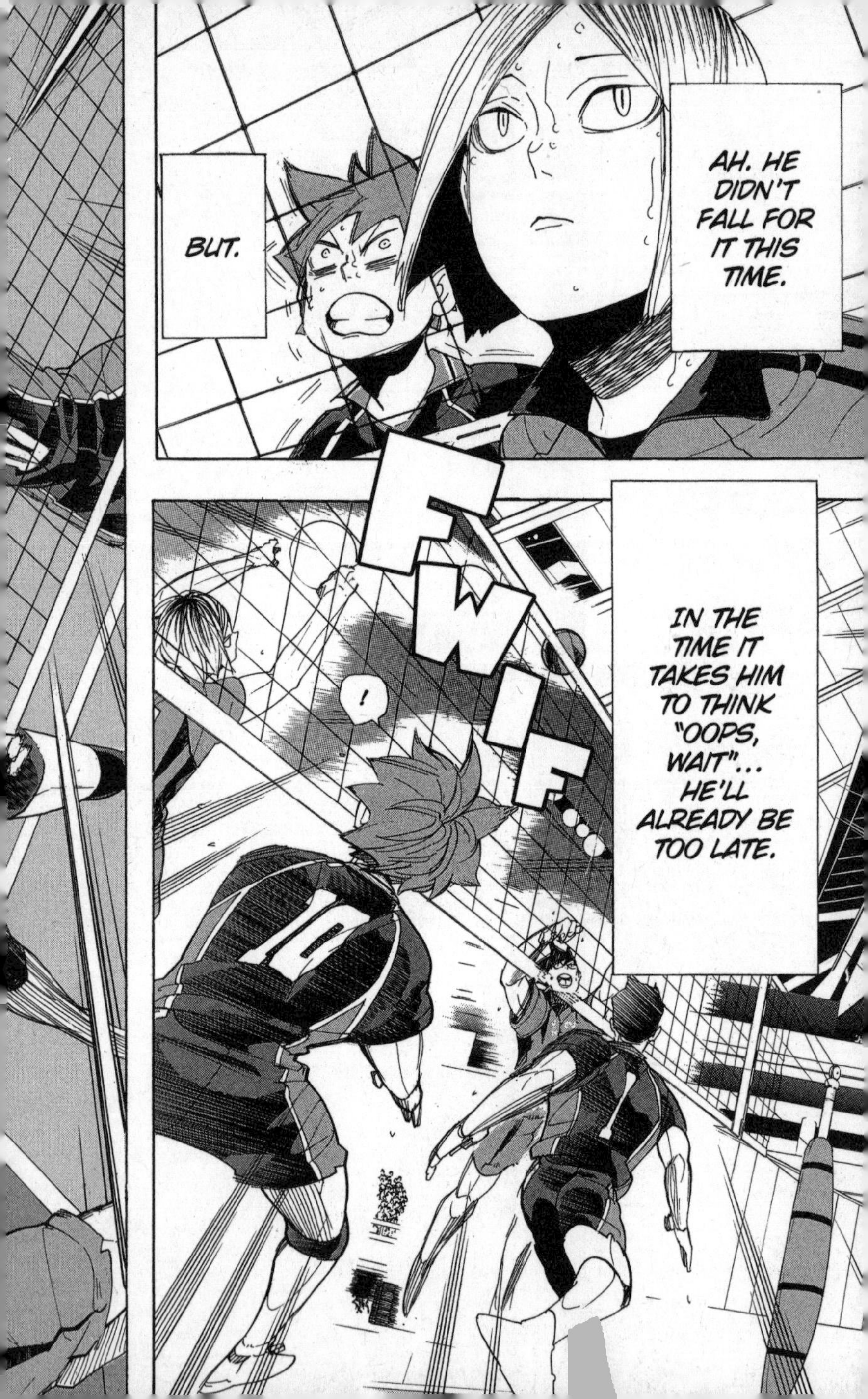
AH. HE DIDN'T FALL FOR IT THIS TIME.
BUT.
IN THE TIME IT TAKES HIM TO THINK "OOPS, WAIT"... HE'LL ALREADY BE TOO LATE.
FWIF...
!

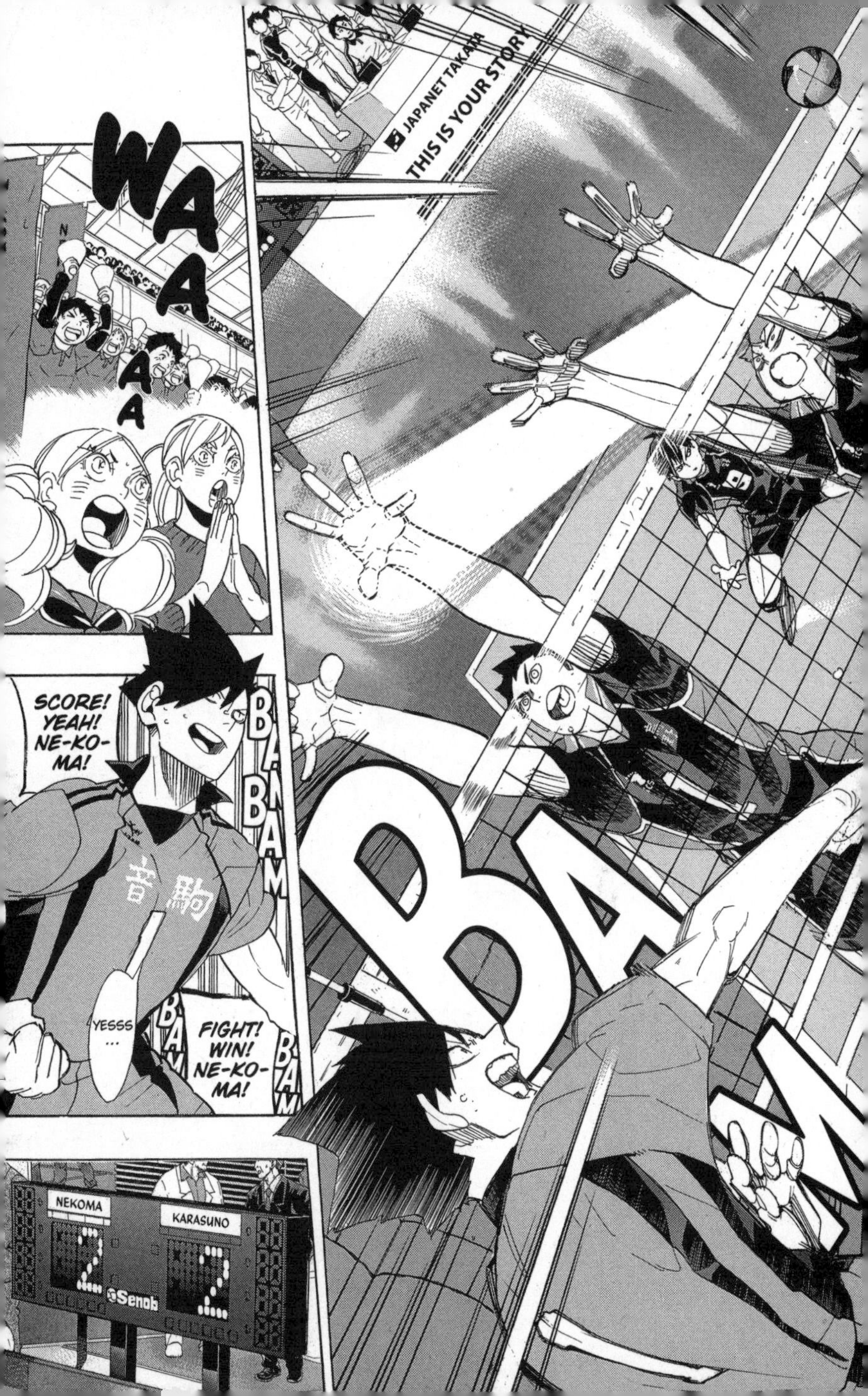
JAPANET TAKATA
THIS IS YOUR STORY
BAM
WAAAA
SCORE! YEAH! NE-KO-MA!
BAM
BAM
YESSS ...
FIGHT! WIN! NE-KO-MA!
BAM
BAM
NEKOMA
KARASUNO
2
2
Senob

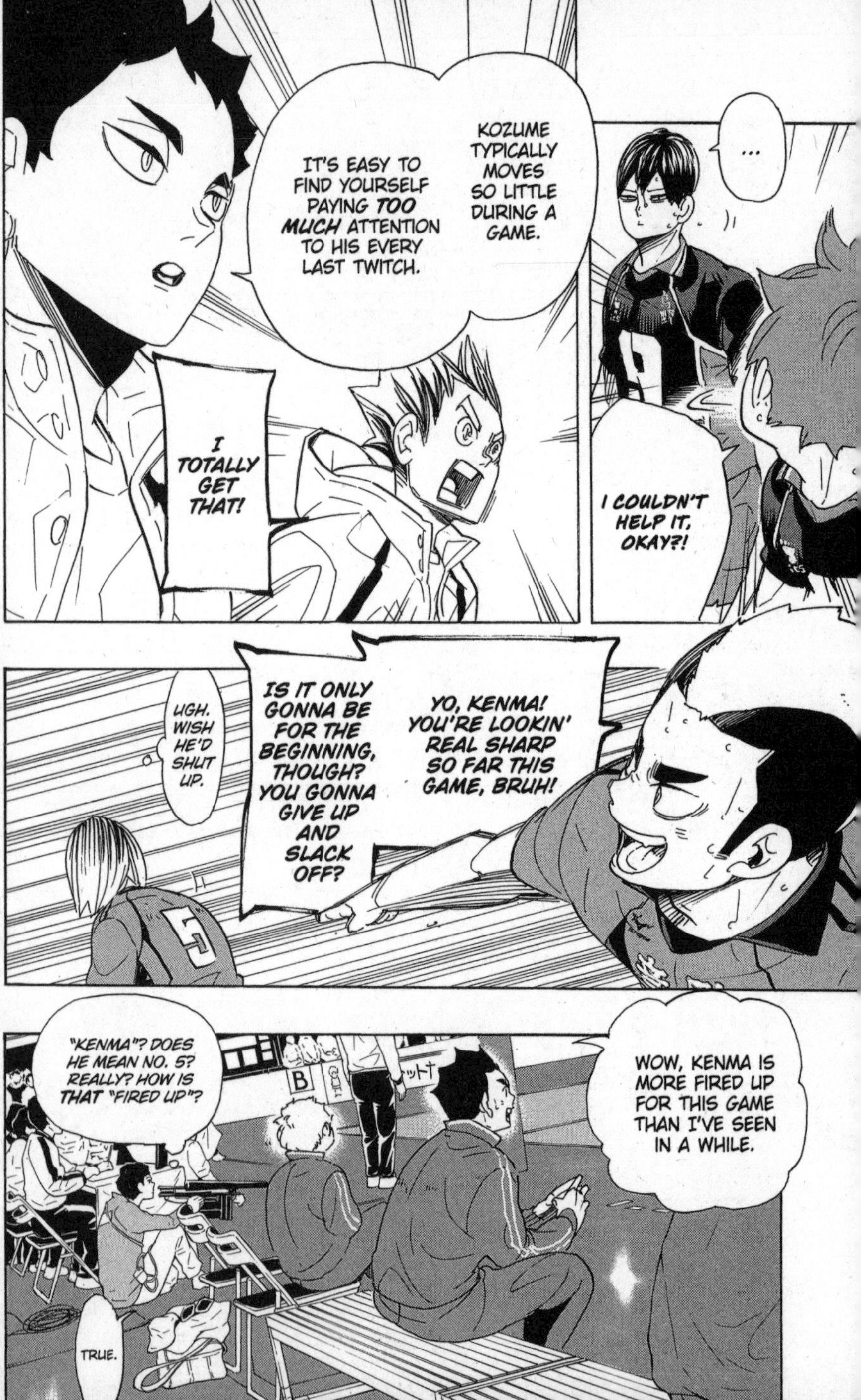
...
I COULDN'T HELP IT, OKAY?!
KOZUME TYPICALLY MOVES SO LITTLE DURING A GAME.
IT'S EASY TO FIND YOURSELF PAYING *TOO MUCH* ATTENTION TO HIS EVERY LAST TWITCH.
I TOTALLY GET THAT!
YO, KENMA! YOU'RE LOOKIN' REAL SHARP SO FAR THIS GAME, BRUH!
IS IT ONLY GONNA BE FOR THE BEGINNING, THOUGH? YOU GONNA GIVE UP AND SLACK OFF?
UGH. WISH HE'D SHUT UP.
WOW, KENMA IS MORE FIRED UP FOR THIS GAME THAN I'VE SEEN IN A WHILE.
"KENMA"? DOES HE MEAN NO. 5? REALLY? HOW IS THAT "FIRED UP"?
TRUE.

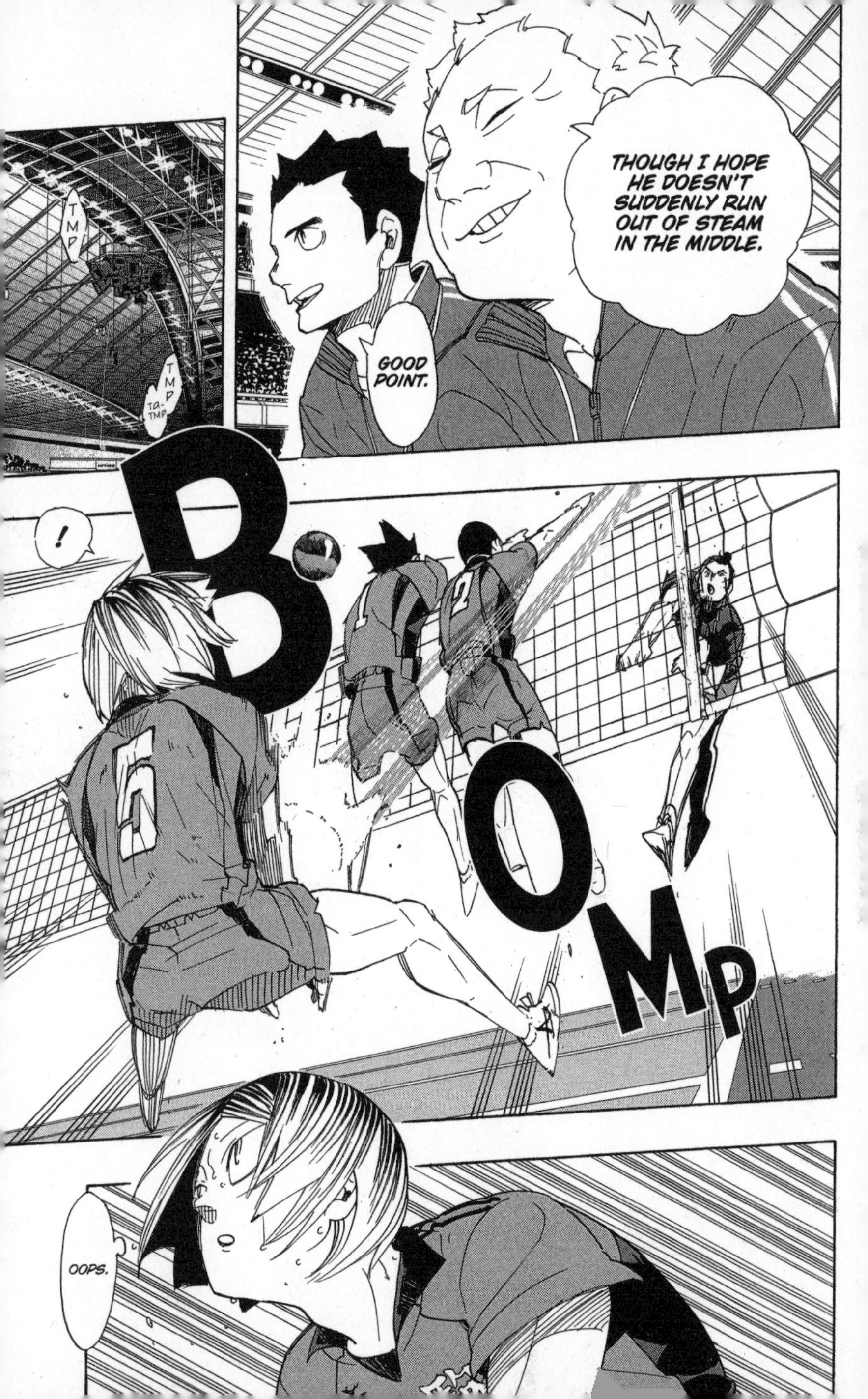
THOUGH I HOPE HE DOESN'T SUDDENLY RUN OUT OF STEAM IN THE MIDDLE.
GOOD POINT.
TMP
TMP
Ta-TMP
!
BOOMP
OOPS.

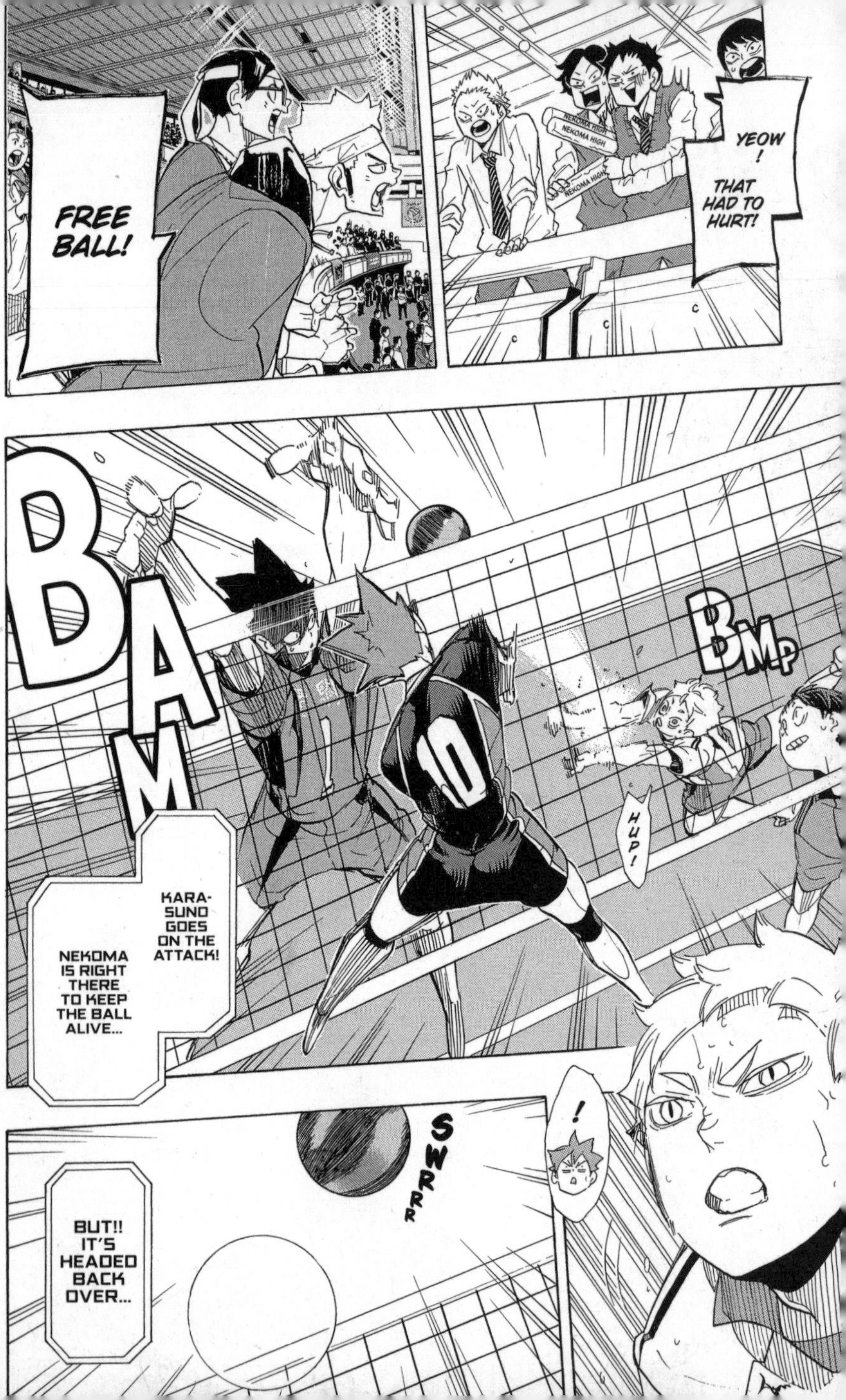
YEOW! THAT HAD TO HURT!
FREE BALL!
BAM
BMP
HUP!
KARA-SUNO GOES ON THE ATTACK!
NEKOMA IS RIGHT THERE TO KEEP THE BALL ALIVE...
!
SWRRR
BUT!! IT'S HEADED BACK OVER...

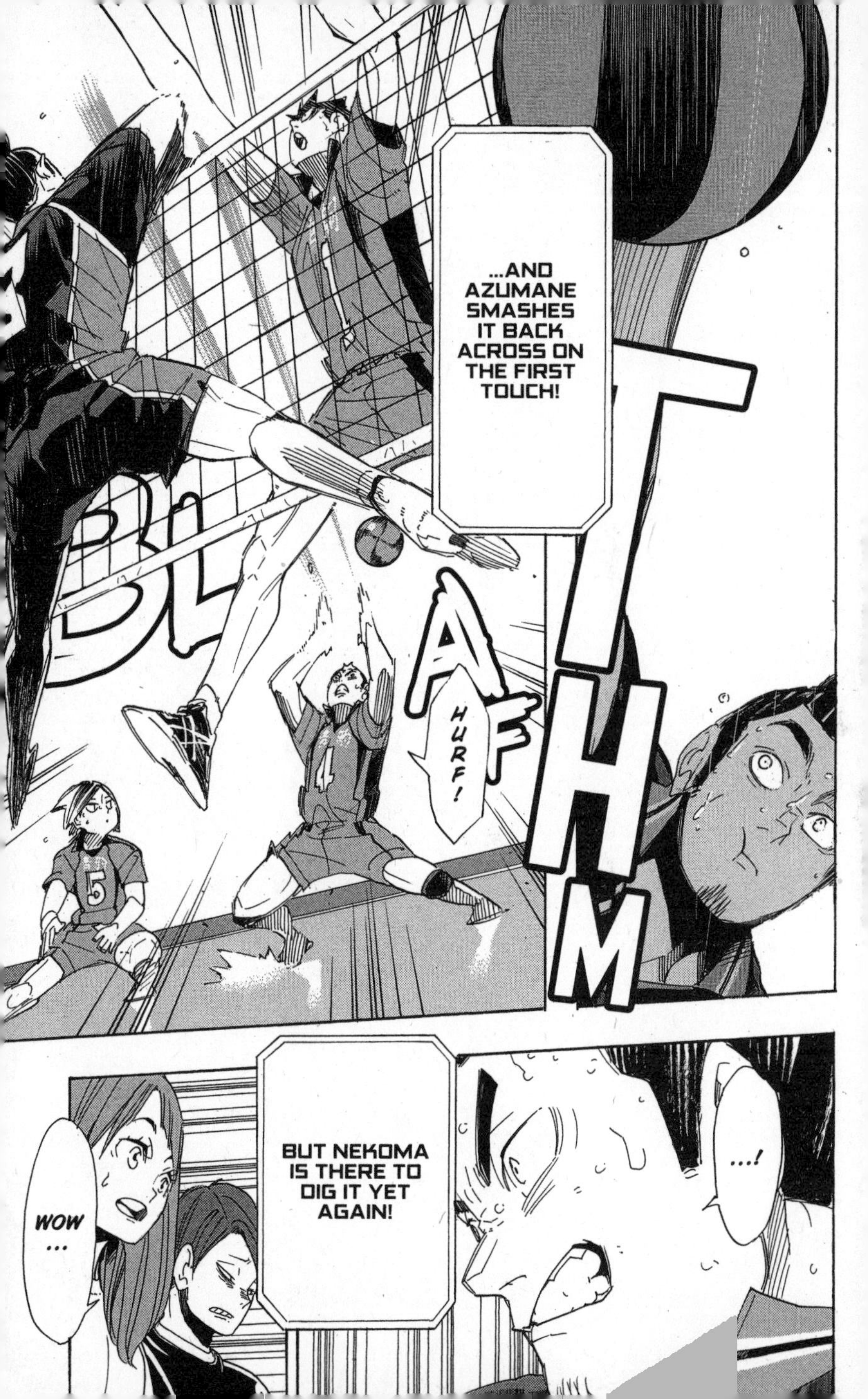
...AND AZUMANE SMASHES IT BACK ACROSS ON THE FIRST TOUCH!
HURF!
BUT NEKOMA IS THERE TO DIG IT YET AGAIN!
...!
WOW ...

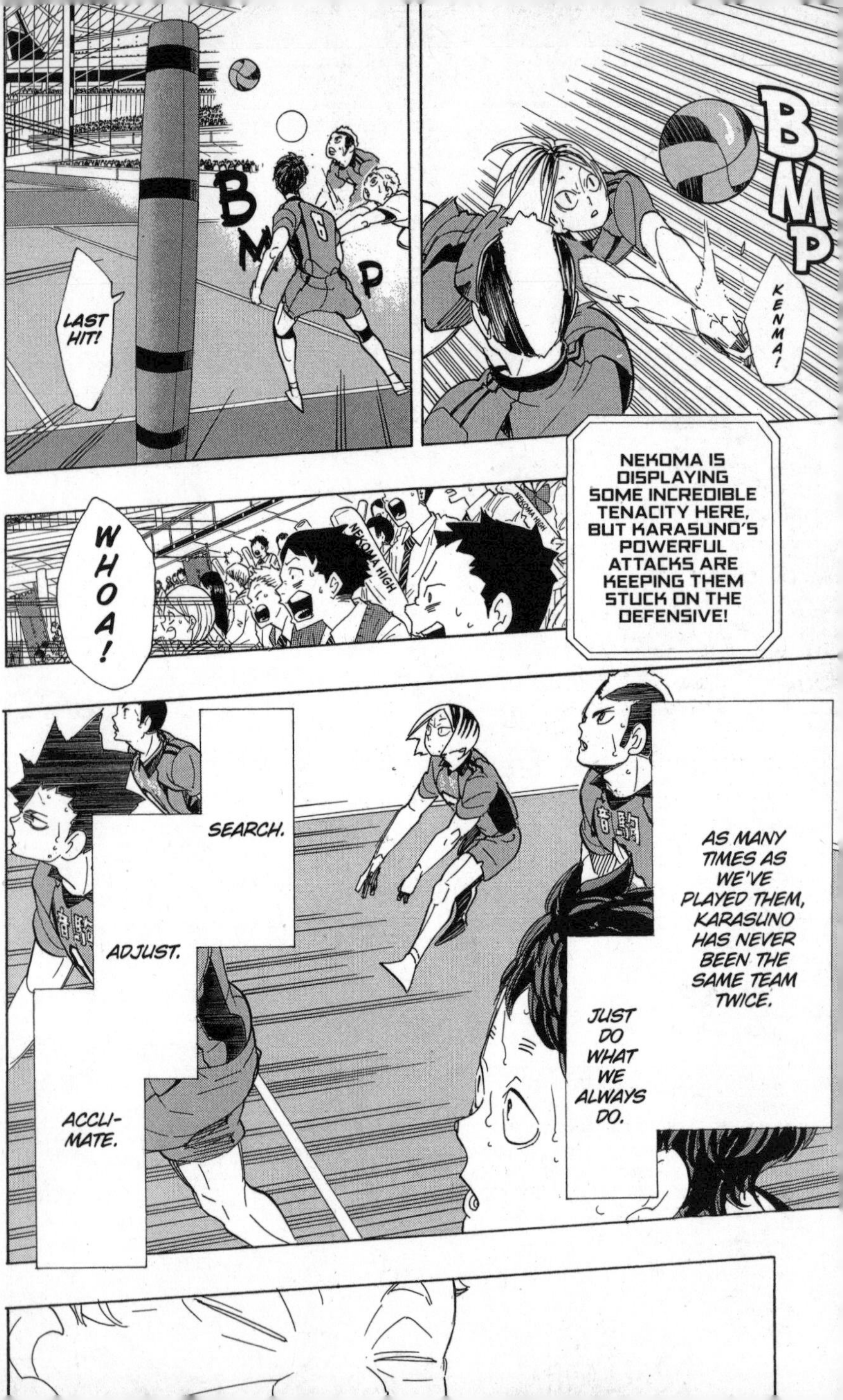
BMP
KENMA!
BMP
LAST HIT!
NEKOMA IS DISPLAYING SOME INCREDIBLE TENACITY HERE, BUT KARASUNO'S POWERFUL ATTACKS ARE KEEPING THEM STUCK ON THE DEFENSIVE!
WHOA!
AS MANY TIMES AS WE'VE PLAYED THEM, KARASUNO HAS NEVER BEEN THE SAME TEAM TWICE.
JUST DO WHAT WE ALWAYS DO.
SEARCH.
ADJUST.
ACCLI-MATE.

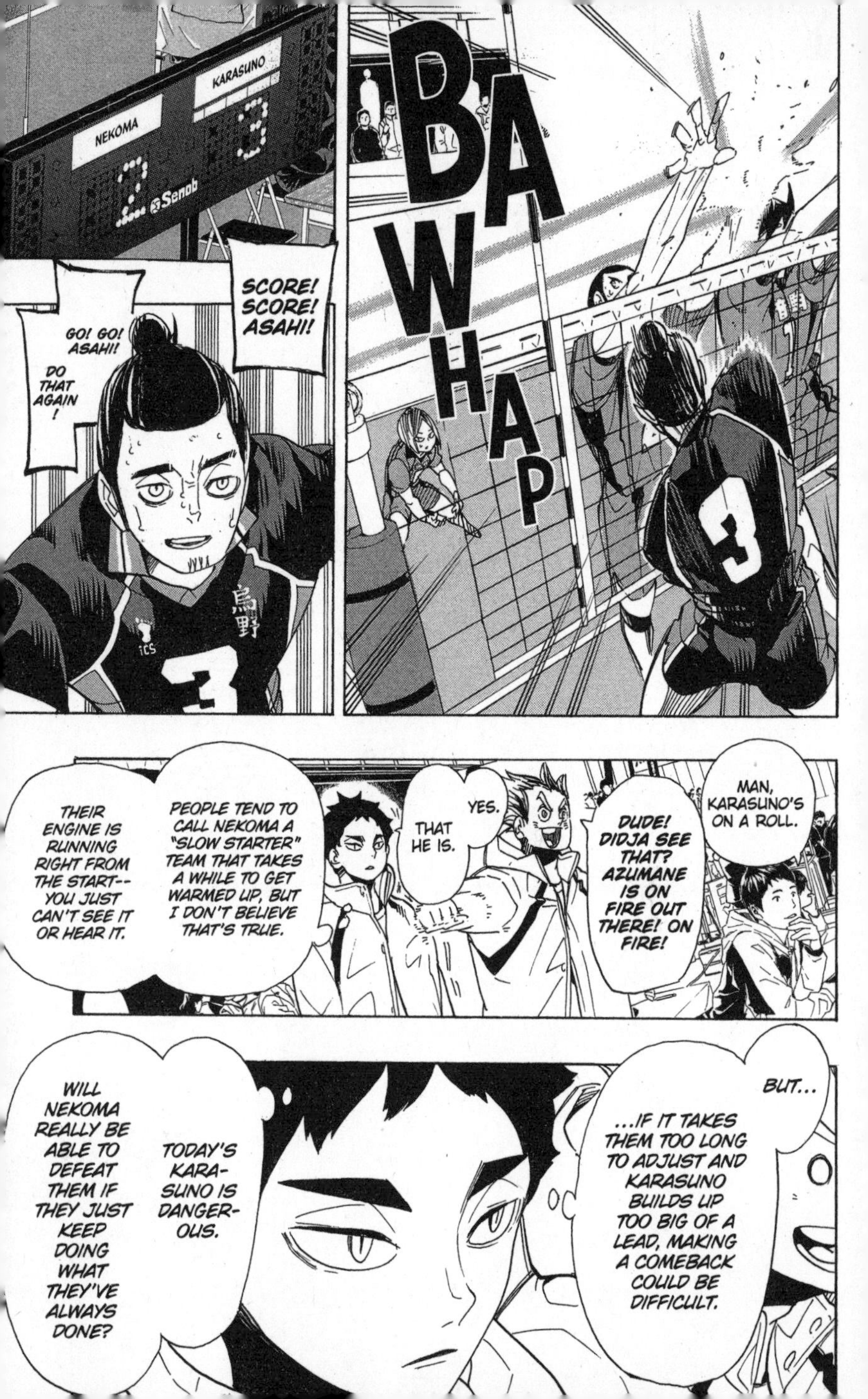
BAWHAP
KARASUNO
NEKOMA
SCORE! SCORE! ASAHI!
GO! GO! ASAHI! DO THAT AGAIN!
MAN, KARASUNO'S ON A ROLL.
DUDE! DIDJA SEE THAT? AZUMANE IS ON FIRE OUT THERE! ON FIRE!
YES.
THAT HE IS.
PEOPLE TEND TO CALL NEKOMA A "SLOW STARTER" TEAM THAT TAKES A WHILE TO GET WARMED UP, BUT I DON'T BELIEVE THAT'S TRUE.
THEIR ENGINE IS RUNNING RIGHT FROM THE START-- YOU JUST CAN'T SEE IT OR HEAR IT.
BUT...
...IF IT TAKES THEM TOO LONG TO ADJUST AND KARASUNO BUILDS UP TOO BIG OF A LEAD, MAKING A COMEBACK COULD BE DIFFICULT.
TODAY'S KARA-SUNO IS DANGER-OUS.
WILL NEKOMA REALLY BE ABLE TO DEFEAT THEM IF THEY JUST KEEP DOING WHAT THEY'VE ALWAYS DONE?

THIS IS YOUR STORY

NISHINOYA OUT

HINATA SERVE

TSUKISHIMA IN

SERVE		
HINATA	TANAKA	KAGEYAMA
SAWAMURA	AZUMANE	TSUKISHIMA

NET		
FUKUNAGA	KUROO	KAI
KOZUME	HAIBA (YAKU)	YAMAMOTO

*CURRENT ROTATION

NO. 11 IS THE KEYSTONE OF KARASUNO'S BLOCKING SCHEME!

DON'T ASK ME WHY, BECAUSE I DON'T KNOW. I JUST DON'T LIKE HIM.

NOW I'VE NEVER PLAYED AGAINST KARASUNO, BUT THERE'S JUST *SOMETHING* ABOUT THAT ROOKIE IN THE GLASSES THAT BUGS ME.

I ALREADY DON'T LIKE HIM.

DID I GET IT RIGHT?

I remember what you said yesterday.

!

OH! YEAH, YOU DID, YOU DID!

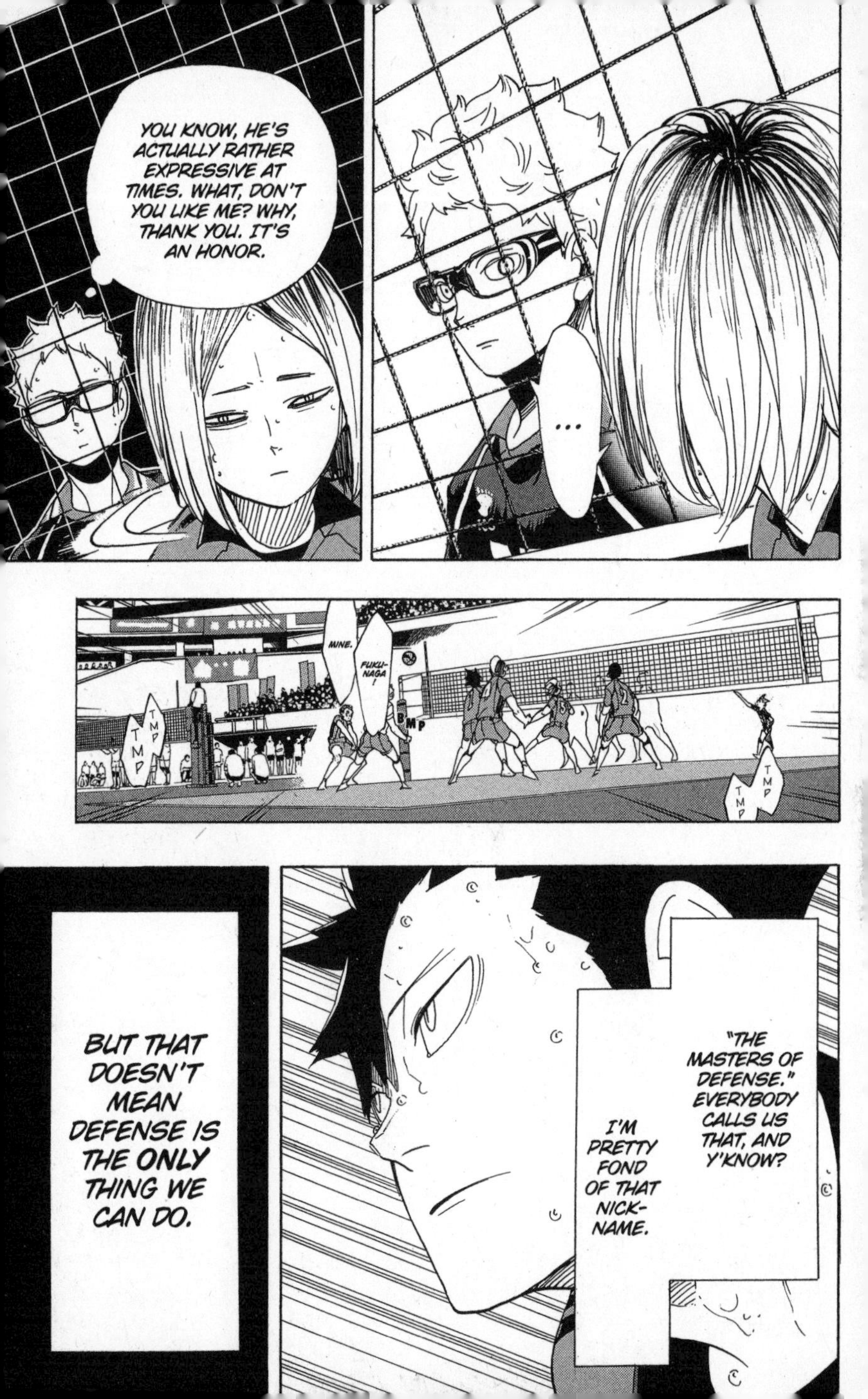
...
YOU KNOW, HE'S ACTUALLY RATHER EXPRESSIVE AT TIMES. WHAT, DON'T YOU LIKE ME? WHY, THANK YOU. IT'S AN HONOR.
TMP TMP
FUKU-NAGA!
MINE.
BMP
TMP TMP
"THE MASTERS OF DEFENSE." EVERYBODY CALLS US THAT, AND Y'KNOW?
I'M PRETTY FOND OF THAT NICK-NAME.
BUT THAT DOESN'T MEAN DEFENSE IS THE ONLY THING WE CAN DO.

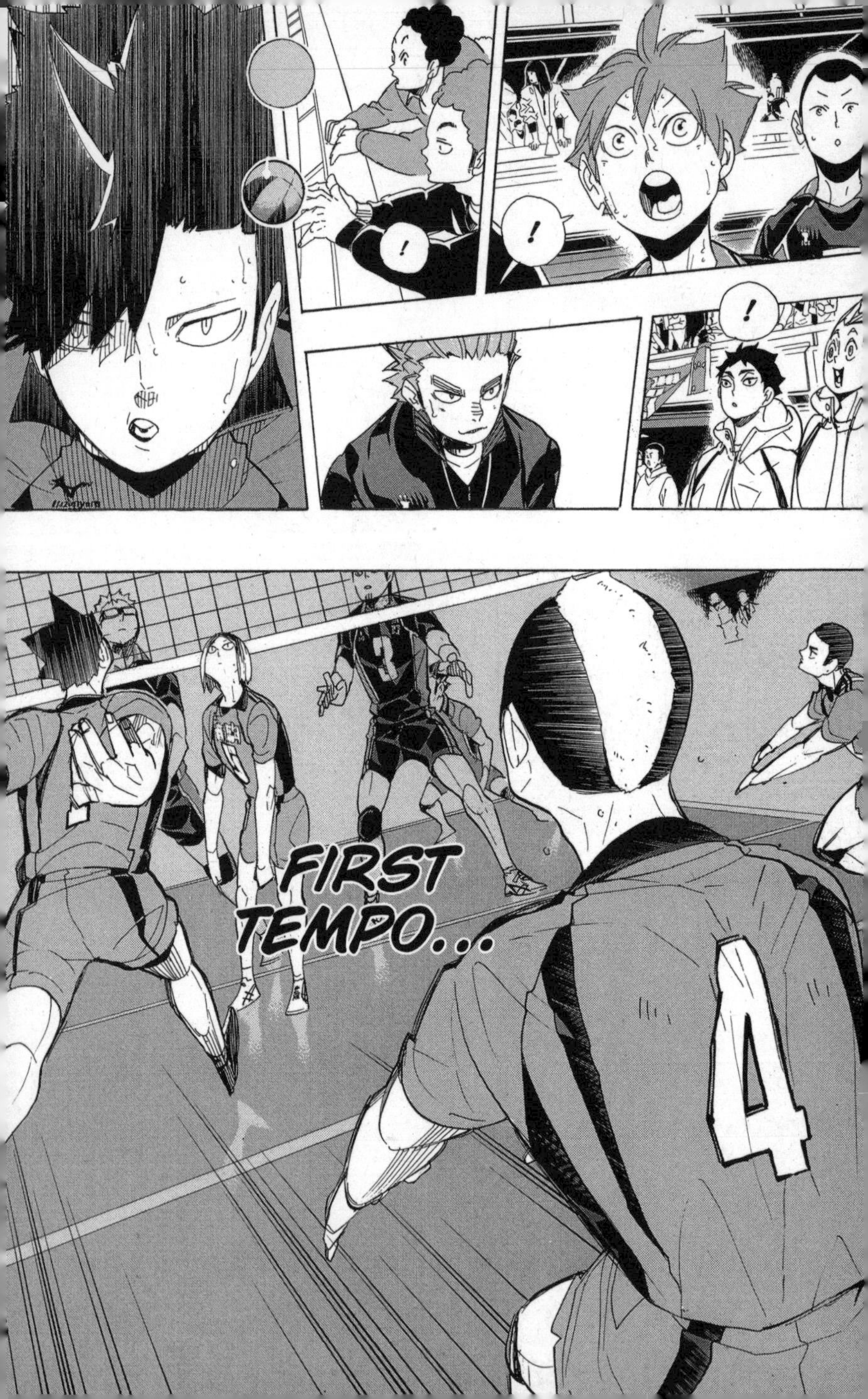
!
!
!
FIRST TEMPO...

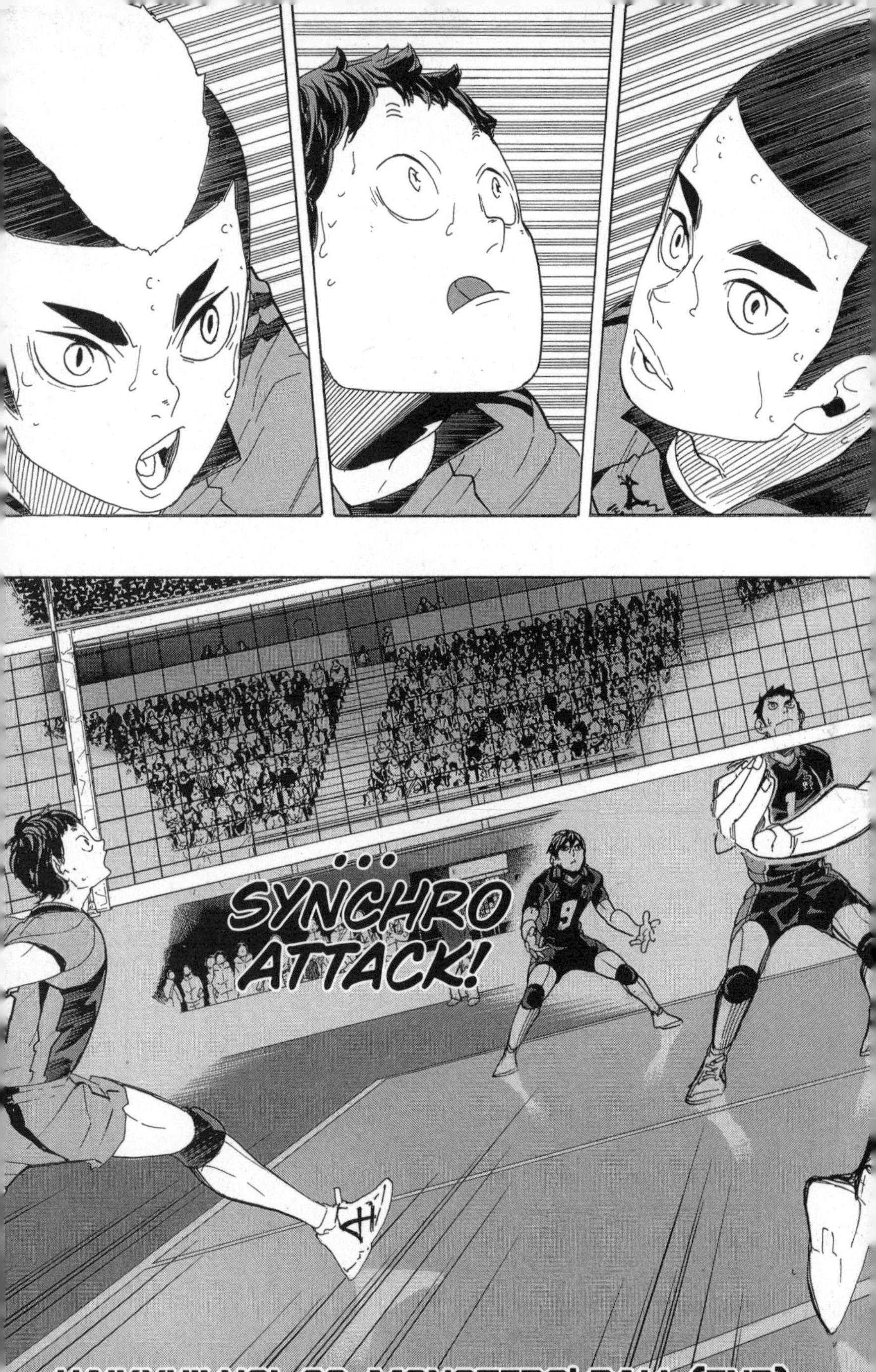
...
SYNCHRO ATTACK!

HAIKYU!! VOL 33: MONSTERS' BALL (END)

You thought the volume was over, but no!

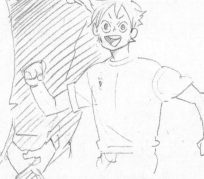

← **BONUS STORIES AHEAD!**

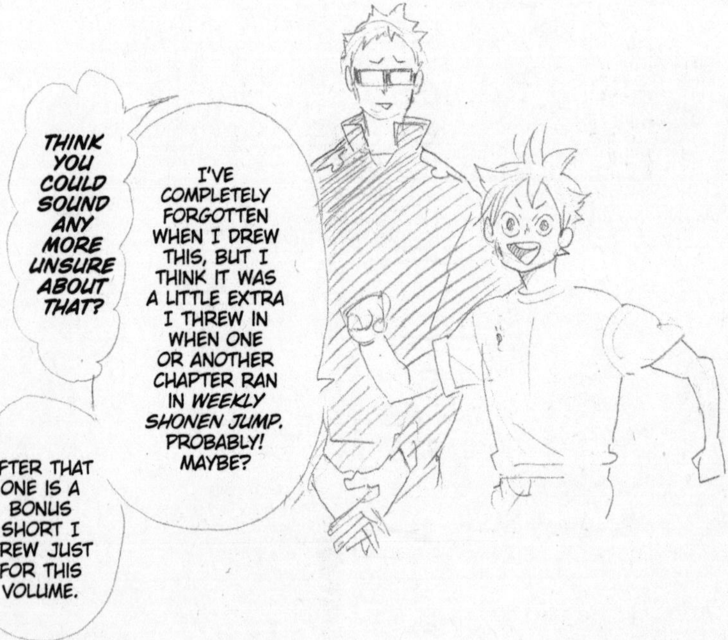

I'VE COMPLETELY FORGOTTEN WHEN I DREW THIS, BUT I THINK IT WAS A LITTLE EXTRA I THREW IN WHEN ONE OR ANOTHER CHAPTER RAN IN *WEEKLY SHONEN JUMP*. PROBABLY! MAYBE?
THINK YOU COULD SOUND ANY MORE UNSURE ABOUT THAT?
AFTER THAT ONE IS A BONUS SHORT I DREW JUST FOR THIS VOLUME.

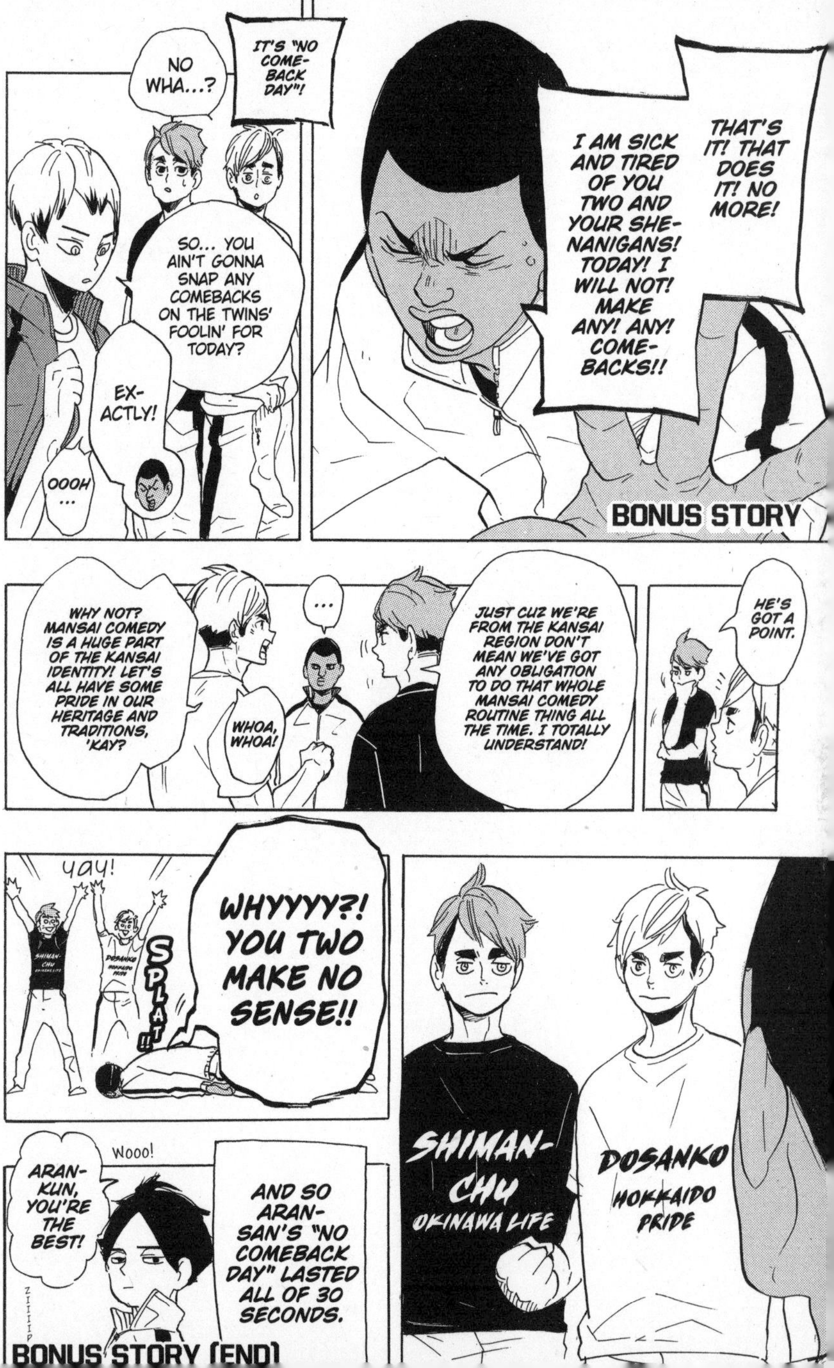

BONUS STORY
THAT'S IT! THAT DOES IT! NO MORE!
I AM SICK AND TIRED OF YOU TWO AND YOUR SHE-NANIGANS! TODAY! I WILL NOT! MAKE ANY! ANY! COME-BACKS!!
NO WHA...?
IT'S "NO COME-BACK DAY"!
SO... YOU AIN'T GONNA SNAP ANY COMEBACKS ON THE TWINS' FOOLIN' FOR TODAY?
EX-ACTLY!
OOOH ...
HE'S GOT A POINT.
JUST CUZ WE'RE FROM THE KANSAI REGION DON'T MEAN WE'VE GOT ANY OBLIGATION TO DO THAT WHOLE MANSAI COMEDY ROUTINE THING ALL THE TIME. I TOTALLY UNDERSTAND!
...
WHY NOT? MANSAI COMEDY IS A HUGE PART OF THE KANSAI IDENTITY! LET'S ALL HAVE SOME PRIDE IN OUR HERITAGE AND TRADITIONS, 'KAY?
WHOA, WHOA!
SHIMAN-CHU OKINAWA LIFE
DOSANKO HOKKAIDO PRIDE
WHYYYY?! YOU TWO MAKE NO SENSE!!
SPLAT!!
yay!
AND SO ARAN-SAN'S "NO COMEBACK DAY" LASTED ALL OF 30 SECONDS.
Wooo!
ARAN-KUN, YOU'RE THE BEST!
ZIIIIP
BONUS STORY (END)

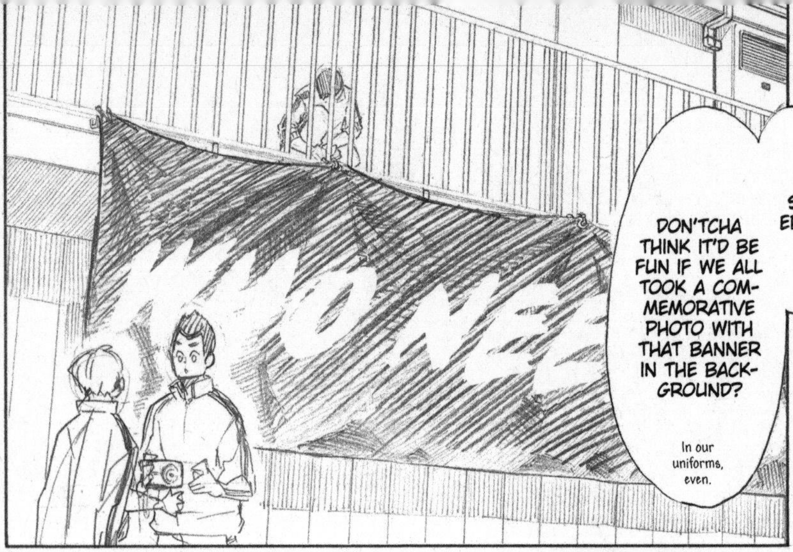
SO, ER...
DON'TCHA THINK IT'D BE FUN IF WE ALL TOOK A COM-MEMORATIVE PHOTO WITH THAT BANNER IN THE BACK-GROUND?
In our uniforms, even.

BONUS STORY 2

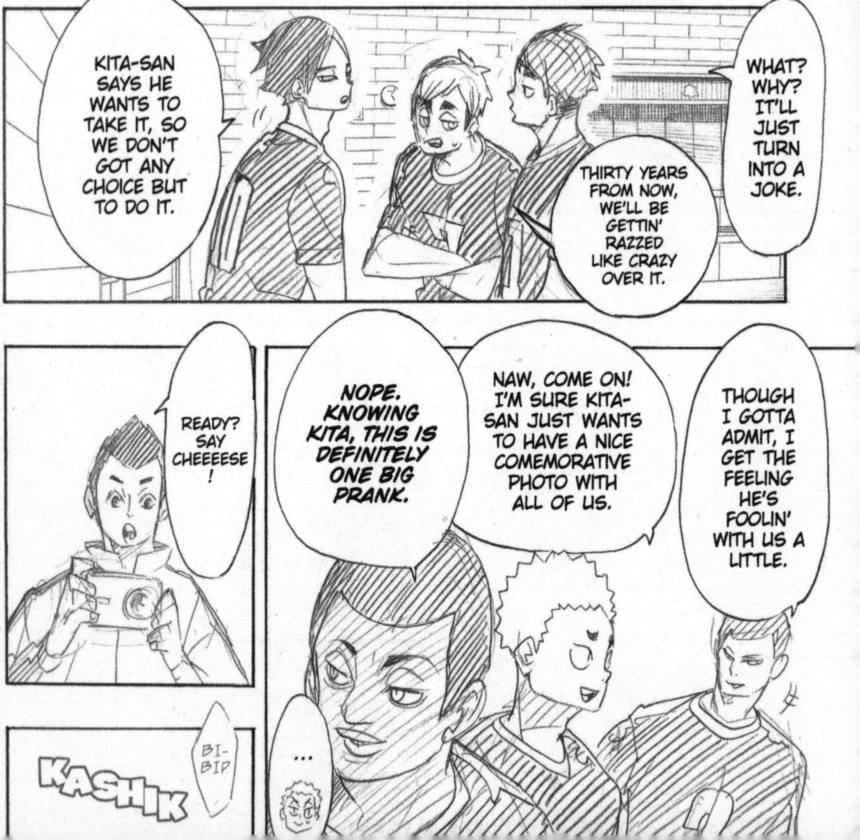
WHAT? WHY? IT'LL JUST TURN INTO A JOKE.
THIRTY YEARS FROM NOW, WE'LL BE GETTIN' RAZZED LIKE CRAZY OVER IT.
KITA-SAN SAYS HE WANTS TO TAKE IT, SO WE DON'T GOT ANY CHOICE BUT TO DO IT.
THOUGH I GOTTA ADMIT, I GET THE FEELING HE'S FOOLIN' WITH US A LITTLE.
NAW, COME ON! I'M SURE KITA-SAN JUST WANTS TO HAVE A NICE COMEMORATIVE PHOTO WITH ALL OF US.
NOPE. KNOWING KITA, THIS IS DEFINITELY ONE BIG PRANK.
...
READY? SAY CHEEEESE!
BI-BIP
KASHIK

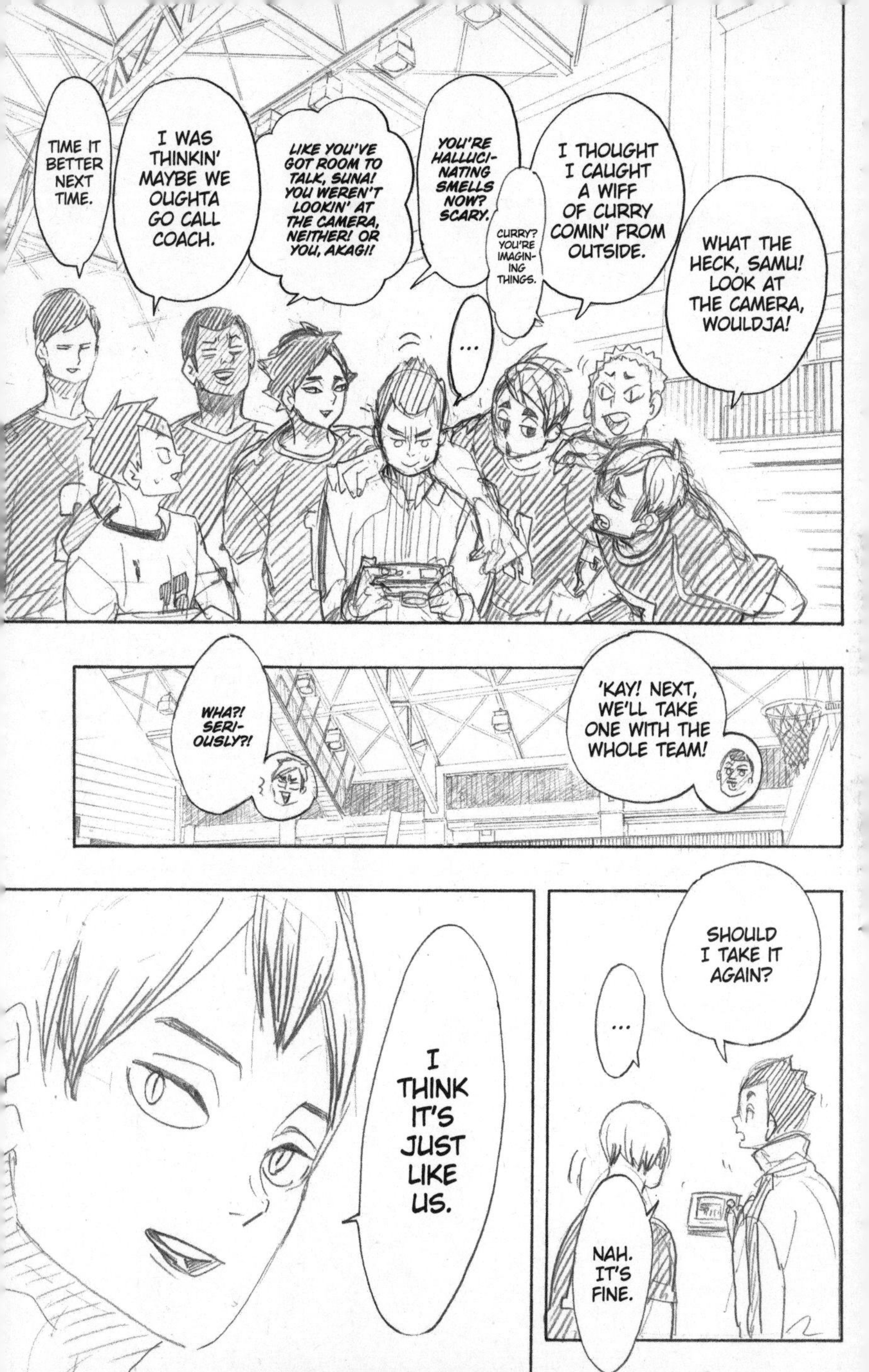
WHAT THE HECK, SAMU! LOOK AT THE CAMERA, WOULDJA!
I THOUGHT I CAUGHT A WIFF OF CURRY COMIN' FROM OUTSIDE.
CURRY? YOU'RE IMAGIN-ING THINGS.
YOU'RE HALLUCI-NATING SMELLS NOW? SCARY.
...
LIKE YOU'VE GOT ROOM TO TALK, SUNA! YOU WEREN'T LOOKIN' AT THE CAMERA, NEITHER! OR YOU, AKAGI!
I WAS THINKIN' MAYBE WE OUGHTA GO CALL COACH.
TIME IT BETTER NEXT TIME.
'KAY! NEXT, WE'LL TAKE ONE WITH THE WHOLE TEAM!
WHA?! SERI-OUSLY?!
SHOULD I TAKE IT AGAIN?
...
NAH. IT'S FINE.
I THINK IT'S JUST LIKE US.

BONUS STORY 3 [END]

EDITOR'S NOTES

The English edition of Haikyu!! maintains the honorifics used in the original Japanese version. For those of you who are new to these terms, here's a brief explanation to help with your reading experience!

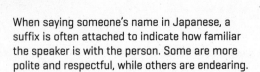

When saying someone's name in Japanese, a suffix is often attached to indicate how familiar the speaker is with the person. Some are more polite and respectful, while others are endearing.

1 **-kun** is often used for young men or boys, usually someone you are familiar with.

2 **-chan** is used for young children and can be used as a term of endearment.

3 **-san** is used for someone you respect or are not close to, or to be polite.

4 **Senpai** is used for someone who is older than you or in a higher position or grade in school.

5 **Kohai** is used for someone who is younger than you or in a lower position or grade in school.

6 **Sensei** means teacher.

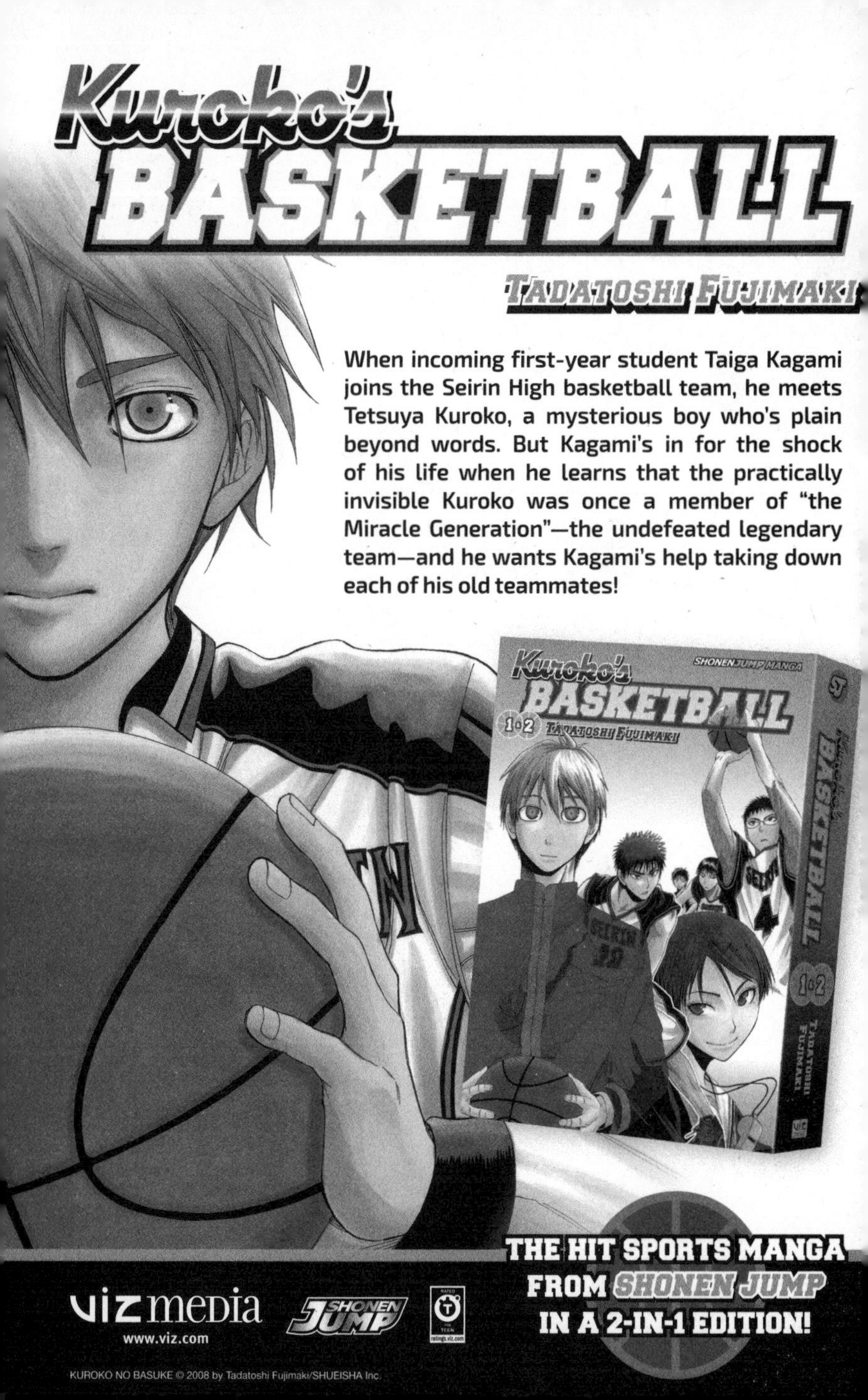
Kuroko's BASKETBALL
TADATOSHI FUJIMAKI
When incoming first-year student Taiga Kagami joins the Seirin High basketball team, he meets Tetsuya Kuroko, a mysterious boy who's plain beyond words. But Kagami's in for the shock of his life when he learns that the practically invisible Kuroko was once a member of "the Miracle Generation"—the undefeated legendary team—and he wants Kagami's help taking down each of his old teammates!
SHONEN JUMP MANGA
Kuroko's BASKETBALL
1•2
TADATOSHI FUJIMAKI
THE HIT SPORTS MANGA FROM SHONEN JUMP IN A 2-IN-1 EDITION!
viz media
www.viz.com
SHONEN JUMP
RATED T FOR TEEN
ratings.viz.com
KUROKO NO BASUKE © 2008 by Tadatoshi Fujimaki/SHUEISHA Inc.

You're Reading the WRONG WAY!

HAIKYU!! reads from right to left, starting in the upper-right corner. Japanese is read from right to left, meaning that action, sound effects and word-balloon order are completely reversed from English order.

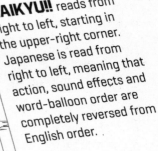